Praise for *Patterns-Based Engineering*

"This book introduces a new and important idea, providing a rigorous approach to Patterns-Based Engineering. As the number of published patterns has increased, understanding how to apply them across all parts of the software development life-cycle has become critically important."

—Kyle Brown, Distinguished Engineer, IBM Software Group,
Author of *Persistence in the Enterprise*

"To misquote Confucius, 'Give a man a solution and you solve his problem for a day. Teach a man a pattern and you've solved his problems for a lifetime.' The guidance provided by Lee and Celso in this book should help solve many lifetimes' worth of software development problems. The book's combination of solid theory coupled with practical implementation makes for an essential reference if you ever plan on trying the benefits of Patterns-Based Engineering. Well done guys!"

—Gregory Hodgkinson, Practice Director for the
Lifecycle Tools and Methodology Practice at Prolifics

"Ever since the GOF patterns book, software design patterns have been a great way to codify best practices to solve specific problems. *Patterns-Based Engineering* gives practical advice on how to manage design patterns for your organization and codify your best practices."

—Dave Hendricksen, Software Architect, Thomson-Reuters

"Ackerman and Gonzalez have provided a well-written book, which describes a process that at a minimum can be used by any software development organization. The authors provide valuable case studies, detailed analysis, and the required governance to define new patterns or fully utilize the patterns already existing within an organization. As software professionals, we recognize the necessity and advantages for the usage of patterns; PBE provides a framework to dramatically enhance the productivity and reusability of those patterns within our projects."

—Davie Sweis, IT Manager, North America and
Worldwide Solutions Architect, Robert Bosch LLC

Patterns-Based Engineering

Patterns-Based Engineering

Successfully Delivering Solutions via Patterns

Lee Ackerman
Celso Gonzalez

✦Addison-Wesley

Upper Saddle River, NJ • Boston • Indianapolis • San Francisco
New York • Toronto • Montreal • London • Munich • Paris • Madrid
Capetown • Sydney • Tokyo • Singapore • Mexico City

Many of the designations used by manufacturers and sellers to distinguish their products are claimed as trademarks. Where those designations appear in this book, and the publisher was aware of a trademark claim, the designations have been printed with initial capital letters or in all capitals.

Figures 13.7 and A.3 are reproductions of Figure 29-1 from page 531 of Martin, R. C., D. Riehle, and F. Buschmann. 1998. "Context-Setting Patterns." In *Pattern Languages of Program Design 3*. Boston: Addison-Wesley. Reproduced by permission of Pearson Education.

The authors and publisher have taken care in the preparation of this book, but make no expressed or implied warranty of any kind and assume no responsibility for errors or omissions. No liability is assumed for incidental or consequential damages in connection with or arising out of the use of the information or programs contained herein.

The publisher offers excellent discounts on this book when ordered in quantity for bulk purchases or special sales, which may include electronic versions and/or custom covers and content particular to your business, training goals, marketing focus, and branding interests. For more information, please contact:

U.S. Corporate and Government Sales
(800) 382-3419
corpsales@pearsontechgroup.com

For sales outside the United States please contact:

International Sales
international@pearson.com

Visit us on the Web: www.informit.com/aw

Library of Congress Cataloging-in-Publication Data

Ackerman, Lee, 1971–
  Patterns-based engineering : successfully delivering solutions via patterns / Lee Ackerman, Celso Gonzalez.
      p. cm.
  Includes bibliographical references and index.
  ISBN 978-0-321-57428-2 (hardcover : alk. paper) 1. Computer software—Development. 2. Software patterns. I. Gonzalez, Celso, 1969– II. Title.
  QA76.76.D47A255, 2010
  005.1—dc22

2010013630

ISBN-13: 978-0-321-57428-2
ISBN-10:   0-321-57428-1
Text printed in the United States on recycled paper at Courier in Westford, Massachusetts.
First printing, June 2010

To Shawna, Katie, Hannah, and Aidan
No matter the distance, no matter the destination,
I cherish our journey.
—Lee Ackerman

A Chantal, Jordan, Duncan, Gwendolyn, et Gabriel
Vous avoir dans ma vie me rend meilleur.
—Celso Gonzalez

Contents

Foreword

Developing, deploying, operating, and evolving software-intensive systems are problems of engineering: One must devise a solution that reasonably balances the forces upon that system. Every individual system faces its own unique set of forces, and thus every system presents a unique engineering problem. Nonetheless, these are not all problems of singularity: Over time, common solutions to common problems emerge, and these become part of the institutional memory of that system space. Insofar as we can make those patterns manifest, we can improve the manner in which we develop, deploy, operate, and evolve systems. Indeed, this too is the nature of engineering: For every new system, we look back on things that didn't work (and try alternatives) as well as things that did (and improve them).

Lee and Celso have considerable industrial experience in delivering software-intensive systems, and in this book they bring the best practices they have learned to the problem of engineering software-intensive systems. If you are are unfamiliar with the nature of patterns, this book will help you understand how to discover, design, create, package, and consume these common solutions to common problems. Their extended case study demonstrates how to pragmatically apply these ideas; their guidelines offer patterns and antipatterns for engineering systems using patterns. Finally, Lee and Celso attend to the softer issues of Patterns-Based Engineering: its value, its risks, and its economic return.

As software-intensive systems continue to grow in complexity and in their importance to the world, it is our responsibility as software engineers to deliver systems of quality. Lee and Celso's work will help you along that path.

—*Grady Booch*
IBM Fellow
February 1, 2010

Preface

Increasing and unending pressure exists in software development to finish more quickly, to produce higher-quality solutions, and to do so with fewer resources. We can use patterns, proven best-practice solutions to known problems, as a powerful tool to help address these challenges. However, if the answer were as simple as "Just use patterns," we would already have dealt with these challenges.

There is complexity, depth, and nuance to using patterns, and succeeding with them requires knowledge, expertise, and guidance. And not only do we want to succeed with patterns, we want to do so in a fashion that is scalable, repeatable, and predictable. This book introduces an approach known as Patterns-Based Engineering (PBE) that provides guidance on how to successfully incorporate and leverage patterns in software development. We don't just use patterns; we think, evaluate, create, innovate, collaborate, abstract, simplify, justify, automate, and reuse.

Patterns-Based Engineering

PBE is a specialized approach to asset-based development that focuses on patterns, a specific type of reusable asset. PBE provides guidance and support for using patterns in a systematic, disciplined, and quantifiable way. With PBE an organization uses patterns in multiple forms, for numerous purposes, and in a number of ways. More specifically, we look at two specific types of patterns: pattern specifications and pattern implementations. We use these types of patterns to support design, testing, deployment, and other aspects of the software development lifecycle. In performing these tasks, we use patterns in many ways such as documenting, generating, refactoring, and harvesting. As a result, we are able to use patterns to boost productivity, improve quality, leverage expertise, simplify, and improve communication within an organization. The goal is to ensure that as we use and create patterns, we are doing so in a way that adds value and boosts the agility of our projects and organization.

An important aspect of PBE is that it goes beyond just the technology. Success on a project has never been and will never be just about the technology. We need to ensure that the team is able to work together; that we all know the roles we are to play, the tasks to be done, the work products to create along the way; and that we can communicate with one another.

How to Read This Book

This section starts with an overview of the book's structure. We then provide a guide to reading the book based on role, and we finish with suggestions for the background needed to get the most out of the book and a list of learning objectives.

Book Structure

This book is divided into four parts. Part I provides an introduction to PBE. Within this part, Chapter 1 starts by defining PBE and Chapter 2 follows by providing some examples of pattern implementations, as this is a new concept for most and is an important aspect of PBE. Chapters 3 through 7 then show an example of PBE in action through a case study. Chapter 8 concludes Part I with a discussion of the process aspects of PBE and how it could fit into existing software development processes, including coverage of Extreme Programming, Scrum, and OpenUP.

Part II describes some of the best practices related to PBE in the form of patterns and guidelines. Chapter 9 explains the organization and summarizes each of the patterns and guidelines. Chapters 10 through 16 detail the patterns and guidelines, each chapter focusing on a specific category.

Part III covers additional topics that provide a deeper examination of PBE, particularly the nontechnical aspects. We detail some of the PBE benefits in Chapter 17, move to the economic aspects of PBE in Chapter 18, and finish Part III with Chapter 19, which takes a look at some of the PBE misconceptions that may be faced in rolling out PBE within an organization.

Part IV wraps up the book with a set of appendices that provide supporting materials and references. Appendix A summarizes the main PBE definitions to provide quick access to some of the terms and concepts used throughout the book. Appendix B takes a look at PBE in comparison to other software development approaches. Appendix C provides a nonexhaustive list of tools available to help in applying PBE within an organization. Appendix D provides a set of PBE Patterns and Guidelines overview diagrams. Appendix E provides the pattern specification for the Subsystem Façade pattern created and used in the case study. Appendix F serves as a companion to Chapter 8, adding more details to support our understanding of the PBE Practice.

To get a high-level understanding of PBE, read all of Part I and Chapter 9 from Part II, which provides a high-level summary of the PBE Patterns and Guidelines.

For a deeper understanding of PBE you should go at least once through the PBE Patterns and Guidelines to get a better idea of what problems they address and the associated solutions. And if you are interested in some of the nontechnical aspects of PBE, Part III is a must read.

Who Should Read This Book

Patterns surface and are applicable throughout the development lifecycle and for multiple purposes. Thus, there is a wide audience for this book, including

- Software architects, designers, and developers: Read all parts.

- Project managers: Read Part I, at least Chapter 1, and Part III.

- Process engineers: Read all parts with a focus on Chapter 8 and Appendix F.

- Analysts, including those responsible for testing, requirements, and business: Read Part I, at least Chapter 1.

Suggested Background

To get the most from this book, we suggest that you have basic familiarity with the following topics:

- Object-oriented programming with a language such as Java or C#

- Patterns

- Unified Modeling Language (UML)

- XML

Learning Objectives

Upon completion of the book, you will be able to

- Describe ways in which patterns can be leveraged in delivering software

- Describe the roles, tasks, work products, and best practices defined within PBE

- Describe the factors that help decision making about investments driven by PBE as well as the expected implications of such decisions

- Describe the value and purpose of using patterns (implementations and specifications)

- Successfully identify, specify, and implement patterns

- Understand that patterns are for all roles and projects

Why This Book?

So, why this book? Why does the world need another patterns book? Aren't there enough already? One way to answer these questions is to say that we do not like solving the same problems over and over again. As a matter of fact, we struggle a bit dealing with the mechanical and mundane aspects of writing software. We are big fans of trying to be creative and solving new and unique problems. And we like to leverage automation to help us minimize and avoid having to work on those mechanical and mundane tasks.

Another way to answer these questions is that it's not enough to be passionate. It's not enough to be creative. It's not enough to use tooling and automation. There's already content in many forms—books, courses, and articles—that touches upon these topics. However, we were not able to find content that brings these ideas together. A holistic approach is needed to discuss how we can use patterns more strategically, more systematically. We need to be able to scale the use of patterns across the organization and ensure predictability and repeatability in our pattern-infused projects.

Downloadable Content

There are three downloads associated with this book, available from www.Patterns BasedEngineering.net. These downloads include

- Source artifacts for the pattern implementation that is discussed in the case study

- The source plug-in for a PBE Practice to be used with Eclipse Process Framework Composer

- A published configuration of the PBE Practice composed of a set of HTML pages that can be viewed with a standard web browser

Writing Style

Software development is a team sport; we present the rest of the book as a team effort. We are in this together, having a chat about how we can better leverage patterns in our projects.

Acknowledgments

There is no way that this book would have been completed without contributions from many people. With immense gratitude we would like to offer our appreciation to those who have supported us in this journey and provided suggestions, discussions, and questions that have helped to shape our efforts:

- Our reviewers via Addison-Wesley: Brian Foote, Dave Hendricksen, Peter Kovari, Davie Sweis, and Rebecca Wirfs-Brock

- The many folks from within IBM who have taken the time to help us: Jonathan Adams, Dan Berg, Andy Berner, Craig Branham, Alan Brown, Kyle Brown, Peter Coldicott, Jim Conallen, Dino D'Agostino, Dwayne Dreakford, Todd Dunnavant, Peter Eeles, Paul Elder, Jeff Fischer, Chris Gerken, Geoffrey Hambrick, Michael Hartmann, Michael Holmes, Derek Holt, James Jamison, Claus Jensen, Eoin Lane, Grant Larsen, Jean-Michel Lemieux, Dan Leroux, Bertrand Portier, Valerio Rosati, Jim Ruehlin, Guenter Sauter, Scott Schneider, Ralph Schoon, Darrell Schrag, James Siddle, Bill Smith, Jason Smith, Doug Stewart, Nansi Stretcher, Cindy VanEpps, Paul Verschueren, Janette Wong

- Our colleagues from across the industry who have shared their experiences and expertise: Regis Coqueret, Johan den Haan, David Dossot, Jonathan Harclerlode, Greg Hodgkinson, Darcy Jouan, Peter Kovari, Randy Lexvold, Mark Lines, Michael Sikorsky, Michael Wahler

- Our team at Addison-Wesley who have helped to guide this project from proposal through to completion: Raina Chrobak, Chris Guzikowski, Laurie McGuire, Anna Popick, and Barbara Wood

- And a special thank you to Grady Booch for his input, comments, and, of course, the Foreword

About the Authors

Combined, Lee and Celso have been working in the software industry for close to 30 years. During that time they have worked in development, services, and enablement organizations. Along the way they have used patterns in their projects and resulting solutions.

More recently, they've been building out PBE within IBM. During this time they have delivered enablement sessions, built courses, delivered conference presentations and workshops, written articles and Redbooks, participated in pattern-related studies, supported governance efforts, and contributed to IBM software products. In these efforts they have created patterns, used patterns, and helped others to use and build patterns.

Most of their PBE efforts have involved the use of IBM products such as IBM Rational Software Architect, Rational Application Developer, Rational Method Composer, and Rational Asset Manager. Because patterns are based on experience, the examples discussed use IBM Rational tools. However, the majority of the concepts, ideas, and guidance presented are applicable to tools provided by multiple vendors and the open-source community. Appendix B and Appendix C relate PBE to other approaches and provide tooling options.

Part I

Understanding PBE

This part of the book introduces Patterns-Based Engineering (PBE). We start by defining PBE (Chapter 1) and then review a set of pattern implementation examples (Chapter 2). We continue with a case study to illustrate PBE in action (Chapters 3 through 7) and conclude with a discussion of the process aspects of PBE, including how it can integrate with Extreme Programming, Scrum, or OpenUP.

Chapter 1

Defining Patterns-Based Engineering

Beginnings are tough. Where to start? Is the necessary expertise available? Will we finish on time? Will the quality be there? Will everyone on the project follow best practices? Will the team get a chance to be creative while using and improving their skills? Are the requirements really known and understood?

As software engineers, we find ourselves asking such questions whether we are working on a greenfield project or maintaining a legacy application. Often the answers are not to our liking. As we start the project, we often joke about missing deadlines and are anxious about whether we will get the job done. Experience has taught us that the road ahead is going to be difficult and frustrating. To quote Grady Booch: "Software development has been, is, and will remain fundamentally hard."[1]

We know that we are not alone. We need to improve how we deliver our software projects. We need to improve productivity, enhance quality, hasten time to market, have better governance, and do all of this while dealing with a challenging set of constraints,[2] such as not enough expertise, daunting timelines, ambiguous and changing requirements, and ever-increasing solution scope and complexity.

Over the years we have tried to take steps to address these issues. We've adopted Agile processes, as who wouldn't want their projects to be more agile? We've tried model-driven development (MDD); as they say, "A picture is worth a thousand words." We've incorporated the leading industry frameworks, including .NET and Java EE, as well as the frameworks within these domains that further support our efforts, including Spring, Hibernate, and JavaServer Faces (JSF). We've adopted the best approaches to development as they've emerged, such as object-oriented (OO), component-based development (CBD), and service-oriented architecture (SOA). We've outsourced and off-shored, looking outside our organization for support,

---

1. Booch (2007).

2. For a look at a selection of notable software failures, refer to Charette (2005).

3

skills, and cost management. However, we continue to come up short—all while the complexity of what we are asked to build continues to advance.

This book discusses Patterns-Based Engineering (PBE), an approach to software development. It is not the silver bullet; it is not the magic elixir that will cure all that ails our projects. However, PBE, as demonstrated in real-world projects, takes a systematic and disciplined approach to using patterns—proven, best-practice solutions—to deliver software. A key and unique aspect of this approach is that in addition to using existing patterns from the community, we identify and create patterns within the organization, codifying, automating, and leveraging our own best practices. Organizations that have adopted this practice have seen improved productivity, increased quality, better utilization of expertise, and improved governance.

Asset-Based Development

A good place to start in gaining an understanding of PBE is to look at asset-based development (ABD). There is a strong connection between PBE and ABD. ABD is focused on how to leverage investments made in software artifacts in future projects. However, the guidance related to ABD is typically focused on assets in general, which is useful when the focus is on promoting reuse across many types of artifacts. PBE builds on the foundation provided by ABD and provides guidance for how we can succeed with a specific type of asset—specifically, patterns. With this relationship in mind, let's take a more detailed look at ABD.

ABD includes four major areas—process, standards, tooling, and assets—all of which are focused on how to successfully reuse and benefit from assets. An asset is "a collection of artifacts that provides a solution to a problem. The asset has instructions on how it should be used and is reusable in one or more contexts, such as a development or a runtime context. The asset may also be extended and customized through variability points."[3] A variability point is a part of the asset that is purposely provided by the creator of the asset and allows for later configuration or extension of the asset. Variability points are key to success with ABD, and in turn PBE, as they allow us to take a proven solution and easily tailor, customize, and adapt it to the specifics of our situation.

Generally a team produces numerous different types of artifacts as they look to deliver software solutions, ranging from requirements, to models, code, tests, and even deployment scripts. Each of these investments could potentially become a reusable asset. We need to evaluate specific instantiations of these artifacts to determine which would warrant an investment.

---

3. Larsen (2006).

As shown in Figure 1.1,[4] when following an ABD approach, we look at four areas of effort related to the assets, including

- **Asset identification.** We need to identify potential assets and determine which are suitable for investment.

- **Asset production.** After we have identified candidate assets, we need to produce those assets.

- **Asset management.** As assets are produced, we take appropriate steps to manage them and make them available for others to reuse. This includes support for searching, reviewing, and providing feedback. An asset repository is typically used to assist with this effort.

- **Asset consumption.** Once a set of assets is made available, the team accesses the asset repository and reuses the assets in their projects. Users of the assets are expected to provide feedback to the asset producers. This feedback is used to improve the assets and increase their value to the organization.

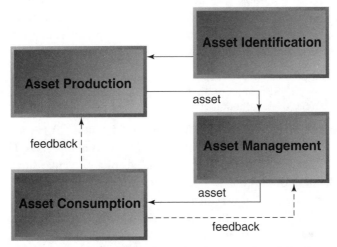

Figure 1.1 *Overview of major areas of effort related to asset-based development*
Credit: Grant J. Larsen, IBM.

Typically, we consider ABD from two perspectives. In one perspective we are concerned with the available tools, processes, standards, and assets. In the other perspective

---

4. Larsen (2003).

we focus on the efforts that we put into the identification, production, management, and consumption of assets.

If an organization already has an ABD program in place, PBE is a quick addition to the effort. If an organization has not yet adopted ABD, PBE is a very good place to start learning, adopting, and succeeding with assets.

Patterns

Let's take a look at what a pattern is and why it is important. A simple definition that we can start with is this: A **pattern** is a proven best-practice solution to a known, recurring problem within a given context. This definition still leaves a bit of ambiguity about patterns. There are many best-practice solutions out there that apply to a context but may not be considered to be patterns. To help further refine and expand our understanding of what a pattern is, we can refer to some of the work done by Christopher Alexander. The patterns movement started with his book *The Timeless Way of Building*. In the book Alexander looks at how we can build better architectures. Although the book addresses civil architecture and not software architecture, its ideas and guidance can be adapted and applied to software. In a subsequent book, titled *A Pattern Language*, Alexander states that a pattern

> . . . describes a problem which occurs over and over again in our environment, and then describes the core of the solution to that problem, in such a way that you can use this solution a million times over, without ever doing it the same way twice.[5]

At this point we are starting to get a more precise definition. A key idea that surfaces from Alexander's statement is that a pattern can be used many times. However, when applying it, we can adapt it so that it suits the needs of a particular situation. Although we may use the pattern multiple times, each instance of the pattern is unique.

Building on this definition, we can add a few ideas provided by John Vlissides.[6] He points out that a pattern needs to support teaching and have a name. In this way we can refer to the entire pattern by just its name and still convey meaning. The detail provided with the pattern can also be used to teach the pattern user about the best practices associated with the pattern, when to use the pattern, and the implications of doing so.

In the software world, the most-referenced book on patterns is *Design Patterns: Elements of Reusable Object-Oriented Software* written by Erich Gamma, Richard

---

5. Alexander (1977).
6. Vlissides (1998).

Helm, Ralph Johnson, and John Vlissides—known as the Gang of Four (GoF).[7] This book contains 23 design patterns that are widely used and referenced, including patterns such as Abstract Factory, Bridge, and Observer. These patterns and others are often embedded within the frameworks that we depend upon for building our solutions, like the Model-View-Controller pattern, which is the basis of Struts and JSF. Odds are that we've already been using patterns in our projects.

Engineering

As we build a definition of PBE, let's next define engineering. **Engineering** is "the application of a systematic, disciplined, quantifiable approach to structures, machines, products, systems, or processes."[8]

As we are dealing with software, it makes sense to look at a definition that is a little more targeted to the work we do. So **software engineering** is defined as "the application of a systematic, disciplined, quantifiable approach to the development, operation, and maintenance of software; that is, the application of engineering to software."[9]

With definitions of patterns and engineering as they relate to software development in mind, we are now in a position to consider a definition for Patterns-Based Engineering.

Patterns-Based Engineering

Let's start with a short definition. PBE is

a systematic, disciplined, and quantifiable approach to software development that leverages the use of pattern specifications and implementations throughout the software development and delivery process.[10]

---

7. Gamma et al. (1995).

8. IEEE Standard Glossary of Software Engineering Terminology, www2.computer.org/portal/web/seonline/glossary.

9. Ibid.

10. This definition reflects this book's focus on the use of patterns for building software solutions. However, we could replace the term *software development* in this definition with *enterprise architecture* or *operational modeling*, for example. The use of patterns is applicable across many aspects of the IT domain.

When we dig into this definition, a number of key ideas surface:

- PBE augments the overall software development and delivery process. We take a wide view of how patterns support us in developing and delivering software.

- PBE unifies the use of patterns in their different forms, using pattern specifications as blueprints as well as using pattern implementations to automate the application of those blueprints.

- PBE focuses on the systematic, disciplined use of patterns while enabling us to quantify the impact of using the patterns.

Pattern Specifications and Pattern Implementations

Design patterns from the GoF book were the first patterns to gain significant attention. Since that time, many other patterns have been identified and documented, as evidenced by the large number of results from online pattern searches. Generally, these patterns are presented in formal, written documentation that explains the pattern. We refer to these documents as **pattern specifications**.

There is some variation in how pattern specifications appear, but the following information is usually included:

- The *name* of the pattern

- A description of the *problem* the pattern solves

- A description of the *solution* that the pattern provides

- A discussion of the *consequences*, the advantages and disadvantages, of applying the pattern

Pattern specifications provide a great deal of value, as they

- Support learning about the best-practice-based approach to a recurring problem

- Simplify communication, since the name of the pattern can be used in place of repeating all of the pattern details

- Enable people to easily read and learn about a pattern

- Detail a best-practice approach to solving a recurring problem

However, there are a number of limitations to just using pattern specifications:

- Pattern Users need to be aware of what patterns exist and how they can be applied.

- Because patterns are tailored to the context in which they are used, it is highly likely that each person who uses a pattern will create slightly different solutions.

- If a pattern needs to be reapplied to a solution, it is a manual effort to update all the areas of the solution that leverage the pattern.

- Because the pattern is applied manually, human error is likely to creep into the application of the pattern. Even a small percentage of errors become significant over a large number of applications.

- It is difficult for individuals and teams to use a selection of patterns together. All the complexity of the combination surfaces as we are unable to easily encapsulate and shield Pattern Users from such complexity.

With the limitations of pattern specifications in mind, we are left to wonder how tooling and automation could assist. To that end, we look to the idea of **pattern implementations**. A pattern implementation automates the application of a pattern in a particular environment. Thus, patterns become tools themselves, concrete artifacts within the development environment.

From a Pattern User perspective, there are a number of different ways in which a pattern implementation can be manifested. A pattern implementation may surface as a wizard, a model transformation, a UML pattern, a web page, or even something as simple as a right-click with the mouse.

Benefits of using pattern implementations include

- **Increased productivity.** Using pattern implementations simplifies and accelerates how we deliver software. We are able to automate our best practices, which allows us to dramatically reduce repetitive and manual efforts. In addition, we reduce the skill requirements for working with and applying a pattern correctly.

- **Increased quality.** Pattern implementations allow us to consistently create solutions that adhere to architectural, design, and coding standards. In addition, as the pattern implementation embodies our best-practice approach to solving a problem, we are by definition increasing the quality of our solutions.

- **Better leveraging of skills and expertise.** With a pattern implementation we are able to capture our best practices and then make them available to the rest of the team for reuse. Others easily reuse the expertise that goes into the pattern, without the need for the experience, trial and error, and research that went into creating the pattern.

- **Improved governance.** Not only are we able to use tooling to apply our best practices, but we can also check that the resulting solution adheres to these best practices.

- **Reduced cost.** We can reduce the cost of the solutions we build as we are able to be more productive, increase quality, better leverage skills, and improve the governance associated with best practices.

A Model for Succeeding with PBE

With this background in mind, we can state that a pattern is a specific type of asset, and we can state that PBE is a specialized form of ABD. The main difference is that we focus on a specific type of asset, namely, a pattern. We still look at and work with all of the other types of artifacts that could be assets, such as requirements, models, code, tests, deployment scripts, and so on. Within PBE, these other types of assets either are used in association with patterns or are used as input into our efforts to create new patterns.

However, we still need to find answers to questions such as these:

- How do we perform PBE? That is, how can we take a systematic, disciplined, and quantifiable approach to using patterns to develop and deliver software?

- How do we succeed in taking on a PBE approach and improving how we deliver software?

- What are the best practices associated with PBE?

- What are the roles and tasks associated with PBE?

- How can we adopt and succeed with PBE as a team?

As we work our way through the rest of the book, we will discuss answers to these questions. As is the case with ABD, we can consider PBE from two perspectives. First, we are concerned with the available tools, processes, standards, and assets. Second, we look at the effort that we put into the identification, production, management, and consumption of patterns.

We can also leverage a model, as shown in Figure 1.2, to help us understand and position the content found in the rest of the book. The elements in the model build out from the base, leveraging the elements contained within. Starting with the innermost circle, we can see that there is a set of PBE Core Values. These core values form the basis of how we approach PBE. The goal is to ensure that we are able to quickly understand, remember, and relate a small and simple set of values that will influence all of our PBE efforts.

Figure 1.2 *A model bringing together the key elements that support our PBE efforts*

There is then a set of PBE Patterns that build upon the PBE Core Values. These patterns, as expected, provide a set of proven best-practice solutions to recurring PBE problems. There are patterns that support us in identifying, producing, managing, and consuming patterns.

Beyond the PBE Patterns there are PBE Guidelines to further assist us in performing PBE. The PBE Guidelines provide advice on PBE, including how to use the patterns and core values.

The final element shown in Figure 1.2 is the PBE Practice. In general, a practice is a process component; that is, it is a building block to help in building out a software development process. Typically a software development process is composed of a number of process components. Some of the components are focused on testing, others on deployment; in this case we will look at a process component focused on PBE. The PBE Practice looks at the tasks, work products, roles, artifacts, and associated guidance, patterns, and core values that we can use in successful PBE efforts.

The following sections take a closer look at each of the constructs from Figure 1.2.

PBE Core Values

With an overall model of PBE in place, we can now start to take a more in-depth look at each of the components within that model. We start with the PBE Core Values, as they serve as the basis for the other elements. These are the PBE Core Values:

1. **Patterns are best used in combination, rather than in isolation.** When building a solution, we expect to use many patterns. The patterns selected will vary in size and occur at multiple levels of abstraction, so we expect that the patterns will both connect and overlap. As stated by Christopher Alexander: "But it is also possible to put patterns together in such a way that many patterns overlap in the

same physical space: the building is very dense; it has many meanings captured in a small space; and through this density, it becomes profound."[11]

2. **Always identify and build new patterns.** We need to always be on the lookout for potential pattern opportunities across repetitive scenarios, repetitive code, repetitive solutions, and areas where we are just mechanically participating in the development effort.

3. **Patterns can be built and used within the same project.** A challenge that has traditionally surfaced in building reusable assets is determining when we should harvest them. Harvesting, whereby we identify and then extract reusable assets from existing solutions, is a significant effort and expense. We thus look for ways to justify the time and monetary expenditure for the asset harvesting. Often we decide that we should just wait until the end of the project and then harvest the assets for reuse on a later project. With PBE we can identify and build patterns within the current project. The assets thus pay for themselves during the current project and are then also available for other projects to use.

4. **Make your patterns live.** A good place to start with this principle is with a quote from Christopher Alexander: "You see then that the patterns are very much alive and evolving. In fact, if you like, each pattern may be looked upon as a hypothesis like one of the hypotheses of science."[12] Much like our development efforts, when we build patterns we leverage an iterative and incremental approach with a focus on always delivering value. In addition to building a better pattern over time, this approach also allows us the opportunity to look at ways in which we can increase the scope of the pattern. This also reduces pressure— we do not need to produce the perfect pattern on the first attempt. We are also able to collect feedback from the Pattern Users, leading to enhancements in future releases. As a result, the portfolio of patterns will grow and mature over time.

5. **Focus on making patterns consumable.** All the effort of identifying and building patterns is pointless if Pattern Users are unable to work with the patterns. Pattern consumability touches upon many aspects such as ease of use, enablement materials, and the ability to find the right pattern at the right time.

6. **PBE can fit into many different development processes.** PBE itself is not a process. It is a development practice that can be combined with and leveraged by other practices and processes. The PBE Core Values, Patterns, Guidelines, and Practice can be leveraged within most other modern software development processes.

---

11. Alexander (1977).

12. Ibid.

PBE Patterns and Guidelines

The PBE Patterns and Guidelines support us in identifying, producing, consuming, and managing patterns. The patterns and guidelines support one another. The guidelines help us to succeed with the patterns, and the patterns in turn help with the guidelines. Why patterns and guidelines? PBE has a set of patterns that have surfaced over the years. It makes sense to discuss patterns that can help us follow PBE; think of them as metapatterns. Also, it is important to see that new patterns are discovered and created; we are not restricted to using patterns that have been discovered by others. Patterns are for everyone; we all need to be on the lookout for pattern opportunities.

Guidelines are also needed to provide advice on how to successfully apply PBE. Not everything needs to be or should be a pattern. We need to evaluate and review patterns to ensure that they are worthy of the name and add value. We don't want to get into a situation where everything is a pattern (think Maslow's Hammer[13]) and end up diminishing the value of the term and concept.

Additional details for each of the patterns and guidelines are provided in Part II. More specifically, Chapter 9 provides an overview of the entire set of patterns and guidelines. The following chapters then provide details on each of the patterns and guidelines based on categories, including foundational patterns, pattern discovery and identification, designing patterns, creating patterns, pattern packaging, using domain-specific languages (DSLs) and patterns, and consuming patterns.

PBE Practice

Typically, a software development process provides guidance regarding the roles, tasks, work products, and workflow needed to develop software. However, PBE is not a full-fledged process; it is a practice. In essence, a practice is a process component that is used in conjunction with other process components (practices) to create a process. The practice still looks at the roles, tasks, work products, and workflows needed; however, the focus is entirely on PBE and not all of the other things that you would normally do when developing software. If we view the software development process as a set of components—some on testing, others on writing code, and some on source code management—we will focus on the PBE component. To that end we will look at the roles, tasks, work products, and workflows associated with PBE.

---

13. The idea that if all you have is a hammer then everything looks like a nail is referred to as Maslow's Maxim or Maslow's Hammer. More information regarding Abraham Maslow and Maslow's Hammer is available at www.abraham-maslow.com/m_motivation/Maslows_Hammer.asp.

The PBE Practice is available in source form that can be modified, configured, and integrated with other practices. Figure 1.3 provides a view of a published default configuration of the PBE Practice. This published configuration is a set of interconnected HTML pages that can be viewed through a standard web browser. As seen in the figure, we are able to use the navigation tree on the left-hand side of the screen to quickly access information about the concepts, roles, tasks, work products, tool list, checklists, and templates that the practice provides. Chapter 8, "PBE and the Software Development Process," provides more details on the elements in the PBE Practice and how to integrate this practice with a software development process.

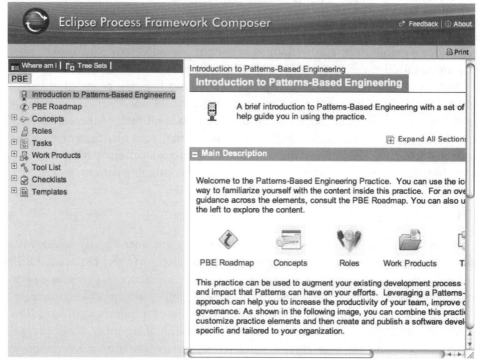

Figure 1.3   *A view of the published PBE Practice from within a standard web browser*

Examples of PBE Results

Chapters 3 through 7 present a case study in which a fictional organization leverages PBE in delivering a software solution. The case study is valuable because it pulls together a range of real-world experiences, ideas, and guidance within the context of one example. However, it has the disadvantage of being a fictional example.

This section provides a brief discussion of real-world examples where teams and organizations have used PBE Core Values, Patterns, Guidelines, and aspects of the Practice in delivering solutions. Each of the examples comes from real-life projects; however, the names of the companies have been left out.

Services Team: Portlet Proof of Concepts

In the first example, a software vendor's services team needed to build custom portlets to support proof-of-concept engagements. Before they used patterns, the work was performed manually, and it would take about 40 hours to create and test a custom portlet. In a proof-of-concept environment, this is unacceptable as it significantly increases the cost and time to complete the proof of concept. This was identified as an opportunity to build a pattern as there was an existing and recognized best practice that was used many times. The pattern was responsible for creating a large number of files (approximately 95) needed for the portlet, code was added to handle common configurations and errors, and the pattern would also generate optimized and tested code. After the pattern was applied, the Pattern User would add business logic to the portlet. Using the pattern to build the portlet took approximately 20 minutes, and the majority of that time was spent on adding the business logic and then deploying the portlet. The pattern was used over a number of years and resulted in over 80 portlets being generated, saving over 3,000 hours of development time.

Software Vendor: Product Update

The second example is based on a team working for a software vendor. The application that they worked on needed to meet a hard deadline for a customer and ship with a set of 130 SOA-based services that adhered to the OAGIS message format. A significant number of steps were needed to create each of the services, resulting in over 100 pages of documentation. The team discovered that performing this work manually would push them three months beyond the customer-imposed deadline.

The team spent a day learning how to create pattern implementations and then went to work applying those skills. The resulting pattern generated a significant portion of the required code, including data objects, client code, server code, and even unit tests. When using the patterns, the team was able to reduce the documentation from over 100 pages to 2 pages. They were able to save over 1,400 hours in their project and deliver the solution to the customer in time to meet the deadline. They also ended up shipping the patterns with the product, enabling customers and business partners to benefit from the patterns.

Entertainment Industry: Enhancing MDD

Let's take a look at a couple of additional examples that go beyond companies that sell and service software.[14] First we'll look at a company in the entertainment industry. In this case the organization was following an MDD approach. More specifically, the team used a UML modeling tool for creating models that would then drive their development. The models were used for documentation, and a manual effort was required to follow through and create the solution. The organization had concerns about productivity, quality, and governance. Some patterns were used, but only manually, and they needed interpretation in the transition to development. Development phases were too long, and transcription errors occurred when moving from the models to code. In addition, adherence to corporate architecture standards was inconsistent, and best practices were not always followed.

The organization performed an analysis of its development approach, models, and resulting artifacts. As a result of this analysis a set of patterns was identified and then delivered as pattern implementations. By using these patterns, it was estimated that the architects in the organization were able to achieve up to 50% improvement in productivity, resulting in millions in development savings. In addition, they were able to eliminate many defects from the resulting solution by using automation in place of manual efforts.

Government: Integrating Departments

The last example we'll look at in this section is based on work completed for a European government department. The department was required to externalize its data via SOA-based services so that it could be shared and integrated across the government. Within the department there were multiple divisions, and each was expected to meet this requirement. The planned strategy was to use an enterprise service bus (ESB) to assist in externalizing the services and support integration and sharing. In creating a solution, the department required a development platform that all of its employees could use that would be simple, agile, and highly productive. In addition, they required a strong level of governance and high quality; each member of the team had to adhere to the corporate architectural standards.

During the analysis of the situation it was determined that supporting the integrations would take three days of effort from a highly skilled resource for each of the services. There were a significant number of services to create. Each of the services would be created according to a specific best-practice-based approach. Recognizing a

---

14. For another example from the software vendor realm, we encourage you to read Siddle and Draper (2008).

recurring best-practice approach, they leveraged the work done in the analysis and recognized the opportunity to create a set of patterns to generate the required integrations. Using pattern implementations, rather than performing the work manually, allowed each of the services to be completed in approximately ten minutes and required a much lower skill level. The organization expected to save over 50 person-years of effort by the switch to using pattern implementations.

Why Do We Need PBE?

As with most types of reusable assets, the more generic the asset, the lower the return that each reuse will provide. Many books since the original GoF book have provided guidance on these first 23 patterns. These books have mapped the patterns to numerous languages, detailed the designs of the patterns, and used the patterns to detail how to perform object-oriented development. In addition, many more patterns have been created and shared. A search of the web or a bookstore will lead you to numerous results that list patterns and pattern-related documents. For instance, the *Handbook of Software Architecture* website[15] has cataloged 2,000 patterns so far. So if we have all of these patterns available to us, you might leap to the conclusion that our problems in delivering software have been alleviated. Unfortunately, that is not the situation; the answer is not as simple as just saying, "Use patterns."

As patterns have been available for use in software development for quite some time now, one would expect that there would be a very high adoption rate and that we would have already reached a very high level of maturity in using them successfully. Unfortunately, we have run into a number of issues in using patterns. In practice, we see that

- There is little methodology that actually shows how to use and leverage multiple patterns within a solution. This leads to random and nonstrategic use of patterns.

- Most of the patterns that people use are the GoF patterns.

- In cases where other patterns are used, they are often used in isolation rather than being woven together as part of a larger solution.

- There is little skill in identifying and formalizing patterns that are unique within an organization. In addition, there is little focus on such patterns.

- If patterns are used, they are used only for forward-engineering a solution.

---

15. www.handbookofsoftwarearchitecture.com.

- Abstraction is put to limited use.

- There is concern that restricting the creativity of the developers within the organization will diminish job satisfaction.

- The patterns used are often invented elsewhere.[16]

Would the application of a systematic, disciplined, and quantifiable approach to pattern use solve some of the issues that have limited their success to date?

The Importance of Creativity, Constraints, Rules, and Assumptions

Popular business literature stresses the importance of creativity, and we expect and value it in new team members. However, unmanaged and unfocused creativity can be detrimental to a project. We need to channel and focus the creativity of the team; we want creativity with purpose, creativity that helps us to reach our goals.

We use platform decisions, architectural styles, architectural patterns, and so forth as mechanisms for narrowing the solution space in a collaboratively disciplined way. To support both the production and consumption of patterns, we seek to leverage constraints, rules, and assumptions. To ensure that we are all on the same page, let's take a quick look at the definitions associated with these terms:

- **Creativity:** "Characterized by originality and expressiveness; imaginative"[17]

- **Constraint:** "The state of being restricted or confined within prescribed bounds"[18]

- **Rule:** "A principle or regulation governing conduct, action, procedure, arrangement, etc."[19]

- **Assumption:** "A statement that is assumed to be true and from which a conclusion can be drawn"[20]

---

16. For additional discussion of some of the challenges regarding the use of patterns, see Manolescu et al. (2007).

17. *American Heritage Dictionary of the English Language, Fourth Edition*. Retrieved July 1, 2008, from http://dictionary.reference.com/browse/creativity.

18. *American Heritage Dictionary of the English Language, Fourth Edition*. Retrieved June 24, 2008, from http://dictionary.reference.com/browse/constraint.

19. *Dictionary.com Unabridged (v 1.1)*. Retrieved June 24, 2008, from http://dictionary.reference.com/browse/rule.

20. *WordNet 3.0*. Retrieved June 24, 2008, from http://dictionary.reference.com/browse/assumption.

In addition to using patterns to focus the creativity of the team, we also want to support the consumption of the patterns. Where's the value in cases where a Pattern User is unable to use a pattern? To help support consumption we provide constraints and rules. Constraints and rules ensure that the pattern is used correctly. In the case of a pattern implementation, the assumptions that are found within the pattern help to reduce the amount of information the user of the pattern needs to provide.

When we turn our focus to the building of patterns, we similarly need to look for ways to manage our creativity. We can use patterns to guide us in identifying, documenting, and building patterns. In addition, we need to leverage the creativity of the team to identify, document, and build the patterns that our organization needs.

Important Definitions

The terms defined in this section, as shown in Figure 1.4, are important to PBE and will be referred to in the rest of the book. This section provides brief definitions of these terms to ensure a common understanding. Additional details on these terms and supporting definitions are provided in Appendix A, "PBE Definitions."

Figure 1.4 also shows that there is a relationship between these elements. We use metamodels, DSLs, and patterns to represent solutions within a model. Models that are recognized as representing a best-practice solution are exemplars. With an exemplar in hand, we are able to create a new pattern that can be used to specify future solutions. With these relationships in mind, let's take a look at the definitions for each of these terms.

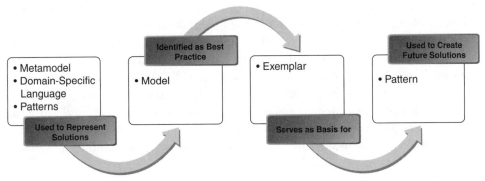

Figure 1.4   *Overview of key concepts related to PBE*

Model

Key to working with patterns is the use of models. Simply put, a **model** is an abstraction or a simplification of reality. A good model includes elements that are relevant at a given level of abstraction, while hiding or ignoring details that are not relevant. A model may be structural, emphasizing the organization of a solution, or behavioral, emphasizing the dynamics of a solution.

Metamodel

The language used within a model can be formalized textual, formalized graphical, or natural language. A formalized language—one that has a detailed and precise description—is helpful in creating models that support communication between people as well as communication with machines. A metamodel is a key mechanism we use in building a formal language. A **metamodel** is a special type of model that describes and specifies a modeling language. Essentially, we use a more abstract model to define the language that is used in another, more concrete model.

Exemplar

When we want to create a new pattern (whether a specification or an implementation), we need to keep in mind that patterns are discovered rather than invented. To this end, we often look for representative reference solutions that we can analyze and use as the basis for the pattern. We call such a reference solution an **exemplar.**

To identify a possible pattern, we are on the lookout for both exemplars and situations where the "Rule of Three" applies. The Rule of Three is used to judge where a possible pattern may exist; in this case we are looking for situations where the same problem/solution set has occurred in three unique situations.

As noted at the beginning of this chapter, starting a project is full of difficulties, including concerns about available expertise. However, what if we take the idea of exemplars and the Rule of Three into consideration? Can we use these ideas to help us find patterns to use on the project? Some of the sources to which we could apply these ideas include past project designs and implementations, as well as some of the artifacts of the current project. For instance, with the current project, we could examine the architectural mechanisms, key use cases, recurring aspects of the solution, and so on.

Domain-Specific Languages

A **domain-specific language (DSL)** is "a programming language or specification language dedicated to a particular problem domain, a particular problem representation technique, and/or a particular solution technique."[21] More simply put, a DSL is a language that we can use to describe a solution that allows us to use terminology from the domain in which we are working.

There are a number of reasons to use DSLs along with PBE, some of which are these:

- We are trying to simplify the lives of pattern consumers and enable them to structure the input model to the pattern in the simplest manner possible.

- Ideally we are able to automate the use of the patterns via the creation and use of pattern implementations.

- DSLs and their underlying metamodels support communication between people as well as with machines.

- A DSL enables us to both speak in terms of the problem domain and to operate at higher levels of abstraction.

Summary

If there is one key idea that you should take away from this book, it is that patterns are for everyone. Whether you are working as an architect, developer, tester, or business analyst, you should be looking at what patterns can be reused and what opportunities present themselves for new patterns. You need to be aware of the best-practice-based solutions and repeating situations where you can apply these best practices. Don't worry about finding the perfect pattern that will work for everyone in all situations. As stated by Alexander:

> You see then that the patterns are very much alive and evolving. In fact, if you like, each pattern may be looked upon as a hypothesis like one of the hypotheses of science.
>
> In this sense, each pattern represents our current best guess as to what arrangement . . . will work to solve the problem presented.[22]

Patterns represent the best thinking currently available. Patterns are alive; they do not start out as perfect entities but improve in quality over time as the community of software engineers investigates and refines them.

---

21. http://en.wikipedia.org/wiki/Domain-specific_language.

22. Alexander (1977).

As you start your journey with PBE, you can leverage tools, processes, standards, and patterns, with a focus on how to identify, produce, manage, and consume patterns. Leveraging the PBE Core Values, Patterns, Guidelines, and associated Practice provides a set of materials you can use to guide you in adopting and succeeding with PBE.

If you already have started an ABD program, PBE makes a logical and easy addition to your efforts. If you have not yet started with ABD, PBE is a great initiative to use to get things going.

Chapter 2

Examples of Pattern Implementations

In this chapter we look at examples of pattern implementations. When working with PBE, we work with both pattern specifications and pattern implementations. However, practitioners are usually more familiar with pattern specifications. So although pattern implementations are just one part of PBE, we focus on them, as not only are they a new concept; they are a critically important part of PBE. Being able to create an automated version of our patterns increases the impact we can have with our patterns and significantly affects our productivity, our ability to consistently apply patterns, and the quality of the resulting solutions.

We will familiarize ourselves with the different types of pattern implementations and their uses. The goal is to help make the different types of pattern implementations more concrete, while showing a variety of ways in which each of the types can be used.

The case study discussed in Chapters 3 through 7 provides a more broadly scoped example of PBE that includes the use of both pattern implementations and specifications.

Types of Pattern Implementations

In the following sections we will look at examples of three different types of pattern implementations: UML pattern implementations, model-to-model pattern implementations, and model-to-text pattern implementations. UML pattern implementations are intra-model pattern implementations, where the pattern adds or updates elements inside the same model, but more important at the same level of abstraction. Model-to-model and model-to-text pattern implementations are pattern implementations that work at an inter-model level and across levels of abstraction.

UML Pattern Implementations

UML pattern implementations are a good place to begin learning about the different types of pattern implementations because they have a limited scope and a visual representation. A UML pattern implementation is a pattern that we use within a UML model. It interacts with the elements within a model and can either update those elements or add new elements to the model. The idea here is not to move from one level of abstraction to another but to add more details within a specific level. The figures we show in this chapter come from Rational Software Architect (RSA); however, this approach is supported by other tools.

Abstract Factory Pattern

Let's start with a well-known pattern, the Abstract Factory pattern. The Abstract Factory pattern was first described in *Design Patterns: Elements of Reusable Object-Oriented Software.*[1] The purpose of this pattern is to enable the creation of families of related objects consistently without dependency on concrete classes.

Figure 2.1 shows an instance of this pattern using the UML pattern implementation approach. In the upper pane of the figure there is a representation of the «Pattern Instance». The different roles that participate in the pattern are shown on the left-hand side of the «Pattern Instance». The right-hand side of the «Pattern Instance» shows the model elements that have been bound to those roles. Once elements from the model have been bound to the roles, the model will be updated as appropriate to adhere to the pattern (relationships added, methods added, possibly even new classes or interfaces created). The bottom half of the figure shows the resulting elements and their relationships once the pattern has been applied.

Once applied, the pattern adds a set of keywords[2] to the model elements, including «AbstractFactory», «AbstractProduct», «ConcreteFactory», and «ConcreteProduct». In this case, we can see that there are a number of roles for the pattern (Abstract Factory, Concrete Factory, Abstract Product, etc.). In addition to adding keywords, the model is modified to support «use» relationships as well as generalization. These changes to the model serve two purposes. First, they assist the model in communicating to others the roles that the elements play in a pattern. Second, they provide additional information

---

1. Gamma et al. (1995).

2. A **stereotype** is the formal mechanism used in UML Profiles to add vocabulary to UML and denote an element as having a specific meaning and eventually specific properties. In contrast, a **keyword** is used as an informal approach to adding markup to a model. Stereotypes and keywords are often represented the same in tooling but are different in meaning.

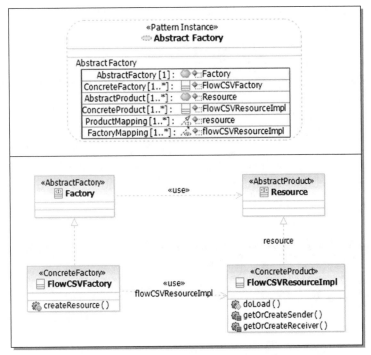

Figure 2.1 *An instance of the Abstract Factory pattern within Rational Software Architect*

to associated pattern implementations and transformations so that they can interpret this markup when generating code associated with the model.

As a result of using this pattern implementation, we are able to quickly and easily apply the pattern to the underlying model and to do so in a consistent manner. In addition, we are able to support using the model to communicate with others and support the use of the model to generate code.

Let's take a look at a few other examples that will help us to expand our thinking about what a pattern implementation can do for us within a model beyond common design patterns.

The No Cyclic Dependency Pattern

When working with models, we want to make sure that the models we create are well formed and support the rules of the business. One approach to making this happen is through the use of constraints. Typically, when working with UML we can use OCL—the Object Constraint Language—to detail and enforce constraints. However, the use of OCL is not widespread, and so most people ignore this capability, asking themselves, "Why learn yet another language?"

However, a set of patterns called the Constraint Patterns[3] has been created to address this issue. The Constraint Patterns simplify how constraints are defined by providing pattern implementations and associated tooling that generate the associated OCL. In this way we can be guided to create better models while not having to find someone who has these rare (yet useful) skills.

As an example, consider the case where we want to ensure that as we create a design there are no cyclic dependencies between elements. As shown in Figure 2.2, we can use a UML pattern in RSA to create a constraint that supports this approach. Using the pattern allows us to have the constraint without having to know how to write OCL.

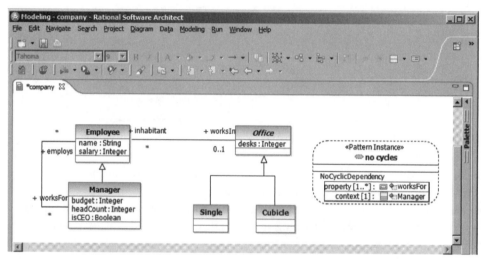

Figure 2.2   *Application of the No Cyclic Dependency pattern within Rational Software Architect*

In the figure we see that we have a Manager who is a specialization of an Employee and could have other employees working for him or her. However, we want to avoid the case where a Manager works for himself or herself. This is where the No Cyclic Dependency pattern comes into the picture. We create an instance of this pattern, bind the property pattern role to the worksFor attribute (the one materializ-

---

3. For more information regarding the Constraint Patterns, please consult Wahler, Ackerman, and Schneider (2008a).

ing the works-for relationship), and bind the context role to the Manager class. This then specifies that the Manager class cannot be linked to itself through the worksFor attribute.

Once the pattern has been applied, we can use additional tooling and pattern implementations to leverage the updated model. For instance, a validator can be used to review the model and ensure adherence to the constraint. We can also use supporting automations that can interpret the OCL and generate code from the model that enforces this constraint.

In contrast to using the pattern, Figure 2.3 shows the OCL that would have to be written to specify the constraint.

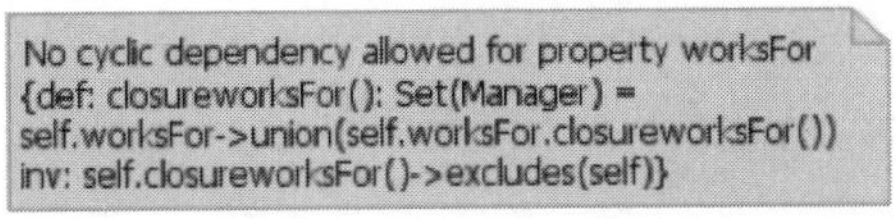

```
No cyclic dependency allowed for property worksFor
{def: closureworksFor(): Set(Manager) =
self.worksFor->union(self.worksFor.closureworksFor())
inv: self.closureworksFor()->excludes(self)}
```

Figure 2.3   *OCL for specifying that cyclic dependency is not allowed for the Manager*

Service Provider Pattern[4]

Next, consider a situation where we are creating SOA-based solutions. In such a situation we can use the UML Profile for Software Services[5] and then model our services and service providers. One approach is to apply the service provider stereotype to a structured class. Once the service provider has been created, we can use ports to detail the interfaces associated with the related services. Although this would be a best-practice approach, we still face a couple of issues:

- Many people are not familiar with the use of structured classes and ports.

- Even those familiar with structured classes and this approach may find it time-consuming to apply the pattern manually.

To solve these issues we can use the Service Provider pattern to assist us in representing services; an example of using the pattern is shown in Figures 2.4 and 2.5. Figure 2.4 shows a pattern instance and the model elements that have been bound to the instance. Figure 2.5 shows the resulting structured class that is created along with the ports and their associated services.

---

4. More information about the Service Provider pattern and guidance on how to create it is available in Ackerman and Portier (2007b).

5. Johnston (2005).

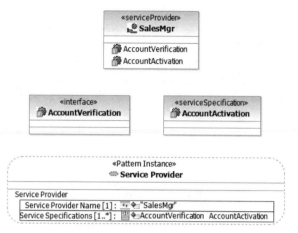

Figure 2.4   *Application of the Service Provider pattern*

Figure 2.5   *Structured class for the ServiceProvider with associated ports for the services*

Master-Detail Pattern

For a final example, let's look at the creation of a user interface. Perhaps we want to use JSF or Struts and start to define the web pages within an application, or even a rich client interface. Although we will perform detailed UI work in a specialized tool, we can spend some time defining the set of pages, flows, and relationships and use a standard template in the resulting web page (which can then be refined).

A common approach to organizing the user interface is to create a master-detail relationship between the pages. In other words, there is a master list of elements on a page, which then provides the option to drill down to a detail page. Figure 2.6 shows a pattern instance for the Master-Detail pattern. In this case the pattern specifies that there are three roles within the pattern: Search Screen, List Screen, and Details Screen. Once the elements are bound to the roles, the pattern will add the appropriate relationships between the screens as well as the «input» MusicForm and the «list» MusicListResults.

From there you can either pass it to your user interface (UI) developers so they can use it as a blueprint while developing the user interface, or perhaps use a custom model-to-text pattern implementation to generate some of the UI code.

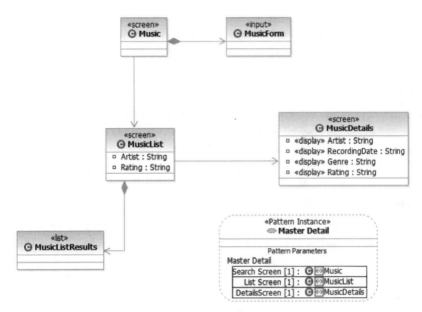

Figure 2.6 *Application of the Master-Detail pattern*

Model-to-Model Pattern Implementations

In this section we look at an example of a model-to-model pattern implementation. Model-to-model pattern implementations are usually used to derive a concrete model from a more abstract model. The example we will look at is the System Use Case to Service Collaboration pattern implementation.

System Use Case to Service Collaboration[6]

Unfortunately, today's tooling does not provide us with strong visual representations of model-to-model pattern implementations. Often they surface only as a configuration file within the environment. To help you better understand the pattern, we will first provide an overview of it, then look at the associated pattern specification, and wrap up with a look at the mapping of elements from the source model to the target model.

---

6. More details about this pattern and related pattern specifications can be found in the RA902 Architecting Services with Rational Software Architect course (www-304.ibm.com/jct03001c/ services/learning/ites.wss/us/en?pageType=course_description&courseCode=RA902). In addition, a version of this pattern implementation is available in Rational Software Architect.

This example comes from the SOA domain; we have created a model representing the key system use cases we have identified and want to progress to a more detailed representation as part of a service model, again applying the Software Services Profile.

Context

A direct linkage exists between the structure of the system use case model and the structure of the service model. For each system use case in the use case model there is a service collaboration in the service model, and for each flow (basic plus alternative ones) there is a service interaction under the service collaboration.

Problem

Creating the service collaborations is simple but can be tedious. We need a way to guarantee that all system use cases become service collaborations in the service model.

Solution

The pattern creates the service collaborations automatically, allowing the developer to focus on the service interaction.

Figure 2.7 provides a graphic view of the mapping of elements in the System Use Case Model to elements in the Service Model. Details on each of the mappings are as follows:

- **System Use Case Model.** The pattern creates a service model based on a model template, with Systems, Service Consumers, Composite Services, and Atomic Services packages.

- **Subsystems.** The pattern creates a UML package under the Systems package with the same name and the «subsystem» stereotype.

- **System Use Cases.** The pattern creates a collaboration stereotyped «serviceCollaboration» from the service profile under the corresponding package in the Systems package, containing an interaction. Both have the same name as the source element.

This same approach could be used to seed any lower level of abstraction from a higher one. One common example is to seed an analysis model from a use case model.

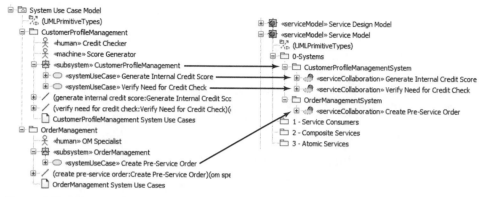

Figure 2.7 *Mapping from System Use Case Model to Service Model*

Model-to-Text Pattern Implementations

Model-to-text pattern implementations help us apply patterns as we move from a model to a text-based representation. This can be a case where we move from UML to a set of text-based artifacts such as code, documentation, configuration files, or deployment scripts.

Bean Factory Pattern Implementation[7]

The first example of model-to-text that we will look at uses an XML file as its input model and is based on the Java Emitter Template (JET)[8] open-source technology.

Bean Factory provides an implementation of the Factory pattern for Beans classes, meaning that the Beans would be created using the factory class.

The beanPackage parameter is used to define the Java package for the Beans as well as the name of the factory. Meanwhile, the bean parameters as well as their properties are then converted into JavaBean files with the right getters and setters, and a corresponding create method is added to the factory class.

Figure 2.8 shows the application of the patterns to the Library package. The package contains two entities, Library and Book. Each of them generates a Java source file containing the Bean properties as well as the corresponding getters and setters. But

---

7. For more details on this pattern implementation see DeCarlo et al. (2008).

8. For a quick introduction to JET, refer to the example section of the Model-to-Text Pattern Implementation pattern in Chapter 13.

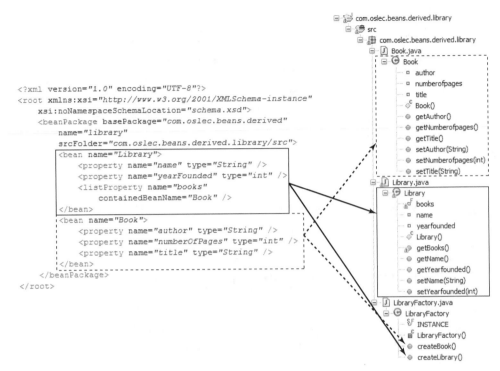

Figure 2.8   *Application of the Bean Factory pattern implementation*

more than a simple generation, the LibraryFactory is created with the methods and the source code to create the different Beans.

Hibernate Pattern Implementation

Transformations help to generate code from UML models, but they usually don't provide rich support for frameworks, configuration files, and associated best practices. The pattern implementation we describe here has been developed to allow the generation of Hibernate configuration files from a UML model.

In Figure 2.9 we can see that the package containing the input entities is used as the basis for the name of the Java project and the folder containing the configuration files. Then each class contained in the package leads to a resulting Hibernate configuration file; the information contained in the file is derived from the class and its relationships.

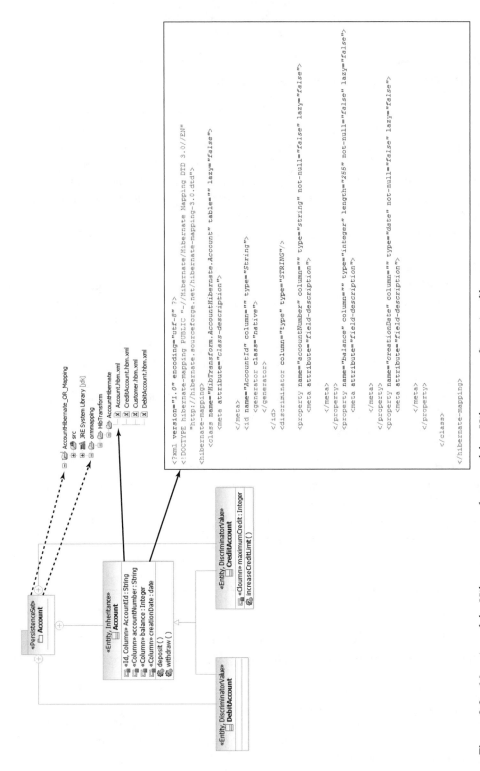

Figure 2.9 *Mapping of the Hibernate pattern from model to Hibernate configuration files*

33

Using Implementations in Combination

As we wrap up this look at examples of pattern implementations, let's look at the result of combining the three technologies. In this example a UML pattern implementation is paired with a model-to-text pattern implementation to generate code.

The pattern implementation we will be looking at is called Requester Side Caching.[9] The objective of this pattern is to increase service performance by providing a cache-aware proxy of the service on the requester side. So if the same request is executed twice, it will be served by the cache instead of being re-emitted.

The Requester Side Caching pattern implementation is composed of two steps:

1. The first step uses a UML pattern implementation to bind the model elements to the pattern instance and create a Cache class as well as an accelerated class implementation for the service. This is shown in Figure 2.10,[10] where the accelerated service is LegacyCatalogApp and the accelerated implementation is AcceleratedLegacyCatalogApp.

2. The second step is the application of a model-to-text implementation that will transform the modified model into Java code, not only translating the model but also filling the methods body of the Cache class and of the accelerated service implementation (AcceleratedLegacyCatalogApp). The code for the caching capabilities is generated by the pattern, so the Pattern User focuses on adding the business logic to the Catalog itself.

Each step provides value; the UML pattern implementation enhances the model, and the model-to-text adds specific method content, but the true value of the pattern is realized when the two steps are combined. In addition, the composition makes the pattern more flexible. If we needed to support .NET technology, we could replace the Java model-to-text pattern implementation with a C# one.

Summary

In this chapter we looked at examples of UML, model-to-model, and model-to-text pattern implementations. We've seen how UML pattern implementations apply

---

9. For more information about the *Requester Side Caching* pattern and its pattern implementation, please see Srinivasan et al. (2005) and Srinivasan et al. (2008). Srivinvasan et al. (2006) provides an example of the application of the pattern implementation.

10. Srinivasan et al. (2006).

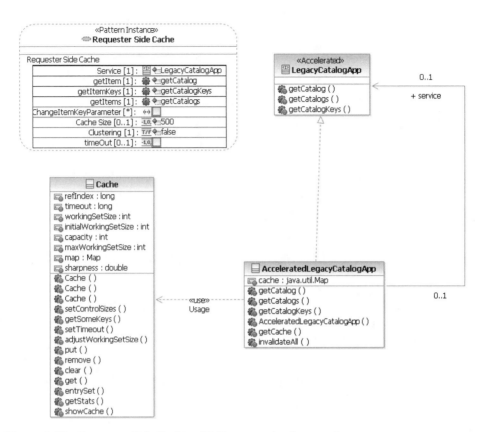

Figure 2.10   *Requester Side Caching UML pattern implementation*
Copyright IBM developerWorks, www.ibm.com/developerworks. Reused with permission.

within a model, whereas model-to-model and model-to-text pattern implementations are used between models.

The examples span multiple technologies and domains, highlighting the fact that we can use pattern implementations in many situations, for many purposes, and for a range of technologies. Recall that in a PBE approach we use both pattern specifications and pattern implementations. However, in this chapter we have provided a more narrow focus, looking specifically at pattern implementations. Pattern implementations are a more recent approach to working with patterns and represent a critical aspect of PBE.

Chapter 3

Case Study Introduction

In Chapters 3 through 7 we will follow an extended case study that illustrates how to apply PBE. The goal of these chapters is to bring together the PBE Core Values, Patterns, Guidelines, and Practice in an example of how they can be applied. This chapter sets the stage by introducing the case study's project team and the application that they will be building. In subsequent chapters we will examine the team's efforts across multiple iterations.

Both the company, Oslec Software, and the application discussed are fictional, but the case study reflects an amalgamation of real-world PBE experiences. The goal in presenting this case study is to provide a balance between real-world applicability and abstracting away details that unnecessarily complicate the scenario. As part of that balance, the case study focuses on the elements that are most important in helping software engineers learn how to adopt and use PBE.

Overview

We'll follow a fictional company, Oslec Software, through the creation of a new software solution. Oslec Software had developed an auction application to allow its employees to purchase corporate logo merchandise. Purchasing via an auction makes everything more exciting, even corporate logo merchandise.

After observing high employee participation and interest in corporate logo merchandise auctions, the company decided to productize the auction application. The application will be sold under the name LogoAuction and will enable other companies to create the same kind of social dynamics achieved within Oslec. We will follow the story of how the company rebuilds the application so that it can be sold as a commercial application. The original application works fine for internal use, but there are numerous issues that prevent an as-is repackaging. We will be exploring some of these issues as we drill down into the architecture of the application.

Because a version of the application already exists, the project team can leverage a number of artifacts in building the commercial version. For instance, there is already a use case model, a domain model, and a code base that they can consult.

The team will be leveraging PBE on the project. This will be a challenge, because the organization is new to PBE and in the past has not excelled in its use of patterns. Any pattern use that has occurred to date has essentially been ad hoc—not systematic, not disciplined—and the company has not quantified the results of any pattern efforts. The team is essentially working from a blank sheet of paper in regard to patterns. Oslec Software has its own methodology and many other tools and assets to support that methodology. An important goal for the organization is to have a successful project while also building out its patterns capability, accelerating this project and future projects.

Meet the Team

Now that we have a better idea of the application scope, let's take a look at the development organization at Oslec Software. The skills, experience, and culture of the organization will play a big role in how successful it is in adopting PBE.

Figure 3.1 depicts a simplified organization chart for the project team and summarizes the names and roles for the team members. Alex, the architect for this effort, has significant experience with the Java EE platform, and he has been a strong proponent of bringing patterns and PBE into the company. Working hand-in-hand with him are Gwen, the requirements analyst, and Michael, the project manager. They are both skilled in their respective domains but are unfamiliar with patterns and PBE. Eight developers are based in three different sites (four in Toronto, two in Boston, and two in Bangalore). Each developer group is led by a team leader: Duncan in Toronto, John in Boston, and Rajesh in Bangalore. The team leaders are familiar with the use of some patterns, but not with PBE. Jade from the testing group has been assigned to the project to assist with the quality assurance effort. Others who will interact with the team include Sam, the asset manager, and Jordan, from the tools group.

As the development team is globally distributed, Michael faces challenges such as differences in language, culture, and time zone that in the past have been difficult for the organization. Designs that have been created in one location are often implemented in another location, based on availability and skills. In many cases the implementations have not stayed true to the design, which has led to rework and missed deadlines.

Because of other project commitments, John's and Rajesh's teams will join the project later. This will give Duncan's team time to define and build the infrastructure that the others will be leveraging.

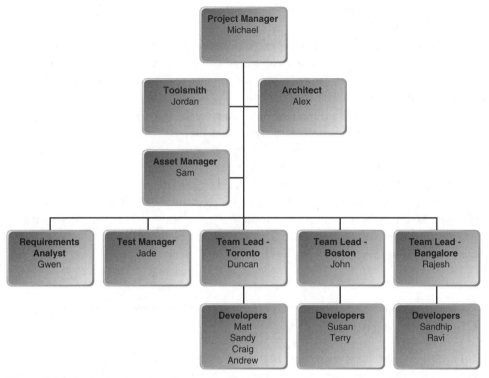

Figure 3.1 *Organization chart for the development team*

Oslec Development Process

Oslec uses an Agile development approach in the majority of its projects. Teams have built out a custom process that brings together a number of Agile practices. Of particular interest is the use of practices such as test-driven development, iterative and incremental development, Agile modeling, and continuous integration.

In terms of planning, they follow iterative and incremental development, with two to three weeks per iteration. The goal is to provide enough time to deliver valuable increments, without going too long between deliveries. They have also adopted Agile modeling[1] for their architecture and design activities. They use UML and have standardized on a modeling platform. Their projects start with Iteration 0: Envisioning, when the teams flesh out the high-level architecture of the application to develop.

---

1. For more information on Agile modeling please see www.agilemodeling.com/. To get an introduction to the design approach used in the case study, please see Ambler and Gonzalez (2008).

The purpose is not to determine all the details but to get a shared vision of the architecture. This architecture will be validated and refined as the application is developed. They have also adopted the practice of recording and specifying requirements with use cases. However, their use cases tend to be high-level; details are fleshed out through discussions and tests. They have adopted a test-driven development approach where they write their tests and test artifacts before developing features. They then work to build a solution that will pass the tests; once the solution passes the tests, they refactor it as necessary. To further support their iterative and incremental approach along with their quest for quality, Oslec uses continuous integration. Each night the application under development is built and tested.

Alex and Michael have worked together, filling the role of process engineer to further customize the Oslec development process to include PBE. They have customized the process and published a configuration that the team will use. The published configuration has been posted to a server that is accessible by all team members so they can refer to it in their day-to-day work.

Overview of the Plan

Up until now, Oslec Software has used patterns in only an ad hoc and isolated manner; for instance, they have previously used Model-View-Controller (MVC) when building their applications. There has also been some use of some of the GoF design patterns. However, this usage has not been systematic or disciplined. When patterns are used, it is an uncoordinated, individual decision, and no rigor is applied to determining the impact of using the patterns. In addition, because of varied skill levels across the team, they've seen inconsistent results related to the application of patterns. Automation has not yet played any role in their pattern efforts, and culturally patterns are not promoted.

As this is the first PBE-based project, the team does not yet have a repository of patterns that they can consult and leverage. The project itself will follow an Agile iterative and incremental approach, and one of the priorities is to build out their PBE capabilities in each iteration; that is, they will not be taking a big-bang approach to the adoption. Instead, within each iteration they will adopt as much as is realistic and worthwhile. By the end of the project, the goal is that they will have substantially increased their capabilities to use patterns. Then, on further projects, they can continue to build on this base and incrementally build out additional capabilities.

In ramping up for the project, the team has taken the following initial steps:

- **Tool selection.** The first step is to determine which tools will be used to help with the creation and management of patterns. For management of patterns, including storage of pattern specifications and implementations, they will use their existing asset repository. A new asset will be created for each pattern they use. If the pattern is not specific to the company (i.e., the source is external to the company) and the specification is already available through the Internet, the entry will contain a brief description of the pattern as well as a reference to the pattern source. Pattern specifications specific to the company will be specified in HTML, to make them easier to consult. The team has also decided to use the pattern specification template as described in the Pattern Specification guidelines (Chapter 13) as their standard with a goal of supporting pattern sharing and comprehension. For pattern implementations, a download link will be provided with the pattern asset page so that people interested in automating the use of the pattern can easily download the implementation. Their standard architecture and design tool is IBM Rational Software Architect as it provides mechanisms to develop model-to-model and model-to-text pattern implementations. The existing configuration management tool will be used to manage the source artifacts related to the development of pattern implementations as for any other development artifact.

- **Collaboration.** On past projects the team extensively used wikis to capture information and collaborate; they want to leverage this positive experience by using wikis to store and discuss candidate pattern specifications. Once the pattern specification has stabilized, it will be moved to the asset repository. However, the wiki entry will be maintained to encourage discussion and feedback on the pattern specification as new versions are pursued. The asset repository will be used for managing feedback on deployed patterns.

- **Enablement.** Alex, Michael, Jordan, and the development team leads have been taking training on PBE, including coverage of concepts, tooling, and implementation skills. This group has learned about the theory behind PBE and the associated patterns, guidelines, core values, and practice. In these efforts they have learned how to identify candidate patterns, how to write pattern specifications, and how to create pattern implementations. In addition, they've been asked to focus on building a culture that will embrace and work with the PBE approach.

Case Study Roadmap

As we move forward with the case study, it is important to remember that PBE is not a one-size-fits-all approach. As we look to apply the lessons from the case study to our own projects, we will need to be pragmatic and pick the aspects that will help us succeed within the specifics of our projects. We will use the PBE Patterns and Guide-lines as well as the PBE Practice highlighted in Chapter 8 as a guide on our journey.

The case study uses a subset of the available PBE guidance. In addition, only a fraction of the thousands of currently available patterns are touched upon. As we embark on our projects, we will need to pick out a subset from this pool of available guidance, a subset that provides value and helps us to get our job done.

The content of the case study is focused in one domain and an application that is limited in applicability. However, the steps taken, the ideas leveraged, and the core values and patterns used can be mapped to many situations.

In the case study we will be following the Oslec team during the first four itera-tions of their project. As we accompany them, we will see how they perform their tasks leveraging PBE practices, patterns, and guidelines. Figure 3.2 summarizes the PBE focus of each iteration of the case study as well as some of the main aspects that will be covered in each iteration.

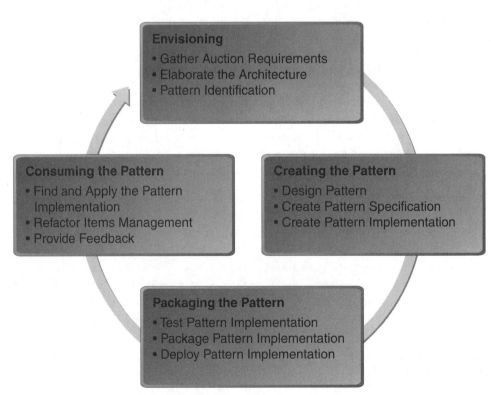

Figure 3.2 *Overview of the case study iterations*

As the team starts envisioning the requirements and architecture of the application, they will use existing patterns and also identify and evaluate new patterns to build. In the second iteration they will work on building the application, while Jordan and Alex design and build a pattern. In the third iteration they will package and deploy the newly built pattern to make it available to others. The last iteration of the case study focuses on how the pattern is used to create a new subsystem as well as to refactor an existing one.

Summary

In this chapter we familiarized ourselves with Oslec, a fictional company. We will follow the project team in the next four chapters as they develop an auction-based application for selling corporate logo merchandise using PBE Core Values, Patterns, Guidelines, and Practice.

Chapter 4

Iteration 0: Envisioning

This chapter describes the activities and tasks performed by the Oslec team during the initial iteration for the LogoAuction project as well as how PBE fits and helps them perform these activities. As stated in the previous chapter, the team is following an Agile development process. In the Envisioning[1] iteration the project team defines the high-level scope and architecture of the project. The purpose is not to define and work through every detail, but to reach agreement on the high-level plan.

Some of the PBE questions that the team will address as they work their way through this iteration include the following:

- Where does it make sense to use patterns?

- Which patterns already exist? Which would need to be created?

- Where does it make sense to use automation along with patterns?

- How much effort will be involved in building our patterns?

- What is the expected ROI associated with the patterns that can be used?

As they answer these questions, they will develop a candidate architecture that includes the set of patterns that they will be using.

Figure 4.1 summarizes the work that will be performed in this iteration.

The team starts their journey in PBE by using patterns to help them gather and organize the requirements for the LogoAuction application and elaborate the architecture. They will also incorporate existing patterns and start to identify and evaluate patterns that need to be created.

---

1. For more information on Agile Modeling please see www.agilemodeling.com/. To get an introduction to the approach we use in the case study please see Ambler and Gonzalez (2008).

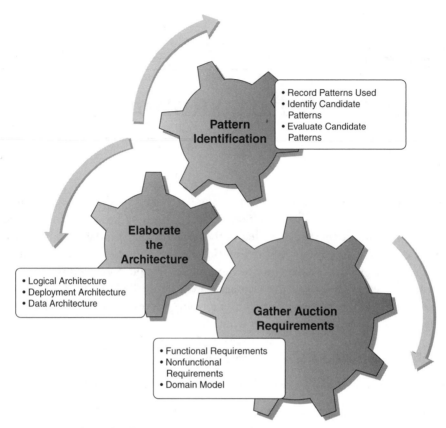

Figure 4.1   *Roadmap for the Envisioning iteration*

Getting Started

As is standard practice at Oslec, Michael, the project manager, starts the iteration by organizing a quick meeting with the team to define the iteration goals and objectives. This iteration will be shorter than the others and will involve a small subset of the team. The purpose of the iteration is to define the high-level requirements and architecture of the LogoAuction application.

Gwen, the requirements analyst, will define the use cases and the business entities for the application based on the artifacts from the existing internal auction application. She also hopes to identify existing patterns she can reuse.

Alex, the architect, will define the architecture and will try to leverage existing patterns as much as possible. In addition to figuring out what patterns he is going to use, he also needs to determine how the patterns will fit together.

PBE Focus

In this iteration the team will leverage the work that has been done in kick-starting PBE within the organization. As mentioned previously, the team has invested time in tool selection, collaboration, process, and enablement. The same team that performed this initial work will continue and drive the LogoAuction project. So the team does not expect to deviate from the output from this initial work effort. If the team members were different, they might evaluate the output from these earlier efforts and tweak the results as needed for the specifics of their project and team composition.

They start the PBE work following the Pattern Search guideline (Chapter 10) by investing in the following actions:

- **Initial identification of external pattern sources.** The team prefers to remain open in terms of pattern sources and will look at many sources. However, with so many possible patterns available, it can be overwhelming and difficult to find the right pattern at the right time. Therefore, they invest some time early in the project in collecting an initial set of pattern sources. It doesn't have to be complete, perfect, or all-encompassing, just a good start. They'll refine, update, and adjust the list as they move through the project. If someone finds a pattern to use outside of these sources, he or she will be able to submit the newly identified source as well as the pattern(s). So far, they have already started using the PBE Patterns and Guidelines and will continue to do so throughout the project. Here are the additional pattern sources they plan to start with:

  - *Patterns for e-Business*[2]: a set of patterns gathered by IBM to help develop web-based applications. The patterns start at the business level and then guide the Pattern User to deployment and runtime aspects of a solution.

  - *Core J2EE patterns*[3]: a set of patterns focused on developing Java EE applications. As these patterns are based on an older version of Java EE, Alex and Duncan review and confirm that the patterns can still be applied with Java EE 5 (requiring modification in some cases).

  - *Analysis patterns*[4]: a set of patterns for using and manipulating domain-related objects.

  - *Gang of Four (GoF) design patterns*[5]: a set of core object design patterns.

---

2. Koushik et al. (2001).

3. Alur et al. (2003).

4. Fowler (1997).

5. Gamma et al. (1995).

- ◦ *Enterprise integration patterns*[6]: a set of patterns to integrate different systems together.

  - ◦ *Patterns of Software Architecture (POSA)*[7]: a set of architecture patterns.

- **Identify initial pattern scope.** The team has been encouraged to use patterns across the software development lifecycle (SDLC), looking beyond just the design discipline. They need to leverage their training and expertise to help identify, acquire, create, and use patterns in other disciplines. For example, they will invest time in using patterns to help them in their test creation efforts.

- **Identify initial focus areas.** The team's focus in the early iterations of the project is on the architecturally significant aspects of the solution, those key elements of the design (and then the implementation) that are the most important—and possibly the most risky—for this project. They will use this focus as their source for identifying unique patterns for their organization as well as for figuring out which external patterns to use.

LogoAuction Application Requirements

We now follow Gwen as she starts gathering the requirements for the LogoAuction application.

The Functional Requirements

As mentioned in the previous chapter, Oslec decided to productize the auction system after seeing the success it had internally. As there is an existing version already in use, the team is not starting from scratch. There are concerns about the implementation of the solution, and the team doubts that it can be repurposed. They need a quality foundation to support the new solution as they build out and up; numerous issues could derail the project, such as requirements related to the size of the user base, application distribution needs, stability, and many others. At a minimum, Gwen expects to reuse some of the requirements that were defined for the internal auction system.

The working principles of the application are simple: the company makes its logo items available for auction, and then an automatic process starts the auction; after a

---

6. Hohpe and Woolf (2004).

7. Buschmann et al. (1996).

certain amount of time, defined for each auction category, the auction is closed and the highest bidder wins the auction.

Figures 4.2 and 4.3 provide an overview of the high-level requirements. Gwen uses use cases to record the requirements, but similar results would arise if she were to use user stories or other requirements-capturing mechanisms.

Figure 4.2 shows the main actors[8] and their relationships. The generalization arrow indicates that a specialized actor can perform all the use cases of a more generic actor. For example, the Administrator actor can perform the use cases of the Registered User (Login, Manage Account, and so on). Nonhuman actors have been identified using the «System» stereotype.

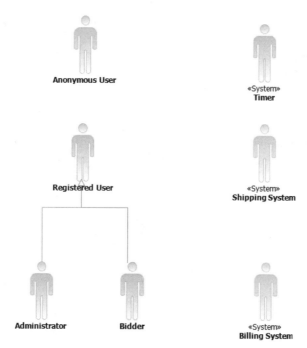

Figure 4.2   *LogoAuction application actors*

Figure 4.3 shows the actors, the use cases, and the relationships among these elements. Tables 4.1 and 4.2 provide brief descriptions of the actors and use cases.

---

8. An **actor** represents a role played by a user or system that is external to the application.

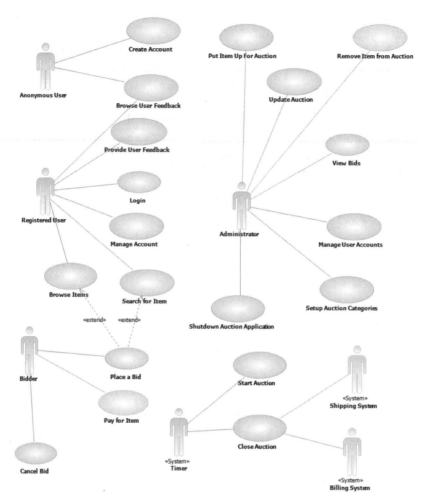

Figure 4.3   *LogoAuction application use cases*

Table 4.1   *Actor Overview for the LogoAuction Application*

Name	Description
Administrator	The Registered User who is in charge of administering the auction application as well as the managed auction items
Anonymous User	A user connecting to the application who does not have an account or who is not logged in
Registered User	A user with an account and who is logged in to the application
Bidder	A registered user who is bidding on one or more items
Timer	A system clock that automatically starts and stops auctions

Table 4.2   *Use Case Overview for the LogoAuction Application*

Name	Description
Create Account	Allow an Anonymous User to create an account.
Provide User Feedback	Allow a Registered User to provide feedback on the auction application as well as any item available for auction.
Browse User Feedback	Allow any user to browse the provided feedback.
Manage User Accounts	Allow the Administrator to create, delete, or modify the user accounts.
Set Up Auction Categories	Allow the Administrator to manage the categories used to group the items for auction. Each category defines the duration of the auction for the items it contains.
Shut Down Auction	Allow the Administrator to shut down the application.
Remove Item from Auction	Allow the Administrator to remove an item from the auction.
Log In	Allow a user to log in.
Manage Account	Allow Registered Users to manage their account; typical actions include changing the password, contact information, etc.
Search for Item	Allow a Registered User to search for an item using one or more keywords.
Browse Items	Allow a Registered User to browse items using the defined categories.
Put Item Up for Auction	Allow the Administrator to make an item available for auction. While putting the item up for auction, the Administrator sets the start date and time.
Update Auction	Allow the Administrator to update an auctioned item.
View Bids	Allow the Administrator to see the bids on an item.
Cancel Bid	Allow a buyer to cancel a previously entered bid.
Place a Bid	Allow a user to place a bid on an item. To place a bid the user needs to add one or more bid increments to the current price of the item.
Start Auction	The auction is started automatically by the system based on the start date and time defined when the auction was created.
Close Auction	After reaching the amount of time specified for the auction, the auction is closed and the highest Bidder becomes the buyer of the item. The system then sends a billing request to the company billing system as well as a shipping request to the shipping system.
Pay for Item	The winning Bidder submits payment for the purchase and provides a credit card, online payment, or payroll deduction.

LogoAuction Domain Model

Gwen inherited a domain model[9] from the original version of the application, so she needs to review it and update it with the latest requirements. Figure 4.4 shows a class diagram representing the main elements of the original domain model.

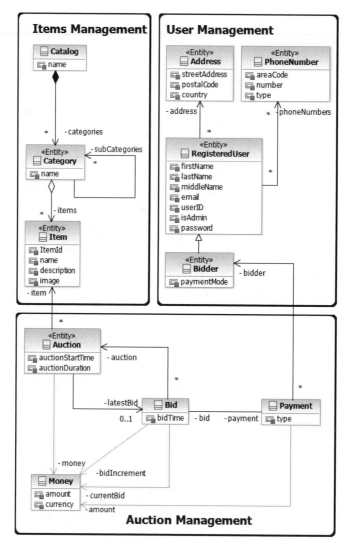

Figure 4.4   *LogoAuction application initial domain model*

---

9. A **domain model** contains the main business objects manipulated by the application.

The domain model can be divided into three areas of responsibility. The first area of responsibility, User Management, is concerned with the management of the users and contains entities to represent the user (RegisteredUser and Bidder) as well as the information that needs to be recorded about a user (Address and PhoneNumber). The second area of responsibility, Items Management, is about the auction-specific items. There we find the entities to describe the items up for auction and the way they are organized (Category and Catalog). The third area of responsibility, Auction Management, is focused on those elements related to auctions, including Bid, Payment, and information about the auction itself.

From discussions with stakeholders Gwen learns that the relationships between RegisteredUser, Bidder, and Administrator were a problem because the Administrator needed to create another account to be able to bid. This could become an even bigger problem for the next release, as a planned enhancement is to give employees the ability to use the auction application to sell logo items they own. Based on past project experience, Gwen recognizes that the Role[10] pattern might apply here. The Role pattern is an alternative to specialization/generalization, where an abstract role class is specialized to allow a user to have different concurrent roles. Figure 4.5 shows the existing implementation as well as the changes once the Role pattern is applied. As she adds the Seller role, Gwen also updates the Item class to add a reference to the Seller, even though in the first release the seller would always be the company.

Working with Craig, Gwen also notes that they are using quite a few attributes related to money. As they plan to internationalize the application, they will need to record the currency used for the prices. Gwen was unsure of how to solve this issue.

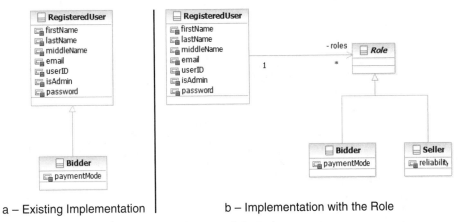

a – Existing Implementation   b – Implementation with the Role

Figure 4.5 *Before and after the application of the Role pattern*

---

10. For more information about the *Role* pattern please see www.martinfowler.com/apsupp/roles.pdf or Baumer et al. (2000).

She decided to search through the previously identified pattern sources. Based on her search, she found that the Quantity[11] pattern could help. The Quantity pattern proposes to use a Quantity class that combines the amount with the corresponding unit. So Gwen decides to create a Money class that will have two attributes, amount and currency. This class will be used whenever there is a need to represent money amounts. Figure 4.6 shows the new version of the domain model with the instances of the Role and Quantity patterns.

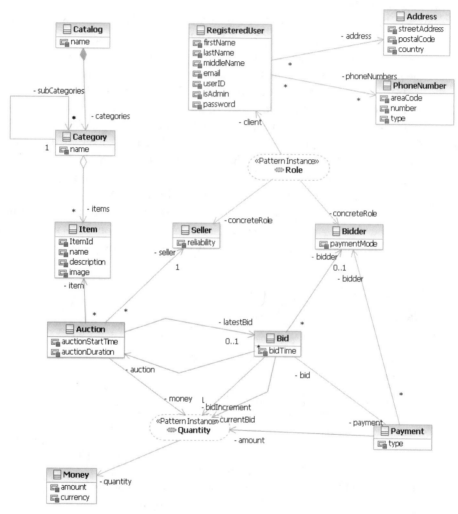

Figure 4.6   *The new version of the domain model including use of the Role and Quantity patterns*

11. Fowler (1997).

The Nonfunctional Requirements

Some of the nonfunctional requirements come from the internal implementation of the auction application. Additional requirements related to the planned productization of the application also need to be supported. Some of the key areas include these:

- **Usability.** The project team knows that the success of the auction application is based on the ability of the system to create interest for the bidders. One way to positively influence user interest is to make the application easy to access and use.

- **Connectivity.** Bidders must be able to connect to the application using a standard browser via the company network or the Internet.

- **Internationalization/localization.** Now that the organization plans to sell the application worldwide, it will need to support multiple languages and currencies.

- **Scalability and performance.** Scalability is also a concern as Oslec expects companies of varying size to use the application. The team needs to ensure that the resulting application will work for both small and large businesses.

- **Security.** Security is a top concern for the application. The team needs to ensure that buyer payments and personal information are kept secure.

- **Portability.** Last but not least, the resulting application is required to support multiple platforms. This has led to the selection of Java EE. Fortunately, the organization has some expertise in this area.

Elaborating the Architecture

In these early stages of the new application, Oslec will focus on a small number of architectural views, including the logical, deployment, and data architecture. The following sections look at how Oslec Software can leverage patterns in each of these views. Alex performs this architectural work in concert with the requirements work performed by Gwen. As in every Oslec project, even if Alex has primary responsibility for the architecture, he will not work in isolation; he will involve the developers and the team leads as much as possible.

To start the effort, he refers to the PBE Patterns and Guidelines and picks the Select Large-Scope Patterns First guideline (Chapter 16) that recommends focusing first on high-level, large-scope patterns, which in his case means identifying architecture patterns that will help define a solid and resilient architecture for the application. The entire team will come together to choose additional patterns that will help to embellish the solution. Those smaller-scope patterns will build upon the structure that is put in place by the larger-scope patterns.

Alex will also be working with the team to start identifying candidate patterns that may fit within the project but that have not yet been built. As part of the effort they will determine which of these patterns will be worth creating as pattern specifications and/or implementations, as described in the Pattern Creation Lifecycle guideline (Chapter 12).

As Alex starts to pull together the patterns that will form the basis for the solution, he also needs to ensure that he documents the design, the patterns, and how they fit together. Others who want to understand or enhance the solution will need to understand what patterns are being used and how they relate. To support this need, he selects the Communicate Design with Patterns guideline (Chapter 16).

LogoAuction Logical Architecture

First, Alex explores the logical architecture of the application, focusing on the major components of the system.

Alex selects the Layers[12] pattern, as it supports separation of concerns, reuse, and flexibility. The Layers pattern is a well-known architecture pattern that "helps to structure applications that can be decomposed into groups of subtasks in which each group of subtasks is at a particular level of abstraction."[13]

Alex decides to use three layers: Presentation, Business, and Data Access. The Presentation layer contains the user interface components, the Business layer contains the components implementing the business logic, and the Data Access layer contains the components providing access to the different data sources. Figure 4.7 highlights the layers and their relationships.

Figure 4.7 *LogoAuction application layers*

---

12. Buschmann et al. (1996).

13. Ibid.

Alex continues by focusing on the Presentation layer. The web interface is a top priority, as all users, including the administrators, will use it.

Following the same approach as followed with the domain model, Alex groups the use cases by area of responsibility. Figure 4.8 shows the use cases mapped to User Management, Items Management, and Auction Management.

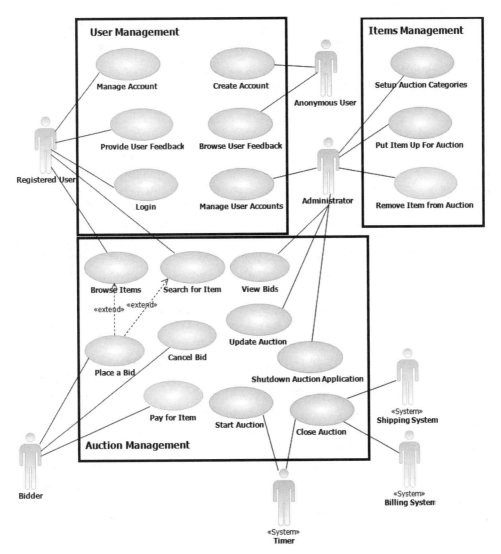

Figure 4.8 *Use cases distributed by areas of responsibility*

Pattern Impact: Areas of Responsibility

Keep in mind that we can find patterns that exist within an area of responsibility as well as patterns that apply across multiple areas of responsibility. Here are some of the consequences of failing to consider both perspectives:

- We may end up assigning areas of responsibility to different teams, where each becomes inwardly focused and we lose opportunities for identifying higher-order patterns.

- Each team re-creates the solution, leading to wasted effort, introduction of unnecessary variation in the solution, and increased complexity.

Each of the three areas—User, Auction, and Items—will be realized by a subsystem with its own business components, as well as persistence counterparts in the Data Access layer. The business components—User Management, Auction Management, and Items Management—will contain the business logic to implement their respective use cases. The persistence components will provide the create, read, update, and delete (CRUD) operations to the entities falling into the business component area. Figure 4.9 summarizes the layers as well as the main components and their dependencies.

The logical architecture described so far is an initial cut that will be refined as the team progresses. However, the team notes that there are some similarities across the areas of responsibility. In particular, each area has a Data Access layer and related business components. Alex considers whether they can benefit from recognizing that this solution recurs across a large part of the system.

Next, Alex adds technology concerns to the logical architecture. As mentioned earlier, one of the design constraints of the project is the use of Java EE 5. So he chooses Enterprise JavaBeans (EJB) 3[14] for the Business layer components and Java Persistence API (JPA) for the Data Access components. Now he needs to decide on a technology for the Presentation layer components. Over the years he has grown to like the Model-View-Controller[15] pattern as it provides a clear separation between the different pieces involved in interacting with a user. The pattern leads to solutions where a model element contains the core functionality and data, the view elements display information to the user, and controllers handle user input. Views and controllers together constitute the user interface and provide flexibility between the Presentation

---

14. For a good introduction to EJB 3 consult Panda et al. (2007).

15. Buschmann et al. 1996.

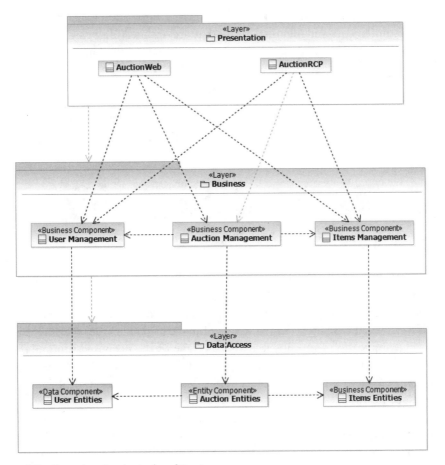

Figure 4.9   *LogoAuction logical architecture*

and the Business layers. Alex chooses JSF[16] as the technical implementation as it is part of Java EE 5 and it implements the MVC pattern.

LogoAuction Deployment Architecture

The next task for Alex is to look at the component distribution and the associated deployment architecture. First, he needs to understand the architecturally significant requirements that will impact the deployment architecture. As stated in the Pattern Selection Driven by Requirements guideline (Chapter 16), often pattern selection results from a combination of functional (business) requirements and nonfunctional

16. Additional details regarding JSF are provided at http://java.sun.com/javaee/javaserverfaces/.

requirements. With this guideline in mind, he works with Gwen to start exploring the gathered requirements and identifies those that are architecturally significant.

Gwen and Alex follow Pattern Search to help identify the patterns to use. They identify the Self-Service pattern from IBM's Patterns for e-Business,[17] and more precisely the Stand-Alone Single Channel application pattern, as a possible fit. This pattern addresses the general case of internal and external users interacting with enterprise transactions and data through a single channel.[18] That's a good start! Now Alex has a conceptual view of the deployment architecture, as shown in Figure 4.10.

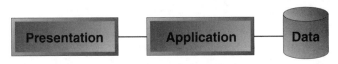

Figure 4.10   *The Self-Service Stand-Alone Single Channel pattern*

However, there are different ways to refine this specific pattern into a concrete deployment architecture. While reading the description of the pattern, Alex remembers the need to provide bidders with a way to make bids or view bids via the company intranet or the Internet. So the team will have to define strict security rules and protect the application from possible attacks. One of the proposed runtime patterns will help secure Internet access to the application by putting a web redirector into the demilitarized zone (DMZ). Figure 4.11 replicates the information available from the pattern specification.

As Alex is using a well-described pattern, he looks to minimize the architecture's documentation. Figure 4.12 shows the diagram he creates, which includes only the pattern instance and its related parameters. Alex is confident that with these two perspectives, others in the organization will be able to easily understand the pattern itself and how it is used in the LogoAuction application.

Now that he has defined the deployment architecture for the type of user interaction needed, Alex must introduce the integration with the Billing and Shipping systems. The Close Auction use case states that when the auction on an item is closed and the winner identified, messages are sent simultaneously to the Shipping and Billing systems to request that the item be shipped to the winner and a bill be sent. Alex selects the Exposed Broker ESB[19] pattern to support the integration between systems

---

17. Koushik et al. (2001).

18. For more details about the Stand-Alone Single Channel pattern consult www.ibm.com/developerworks/patterns/u2b/select-application-topology.html.

19. For more details about the Exposed Broker ESB pattern consult www.ibm.com/developerworks/patterns/.

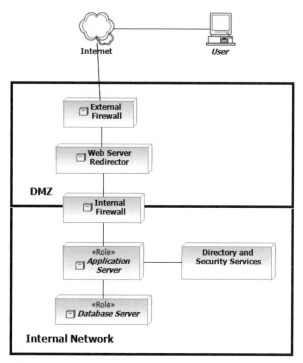

Figure 4.11   *The Self-Service Stand-Alone Single Channel pattern definition with a web server redirector*

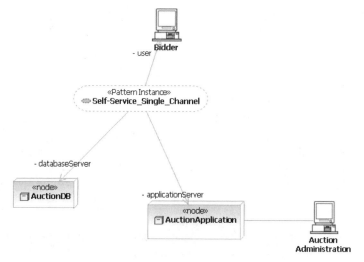

Figure 4.12   *The Self-Service Stand-Alone Single Channel pattern instance with associated database and application server roles*

by connecting them through an ESB. Figure 4.13 shows the Exposed Broker ESB pattern instance with the Source role bound to the `AuctionApplication` and the Targets role bound to the `ShippingSystem` and the `BillingSystem`.

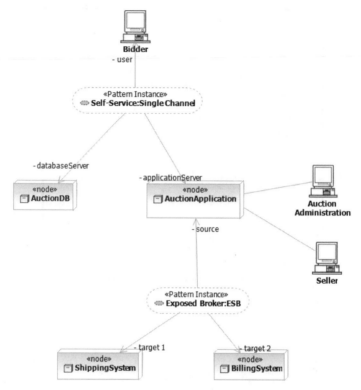

Figure 4.13 *Overview of the final LogoAuction deployment architecture*

Staying consistent with his earlier decision regarding how to model the Self-Service Single Channel pattern, Alex chooses to minimize the details for the Exposed Broker ESB pattern. In following the Use Models in Documenting Patterns guideline (Chapter 14), Alex is confident that he has used the correct level of detail. His models are concise, and details supporting the pattern definitions are available in the respective pattern specifications.

In reviewing the logical architecture, Alex can see that parts of the solution will be deployed to multiple places, such as application servers, web servers, databases, the client, and so on. The team will have to make deployment and configuration efforts in multiple places. In addition, as the team looks to support multiple environments (development, QA, preproduction, production) and multiple versions (how many applications get released only once?), it quickly becomes obvious that they have a recurring problem that needs to be addressed. Perhaps this is a pattern opportunity? Some additional questions then come up:

- Is there a proven best-practice solution that can be applied?

- Are there standards and best practices in these architectural components that would constitute such a best-practice solution? Are there organizational standards for handling deployments? Are there industry standards?

- How much effort does it take to handle these deployments manually?

- How much can they expect this deployment to change over time? Are there some points in time when things are more fluid? More solid? Is there a maturation that occurs?

- How will purchasers of the solution handle the deployment?

Before proceeding, Alex captures details on these scenarios and adds them to the candidate pattern list. As discussed in the Pattern Opportunity pattern (Chapter 11), as the team identifies potential patterns, they are briefly noted. Once the team is comfortable with the effort that has gone into identifying potential patterns, they will evaluate the list to determine which warrant further investigation and investment.

LogoAuction Data Architecture

Now, Alex can work on the data model. Because data architecture is not his specialty, Alex will work with Paul, one of the company's database administrators, to help him turn the domain model into a data model. Figure 4.14 shows the physical data model resulting from their work.

Because of Paul's extensive experience in database design, many of these mappings were straightforward. However, some of them are based on patterns. For example, there isn't a Money table; instead Money values have been defined in the appropriate entity tables. To handle Money values, the ITEM table has two fields, CURRENCY and INITIALPRICE, that will be converted into a Money object when the Item is loaded; the same is true for PAYMENT and BID tables. The Embedded Value[20] pattern is used for dealing with one-to-one relationships between two objects. The Foreign Key Mapping[21] pattern is used to represent many-to-many relationships as join tables, as seen with REGISTEREDUSER and

---

20. Fowler (2003).

21. Ibid.

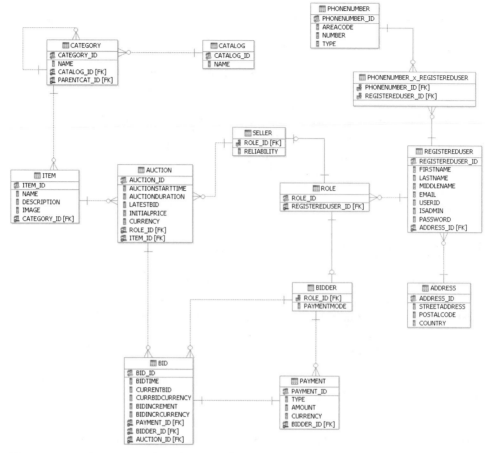

Figure 4.14   *The LogoAuction physical data model*

PHONENUMBER. The last pattern that Paul uses is related to the mapping of the Role hierarchy. To support flexibility, each class is stored in its own table following the Class Table Inheritance[22] pattern.

While reviewing the model and the patterns used within, Alex recognizes that the Money[23] pattern matches Gwen's use of the Quantity pattern in the domain model. The Money pattern is more specific to the situation, so he decides to use it to replace the Quantity pattern reference in the domain model.

---

22. Ibid.

23. Ibid.

Recording the Patterns Used

To define the different aspects of the architecture, Alex, Gwen, and Paul use a selection of patterns. They ensure that the pattern repository has an entry for each of the patterns that were used. So far, each pattern used has been a pattern specification from an external source. A brief description of the pattern is recorded along with a pointer to further details. In addition, they add feedback regarding the pattern and its usefulness with the goal of helping others understand the value of the patterns.

Opportunity Identification

Accessing the PBE catalog once again, Alex is ready to apply the Pattern Opportunity pattern (Chapter 11).

To start a list of candidate patterns, Alex organizes a brainstorming session with the development teams. He comes to the meeting with a few ideas based on the work done so far but uses them as a mechanism to get the discussion going. The goal is to bring the teams together to discuss the opportunities for using patterns. The teams can discuss the overall project, recurring problems, possible solutions, applicability for reuse, and similar issues. It's a chance for the teams to be creative and have a significant impact on the project.

The session provides Alex with a list of candidate patterns based on suggestions from many team members. One issue that comes up is trying to figure out how to organize all of the candidates. In reading about pattern categorization, Alex realizes that finding the right taxonomy could be a long and difficult task. It turns out that patterns can be organized by discipline (assessment, design, implementation, etc.), level of abstraction (architecture, design, idioms), and a number of other ways. As there is not a single agreed-upon approach, he decides to make an initial best effort, recognizing that this is something that can be refined as they gain experience with patterns. They don't want to waste time on a decision that currently has little impact on their project deliverables. He decides to group the patterns by the area where they apply, making clear to the team members the meaning of each category. The organized list of possible candidate patterns is shown in Table 4.3.

Although the project team hasn't yet evaluated all of the candidates in Table 4.3, the ideas are good and warrant further investigation. The team will keep track of the candidates by using a wiki to capture the name and a short description of each.

Table 4.3 *Possible Candidate Patterns for the Oslec Software Project*

Name	Brief Description
Design	
Subsystem Façade pattern	Duncan, the Java EE expert, highlights the fact that in past projects the Session Façade and the Data Access Object (DAO) patterns have been used together. He also notes that with Java EE 5 the DAO pattern has been slightly modified in its application, the DAO class being replaced by a JPA manager.
Generate code for data access	The team wants to ensure that all of their data access is handled consistently. They'll use JPA and expect to be able to abstract away many of the details associated with data access through patterns and JPA. They expect to see some of this surface with the Subsystem Façade pattern as well.
Assessment	
Unit test case generation (JUnit/Groovy)	In the past, the organization has seen inconsistent adherence to the idea of creating unit tests. This is an important best practice and they want to achieve 100% code coverage.
Test Data Reset pattern	There will be a number of test cycles and associated test data that need to be managed across a number of environments. How will data get loaded into the database? How will that data get refreshed?
Deployment	
Configure the firewall	The team has a number of components that will need to be deployed and configured. They want to streamline and simplify the process of moving components through the various testing environments and then to deployment (for both the organization and customers who purchase the LogoAuction application).
Configure the application and web servers	
Deploy files to application and web servers	

Evaluating the Candidate Patterns

In the real world, the Oslec team would look into each of the patterns on the candidate patterns list and evaluate them. In our simple case study, we are going to follow them as they focus on just one pattern, the Subsystem Façade pattern.

A first step in evaluating the pattern is to get a solid understanding of it. Alex works with Duncan to write an initial version of a pattern description, shown in Figure 4.15, following the Pattern Description guideline (Chapter 11).

Now that the essence of the pattern is captured, Alex takes another look at the domain model, shown in Figure 4.16. In this analysis he can see that there are many

---

Pattern: *Subsystem Façade*

Summary: To allow loose coupling between subsystems, subsystem entities will be exposed through a façade and persistence of the entities will be abstracted via a `Data Access Object` (DAO) class. This pattern is a composition of the Core J2EE Session Façade and DAO patterns.

Subject Matter Expert: Duncan

Areas of Applicability: This pattern can be used for all the subsystems identified in the project as well as other Java EE subsystems that could be developed for future projects.

Figure 4.15 *The initial Subsystem Façade pattern description*

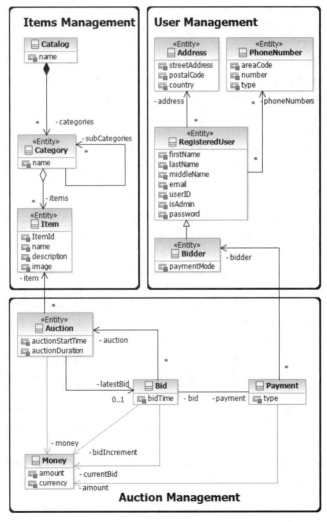

Figure 4.16 *LogoAuction application domain model*

entities within the LogoAuction domain. Each of these entities will need to have data persisted to the database and will also need to be involved in the 19 application use cases. Getting a little deeper into the application, such responsibilities will map to components within two of the layers of the layered architecture, namely, the Business and Data Access layers.

With such a wide impact on the solution, it appears that the team has come across a pattern that is architecturally significant, and more specifically a pattern that would be worth automating. They know that numerous people will work on the set of use cases, and they want to ensure that they are able to consistently build these needed components following best practices.

Alex and Duncan estimate that it will take them approximately two days to create the exemplar for this solution and another day to test the implementation. They already are familiar with the patterns that are used in composing the Subsystem Façade pattern. They will just need to apply those patterns and apply some additional best practices that are unique to Oslec. These are Oslec's top experts, and they expect that once the exemplar is built, others in the organization can manually replicate their efforts for the other subsystems, each subsystem requiring about 9 or 10 days. They also expect that they would spend 6 days in testing and inspecting the solution to ensure that quality goals have been met. Based on past experience, they expect to find errors and inconsistencies in the implementation, adding 4 days to the effort. Overall, they expect that it will take approximately 25 to 26 days of effort to create, test, and debug the solution manually.

Alex and Duncan ask Jordan to assist with the estimate for the creation of a pattern implementation. From a technology point of view, Jordan tells them that he would build the model-to-text pattern implementation combining JET and model-mapping components. He estimates that it will take approximately 3 to 4 days to build the JET portion of the solution and another 3 to 4 days to build the model-mapping portion. Testing will take 1 to 2 days, and addressing defects should take about a day. Once the pattern implementation is created, others should be able to learn and then apply the pattern to the other entities in a couple of hours. They expect that creating and using the pattern implementation will take approximately 17 days of effort. They expect to have a positive ROI on this pattern implementation within the current project as the automation should allow them to save 8 to 9 days of effort. In addition, they will have an asset available to use if additional subsystems are added to this application or to use on other applications. Since the organization is standardizing on Java EE, there is a strong likelihood that the pattern will get reused on other projects.

For Alex this is also an opportunity to spread another important practice: unit testing. He's noted that on past projects there was a lack of unit testing. Having the pattern implementation automatically generate unit tests for the Façade and the DAO patterns would provide basic tests that the developers could easily extend, leading to a higher percentage of unit testing coverage.

Based on Alex's analysis so far, it's clear that Oslec Software needs to build the Subsystem Façade pattern implementation. The savings are significant, and they can make a strong business case for the effort. The one other step they perform is checking to see if other options exist aside from building the pattern. They ask a number of questions: Is there already a similar pattern that is available? How similar? What would be the effort in using it as is? What would be the effort if the pattern was modified? In following through on this analysis, they discover that an existing pattern implementation that meets their needs does not yet exist, so they can continue to move ahead with the idea of building this pattern.

Summary

Much of the effort in PBE aligns with what we would see in traditional projects, except that we have a mind-set of reuse. We are consciously looking for opportunities to reuse existing patterns as well as identifying instances where a new and unique pattern may exist within our organization.

However, we are not just using patterns for the sake of patterns. We don't want to get into a mind-set where we see patterns as our hammer and every problem a nail. We need to continue to evaluate where it makes sense to use a pattern. Is it the right solution? Does it add sufficient value? If not, we need to look elsewhere for our solution.

In addition, we are looking beyond the scope of just design and implementation for opportunities for automation, best practices, and reuse. Design and implementation account for only 40% of the overall effort during the project. If we focus on patterns within that space to the exclusion of others, we unnecessarily minimize the impact that patterns can have on the project.

Oslec Software successfully qualified a pattern from the candidate pattern list and moved forward to create that asset. As a key step in improving the culture of the organization, they also ensured that similar assets didn't already exist.

Figure 4.17 on the next page summarizes the PBE roles, tasks, Patterns, and Guidelines that have been covered in this iteration.

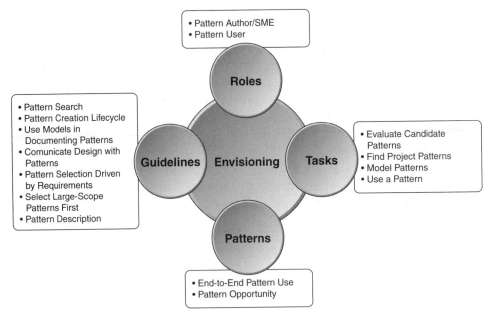

Figure 4.17   *Summary of the PBE elements used in this iteration*

Chapter 5

Iteration 1: Creating the Pattern

So far, the Oslec Software team has started to model some of the architecturally significant aspects of the solution, giving thought to the deployment, logical, and data aspects. While working on the architecture, they have begun to use patterns from outside sources (vendor and community) and have identified some patterns that are unique to their organization.

In this chapter we will follow the Oslec team as they continue to refine the work that has been completed so far. More specifically, they will give further thought to the design of the LogoAuction application and identify any shortcomings in the requirements and the architectural work done so far. In addition, they will pursue the implementation of the use cases, iteratively building the solution.

They will also continue their PBE work, as summarized in Figure 5.1.

The first step will be to design the Subsystem Façade pattern, focusing first on understanding the different pieces of the pattern; then they will analyze an exemplar and finish with the pattern implementation design.

With the design in hand the team can then start working on the specification as well as building the pattern implementation.

These steps will be shown sequentially; however, they are usually done in an iterative manner with some back-and-forth.

Launching the Iteration

Michael explains to the team that this iteration has two main goals. The first goal is to flesh out more solution details. In particular, Duncan's team will focus on the Items Management subsystem, through the implementation of the main flow of the Put Item Up for Auction use case. This subsystem has been chosen because it is independent from, yet still representative of, the other subsystems. It provides a good way to validate the planned architecture without introducing unnecessary complexity. In addition, the work done by this team will serve as the basis for the exemplar for the Subsystem Façade pattern.

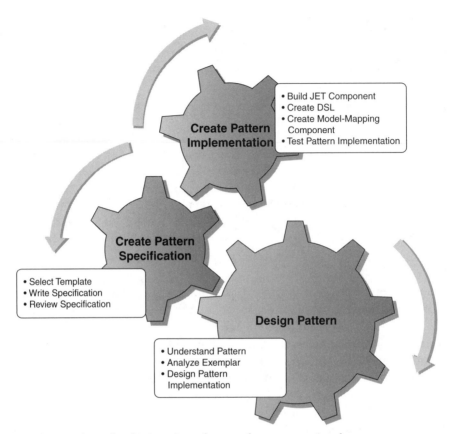

Figure 5.1 *Roadmap for this iteration where we focus on creating the pattern*

The second objective of the iteration is to build the Subsystem Façade pattern implementation. Alex and Jordan will lead the effort to design the pattern and will take advantage of the work done by Duncan's team to validate the pattern and its variability points. Duncan is Oslec's Java EE expert, so he will also provide assistance to Alex and Jordan in their efforts. In this collaboration Duncan is the Pattern Author/ SME, Alex is the Pattern Specification Author, and Jordan is the Pattern Implementation Author.[1]

As mentioned earlier, Duncan and Alex have already been collaborating on the initial work on the pattern description and will continue to do so with the pattern specification. As they get into more detailed design, that collaboration effort will continue, and Jordan will join the discussions.

---

1. As will be discussed in Chapter 8, three roles often come together to create a pattern implementation: the Pattern Author/Subject Matter Expert (SME), the Pattern Specification Author, and the Pattern Implementation Author.

Designing the Subsystem Façade Pattern

Now that it has been deemed worthwhile to invest in the Subsystem Façade pattern, Alex and Jordan need to work on the design of the pattern.

Understanding the Essence of the Subsystem Façade Pattern

Before getting into the creation and analysis of the exemplar, Alex and Jordan want to ensure that they understand the essence of the pattern. To do so, they review the description of the Subsystem Façade pattern that was created in the previous iteration.

The pattern description indicates that the Subsystem Façade pattern results from the composition of the Session Façade and Data Access Object (DAO) patterns.[2] Alex reviews the specifications of these existing patterns to ensure that he understands them. Figures 5.2 and 5.3 provide summaries of the patterns.

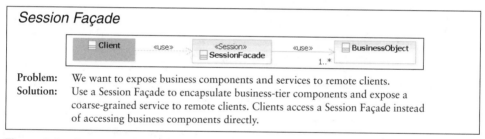

Problem: We want to expose business components and services to remote clients.
Solution: Use a Session Façade to encapsulate business-tier components and expose a coarse-grained service to remote clients. Clients access a Session Façade instead of accessing business components directly.

Figure 5.2 *Overview of Session Façade pattern*

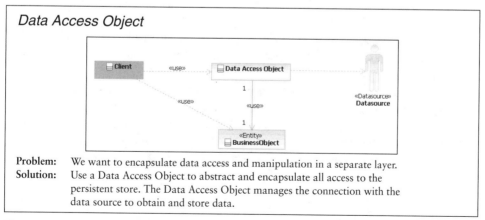

Problem: We want to encapsulate data access and manipulation in a separate layer.
Solution: Use a Data Access Object to abstract and encapsulate all access to the persistent store. The Data Access Object manages the connection with the data source to obtain and store data.

Figure 5.3 *Overview of Data Access Object (DAO) pattern*

---

2. The Session Façade and *DAO* patterns are specified in the Core J2EE patterns. For more details see Alur et al. (2003).

Alex determines that the way to connect these two patterns seems to be the BusinessObject class. The Session Façade can be used as is; however, the DAO pattern needs to be adapted to Java EE 5. Java EE 5 provides a new persistence framework called the Java Persistence API (JPA). One of the features provided by JPA is the JPA manager, which provides the same services as the DAO class in the DAO pattern. So while specifying the Subsystem Façade pattern, Alex replaces the DAO class with a JPA manager. He also notes that the goal of the Subsystem Façade pattern is to shield the content of a subsystem, so the Business Objects role will be fulfilled by the entities in the subsystem.

Alex updates the existing pattern description, which is shown in Figure 5.4. The effort has allowed him to gain a better understanding of the pattern and produce an artifact that can be used to solicit feedback from others.

The team will use the pattern description in creating the related pattern specification and implementation. Following the Pattern Specification guideline (Chapter 13), the team decides to use a template with the following fields: Pattern Name, Context, Problem, Forces, Solution, Example, and Related Patterns.

▼ ──

Services: Dealing with an Overloaded Term

In working with the Façade[3] pattern, we look to expose a set of services, hiding the underlying implementation. The Pattern User needs to worry only about the interface that is exposed by the façade, not the underpinnings. If we consider SOA-based solutions, we find a similar approach in use—we define a set of interfaces for a service, which becomes the contract that enforces the relationship between the service and a service consumer. However, in this case, when we use the term *service,* we usually mean something more specific than when discussing the Façade pattern (which is more general in its applicability).

In the case of Oslec, they are initially looking at using a more generic implementation of the Façade pattern. However, they could easily extend their solution later for SOA-based solutions. For example, if we look at the SOA Reference Architecture from IBM, shown in Figure 5.5[4] on page 76, we can see that the service components layer contains one or more components that provide implementations that get exposed as SOA services in the services layer. In this case it is likely that they will end up being web services. With the Subsystem Façade pattern, however, the Oslec team is focused on creating elements that live in the service components layer. They can later extend the pattern to support the services layer as well. Doing so would allow them to support an SOA initiative and provide a set of services for others to consume.

── ▲

───────────

3. Gamma et al. (1995).

4. Arsanjani et al. (2007).

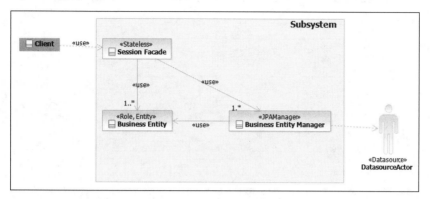

Context: A set of database-stored business entities that need to be made accessible.

Problem: Entities and services need to be exposed to remote clients without binding the clients to the entities.

Solution: Group related business entities into a subsystem and use a Session Façade to encapsulate the business entities. Remote clients interact with the Session Façade via a coarse-grained service. Access to the database is abstracted away by the Business Entity Manager.

Subject Matter Expert: Duncan

Areas of Applicability: This pattern can be used for all the subsystems identified in the LogoAuction project. Likely that it can also be used for Java EE subsystems in other projects.

Related Patterns: The Subsystem Façade pattern composes the Session Façade and the Data Access Object patterns together as shown below.

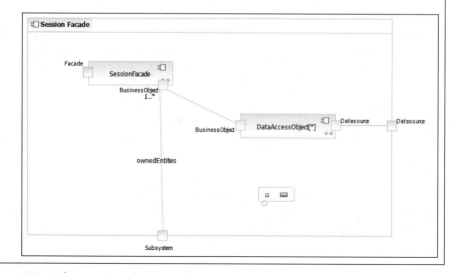

Figure 5.4 *Subsystem Façade pattern description*

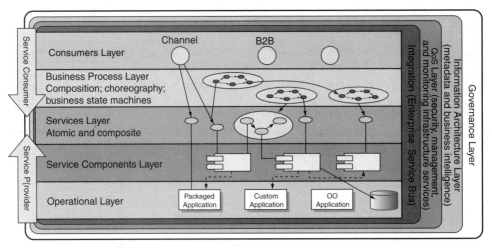

Figure 5.5 *IBM SOA Reference Architecture*
Copyright IBM developerWorks, www.ibm.com/developerworks. Reused with permission.

The Subsystem Façade Exemplar

With the pattern description for the Subsystem Façade pattern completed, the project team now needs to come up with a design for the pattern. The next step for Alex and Jordan is to acquire an exemplar.

Finding an Exemplar

Patterns are not invented, but rather discovered; we harvest them from existing solutions. As discussed in the Pattern Creation Lifecycle guideline (Chapter 12), there is a flow where we use patterns in creating a solution, which in turn may end up serving as an exemplar that is used in the creation of a new pattern.

The Oslec team has recognized that a number of patterns will come together in building a solution. Once they are satisfied with the solution, they will transition it to an exemplar, ensuring that it represents best practices while providing appropriate variability and scope.

Duncan's team is currently working on the Put Item Up for Auction use case, which requires the Items Management subsystem. Alex and Jordan plan to use this subsystem as the basis for the Subsystem Façade exemplar. Figure 5.6 shows that this subsystem contains three entities: Catalog, Category, and Item.

The team likes this approach, as the subsystem needs to be built anyway, they are supporting a key use case, and Duncan—the resident Java EE expert—is helping

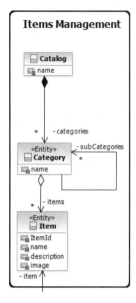

Figure 5.6   *The elements associated with the Items Management subsystem*

them build the solution. Alex, Jordan, and Duncan recognize that some variations will exist in the other subsystems that do not show up in Items Management. Once the subsystem is built, the three of them will review the solution, looking for areas where they need to augment and embellish it, creating an exemplar that suits the needs of all of the subsystems.

Figure 5.7 shows an overview of the structure of the resulting exemplar. There are many elements in the exemplar—projects, configuration files, XML files, Java files, test cases, referenced JAR files, packaging elements, and others. For a simple subsystem and pattern, they actually end up with many moving parts; if they were to replicate this work many times manually across a number of subsystems, there are ample opportunities for introducing errors.

Analyzing the Exemplar

In this section we focus on following the Exemplar Analysis pattern (Chapter 12). The focus is to "identify the key entities involved in the pattern, specify the points of variability, define the information that the Pattern User provides, recognize the rules we can use to derive any additional information needed by the pattern, and identify the aspects of the pattern that stay the same across applications of the pattern."[5]

---

5. From the "Solution" section of the Exemplar Analysis pattern specification.

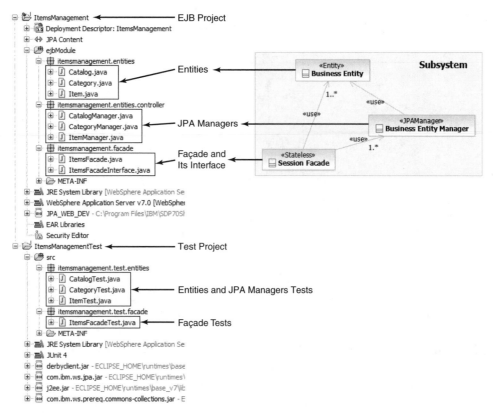

Figure 5.7   *Structure of the exemplar project*

Looking at the project structure, shown in Figure 5.7, Alex, Jordan, and Duncan identify the following roles:

- **EJB project:** defines the subsystem that will be encapsulated by the façade. It also contains libraries and JPA-related files such as orm.xml and persistence.xml.

- **Entities:** the business entities that are exposed by the façade. The exemplar contains three entities: Catalog, Category, and Item. Each entity has a JPA manager to abstract CRUD operations: CatalogManager, CategoryManager, and ItemManager.

- **Façade:** There is only one façade per subsystem, and its name can be derived from the name of the EJB project. A pair of elements, including a class and an interface, represents the façade.

- **Test project:** This project contains the tests that will be run against the EJB project elements. It also contains libraries and JPA configuration files to support the execution of JUnit tests outside the Java EE container. The name of the Test project can be derived from the name of the EJB project.

- **Tests:** These are the JUnit tests used to test the subsystem. There is one test for the façade and one test for each of the entity managers. Entities are usually simple enough that they don't require a unit test of their own.

Using these roles, Alex and Jordan can start to define the input model. They need a subsystem parameter that helps them define the name of the EJB and Test projects as well as the name of the façade and its associated tests. That parameter will have a child parameter that will specify the entities and the managers that the façade will expose. With this relationship a subsystem can have many entities. Figure 5.8 shows the parameters and attributes that have been identified so far. A goal is to keep the input model as simple as possible. They look for opportunities to reuse information either as is or via calculations.

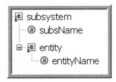

Figure 5.8 *Current list of parameters*

With this simple list of parameters and support from RSA, they determine the following:

- The Tests role does not require any additional information. Creating the initial testing infrastructure for the Pattern User will be seamless and encapsulated by the pattern.

- Infrastructure artifacts, such as Eclipse project elements and JAR files, are supported by RSA. It is unlikely that they will require any information from the Pattern User beyond what is provided for the subsystem entities.

- JPA persistence framework configuration files will use details directly related to the entities and the entity test cases. No additional parameters are required.

A More Detailed Look at the Exemplar

To dig deeper into the design Alex and Jordan need to start analyzing the internals of the exemplar artifacts. The focus of the effort is on identifying additional parameters. They want to ensure that they are finding all of the variations within the files. For example, even though each of the entity files is similar, there might be variations that are not present in all entities. As they work through the design, they will validate their findings with Duncan.

They start with the JPA entities as they are simple Java files. First they review the Item.java file, shown in Figure 5.9, and identify higher-order elements and relationships.

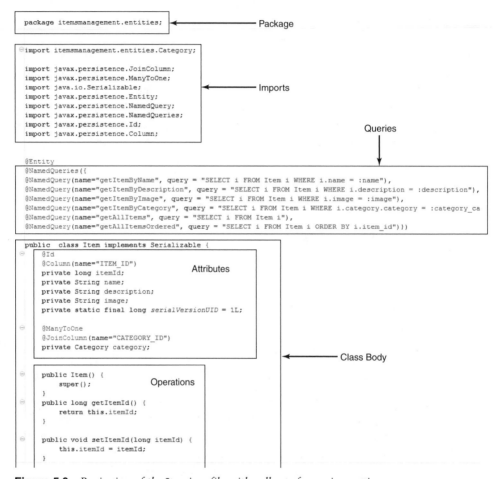

Figure 5.9   *Beginning of the* Item.java *file with callouts for major sections*

They identify six parts in the Item.java file: Package, Imports, Queries, Class Body, Attributes, and Operations. They examine each section to look for points of variability, those things that change as the pattern is applied. Here are their findings for each part:

- **Package.** They notice that the package name is similar to the project name except for two differences. The first difference is that the package name is shown entirely in lowercase letters. The second difference is that the package name is longer than the project name as it has .entities appended. Both of these differences from the project name are simple and can be calculated.

- **Imports.** Some of these imports are going to be easy to figure out based on the standard relationships between the entities in the solution. They are relatively static, requiring only the project name. Things get more interesting as they start to think about the entity's attributes, since the Pattern User can specify a range of attribute types. Depending on the types that are specified, they may need to add more import statements. Based on this discovery, Duncan confirms that an attribute parameter is needed to provide the name and type of the attribute.

- **Queries.** The Queries section is new to Alex and Jordan, so they turn to Duncan for advice. Duncan explains that queries are based on JPA's Java Persistence Query Language (JPQL). The purpose of JPQL is to allow the use of queries to retrieve entities from the data store without caring about the underlying implementation. Duncan explains that there are usually two kinds of queries. The first is linked to the entity's attributes, such as getItemByName, and is used to retrieve entities using the attribute as a filter. The second query type is based on the entity, such as getAllItems and getAllItemsOrdered. This type of query is used to retrieve all the entities, ordered or unordered. Since they already have the attribute names, they are able to calculate the query names; there's no need for a new parameter.

- **Class Body.** The class name needs to match the name of the entity. This is information they are already looking to capture, so no additional parameters are needed.

- **Attributes.** They recognize that there are two kinds of attributes. The first kind are the standard class attributes and will be tackled by the attribute parameter defined earlier. However, one of the attributes is special in the sense that it identifies the attribute/column used as an ID for persistence. This attribute is identified by the @Id annotation and will require a specific parameter identifying its name and type.

  The second kind of attribute is based on associations. An association has a name and a type, but it also has an indicator for multiplicity (@ManyToOne), as well as an indicator of a mapped column (CATEGORY_ID). So they need to add an association parameter with four attributes: name, type, multiplicity, and target column.

- **Operations.** Operations are straightforward as they are dealing with entities. Entity operations consist of only get and set operations to retrieve and set the entity attributes.

The resulting set of parameters and attributes is summarized in Figure 5.10. The changes that have been made to the input model include

- attribute, described by its name (attrName) and type (attrType)

- id, described by its name (idName) and type (idType)

- association, described by its name (assoName), type (assoType), multiplicity (multiplicity), and table column name (targetField)

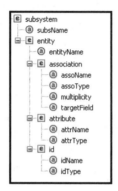

Figure 5.10 *Summary of the identified parameters and their attributes*

Using the same approach, Alex and Jordan look at the JPA managers in the controllers package. They do not find any new parameters, as the managers mainly provide the CRUD operations for the entity. The exemplar contains three controllers, and after checking with Duncan, they decide to use the ItemManager as a base for the manager template as it is the most representative.

The façade in the exemplar is pretty basic and provides operations to access an entity using its id and to retrieve all the entities. When looking at the façade, they note that there is a pairing between a class and an interface. The relationship between the two is quite direct; Jordan notes that he will need the pattern implementation to generate them as a pair.

Duncan points out that a variation they need to add to the exemplar is the use of the Embedded Value pattern. The pattern currently is used only in the Auction Management subsystem. Figure 5.11 shows an example of the application of the pattern to the Money class. A key aspect of the pattern is that the Money class does not have its own table in the database. Instead, the values associated with an instance of Money are stored along with the object that uses that instance of Money, in this case the Payment class.

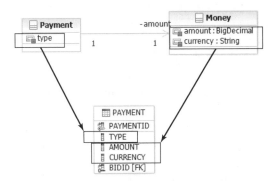

Figure 5.11 *Example of the application of the Money pattern*

The Money class has two attributes: amount and currency. Duncan provides Alex and Jordan with Listing 5.1, which includes two examples of using the Money pattern. Alex and Jordan also notice that the Money class, among other utilities, is stored in the AuctionUtility Java project. Duncan explains that the first example in the Payment.java file is the simple case. In this case the column names are the same as the Money class's attributes. The second case, in the Bid.java file, shows how to declare new column names. Duncan also indicates that no queries are created for embedded attributes.

Listing 5.1 *Examples of Using the Money Pattern[6]*

```
============== Payment.java ===========================
@Embedded
private Money amount;


============= Bid.java ===============================
@Embedded
   @AttributeOverrides( {
      @AttributeOverride(name="amount", column=@Column(name="CURRENTBID")),
      @AttributeOverride(name="currency", column=@Column(name="CURRBIDCURRENCY"))
   })
   private Money currentBid;
```

Based on their analysis of Listing 5.1, Alex and Jordan recognize that they need to update their input model. First they will need a new parameter to identify embedded value attributes. The new parameter should capture the embedded value's name and type as well as an optional child parameter in cases where the column names are overridden. This parameter for overridden names will need two attributes, one for the name of the overridden attribute and one for the name of the corresponding column.

---

6. The format of some of the code listings has been altered to fit the book pages.

Another change they need to make is to support project dependencies, as seen with the import of the Money class, which is stored in the utility project. Jordan creates a dependency parameter under subsystem, allowing him to dynamically add dependencies.

To ensure that they did not overlook anything, Alex and Jordan consult the domain model to validate that all its elements can be mapped to the points of variability identified as well as the other way around—all the variability points can be derived from the model. In doing so, they notice that there is no identification of the subsystems in the domain model, so they consult with Gwen to determine how to address this issue. After learning the role of the subsystems, Gwen finds that they directly map to the responsibility areas she has been identifying on the main domain model diagram. To make the domain model easier to transform, she agrees to group the entities by subsystem in different packages.

Looking at the domain model again, they see that there is no mechanism on the current list of parameters to address inheritance or abstract classes such as the Role class. Adding an abstract attribute to the entity easily solves supporting abstract classes. Inheritance turns out to be more complex, so they ask Duncan for assistance. Duncan provides Listing 5.2 as an example of inheritance between User (the parent) and Administrator (the child).

Listing 5.2 *Example of Inheritance Use*

```
============= User.java ====================
@Entity
@Inheritance(strategy=JOINED)
public class User implements Serializable {
    @Id
    @Column(name="USER_ID")
    private long userId;
    private String name;
============= Administrator.java =============
@Entity
public class Administrator extends User implements Serializable {
    private boolean admin;
```

When they review the example, Alex and Jordan see that the parent, User, has an @Inheritance(strategy=JOINED) annotation and that the child, Administrator, extends the parent class but does not have an @ID annotation. Duncan explains that only the JOINED inheritance strategy is used at Oslec, so there is no need to parameterize it. To support these discoveries they decide to add to the input model. They will need to add two attributes to the entity parameter—hasChild, to identify an entity that has children, and parent, to identify that a class is part of an inheritance tree—and provide the name of the entity it needs to extend. The bidirectional nature of the parameters simplifies capturing and processing the relationship in XML.

Figure 5.12 shows the list of parameters at the end of exemplar analysis. The changes that have been made to the input model include the following:

- dependency, with one attribute for the name of the project the subsystem depends on (depName).

- Three attributes for the entity node to indicate its abstractness (isAbstract) and inheritance (hasChild and parent).

- embeddedAttribute captures the name (embAttrName) and type (embAttrType) of the embedded attribute. It also contains an optional node (attrOverride) to specify cases where the name of an attribute has been overridden. The attrOverride node captures the name of the corresponding column in the database (attrLocalName), as well as the name (attrName) and the type (attrType) of the overridden attribute.

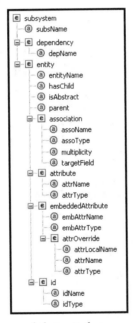

Figure 5.12 *Identified parameters and their attributes*

The design work done so far has more or less been common to the pattern implementation and specification. It is now time for Jordan to look at design decisions specific to the pattern implementation.

Design of the Pattern Implementation

Jordan's first step in designing the pattern implementation is to determine the type that should be built. Two factors influence the decision. The first is that Oslec used UML and models to design its applications. The second is that the exemplar contains many text-based artifacts. With these two considerations in mind, Jordan decides that he will follow the Model-to-Text Pattern Implementation pattern (Chapter 13). The pattern implementation will be applied to the domain model and will generate a set of text-based artifacts.

To implement the pattern Jordan decides to combine two technologies provided by Rational Software Architect. He will use JET to create the text-based artifacts, including Java code and XML-based configuration files. To simplify the user experience in creating the input model, Jordan will leverage RSA's model-mapping capabilities. This will allow the Pattern User to specify a UML model, known as the user model, which will then be translated by the pattern into the input model that is needed for the JET-based portion of the pattern implementation. He also plans to use the Integrated Patterns and DSLs pattern (Chapter 15) to help ensure that the user model is built out as simply—and correctly—as possible.

Jordan also wants to ensure that he is simplifying the set of patterns that he is providing to the Pattern Users. He selects the Compound Pattern pattern (Chapter 12) to help him meet this goal. So far, the Subsystem Façade pattern implementation includes the Session Façade, DAO, Role, Money, Embedded Value, and Class Table Inheritance patterns, as shown in Figure 5.13.

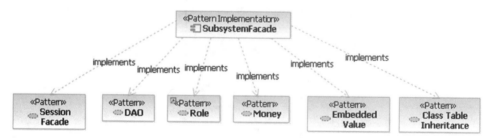

Figure 5.13   *Patterns included in the Subsystem Façade pattern implementation*

Because the LogoAuction project is using an iterative approach, there is a need to ensure that the pattern implementation will provide support for reapplication so that the pattern implementation can be reapplied on components while preserving hand-written code that's been added to designated areas. Code that exists outside the designated areas is owned by the pattern implementation and will be overwritten each time the pattern is applied. Jordan leverages the Team Pattern Implementation Use guideline (Chapter 12) to help him design this aspect and will also use it in enabling the Pattern Users.

Creating the Subsystem Façade Pattern Specification

While Jordan is working on the design of the pattern implementation, Alex continues working on the pattern specification.

At this point in its PBE adoption, Oslec has not yet selected a pattern specification template. Alex reviews some of the available templates and decides to create a template reusing the sections he found meaningful and useful from the available templates. Then, using the pattern design and with some help from Duncan on the examples, he writes the pattern specification.

When he has a stable enough pattern specification, Alex organizes a peer review of it with Jordan, Duncan, Sandy, and Craig. The final version is provided in Appendix E.

Building the Subsystem Façade Pattern Implementation

With the initial design in hand and his notes resulting from the exemplar analysis, Jordan can start building the pattern implementation, beginning with the JET component.

Building the JET Component

Test-Driven Development

Jordan has experienced the benefits of using test-driven development in previous projects and would like to apply it in this effort. He decides to use the ItemsManagement project as his reference for the test case. This will allow him to compare the pattern output to the exemplar project. However, to avoid overwriting the exemplar within his workspace, he names the subsystem Items2.

To identify the content of the input model for the test case, he returns to the domain model and focuses on the business entities within the Items Management subsystem. These entities and their relationships are shown in Figure 5.14.

Using the diagram shown in Figure 5.14, Jordan creates the test input model. He uses XML to specify the test input model, as that is the default language that JET

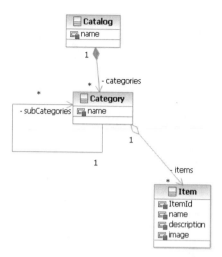

Figure 5.14   ItemsManagement *entities*

accepts. The first version of the test input model is shown in Listing 5.3. It's a simple test that creates the subsystem.

Listing 5.3   *Initial Test Input Model*

```
<?xml version="1.0" encoding="UTF-8"?>
<root xmlns:xsi="http://www.w3.org/2001/XMLSchema-instance"
      xsi:noNamespaceSchemaLocation="schema.xsd">
      <subsystem subsName="Items2" />
</root>
```

As he proceeds through the creation of the JET component, he enhances the test case. He alternates test case enhancement efforts with JET component enhancements, ensuring that the component passes the test before adding functionality. Listing 5.4 shows the final test input model.

Listing 5.4   *Final Test Input Model*

```
<?xml version="1.0" encoding="UTF-8"?>
<root xmlns:xsi="http://www.w3.org/2001/XMLSchema-instance"
      xsi:noNamespaceSchemaLocation="schema.xsd">
      <subsystem subsName="Items2">
        <entity entityName="Item">
           <attribute attrName="name" attrType="String" />
           <attribute attrName="description" attrType="String">
           </attribute>
```

```
            <attribute attrName="image" attrType="byte[]" />
            <id idName="Item_Id" idType="long"></id>
            <association assoName="categoryId"
               assoType="items2management.entities.Category"
               multiplicity="manyToOne"
               targetField="CATEGORY_ID" />
        </entity>
        <entity entityName="Category">
            <attribute attrName="name" attrType="String" />
            <id idName="category_Id" idType="long" />
            <association assoName="catalogId"
               assoType="items2management.entities.Catalog"
               multiplicity="manyToOne"
               targetField="CATALOG_ID">
            </association>
            <association assoName="parentcatId"
               assoType="items2management.entities.Category"
               multiplicity="manyToOne"
               targetField="PARENTCAT_ID">
            </association>
            <association assoName="subcategories"
               assoType="java.util.Set
                  &lt;items2management.entities.Category&gt;"
               multiplicity="oneToMany"
               targetField="parentcatId">
            </association>
            <association assoName="items"
               assoType="java.util.Set
                  &lt;items2management.entities.Item&gt;"
               multiplicity="oneToMany"
               targetField="categoryId">
            </association>
        </entity>
        <entity entityName="Catalog">
            <attribute attrName="name" attrType="String" />
            <id idName="catalog_Id" idType="long" />
            <association assoName="categories"
               assoType="java.util.Set
                  &lt;items2management.entities.Category&gt;"
               multiplicity="oneToMany"
               targetField="catalogId">
            </association>
        </entity>
    </subsystem>
</root>
```

Getting Started with the JET Project

To create the JET component, Jordan uses the Exemplar Authoring capability in RSA. To get started, he creates an Exemplar Authoring[7] project and links it to the ItemsManagement exemplar project. Once the project is set up, Jordan specifies the parameters (called types in JET) and attributes that were identified during the exemplar analysis efforts in the design phase.

Figure 5.15 shows the main view of Exemplar Authoring. The left pane contains the two projects identified as the exemplar, and the right pane contains the initial list of types and attributes. As the team works through Exemplar Authoring, they will add more details to the types and attributes, defining attributes that can be calculated or derived from other attributes as well as defining actions that the pattern implementation needs to take to create files.

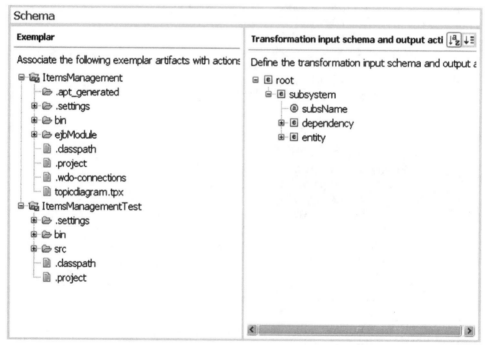

Figure 5.15   *Exemplar Authoring main view*

---

7. What Jordan will do with Exemplar Authoring could be done using the JET Eclipse tooling. However, it would be a manual effort and take longer as only basic text editors are available. The JET runtime is available in Eclipse; however, no specialized authoring tools are provided.

Creating Elements

Jordan recognizes that he has to create an EJB project for each subsystem. To do so, he drags the ItemsManagement project from the Exemplar pane and drops it on the subsystem element in the right-hand pane. A Create action for the EJB project is added to the right-hand pane, indicating that for each subsystem type specified by the Pattern User, an EJB project will be created. The name of the EJB project is of the form <Subsystem_Name>Management, which Jordan parameterizes to ensure that the correct name is assigned. This is done in the Exemplar Authoring tool by replacing the name with a model reference in the properties of the Create action. Note that such customization of the pattern implementation to support dynamic data access and calculations is done using XPath, since the input model is an XML file. When the input model provided by the user is made available to the pattern implementation, it is presented as a Document Object Model (DOM), essentially a tree structure.

There are two options for customizing this attribute:

1. Replace ItemsManagement in the name property field with {$subsystem/@subsName}Management, appending the string Management to the subsName attribute.

2. Create a new derived attribute projectName set to {$subsystem/@subsName}Management and then replace ItemsManagement in the name property field with a reference to this variable ({$subsystem/@projectName}).

Jordan chooses the second option,[8] using a derived variable, as there is more than one place where he will need this value. Figure 5.16 shows the updated Exemplar Authoring view as well as an example of the parameterization of the project name.

Next, Jordan needs to identify all the elements inside the project that are created only once per subsystem and drag them under the subsystem type. Some obvious ones are the project metadata files (.project, .classpath, .settings, etc.) and the ejbModule source directory. These elements have names that are not dependent on the subsystem; regardless of the subsystem name, the project configuration file will be called .project and the source directory ejbModule. What is important to understand here is that we are looking only at the names of the elements, not the content. The content of some of the files will change based on the projectName attribute.

There is no variability associated with the file names, so Jordan just has to drag them under the Create Project: ItemsManagement node and does not need to make any modifications. Another set of elements that falls into that category is the META-INF directory and its content (orm.xml and persistence.xml); he treats them in the same fashion.

---

8. As a rule of thumb, when dealing with Eclipse projects, you usually are better off creating a derived attribute. The reason is that some of the Eclipse metadata files also use the name of the project.

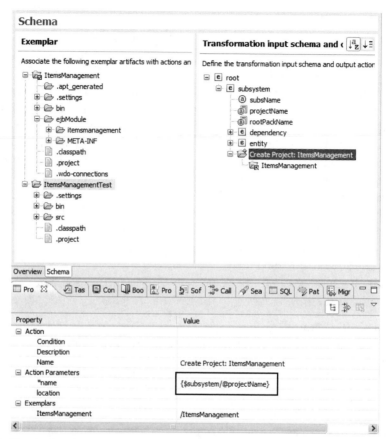

Figure 5.16   *Updated Exemplar Authoring view*

So far the changes have been pretty simple. Now Jordan explores the content of the source directory, and things start to get a little more involved. As shown in Figure 5.17, the source directory contains three packages: itemsmanagement.entities, itemsmanagement.facade, and itemsmanagement.entities.controller. In Eclipse, packages are physically represented by directories, so the pattern implementation must create these four directories (items-management is also a directory). From the content of these different packages, only the façade and its interface need to be added to the list as they are created once per subsystem. Jordan drags all the identified directories and files under the subsystem type and parameterizes them the same way he did for the project.

Now that he is done with the subsystem-dependent elements, Jordan decides to tackle the entity-dependent elements before starting to parameterize the different files.

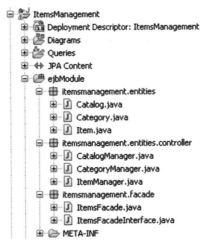

Figure 5.17 `ItemsManagement` *source directory*

Entity-dependent elements are those that are typically associated with an entity. Within the exemplar project there are three entities to choose from: `Catalog`, `Category`, and `Item`. There is no need to add all of them to the output actions as they represent variations of the same type of artifact. Jordan needs to drag only one of the entities and the corresponding manager to the right-hand pane under the entity type and then parameterize it. Jordan selects `Item` as it is most representative of the type, the one that is the most complete and displays the most variability. Jordan adds `Create File` actions for the `Item.java` and `ItemManager.java` classes under the entity element. These actions will create the two files for each entity. Figure 5.18 shows the updated content in the Exemplar Authoring view.

Next, Jordan needs to parameterize the JET templates. To get the process started, he generates an initial version of the templates from the Exemplar Authoring view.

Updating the Elements Templates

At this point Jordan turns his focus to the JET templates and the content within. He starts the process by generating the JET templates.

Note

We will not detail all of the template editing and parameterization that Jordan performs as the work gets repetitive—and there are quite a few templates. Instead, we will look at a few examples of some of the possible and likely scenarios when working with JET files.

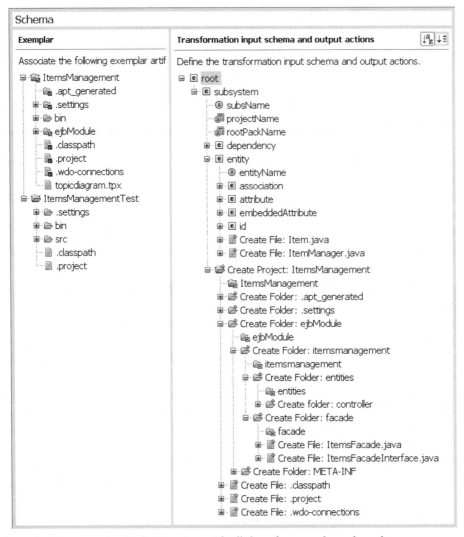

Figure 5.18 *Exemplar Authoring view with all the subsystem-dependent elements*

Jordan starts with the project.jet file that generates the .project file of the Eclipse project. This is good place to start, as the contents of this file are relatively static; the only thing that will need to be modified is the name of the project. In JET this is done using the <c:get> tag to reference the projectName attribute from the subsystem type. Recall how Jordan customized the derived attributes associated with the input model; he used XPath for calculations and data access via the DOM-based input model. Listing 5.5 shows the beginning of the project.jet file with the use of the <c:get> tag that Jordan has used to access the projectName attribute of the subsystem entity.

Listing 5.5   *Beginning of* project.jet *File[9]*

```xml
<?xml version="1.0" encoding="UTF-8"?>
<projectDescription>
   <name><c:get select="$subsystem/@projectName" /></name>
   <comment></comment>
   <projects>
   </projects>
```

Another interesting file to examine is the Item.java.jet template, shown in Listing 5.6.

Listing 5.6   *Beginning of* Item.java.jet *File*

```java
package itemsmanagement.entities;

import itemsmanagement.entities.Category;

import javax.persistence.JoinColumn;
import javax.persistence.ManyToOne;
import java.io.Serializable;
import javax.persistence.Entity;
import javax.persistence.Id;
import javax.persistence.NamedQuery;
import javax.persistence.NamedQueries;
import javax.persistence.Column;

@Entity
@NamedQueries( {
   @NamedQuery(name = "getItemByName",
      query = "SELECT i FROM Item i WHERE i.name = :name"),
   @NamedQuery(name = "getItemByDescription",
      query = "SELECT i FROM Item i
        WHERE i.description = :description"),
   @NamedQuery(name = "getItemByImage",
     query = "SELECT i FROM Item i WHERE i.image = :image"),
   @NamedQuery(name = "getAllItems",
     query = "SELECT i FROM Item i"),
   @NamedQuery(name = "getAllItemsOrdered",
     query = "SELECT i FROM Item i ORDER BY i.Item_Id")
})
public class Item implements Serializable {
  @Id
  @Column(name = "ITEM_ID")
  private long itemid;
```

---

9. In this listing and all the remaining ones in this chapter, **bold** text is used to denote dynamic content and normal text denotes static content.

```
private String name;
private String description;
private byte[] image;
private static final long serialVersionUID = 1L;

@ManyToOne
@JoinColumn(name = "CATEGORY_ID")
private Category categoryId;

public Item() {
  super();
}

public long getItemid() {
  return this.itemid;
}

public void setItemid(long itemid) {
  this.itemid = itemid;
}
```

Jordan looked at the file during the exemplar analysis activity; now he uses the parameters he identified to add variability to the template. He notices that there is an attribute declaration for each attribute, so he will need to use the <c:iterate> tag to iterate through an input model type (in our case the entity attributes). Listing 5.7 shows the use of <c:iterate> for the attributes declaration. In this way Jordan dynamically builds the attributes owned by the entity.

Listing 5.7 *Example of the* <c:iterate> *Tag for Attributes in* Item.java.jet

```
<c:iterate select="$entity/attribute" var="attribute">
   private <java:import><c:get select="$attribute/@attrType"/>
      </java:import> <c:get select="$attribute/@attrName" />;
</c:iterate>
```

There is also one query per attribute, so Jordan adds an iterate tag to add the attribute name and type to the entity file, as shown in Listing 5.8.

Listing 5.8 *Example of the* <c:iterate> *Tag for Queries in* Item.java.jet

```
<c:iterate select="$entity/attribute" var="attribute">
@NamedQuery(name="get<c:get select="$entity/@entityName" />By
   <c:get select="uppercaseFirst($attribute/@attrName)" />",
query = "SELECT <c:get select="lower-case(substring($entity/@entityName,1,1))" />
FROM <c:get select="$entity/@entityName" />
   <c:get select="lower-case(substring($entity/@entityName,1,1))" />
WHERE <c:get select="lower-case(substring($entity/@entityName,1,1))" />.
   <c:get select="$attribute/@attrName" /> = :
   <c:get select="$attribute/@attrName" />"),
</c:iterate>
```

Next, Jordan examines the relationships within this entity. By looking at the many-to-one relationship within Item.java, shown in Listing 5.9, Jordan realizes that he must update the input model with a new association attribute to store the name of the join column. He also suspects that there are other multiplicities, so he starts looking at the other entities that were provided in the exemplar. In the Category entity he finds an example of a one-to-many relationship, reproduced in Listing 5.10.

Listing 5.9   *Example of Many-to-One Association*

```
@ManyToOne
@JoinColumn(name="CATEGORY_ID")
private Category categoryId;
```

Listing 5.10   *Example of One-to-Many Association*

```
@OneToMany(mappedBy="categoryId",fetch=FetchType.EAGER)
private Set<Item> items;
```

Jordan notices that the code for a one-to-many relationship has the same number of variables as the code for the many-to-one relationship. The only difference is that the join column is replaced with a mapping attribute. Since the meaning of the attribute is similar between the two, Jordan decides to reuse the attribute created for specifying the join column, keeping things simple.

In a further review of the entities, Jordan does not find any additional examples of different types of relationships. Before moving ahead, he asks Duncan to confirm that all relationship types have been identified. Duncan tells him that a third type of association is used in the company: a many-to-many relationship. A many-to-many relationship is created by annotating both classes in the relationship. One of them defines the join table using an @JoinTable annotation. The other class makes a reference to the join table attribute much like a one-to-many relationship (except that @OneToMany is replaced with @ManyToMany). Duncan provides the example shown in Listing 5.11, further explaining that the only fetching option they use is EAGER.

Listing 5.11   *Example of Many-to-Many Association*

```
@JoinTable(name="PHONE_X_USER",

    joinColumns=@JoinColumn(name="PHONE_ID"),

    inverseJoinColumns=@JoinColumn(name="USER_ID"))
@ManyToMany(fetch=FetchType.EAGER)
private Set<User> users;
```

Jordan notices that there are three variability elements, as shown in Listing 5.11: the name of the join table, the name of the join column, and the name of the inverse join column. The only information not yet available in the association type is the join table and the inverse join column names. So he adds them to the input model.

Listing 5.12 shows the parameterization of the associations inside the entity Java class using the following JET tags:

- <c:iterate> to iterate through the associations

- <c:choose> and <c:when> to provide a behavior depending on a test (here the value of the multiplicity)

- <java:import>, allowing the addition of an import statement for the type of the entity

Listing 5.12 *Parameterization of the Association*

```
<c:iterate select="$entity/association" var="association">
   <c:choose select="$association/@multiplicity">
     <c:when test="'oneToMany'">
@<java:import>javax.persistence.OneToMany</java:import>
   (mappedBy="<c:get select="$association/@targetField" />",
   fetch=<java:import>javax.persistence.FetchType</java:import>.EAGER)
private <java:import><c:get select="$association/@assoType"/>
</java:import> <c:get select="$association/@assoName" />;
     </c:when>

     <c:when test="'manyToOne'">
@<java:import>javax.persistence.ManyToOne</java:import>
@<java:import>javax.persistence.JoinColumn</java:import>
   (name="<c:get select="$association/@targetField" />")
private <java:import><c:get select="$association/@assoType"/>
</java:import> <c:get select="$association/@assoName" />;
     </c:when>

     <c:when test="'manyToManyRef'">
@<java:import>javax.persistence.ManyToMany</java:import>
   (mappedBy="<c:get select="$association/@inverseField" />")
private <java:import><c:get select="$association/@assoType"/>
</java:import> <c:get select="$association/@assoName" />;
     </c:when>

     <c:when test="'manyToMany'">
@<java:import>javax.persistence.ManyToMany</java:import>
@<java:import>javax.persistence.JoinTable</java:import>
   (name=" <c:get select="$association/@joinTable" />",
       joinColumns=@<java:import>javax.persistence.JoinColumn</java:import>
   (name="<c:get select="$association/@targetField" />"),
       inverseJoinColumns=@<java:import>javax.persistence.JoinColumn
   </java:import>
   (name="<c:get select="$association/@inverseField" />"))
```

```
private <c:get select="$association/@assoType" /> <c:get select="
$association/@assoName" />;
    </c:when>

  </c:choose>
```

```
</c:iterate>
```

One of the requirements outlined in Chapter 4 was the ability to reapply the pattern while preserving any modifications to the generated code. To support this requirement, Jordan leverages the Team Pattern Implementation Use guideline (Chapter 12). The idea is to provide a way for developers to modify the code within generated files without having the pattern overwrite or delete the modification upon reapplication of the pattern. Implementing such a solution with JET consists of defining user-preserved areas within the templates. The corresponding JET tag is <c:userRegion>. The <c:initialCode> tag specifies content to be written to the file the first time the pattern implementation is executed. Listing 5.13 provides an example of the use of these tags in the JET template of the façade (AuctionFacade.java.jet).

Listing 5.13   *Use of the Preserved Area Tag in the Façade JET Template*

```
<c:userRegion>
    // BEGIN user-region operations
    <c:initialCode>
    /*
     * Add your business methods between the BEGIN and END tags
     */
    </c:initialCode>
    // END user-region operations
</c:userRegion>
```

Jordan will go through the remaining files to add variability where it makes sense. The work will involve repeating the steps that we've discussed here, using JET tags to access and work with the data from the input model. In this way he will be able to inject dynamic elements into the static structure of the templates.

Unit-Testing the JET Implementation

As part of his development approach Jordan has been regularly testing with the test input model as described earlier. At this stage he will perform a test with the complete input model that was shown in Listing 5.4.

Jordan runs the JET pattern implementation and compares the results with the exemplar project. As this is a case study, they conveniently match on first testing! Figure 5.19 shows the structure of the generated project.

Figure 5.19   `Items2Management`-*generated project*

Jordan plans additional tests, including

- Changing one of the associations to be a many-to-many association (remember that there was no such association in the exemplar, which is why it was not identified during the design)

- Adding an embedded attribute to the `Item` entity to check that the JET component generates the appropriate code

JET Implementation for the Test Project

Now that the pattern seems to work fine for the EJB project, Jordan turns to the Test project. He repeats the steps described previously to parameterize the generation of the Test project. The input model stays essentially the same, aside from `Create File` actions to support the creation of the Test project and associated files. Figure 5.20 shows the resulting Exemplar Authoring view.

Now that the implementation of the JET piece of the pattern implementation is developed and tested, Jordan can move on to developing the UML front end for the

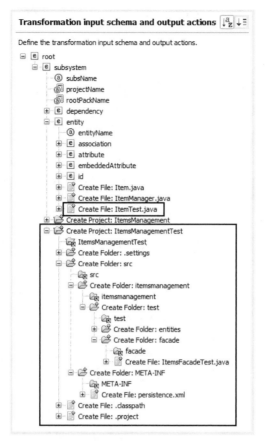

Figure 5.20 *Resulting Exemplar Authoring view*

pattern. He will reuse an Eclipse Modeling Framework (EMF)[10] model (input.ecore) corresponding to the JET input model as he works on the UML front end. The EMF model was automatically generated by the Exemplar Authoring tool and formally specifies the input model.

Implementing the UML Front End for the Pattern

In this section we follow Jordan as he creates the model-mapping component that will process UML and connect to the JET component within the pattern implementation. As discussed in the previous chapter, the input for the Subsystem Façade pattern

---

10. For more information about EMF see www.eclipse.org/modeling/emf/.

implementation is the domain model. The domain model is defined using UML and is maintained by Gwen.

Building the DSL[11]

Reading the Integrated Patterns and DSLs PBE Pattern (Chapter 15), Jordan realizes that he should develop a DSL that Gwen can use to mark up the domain model and make the Subsystem Façade more consumable. Because they use UML, he chooses to use a UML Profile as the basis for the DSL.

The first thing Jordan does is to go back to the JET component of the pattern implementation to look at the input model and identify what elements can be directly derived from UML and what would need a specific stereotype to denote them. Figure 5.21 shows a summary of the JET input model types and attributes.

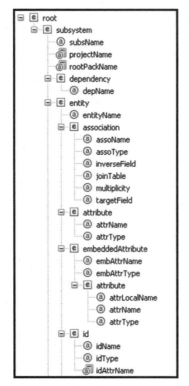

Figure 5.21 *Input model parameters and attributes*

---

11. To make the reading of the chapter easier, we first tackle building the DSL, then the creation of the model mapping, but in real life those two activities are usually done simultaneously.

When they analyze the input model and the domain model, Jordan and Gwen make the following decisions:

- Previously, Gwen had agreed to use packages to organize the subsystems in the domain model. However, not all of the packages in the domain model will be subsystems. So Jordan creates a «Subsystem» package stereotype that Gwen will use to identify the packages corresponding to subsystems.

- Dependencies can be derived from the UML dependencies between two subsystems, so no stereotype is needed.

- Not all classes inside a subsystem package are necessarily entities, so Jordan creates an «Entity» class stereotype to be applied to entity classes.

- Entity attributes and relationships can be derived from the UML attributes and relationships, so no additional markup is required.

- Embedded attributes, attributes of a related class that are persisted into the table of the containing class, will need to be denoted. To identify them, Jordan adds an «EmbeddedAttribute» property stereotype.

- The last stereotype that Jordan provides is «Id». The «Id» property stereotype is used to support the specification of a particular database table ID. The rule in the company is to name the ID of a column following the pattern <TABLE_NAME>_ID (i.e., the ADDRESS table leads to ADDRESS_ID). However, Jordan wants to allow the opportunity to enter a specific ID in case someone has to use a legacy database that does not adhere to the naming convention.

With these four basic stereotypes and the UML syntax, Jordan should be able to gather all the information he needs for the input model. Figure 5.22 summarizes the stereotypes Jordan creates as well as the relationships between them. The metaclasses are used to identify the type of UML elements to which the stereotype can be applied. Jordan does not want to overinvest in the profile and create specific icons because there are only a few users of the profile.

With the profile in hand, Jordan works with Gwen to test the pattern. The goal of the test is to ensure that the profile contains only those elements that are meaningful to her domain. They decide that the best way to validate the profile is to try to apply it to one of the subsystems. Jordan and Gwen choose the Auction subsystem as it contains the most variability. The result of this test is shown in Figure 5.23.

They are both pleased with the results of the test. Jordan can now move to the implementation of the UML front end of the pattern implementation while Gwen continues applying the profile to the rest of the domain model.

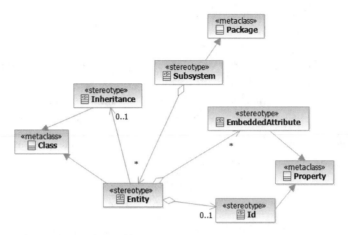

Figure 5.22 *Subsystem Façade profile stereotypes*

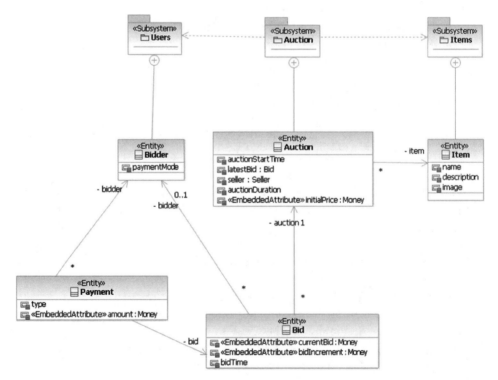

Figure 5.23 Auction *subsystem entities with their stereotypes and dependencies*

Test-Driven Development

Jordan realizes that he needs to put together his plans and test cases for this portion of the pattern implementation. One test case is already available: he can test the Auction subsystem that was used to test the new profile.

In addition to looking at the input models for the test cases, he knows that he wants to isolate the component under test as much as possible. To that end, he decides to leverage the Ecore model that was generated along with the JET component.

Implementing the Model-Mapping Component

Building the model-mapping component consists mainly of mapping UML elements (with or without a stereotype applied) to the corresponding elements defined in the Ecore model that represents the input model of the JET component. We will refer to the UML model as the user model because it is the model that the Pattern User will work with. This model may end up containing more information than is needed for the input model, that is, the model that is required for the JET component. Thus, a single user model may work with multiple pattern implementations and support the generation of a wide range of output artifacts. Also, it allows the team to focus on creating a user-friendly representation of the user model, without being overly constrained by the input model needed by the JET component.

The easiest way to perform this with RSA is by using the Model to Model Mapping feature. Jordan uses the UML Interface to a JET Transformation wizard to generate the needed infrastructure for the Model-Mapping project. This infrastructure contains the UML front end project itself, the model project providing a Java API to navigate the Ecore input model, as well as a feature packaging them with the JET component, making the packaging and deployment easier. The resulting projects are shown in Figure 5.24.

> **Note**
>
> When creating a model-mapping project, the project creation wizard expects to have an input and output model. We can assign one or more metamodels to each of these models. Things can get a little confusing when we connect this component with a JET component. The JET component also has an input model. Generally the input model for the model-mapping component should be considered the user model. The output model from the model-mapping component is the input model for the JET component.

⊞ 🗁 SubsystemFacadePattern
⊞ 🗁 SubsystemFacadePattern.frontend
⊞ 🗁 SubsystemFacadePattern.model
⊞ 🗁 SubsystemFacadePattern-feature

Figure 5.24   *Pattern implementation projects*

In creating the Model-Mapping project he selects UML and the Subsystem Façade profile as the input model (our user model). He then selects the Eclipse Ecore model representing the input model of the JET transformation as the output model.

When building the model-mapping component with RSA, Jordan will create a series of maps that describe how an element from the input model is translated into one or more elements in the output model. To identify which maps he will need to create, Jordan performs a brief analysis of the elements in his profile and the schema associated with the JET component. In this analysis he identifies which UML elements map to which input model elements. Figure 5.25 shows a conceptual view of the high-level mapping between UML elements and the JET input model. Each of the arrows in the figure represents a mapping that needs to be implemented.

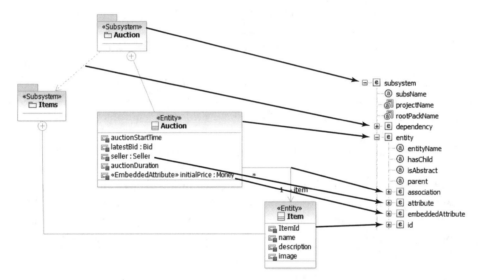

Figure 5.25   *View of the conceptual mappings between UML elements and the input model*

He starts by creating an initial map, called `ModelToRoot`, for extracting the packages with the «Subsystem» stereotype from the input model and feeding them into the subsystem nodes in the output model. Figure 5.26 shows the resulting map. The Submap mapping indicates that the mapping is delegated to another map; this is usually used to iterate through elements where there is a collection of elements. Identification of the packages with the «Subsystem» stereotype is done through a custom extractor[12] retrieving only the relevant packages.

---

12. A custom extractor is a feature provided by RSA Model Mapping Authoring which enables the user to write a custom method to extract the elements that are passed to the submap.

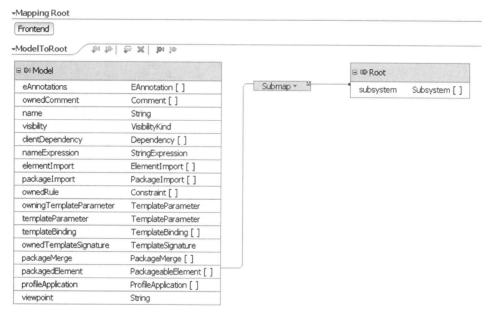

Figure 5.26 ModelToRoot *map*

The subsystem and dependency mappings are straightforward; Jordan just gathers the name of the subsystem and the name of its dependent subsystem.

The entity mapping is interesting, not because it is complex but because it is the hub from where the other maps will be derived and connected. Figure 5.27 shows the («Entity») ClassToEntity map with a set of submaps that allow Jordan to iterate through the different subnodes of the entity (association, attribute, embeddedAttribute, and id). The Move mapping is used to specify that the name of the entity is copied into the entityName attribute.

To create the mapping between UML associations and the associations in the entity element in the output model, Jordan needs to keep in mind the way that this information is modeled in UML. Figure 5.28 provides an overview of how elements are derived from an association. The UML association multiplicities (1–*) are used to define the multiplicity of the association attribute (oneToMany) in the output model. The name and type of the association are defined by the associated UML «Entity», and the targetField attribute is derived from the name of the «Entity» following Oslec Software naming conventions (categoryId).

Another interesting mapping is the one for the embeddedAttribute element. Figure 5.29 provides a conceptual view relating elements in the UML-based input model to elements in the output model. In this case the embedded attribute name and type are derived from the UML attribute with the «EmbeddedAttribute» stereotype. The attributes' names and types are derived from the type class.

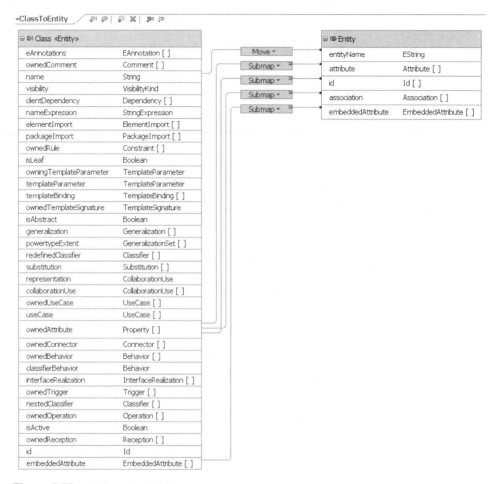

Figure 5.27 «Entity» ClassToEntity *map*

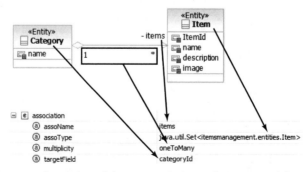

Figure 5.28 *Conceptual mapping of the* UML *association to the input model* association *parameter*

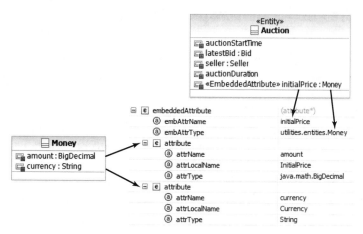

Figure 5.29 *Conceptual mapping of the* «EmbeddedAttribute» *property to the input model* embeddedAttribute *parameter*

Once all of the mappings have been specified, Jordan generates the code for the model-mapping component.

Unit-Testing the Model-Mapping Component

RSA provides an option to save the intermediate Ecore model generated by the model-mapping transformation. This is very useful in unit-testing the model-mapping component. Jordan uses this capability to unit-test the pattern implementation and ensure that it generates a proper Ecore model. To perform this test he uses the portion of the domain model related to the Items subsystem, as shown in Figure 5.30.

Jordan uses the Items subsystem; it will be easy for him to validate the generated Ecore model as it is the same as the one used in the JET testing. When they match, he can then move to the next level of testing.

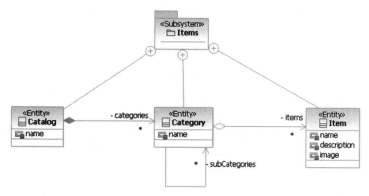

Figure 5.30 Items *subsystem entities with their stereotypes*

Testing the Full Pattern Implementation

After finishing his tests of the model-mapping component, Jordan now turns to testing the full, connected implementation. He uses the Auction subsystem again to help in confirming that there are no errors. The output from running the full pattern implementation is shown in Figure 5.31. He asks Duncan to review the content to check that everything is fine.

As a follow-on step, Duncan, Jordan, and Gwen review the test input artifacts and results. Duncan confirms that the content generated by the pattern indeed aligns with expectations in terms of content, interpretation of user input, coverage of variability, and quality. Gwen reviews the domain model and is satisfied with both the model and the DSL. However, she also requests an enhancement to the profile; she'd like to be able to identify in the model the business services provided by the entities and have

Figure 5.31   Auction-*subsystem-generated projects*

these services generated automatically as exposed operations into the subsystem façade. It is too late to add this feature to this release, but Jordan adds it to the backlog list of future enhancements to the pattern.

Summary

At this point Jordan and Alex have specified the Subsystem Façade pattern and built the corresponding pattern implementation. As mentioned earlier in this chapter, a pattern implementation usually automates more than one pattern, and the Subsystem Façade pattern also follows this rule, encapsulating a number of patterns (as shown previously in Figure 5.13).

Figure 5.32 summarizes the PBE roles, tasks, Patterns, and Guidelines that have been covered in this chapter.

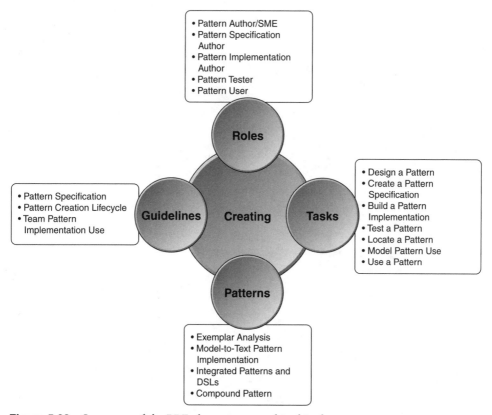

Figure 5.32 *Summary of the PBE elements covered in this chapter*

Chapter 6

Iteration 2: Packaging the Pattern

We pick up with the next iteration of the project. At this point Jordan has built and tested the Subsystem Façade pattern. This model-to-text pattern implementation includes both JET- and model-mapping-based components as well as a UML-based DSL. The pattern has been constructed and tested, and it is ready to be rolled out to the Pattern Users.

In this iteration we wrap up pattern production and transition to pattern management. The focus will be on ensuring that the Subsystem Façade pattern is consumable and accessible by Pattern Users. Jordan will package the completed pattern and then work with Sam, the asset manager, to make the pattern available in Oslec's asset repository.

The main PBE-related activities performed during this iteration are shown in Figure 6.1.

Jordan will start by going through a real-life test of applying the newly developed pattern implementation to the User Management subsystem. Then he will document and package the pattern and work with Sam, the asset manager, to publish it to the asset repository to make it easily accessible.

Launching the Iteration

Michael starts the iteration with a team meeting to define the goals and content of the iteration.

The implementation of the main flow of the Put Item Up for Auction use case has been successful and validated the high-level architecture. With that done, Duncan's team moves to the implementation of the Auction Management subsystem, as it is the next most critical part of the application. Their objective is to implement the Browse Items and Place a Bid use cases. Jordan's objective for the iteration is to package and deploy the Subsystem Façade pattern.

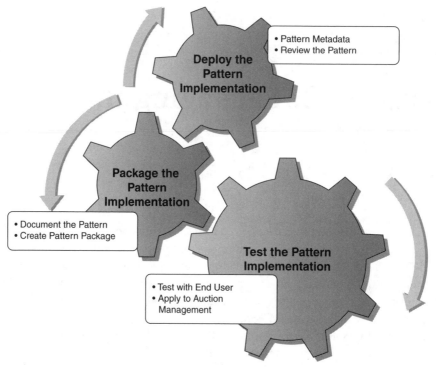

Figure 6.1   *Overview of PBE-related activities in this chapter*

Applying the Subsystem Façade Pattern to the New Subsystem

As Duncan's team is moving to a new subsystem, they need to create all the entities and the façade for this new Auction Management subsystem. Jordan proposes that the team use the Subsystem Façade pattern. This would accelerate the effort, while giving Jordan a chance to get extended feedback based on real-world experience.

Since the pattern is not yet packaged for reuse, Jordan works directly with Matt, guiding him in how to use the pattern. In addition to confirming the quality of the pattern, Jordan hopes to identify content for the supporting collateral. As he works with Matt, he takes notes on the tasks and concepts that Matt asks questions about. Matt also offers a number of suggestions on details that he'd like to see in the documentation, including pointers to details on the encapsulated patterns, information about the profile, and guidance on how to work with the user regions and how they will be affected by the automated build process.

Figure 6.2 shows the Auction-related elements in the domain model, and Figure 6.3 shows the generated Eclipse projects.

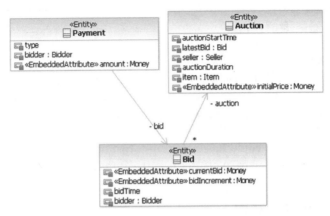

Figure 6.2   *Overview of the Auction subsystem entities*

Figure 6.3   *Overview of the generated Auction subsystem projects*

Packaging the Patterns

Now that Jordan has finished developing and testing the Subsystem Façade pattern implementation, he needs to package it so it can be shared easily with others. In that effort he refers to the PBE Patterns and Guidelines for packaging patterns. The first guideline, Pattern Packaging (Chapter 14), encourages him to be careful with the packaging and to keep in mind that the value of the pattern implementation is based on reuse. The packaging could have a very positive impact on the pattern adoption when done correctly but an even greater negative impact when done poorly.

Document the Pattern

Some of the documentation has already been created while the pattern implementation was being developed, so Jordan does not need to start from scratch.

As stated in the Document Pattern guideline (Chapter 14), the documentation needs to provide different levels of information. The first level is a description of the pattern. To provide a detailed description, Alex suggests that Jordan package the pattern specification with the implementation. Next, for a high-level overview, Jordan decides that the pattern description provides sufficient details on the pattern's context, problem, and solution. And to provide a quick overview of the pattern, he follows the Use Models in Documenting Patterns guideline (Chapter 14) and produces a pattern overview diagram, as shown in Figure 6.4. The diagram provides an overview of the patterns that are encapsulated within Subsystem Façade.

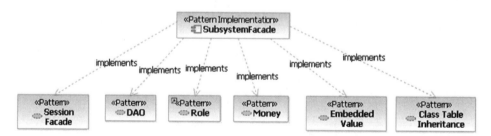

Figure 6.4   *Overview of the patterns that are encapsulated in the Subsystem Façade pattern*

Another important element of the documentation is to explain how to install, use, and uninstall the pattern. Because the developers are using Rational Software Architect, Jordan just has to explain how to install the set of plug-ins that contain the pattern. To simplify the installation, he plans to create two Eclipse features,[1] one with the pattern implementation plug-ins and the other with the profile. With this plan in mind, he writes an initial version of the installation instructions. The instructions guide the Pattern User through the installation of the features. The document is set up to target two roles: those who will use the pattern and the profile, and those who will use only the profile. The plan is to provide the installation documentation alongside the pattern asset.

Following the Embedded Pattern Implementation Guidance pattern (Chapter 14), Jordan develops the rest of the documentation as a set of HTML pages to be attached to the Eclipse help system. This documentation contains details on how to use the profile stereotypes as well as how to create a transformation configuration and launch the pattern. Providing this kind of documentation directly in RSA makes pattern adoption easier and helps the user correctly apply the pattern.

Creating the Pattern Package

Now that the pattern documentation is ready, Jordan can build the package that will be deployed to the pattern repository. In following the Provisionable Pattern Implementation pattern (Chapter 14), he uses a feature to group all the pattern plug-ins, with the exception of the UML Profile, and export them as a single deployable unit. Jordan includes the documentation in the SubsystemFaçadePattern plug-in. Figure 6.5 provides an overview of the feature's content.

He then packages the UML Profile as a separate feature, allowing it to be installed independently from the pattern implementation. The system analysts need to use only the profile and not the pattern implementation, so having the profile and pattern in separate features will allow them to install only what is necessary.

Jordan exports the feature once it has been completely specified. He uses a set of virtual images that contain RSA configurations to test the installation of the feature. As part of the test, he ensures that the pattern installs, the documentation is accessible, and the pattern works successfully with the sample artifacts. He wraps up the testing by ensuring that he is able to uninstall the pattern.

---

1. A feature is a mechanism used in Eclipse to package a set of related plug-ins.

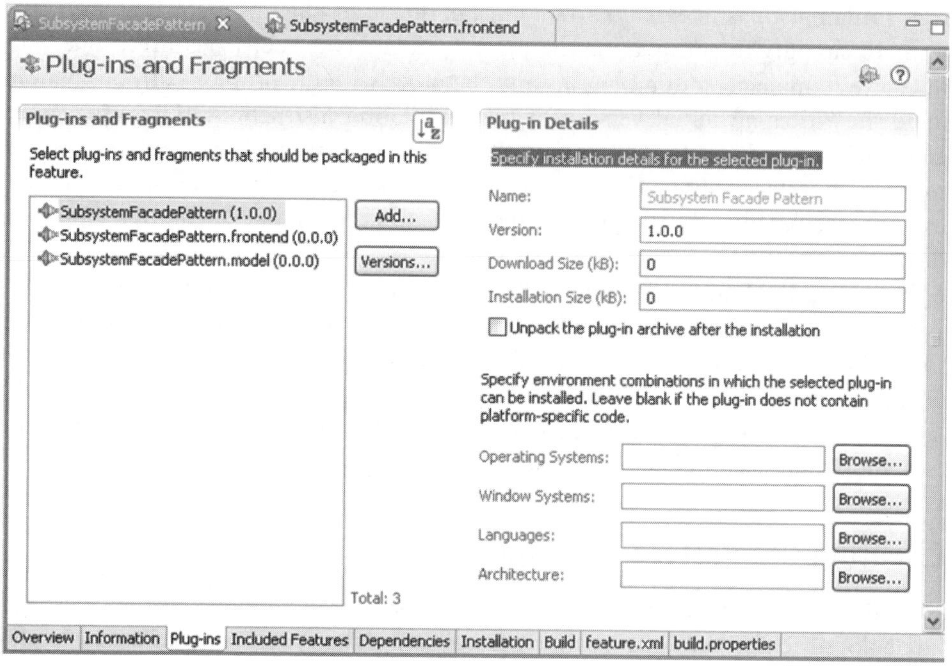

Figure 6.5 *Subsystem Façade pattern feature*

Making the Pattern Available for Reuse

Sam and Jordan decide to collaborate to publish the pattern. The first thing they need to do is figure out where to put the pattern. Recall that Oslec has both a software configuration management (SCM) repository and an asset repository. These two systems appear to have similar purposes; each takes some artifacts, is aware of versions, and is a way to share with a team. However, they serve very different purposes, and so the user interaction with each differs. The SCM repository is responsible for the source artifacts. When Jordan created the pattern, all of the development artifacts were managed using the SCM repository. Now that the pattern is completed, the asset repository will hold the published asset. In making the pattern available as a reusable asset, Sam and Jordan will focus on two key aspects:

1. **Pattern metadata.** The pattern metadata captures information about the pattern, including the pattern description and relationships to other patterns.

2. **Pattern review process.** Patterns added to the repository are not automatically made available to the user community. A review process is used to validate

them. As a result of the review, a pattern can be rejected, sent back for updating, or accepted and made available for reuse.

Pattern Metadata

Making the pattern easy to find is one of the main objectives for Sam and Jordan. With the pattern already packaged, they now focus on adding it to the asset repository. In particular, they want to make sure that the pattern is well described and can easily be found by Pattern Users.

Asset Metadata

Once the asset has been packaged, we post it to a repository. As we post the asset, we want to make sure that we are accurately describing it, detailing relationships, categorizing the asset, and making it available to the correct communities.

The goal is to make the pattern easy to find, and easy for Pattern Users to connect it to their context and other related assets. We want to minimize search errors, including false positives and false negatives. From the Pattern User point of view, the focus is on getting the work done.

From the pattern producer point of view, success is associated with pattern reuse. A producer doesn't want people to rebuild a solution, use the wrong pattern, or copy and paste.

In adding the pattern to the repository, Sam and Jordan specify the following:

- **User community.** The asset repository supports a number of communities within Oslec. Each community has a set of users who have a shared interest, based on a combination of role and project. In this case Sam and Jordan make the pattern available to the LogoAuction team. They decide that they will revisit the scope of availability later on. First they want to ensure that the pattern is successful for the current project.

- **Type of asset.** Sam and Jordan specify that the asset is a pattern.

- **Description of the asset.** In describing the asset, they provide a summary of the pattern, including the pattern's context, problem, and solution. The pattern description provides all the necessary information.

- **Asset relationships.** They specify the asset relationships. In this case they connect the pattern to the documentation that is available externally (installation instructions, pattern specification) and the Façade and DAO patterns.

- **Asset tags.** Sam suggests using the tagging mechanism available in the repository to help categorize the pattern and make the search easier, as the user can filter based on tags. Sam proposes to tag the pattern using the following keywords: Design, Persistence, Subsystem, Façade, Java EE, and JPA.

At this point they are satisfied with the information that's been provided. There are not many patterns in the repository yet, so it should be easy to find this one. After some time they plan to follow up with the team to make sure that the pattern can be found and incorporate feedback into how they create asset entries. With the metadata finalized, they submit the pattern to the asset review process.

Pattern Review Process

Figure 6.6 depicts the review process used for approving the addition of new assets to the asset repository. In this workflow the asset is reviewed by a number of different roles, each providing a different perspective on the suitability of the asset for reuse within the organization. The goal is to confirm that the asset adheres to corporate standards:

- **Legal.** For some Oslec products, the company will ship some of the patterns with the product. In such cases they need to be sure that they are complying with all licensing requirements of any libraries and frameworks that are used. In addition, in the case of a model-to-text pattern implementation, they need to understand the code that is generated and any dependencies on external components.

- **Technical.** The reviewers want to ensure that the pattern embodies best practices and to confirm that standard tests and quality reviews have been performed.

- **Reusability.** The goal is to ensure that the pattern has been properly packaged and documented and that it can be easily consumed and reused.

Asset Review Process

Once the asset has been packaged, we post it to a repository. Although the asset is in the repository, it is not yet available to the Pattern Users. We want to use the repository effectively, so we need to make sure that the assets added have been vetted. As part of the vetting process we make sure that the asset is of sufficient quality, that legal aspects have been reviewed, and that the asset is properly categorized and documented. Such a review effort may lead to the asset being accepted, sent back for modification, or rejected.

A review process also needs to allocate time and attention to assets that have already been approved and are available. In this case the reviewers are looking for assets that should no longer be in the repository and should be retired.

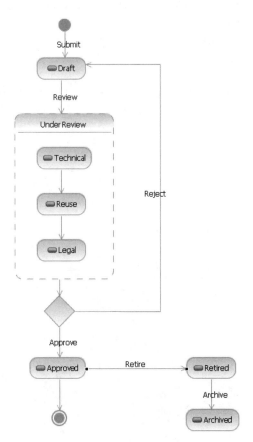

Figure 6.6   *Oslec review process*

The review process goes quickly because Sam and Jordan were well prepared. The asset is approved and made available for reuse.

Summary

In this iteration we have seen how Jordan takes an opportunity to work with Matt in applying the Subsystem Façade pattern. Although the pattern has not yet been officially released, the effort provides two major benefits. First, it allows Matt to benefit from the use of the pattern in creating the Auction Management subsystem. Second, it allows Jordan to gain firsthand experience in helping someone use the pattern. This experience is valuable in helping to crystallize his thoughts about how he will package and document the pattern.

We also followed Sam and Jordan as they worked together to publish the pattern into the Oslec asset repository. They detailed the pattern metadata and successfully guided the pattern through the asset review process.

Figure 6.7 summarizes the PBE roles, tasks, Patterns, and Guidelines that we have seen in this chapter.

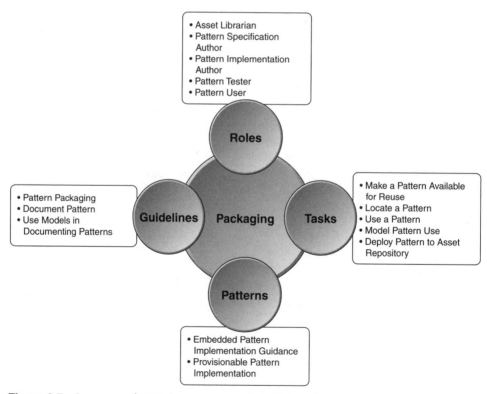

Figure 6.7 *Summary of PBE elements covered in this iteration*

Chapter 7

Iteration 3: Consuming the Pattern

We pick up with the next iteration of the project. At this point Jordan has built, tested, and published the Subsystem Façade pattern.

In this iteration we transition to pattern consumption, where the focus will be on acquiring and using the Subsystem Façade pattern. Rajesh and his team will use the completed pattern implementation to work on the User Management subsystem, and John's team will use it to refactor the Items Management subsystem. Duncan will not be involved in this effort, so the team will get to see if the pattern truly captures his expertise.

Figure 7.1 shows the main PBE activities in this iteration.

In this iteration we will focus on three main scenarios. The first two scenarios are closely related as they both pertain to applying the pattern; however, they differ in terms of the underlying target. In one scenario we look to apply the model where no code for the subsystem has yet been created. In the second scenario we examine a situation where the code for a subsystem already exists and the team plans to refactor to the pattern. The third scenario in this iteration is related to providing feedback and capturing metrics, both of which serve as important inputs to future pattern activity.

Launching the Iteration

Like the other iterations, this iteration starts with Michael leading a team meeting to define the goals and content of the iteration.

John's team and Rajesh's team are driving the effort in this iteration. John's team will take responsibility for the Items Management subsystem, and Rajesh's team will take ownership of the User Management subsystem.

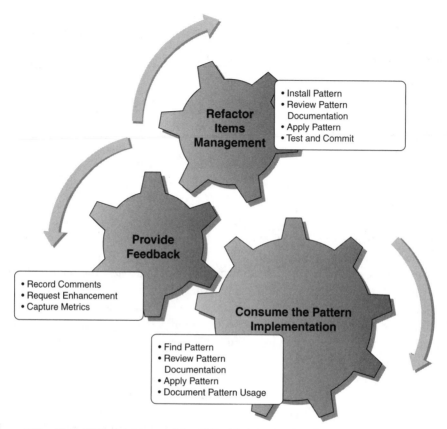

Figure 7.1 *Main PBE activities performed in this iteration*

For this iteration the goal for John's team is to finish the implementation of the Put Item Up for Auction use case as well as implement the Remove Item from Auction use case. One additional task for them as they take ownership of the Items Management subsystem is to refactor it to match the Subsystem Façade pattern. In particular, if modifications are made to the pattern implementation, applying the changes to the Items Management subsystem will be quick and painless. Using the pattern implementation also ensures that all of the subsystems are consistent in their adherence to the pattern.

Rajesh's team will start building the User Management subsystem by implementing the Log In and Create Account use cases.

Duncan will not be involved in John's and Rajesh's efforts. He will focus on the Start Auction and Close Auction use cases. So the organization will see how successful they have been in leveraging his expertise.

With the Subsystem Façade pattern complete, Jordan will start working on the Test Data Reset pattern, which was identified earlier as a candidate pattern (Chapter 4). Recall that this pattern will be important in helping the team to test the LogoAuction application as it makes its way through different environments such as development, testing, and so on.

Using the Pattern in a New Subsystem

In this iteration Rajesh's team is scheduled to work on the User Management subsystem. As they embark on the effort, Rajesh reminds the team that they need to think in terms of finding and using patterns where it makes sense.

Sandhip recalls hearing that a new pattern is available to help with subsystems and, following the Use an Asset Repository guideline (Chapter 16), turns to the asset repository to find the pattern. He accesses the repository and searches using *subsystem* as his keyword and indicates that he is searching for assets tagged *pattern*. The repository returns the Subsystem Façade pattern, which sounds familiar. He sees that there are two related assets:

- Pattern specification

- Pattern documentation

He reviews the details for the pattern and the related assets and then proceeds to download all three. He then reviews the pattern specification to gain a better understanding of the pattern. Rajesh's team, while skilled in a number of areas, does not have anyone with Duncan's skills in Java EE. They view the pattern as a great way to be able to leverage Duncan's expertise without having to compete for his time (or deal with remote collaboration challenges).

Installing the Pattern Implementation

With the pattern implementation now in hand, Sandhip reviews the documentation to understand how to install it. The pattern implementation and the associated profile are packaged within a feature, so he quickly and easily installs the pattern into Rational Software Architect.

Once it is installed, Sandhip reviews the pattern's documentation, which is embedded within RSA (recall that Jordan followed the Embedded Pattern Implementation Guidance pattern; see Chapter 14). He notices that a number of supporting artifacts are installed as well, including a sample input model. He follows the documentation to set up a project, add the sample input model, and test the application of the pattern. Everything works as expected, and Sandhip is confident that the pattern has been installed correctly.

Applying the Pattern to the User Management Subsystem

In the pattern implementation's documentation Sandhip sees Figure 7.2, which shows the roles to which he needs to assign elements.

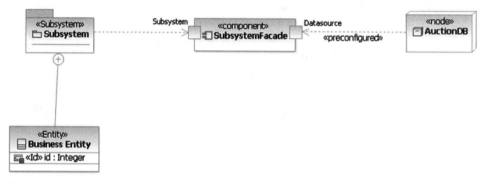

Figure 7.2 *Subsystem Façade roles*

The pattern has two roles, Subsystem and Datasource. However, Datasource is preconfigured, so Sandhip has to focus only on the Subsystem role.

Sandhip accesses the SCM repository and adds the domain model to his workspace. Figure 7.3 shows the domain model entities owned by the Users subsystem.

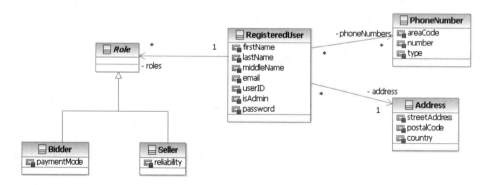

Figure 7.3 Users *subsystem entities*

These are all the entities that the pattern implementation will generate for him; the only thing he has to do is configure the pattern to focus on this subsystem and then apply the pattern.

The first thing that strikes him is the inheritance relationship associated with the Role entity. Sandhip knows that class inheritance can be mapped using different strategies and is curious about how the pattern will handle the situation. He checks the documentation, focusing on the overview shown in Figure 7.4, and finds that the Class Table Inheritance pattern is used. He makes a note to spend some time reading about the Class Table Inheritance pattern to grow his skills in this area.

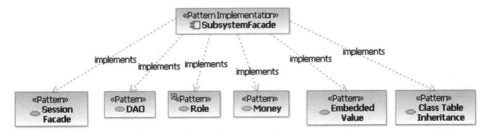

Figure 7.4 *Overview of the patterns that are encapsulated in the Subsystem Façade pattern*

He then creates the transformation configuration for applying the Subsystem Façade pattern to the Users package in the domain model. Running the transformation generates the Java EE projects as shown in Figure 7.5.

Sandhip wants to ensure that it is clear that the pattern is being used, as well as how it is being used. Others on his team will need to understand the usage and its impact on the application. Requirements may change or defects be found once the application is in development. Sandhip follows the Communicate Design with Patterns guideline (Chapter 16). In this case he is using a pattern implementation that allows him to cross levels of abstraction, transitioning from a UML model to a set of text-based artifacts. The tool, by default, has a transformation configuration file to denote the mapping, but he'd like something a little more visual. To that end, he creates a new model that he uses to document patterns that are used across models. He creates a diagram, as shown in Figure 7.6, to denote the use of the pattern and the input and output artifacts.

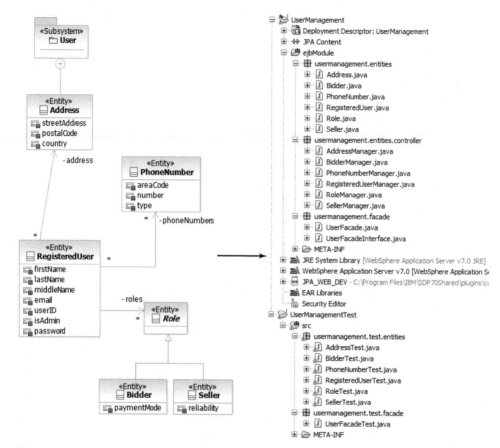

Figure 7.5   UserManagement *entities and the generated projects*

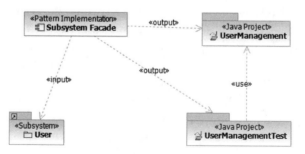

Figure 7.6   *Overview of instantiation of the Subsystem Façade pattern*

Providing Feedback on the Pattern

The last step that Sandhip needs to do is to provide feedback on the pattern. Overall the feedback he provides is positive, as the use of the pattern simplified the work that he had to do. However, it would have been helpful if the business operation signatures were also automatically generated by the pattern implementation. He adds a feature request noting the need for this additional functionality and the value such an enhancement would add to the pattern. In addition, he's heard that there may be a need to support SOA service requests from the subsystems and wonders if it would be possible to have the pattern implementation also generate the web services to support such functionality. He details a feature request for this functionality as well.

He also captures metrics related to his use of the pattern. Finding and downloading the pattern took only a few minutes. He then invested 2 hours in reading the documentation, installing the pattern, and testing the pattern. After that, he spent another 30 minutes applying and running the pattern. Overall, he spent approximately 2.5 hours on finding and using the pattern, the majority of that time on familiarizing himself with it.

Refactor the Items Management Subsystem to the Pattern

During a team meeting, John hears that the Subsystem Façade pattern implementation has been published. He also recalls that the Items Management subsystem serves as the genesis of the pattern's exemplar. However, he is concerned about divergence between the subsystem and the pattern; in particular, what will happen as the pattern evolves over time? How will the two remain synchronized? John quickly confers with Duncan, and they decide that the best path forward is to refactor the Items Management subsystem by using the pattern implementation.

John's first step is to search and retrieve the pattern implementation in the same manner as Sandhip. Once the pattern is found and installed, John spends time reviewing the documentation, particularly the section that explains reapplying the pattern. He focuses on the support for the "user region" tag that is mentioned as a way to preserve manually inserted code. The documentation states that manually added code should be inserted only between // BEGIN and // END lines. He also notices that user regions exist only in the generated façade classes (the session façade and its remote interface) as well as in the JUnit tests.

The next step for John is to test the application of the pattern to the Items Management subsystem. The goal is to see an example of what is generated and further understand the user regions. He applies the pattern in a new workspace, ensuring that he does not impact the actual code base with his test.

After the pattern has generated the subsystem, John starts looking at the ItemsFacadeInterface.java class, shown in Listing 7.1, to identify how and where the user regions // BEGIN and // END are used.

Listing 7.1   *Excerpt of* ItemsFacadeInterface.java

```java
package itemsmanagement.facade;

// BEGIN user-region 01
/*
 * Add your custom imports BEGIN and END tags
 */
// END user-region 01

import itemsmanagement.entities.Item;
import itemsmanagement.entities.Category;
import itemsmanagement.entities.Catalog;
import javax.persistence.PersistenceException;
import java.util.List;

public interface ItemsFacadeInterface {
  public Item getItem(long itemid)
    throws PersistenceException;
  public List<Item> getAllItems()
    throws PersistenceException;
  public Category getCategory(long categoryid)
    throws PersistenceException;
  public List<Category> getAllCategorys()
    throws PersistenceException;
  public Catalog getCatalog(long catalogid)
    throws PersistenceException;
  public List<Catalog> getAllCatalogs()
    throws PersistenceException;


  // BEGIN user-region 02
  /*
   * Add your business methods between the BEGIN and END comments
   */
  // END user-region 02
}
```

In the file he sees that there are two such sections, one for the custom imports and one for the operations exposed by the façade. He also reviews the ItemsFacade.java file and confirms that it is the same. Looking at the tests, he reviews the ItemTest.java and

ItemsFacadeTest.java files. The import user region is still there, but the other user region is at the end of the files to allow for adding new tests.

Now that he knows where to add the user region tags to the actual code base, he can start the refactoring. From past experience in other projects he knows that a successful refactoring always includes tests to ensure that the refactoring does not break anything. Luckily, unit tests already exist and are contained in the ItemsManagementTests project. He can also reuse the web page that was developed to support the Put Item Up for Auction use case as a functional test.

He decides to start with the façade and its interface. He compares the interface of the actual project with the one generated by the pattern implementation. He notices that there is only one operation, addItemToAuction(), that needs to be handled. He checks the imports and notices that no action is needed, so he adds the //BEGIN and //END tags around the operation signature in the ItemsFacadeInterface.java file inside the ItemsManagement project, as shown in **bold** in Listing 7.2.

Listing 7.2 ItemsFacadeInterface.java *with the Added Operation Signature*

```
package itemsmanagement.facade;

// BEGIN user-region 01
/*
 * Add your custom imports BEGIN and END tags
 */
// END user-region 01

import itemsmanagement.entities.Item;
import javax.persistence.PersistenceException;
import itemsmanagement.entities.Category;
import itemsmanagement.entities.Catalog;
import java.util.List;

public interface ItemsFacadeInterface {
  public Item getItem(long itemid)
    throws PersistenceException;
  public List<Item> getAllItems()
    throws PersistenceException;
  public Category getCategory(long categoryid)
    throws PersistenceException;
  public List<Category> getAllCategorys()
    throws PersistenceException;
  public Catalog getCatalog(long catalogid)
    throws PersistenceException;
  public List<Catalog> getAllCatalogs()
    throws PersistenceException;
```

```
// BEGIN user-region 02

public void addItemAuction( String name, String description,
  Category category, byte[] image )
  throws PersistenceException;

// END user-region 02
}
```

He repeats the operation to add the implementation of the method into the ItemsFacade.java file. He then runs the pattern implementation again and validates that the code he added has not been modified or deleted.

He can now go to the next step and validate that the modified code passes the unit tests. To do that he copies the interface and its implementation from the test project to the original project and runs the unit tests. All the unit tests pass, so he can now repeat this approach for the rest of the subsystem. When the original project is updated and tested, he commits the changes to the SCM system.

With success confirmed, John notifies the other team members that they should refresh their ItemsManagement and ItemsManagementTest projects to pick up his changes.

Summary

In this iteration we focused on how the Subsystem Façade pattern was consumed by the Oslec team. Figure 7.7 shows the main PBE elements we have covered in this final iteration.

This wraps up the case study discussion. We went through a few iterations of the project, looking at how the team can adopt PBE and succeed in using it. Their efforts have resulted in the identification of a number of candidate patterns, and then the selection and creation of one of those candidate patterns, the Subsystem Façade pattern. We saw how Alex put thought into and leveraged metrics and ROI as a basis for deciding what pattern to create.

An interesting aspect of the Subsystem Façade pattern implementation is that as the team worked on this pattern, they found and then leveraged a number of related patterns. They were able to encapsulate those patterns, providing the user of the pattern with a simplified experience.

As we've gone through the case study, we've looked at using pattern specifications as an alternative to pattern implementation as well as a complement. There are times when an implementation would not be worthwhile to create; yet we still need to incorporate a best-practice solution. We also looked at using a pattern specification to help Pattern Users understand the details that are captured in a pattern implementation.

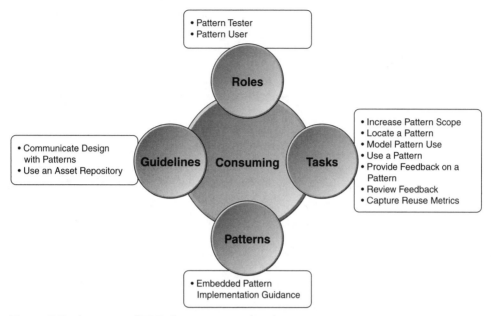

Figure 7.7 *Summary of PBE elements covered in this iteration*

We've also seen some of the ways patterns can be shared with others, supporting reuse of the pattern, where the reuse could be a straightforward application of the pattern or a means to guide a refactoring effort.

Chapter 8

PBE and the Software Development Process

This chapter introduces the process aspect of PBE. Typically, a software development process provides guidance on the roles, tasks, work products, and workflow needed to develop software. This chapter examines the roles, tasks, work products, and workflows associated with PBE.

We can view the software development process as a set of components—some on testing, others on writing code, and others on source code management; each of these process components is known as a **practice**. This chapter provides an overview of the PBE Practice and guidance on how we can leverage the practice in our development efforts. The discussion will also include guidance on how to integrate PBE with some popular processes: Scrum, OpenUP, and Extreme Programming.

To gain a deeper understanding of the elements of the PBE Practice, the follow-on steps are to review Appendix F and then the PBE Practice itself.

Introduction to the PBE Practice

The PBE Practice is authored as a plug-in that can be used with Eclipse Process Framework Composer or Rational Method Composer.[1] The PBE Practice is customizable and configurable, and it can be combined with other practices to create a software development process tailored to the needs of an organization. At a minimum, a default configuration of the content can be published as a set of HTML pages that can be viewed in a standard web browser, as shown in Figure 8.1.[2]

---

1. More information on these tools can be found in Appendix C, "PBE Tooling Options."

2. EPF Composer is open-source and a free download. There are two options for working with the practice: download EPF Composer, or download a published version of the PBE Practice. Details on downloading the practice are provided in the Preface. The goal is to make this content easy to acquire and work with regardless of tooling preferences.

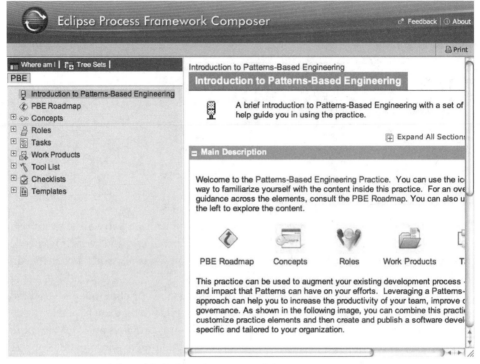

Figure 8.1   *View of the published configuration of the PBE Practice*

With the PBE Practice in hand, we can answer these questions:

- Who is involved in the PBE effort?

- What should each of these roles be doing?

- When should tasks be performed?

- How should tasks be performed?

The rest of the chapter will provide a high-level overview of the practice, focusing on building the base necessary to get started with using PBE without being overwhelmed by too many new concepts and ideas. With this foundation in place, we can gain additional insights about the practice through

- **Oslec case study.** Chapters 3 through 7 illustrate many of the tasks used in the creation of the LogoAuction application. Practice elements introduced in this chapter include references to the case study chapters where the elements are discussed.

- **Appendix F.** Appendix F provides a more detailed look at the roles, work products, and tasks associated with the PBE Practice.

- **Patterns and guidelines.** To successfully complete the PBE tasks, we use one or more of the PBE Patterns and Guidelines. The overview includes references to the chapters where the supporting patterns and guidelines are detailed.

- **PBE Practice.** The PBE Practice is available for download as both an Eclipse Process Framework Composer plug-in and a published configuration. We can review these downloadable elements to gain further insights into the elements within the PBE Practice.

PBE Roles and Tasks in Context

Recall from Chapter 1 that we introduced PBE as a specialized implementation of asset-based development (ABD). Within ABD, there are four key areas that we focus on as we work with assets, as shown in Figure 8.2.[3]

Figure 8.3 shows an instantiation of Figure 8.2 that focuses on patterns as assets.

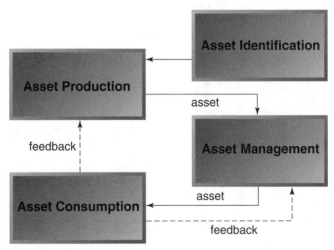

Figure 8.2 *High-level overview of asset-based development efforts*
Credit: Grant J. Larsen, IBM.

---

3. Larsen (2003).

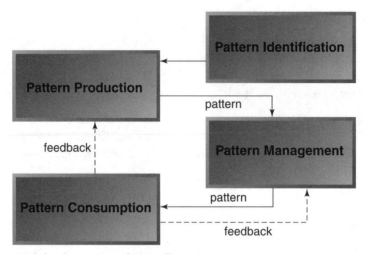

Figure 8.3 *High-level overview of PBE efforts*

And we can take things a step further, as shown in Figure 8.4, and look at the flow between these phases.

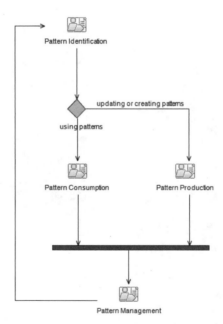

Figure 8.4 *PBE efforts activity diagram*

We can use Figures 8.3 and 8.4 to help us put the elements within the PBE Practice in context. This is particularly useful as we consider the PBE tasks and roles. We can see the details regarding who is doing what, when, and for what purpose. We are also then able to map that understanding into the bigger picture. The roles, tasks, and work products within the PBE Practice support these four major focus areas. It is therefore important that we understand what we are trying to accomplish within each of the areas:

- **Pattern identification.** In this phase we are focused on identifying the patterns that can add value and assist us in successfully completing our projects. These patterns may already exist or may need to be created. We can reuse, as is, those patterns that exist (either from external sources or previously built within our organization) or enhance them. Typically we end up identifying more patterns that are possible to build, enhance, or use; we need to ensure that we are systematic in our efforts and quantify the value of a pattern before we make any investments.

- **Pattern production.** In pattern production our focus is on creating or updating the patterns that have been identified and vetted during pattern identification. In these efforts we look to design, implement, and test the new or extended patterns and their associated artifacts.

- **Pattern management.** In this phase we are focused on managing the patterns that we are making available within the organization. These may be patterns that we have created or patterns that we have acquired. Our focus is on ensuring that we are making it possible for Pattern Users to easily find and then use the patterns that meet the specific needs of their situation.

- **Pattern consumption.** In pattern consumption we are focused on successfully using patterns that have been made available within the organization. Surprisingly, this is often an area of weakness. Typically we find that we are much better at producing patterns than we are at consuming them.

Getting Started with the PBE Practice

To get started with the PBE Practice, there are a number of steps that we can follow to ensure success:

- **Start small.** We are doomed to fail if we attempt to learn, adopt, and integrate all of the content from the PBE Practice at once. To succeed as a team, we need to ensure that we are picking those core elements of the practice and integrating them, and then add further refinements and enhancements in future iterations.

- **Leverage current strengths.** We need to look at our current strengths, while also acknowledging our weaknesses, to help us decide how we will integrate new process elements.

- **Quick wins.** As we adopt and integrate new process elements, we want to ensure that we are setting ourselves up for quick wins. And as these wins occur, we want to ensure that we are communicating these successes to the team at large.

With these steps in mind we can consider Figure 8.5 and Table 8.1, which, respectively, list the roles and tasks within the PBE Practice and map them to the PBE phases. In reviewing these lists and keeping in mind that the roles and tasks continue to fan out to supporting steps, work products, guidelines, and patterns, it is clear that this is beyond starting small. As a matter of fact, we are likely to be overwhelmed if we try to absorb all of this material at once.

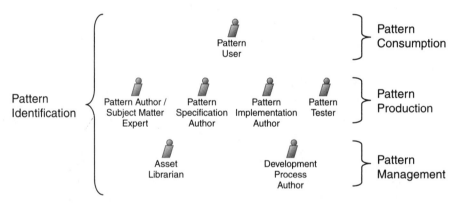

Figure 8.5   *View of the PBE roles and how they map to phases of PBE*

Table 8.1   *Mapping of Tasks to Phases of PBE*

Pattern Identification	Pattern Production	Pattern Consumption	Pattern Management
Find Project Patterns* (Chapter 4)	Design a Pattern* (Chapter 5)	Locate a Pattern (Chapters 4, 5, 6, 7)	Deploy Pattern to Asset Repository (Chapter 6)
Evaluate Candidate Patterns (Chapter 4)	Create a Pattern Specification (Chapter 5)	Use a Pattern* (Chapters 4, 5, 6, 7)	Review Feedback (Chapter 7)

*Indicates a key subset of tasks for initial focus.

Table 8.1 *Mapping of Tasks to Phases of PBE (Continued)*

Pattern Identification	Pattern Production	Pattern Consumption	Pattern Management
Increase Pattern Scope (Chapters 4, 7)	Build a Pattern Implementation* (Chapter 5)	Model Pattern Use (Chapters 4, 5, 6, 7)	Capture Reuse Metrics* (Chapter 7)
	Make Pattern Available for Reuse (Chapter 6)	Provide Feedback on a Pattern (Chapter 7)	Update Development Process (Chapter 4)
	Test a Pattern (Chapter 5)		

*Indicates a key subset of tasks for initial focus.

Sticking with the idea of starting small and providing a solid foundation for successfully adopting PBE, let's focus on a subset of tasks, including Find Project Patterns, Design a Pattern, Build a Pattern Implementation, Use a Pattern, and Capture Reuse Metrics.

Create a Pattern Specification is not part of this list because there are so many available pattern specifications that as we start introducing PBE into our organization, we are better off reusing existing pattern specifications rather than creating new ones. Capture Reuse Metrics is part of the list as we are trying to capture the benefits of using patterns; however, as we get started, we don't necessarily need to record this information formally.

Summaries of these tasks are provided in Tables 8.2 through 8.6. More details on these tasks as well as the others are provided in Appendix F.

Table 8.2 *Summary of Find Project Patterns Task*

Task Name	Find Project Patterns	
Summary	Focus on figuring out the set of patterns that could have an impact on the project. Spend some time and effort in putting together a list of candidate patterns. Perform analysis on the patterns and their possible impact.	
Roles	**Primary performer:**	**Additional performers:**
	Architect	Pattern User
Patterns and Guidelines	Antipatterns (Chapter 11), Domain-Driven Patterns (Chapter 10), Pattern Opportunity (Chapter 11), Recurring Solution (Chapter 11), Use Patterns to Find Patterns (Chapter 16)	

Table 8.3 *Summary of Design a Pattern Task*

Name	Design a Pattern	
Summary	Once we have decided that a pattern is to be built, we have to come up with a design for it. Exemplar analysis plays a key role in this effort.	
Roles	**Primary performer:**	**Additional performers:**
	Pattern Implementation Author	Pattern Author/SME
	Pattern Specification Author	
Patterns and Guidelines	Compound Pattern (Chapter 12), Exemplar Analysis (Chapter 12), Limited Points of Variability (Chapter 12), Meet-in-the-Middle Pattern Design (Chapter 12), Pattern Creation Lifecycle (Chapter 12), Pattern Harvest (Chapter 11), Pattern Implementation (Chapter 12), Pattern Implementation Extensibility (Chapter 12), Team Pattern Implementation Use (Chapter 12)	

Table 8.4 *Summary of Build a Pattern Implementation Task*

Name	Build a Pattern Implementation	
Summary	Create a pattern implementation that has been identified on the list of candidate patterns and has been deemed worthy of investment. Leverage the design that was created in the Design a Pattern task.	
Roles	**Primary performer:**	**Additional performers:**
	Pattern Implementation Author	Pattern Author/SME
		Pattern Specification Author
Patterns and Guidelines	Automate Creation of Pattern Implementations (Chapter 13), Model-to-Model Pattern Implementation (Chapter 13), Model-to-Text Pattern Implementation (Chapter 13), UML Pattern Implementation (Chapter 13), Using DSLs with Patterns guidelines and patterns (Chapter 15)	

Table 8.5 *Summary of Use a Pattern Task*

Name	Use a Pattern
Summary	Use a pattern to assist in completing some task or set of tasks as part of a software delivery effort.
Roles	**Primary performer:**
	Pattern User
Patterns and Guidelines	Design Solutions with Patterns (Chapter 16), Refactor with Patterns (Chapter 16), Single Pattern–Varied Use Cases (Chapter 10), Use Pattern Definitions to Understand Existing Solutions (Chapter 16), Use Patterns to Find Patterns (Chapter 16)

Table 8.6 *Summary of Capture Reuse Metrics Task*

Name	Capture Reuse Metrics	
Summary	When using a pattern, we need to understand its ROI. What was the investment made in acquiring the pattern and then what was the return on that investment?	
Roles	**Primary performer:**	**Additional performers:**
	Pattern Author/SME	Pattern Implementation Author
	Pattern User	Pattern Specification Author
Patterns and Guidelines	Determine Business Impact (Chapter 11), Use an Asset Repository (Chapter 16)	

With this subset of the tasks, we will be well on our way to starting with PBE. Note that there are many other tasks, some of which we will find and perform by default as we follow and complete these key tasks.

The keys to focus on when getting started with these tasks are as follows:

- We are on the lookout for when and where we can use patterns. We adopt a mind-set of using patterns.

- In cases where a pattern does not yet exist, we look to create the pattern—where it makes sense. In particular, the use of model-to-text pattern implementations has proven to be quick and easy to learn while delivering substantial results.

- We need to measure and quantify our efforts. We cannot build or use patterns just for the sake of it. There must be a business result that we can identify, record, and use to justify the investment in our pattern efforts.

In other words, we should find guidance and support in the PBE Core Values.

Appendix F provides additional details on these tasks, along with pointers to the associated roles, work products, patterns, and guidelines needed to successfully complete them.

Leveraging the PBE Practice within Your Own Process

As mentioned earlier, PBE is a practice, not a full-fledged process. A practice can be thought of as a process component. A collection of such components is brought together to create a process specific to the needs of an organization.

To author a process via a set of practices, we use Eclipse Process Framework and Eclipse Process Framework Composer. In doing so, we need to keep in mind that we are working with a process framework, not a one-size-fits-all approach to processes. The goal is to use content building blocks and tools to build a process that works for our situation.

We have a number of practices that we can leverage, including OpenUP, Extreme Programming, and Scrum. Some organizations may prefer not to start with any of these sources, instead sampling from others. The choices depend on the work that needs to be accomplished and the skills and preferences of the team.

PBE is compatible with many other practices. In this section we will take a quick look at how we can integrate with some of them: Scrum, Extreme Programming, and OpenUP.

Building upon our earlier discussion about how to get started with the PBE Practice, here are some additional thoughts to keep in mind as we integrate with other practices:

- An iterative and incremental approach is a key aspect of how we create and work with patterns. We do not expect to find and create all patterns at the beginning of the project, falling into a waterfall approach. Nor do we want to wait until the end of the project to harvest patterns that can then be used on the next project.

- We always aim to be value-driven in deciding which patterns to create and use. We are focused on producing deliverables that meet the needs of our organization. We are not looking to create or use patterns just for the sake of doing so.

Scrum

Scrum is a project management framework that helps manage iterative projects centered on Sprints that are between two and four weeks long. Figure 8.6 provides an overview of a standard Scrum iteration. An iteration has three main elements:

- **Pre-Sprint.** This is when the content planning for the Sprint is done. A Sprint goal is defined, helping the team to understand the objective of the Sprint and to prioritize work. A product backlog tracks all requirements for the project. A Sprint backlog is a subset of the product backlog and is created for each Sprint. This planning is a joint activity between the product owner, who defines the priorities, and the project team, who define and estimate the associated tasks.

- **Sprint.** This is the heart of the Scrum iteration, where the team members sign up for tasks and perform them, providing feedback during a daily Scrum meeting.

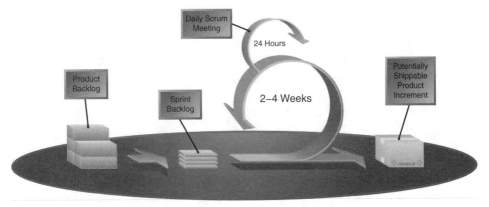

Figure 8.6 *Overview of Scrum*
Copyright 2005, Mountain Goat Software. Reused under the Creative Commons license.

One of the characteristics of a Sprint is that the content of the Sprint backlog cannot be changed during the Sprint, ensuring that the team can focus on the agreed-upon set of requirements.

- **Post-Sprint.** A Sprint is concluded with a potentially shippable increment, a demo to the product owner, as well as a project review. Unimplemented requirements in the Sprint backlog are moved back to the product backlog, ready to be discussed with other requirements in the next pre-Sprint phase.

Integrating PBE with Scrum

Integration between PBE and Scrum starts with the product backlog. The product backlog contains a list of functional and nonfunctional requirements. It is this latter category where we list the patterns that need to be built. In early Sprints we find that we are focused on identifying the patterns that may need to be built. As we progress through our Sprints, we find that we are able to select not only features, but also patterns that need to be built, adding these to the Sprint backlog. We may want to pre-allocate some of each Sprint to working on the patterns that have been identified (for example, within each Sprint, 10% of the effort will go toward building a pattern).

We can also integrate with the planning efforts associated with creating the Sprint backlog. As part of the analysis done for the Sprint, team members will consider how patterns can help them to deliver the elements in the Sprint backlog.

Another integration opportunity is the daily Scrum meeting. We can discuss any patterns that have been identified, those that are in use, and those that are in the process of being built. In this way we can ensure that the entire team is aware of possible patterns, assisting with the evaluation, and contributing to the overall pattern effort.

OpenUP

OpenUP is an iterative, incremental, Agile, and open-source development process that is minimal, complete, and extensible. The OpenUP project lifecycle is split into four phases, each one having its own focus and goal:

- **Inception** focuses on the definition of the high-level scope of the project.

- **Elaboration** focuses on defining and validating the architecture of the project.

- **Construction** focuses on implementing the remaining features, using and enhancing the architecture created during elaboration.

- **Transition** focuses on transitioning the developed product to the users, including deployment, training, and any other activity needed to make the transition as successful as possible.

Figure 8.7 provides an overview of OpenUP. The OpenUP phases drive the project lifecycle, which in turn drives the iteration lifecycle and micro-increments. Corresponding

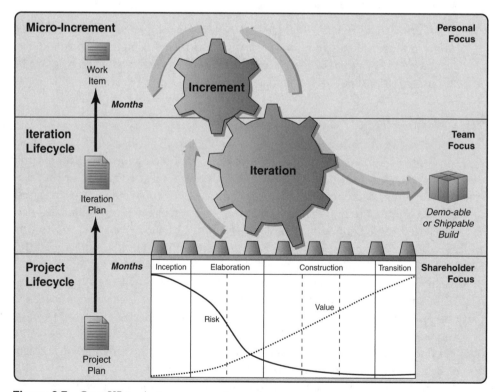

Figure 8.7   *OpenUP project management overview*
> *Reprinted under the Eclipse Public License. Please visit http://www.eclipse.org/epf/downloads/ openup/openup_downloads.php to access this material online.*

to this flow we see that the high-level project plan is used to coordinate the overall project. Each phase is subdivided into one or more time-boxed iterations that target the creation of an executable product increment. The scope and content of an iteration are detailed in an iteration plan. Work is assigned to each team member using work items.

Integrating PBE and OpenUP

There are a number of places where we can integrate PBE with OpenUP. We need to ensure that we map the PBE tasks to the right phases and the right level.

Initial pattern identification tasks are performed during the inception and elaboration phases. However, as new pattern sources or opportunities arise, we can come back to these tasks, regardless of the phase.

Pattern production and consumption tasks are started during elaboration and carried through to the transition phase. Recall that we use patterns across the SDLC, so we may end up building and using patterns targeted specifically at transition activities.

Pattern management tasks occur across all phases and all projects. Funding and staffing models for these efforts determine how these tasks will impact our project plans.

Extreme Programming (XP)

Extreme Programming is an Agile process that is iterative and encourages interaction and communication. As shown in Figure 8.8, it is based on a set of practices that reinforce and counterbalance each other.

The outer circle contains the practices that focus on the overall project and producing incrementally, iteration after iteration:

- **Whole team.** The whole team, usually no more than ten people, sits together in a room. The team includes a customer representative.

- **Planning game.** This is used to plan the content of the release as well as to split the content into two- to three-week iterations. Features to implement are expressed via user stories.

- **Small release.** New versions of the application are released frequently, typically every two or three months.

- **Customer tests.** The customer representative prioritizes the user stories and tests the resulting implementation.

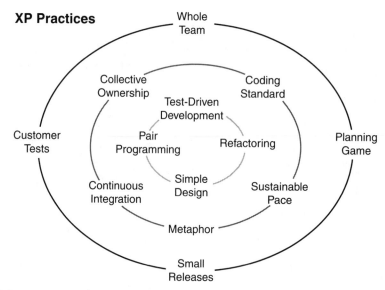

Figure 8.8   *Overview of Extreme Programming practices*
Credit: Ronald E. Jeffries, www.Xprogramming.com.

The middle circle contains a set of supporting practices:

- **Collective ownership.** Source code is modifiable by every team member; code must be well documented and have supporting tests.

- **Coding standard.** The use of standards is encouraged to ensure that code is developed following best practices and supports collective ownership.

- **Continuous integration.** The application is built and tested frequently (at least daily) to avoid late integration and divergence issues.

- **Metaphor.** This is used to help the team stay in unison with one another and the overall project architecture.

- **Sustainable pace.** A sustainable pace discourages team exhaustion by having developers work no more than 40 hours a week.

The inner circle contains the practices that are performed by the developers on a day-to-day basis:

- **Test-driven development.** In this technique development starts with writing tests. The objective of the developers is to write just enough code to successfully pass the tests.

- **Refactoring.** The focus is on improving the quality of existing code without changing its functionality.

- **Simple design.** Design should focus only on current needs. If new needs arise in the future, we can use refactoring to adapt.

- **Pair programming.** Team members are encouraged to work in pairs; one writes the code while the other observes. The observer is tasked with spotting bugs and considering possible tests.

Integrating PBE with XP

PBE is compatible with many of the XP practices. Let's take a look at a few of the possibilities:

- **Planning game.** As part of the planning game we can identify pattern opportunities, determine which patterns to build, and leverage Piecemeal Pattern Creation (Chapter 10).

- **Coding standard.** Model-to-text pattern implementations can be used to ensure that code that is created adheres to the project and organizational standards. As standards evolve, it is easy to reapply them and update the code.

- **Continuous integration.** Pattern implementations can be run in a headless fashion and integrated with an automated build system. User regions in the generated solution ensure that code added by the Pattern User is not overwritten. Tests generated by the pattern can be included in the automated build process and used to report on the quality of the solution.

- **Test-driven development.** Pattern implementations can be set up to generate the test cases that will need to be passed by the solution. Typically the Pattern User will have to add content to the output that is generated by the pattern implementation. Thus, the tests will exist before the solution is created.

- **Pair programming.** PBE uses pair programming in the creation of the patterns themselves. Typically a pairing of a Pattern Implementation Author and a Pattern Author/SME occurs as a pattern is created.

- **Simple design.** Having an approach whereby we create and use patterns within the same project drives us to support our current needs. In addition, patterns such as Exemplar Analysis (Chapter 12) and Pattern Selection Driven by Requirements (Chapter 16) keep us focused on current needs and best practices.

Summary

In this chapter we looked at the process implications associated with PBE. With PBE our focus is on using pattern specifications and pattern implementations, but doing so in a systematic and disciplined manner while quantifying results, impact, and decisions.

The team needs to understand the roles involved in the effort, the tasks that need to be performed, what artifacts are produced and consumed, and how PBE connects with the process that they follow in the larger software delivery effort. There is no single PBE path that all organizations can follow; we need to come up with the approach that works for our team and our situation.

Part II

PBE Patterns and Guidelines

This part describes the Patterns-Based Engineering Patterns and Guidelines. Chapter 9 explains the organization and provides a quick reference to the entire set of patterns and guidelines. Each of the following chapters focuses on one specific category and details the associated patterns and guidelines.

Chapter 9

Introduction to the PBE Patterns and Guidelines

This chapter opens Part II of the book, which discusses the PBE Patterns and Guidelines.[1] The PBE Patterns and Guidelines are to be used in conjunction with the PBE Core Values introduced in Chapter 1 and the PBE Practice discussed in Chapter 8 and Appendix F.

Why patterns and guidelines? PBE includes a set of patterns that have surfaced over the years. It makes sense to discuss patterns that can help us follow PBE; think of them as metapatterns. Also, it is important to see that new patterns are discovered and created; we are not restricted to using patterns that have been discovered by others. Patterns are for everyone—we all need to be on the lookout for pattern opportunities.

Guidelines are also needed to provide advice on how to successfully apply PBE. Not everything needs to be or should be a pattern. We need to evaluate and review patterns to ensure that they are worthy of the name and add value.

Relationship of Patterns and Guidelines to Other Elements within PBE

As a quick refresher, let's review a short definition of PBE and a summary of the PBE Core Values. First, recall that we define PBE as

> a systematic, disciplined, and quantifiable approach to software development that leverages the use of pattern implementations and specifications throughout the software development and delivery process.

---

1. A set of graphics depicting the collection of PBE Patterns and Guidelines is provided in Appendix D.

And, when following a PBE approach, we embrace the following core values:

1. Patterns are best used in combination, rather than in isolation.

2. Always identify and build new patterns.

3. Patterns can be built and used within the same project.

4. Make your patterns live.

5. Focus on making patterns consumable.

6. PBE can fit into many different development processes.

The patterns and guidelines, as shown in Figure 9.1, build upon and leverage the PBE Core Values, while providing details on how we realize the tasks and deliverables associated with the PBE Practice. In this chapter and those that follow in Part II we will discuss the PBE Patterns and Guidelines.

Figure 9.1   *A model bringing together the key elements that support PBE efforts*

Quick Guide to PBE Patterns and Guidelines

In this section we've assembled a quick guide to the PBE Patterns and Guidelines. As discussed earlier, a pattern is a proven best-practice solution to a known recurring problem within a given context. A guideline is less formal; essentially it is a piece of advice or a general rule.

The PBE Patterns and Guidelines are organized into a set of categories, as follows:

- **Foundational.** This is the base set of patterns and guidelines. They form the foundation of our PBE efforts.

- **Discovering patterns.** This set of patterns and guidelines focuses on the discovery of new patterns. To find patterns we need to have the proper skills and focus.

- **Designing patterns.** This set focuses on patterns and guidelines related to the design of patterns.

- **Creating patterns.** With a design in place, these patterns and guidelines focus on successful pattern creation.

- **Packaging patterns.** Once created, patterns need to be packaged and made available for reuse.

- **Using DSLs and patterns.** There is a strong connection between the use of patterns and DSLs. These patterns and guidelines help us in using these two mechanisms together.

- **Consuming patterns.** With thousands of patterns already available and more being identified, we also need to focus on how we can successfully consume patterns. Although just one of the seven categories, it is one of the most important. Our patterns will have little value if we fail to consume them successfully.

The following sections provide an overview of each category along with its patterns and guidelines. The goal is to provide both a summary view and a quick reference.

Chapter 10: Foundational

This chapter focuses on the base, foundational PBE Patterns and Guidelines. These patterns and guidelines will help you incorporate PBE into your projects, guiding your focus, scope, and approach.

Patterns

End-to-End Pattern Use

Problem: How do we accelerate the speed of the project and the quality of the resulting artifacts? And most important, how do we do so across all of the phases and disciplines within the SDLC?

Solution: Use patterns with an end-to-end focus across the entire SDLC and the associated set of tasks and tooling.

Piecemeal Pattern Creation

Problem: How and when do we determine what patterns to use, which ones need to be built, and when and where they should be used?

Solution: Take a piecemeal approach to creating patterns. Analyze and prioritize the development of the pattern features, then map that prioritized effort across a set of iterations and incrementally deliver the needed pattern functionality.

Simple Solution Space

Problem: We use a combination of generic and extremely rich languages to define a solution. In addition, we often work at multiple levels of abstraction. How do we boost productivity, improve quality, and support governance while working in a solution space that is complex?

Solution: Simplify. Reduce the number of moving parts. Review and reduce models, DSLs, diagrams, and elements within diagrams. To assist and accelerate the effort, ensure that you are finding, creating, and applying the correct set of patterns.

Single Pattern–Varied Use Cases

Problem: How do we ensure that we are fully leveraging the investment made in a pattern and that we magnify the impact of the pattern?

Solution: Use a pattern to support multiple use cases in the development effort. Think in terms of the various ways in which you can use the pattern.

Guidelines

Domain-Driven Patterns

Summary: Create, acquire, and use patterns focused on meeting the needs of a domain as well as providing a bridge between domains. Typically, we would look to patterns in the business domain, technology domain, and crossing between these domains.

Pattern Search

Summary: We know that we should be using patterns as we build our solutions. However, it is hard to find patterns to address a problem. Where and how do we find the patterns that we should be using? The short and simple answer is that we need to search for them.

Chapter 11: Discovering Patterns

This chapter focuses on patterns and guidelines that will help in discovering patterns within an organization.

Patterns

Antipatterns

Problem: How do we capture and then share common worst practices with the team? How do we ensure that the team is aware of and then avoids duplicating these worst practices?

Solution: Ensure that you are identifying, detailing, and then communicating the details associated with antipatterns, proven worst-practice solutions applied within a given context.

Pattern Opportunity

Problem: How do we identify the opportunities for using patterns on a project?

Solution: Opportunity identification is all about looking for and finding places where patterns can be used. Tune the creativity and sleuthing skills of the team to be on the lookout for pattern opportunities.

Recurring Solution

Problem: Although we want to use patterns that are specific to a situation and are looking for them, we are not sure when and where the best opportunities to create patterns exist. Where do we find patterns?

Solution: Look for recurring implementations of solutions as a key mechanism for creating patterns. You can use a number of approaches and guidelines such as the Rule of Three, déjà vu, experience, and so on.

Guidelines

Determine Business Impact

Summary: Creating patterns for reuse requires an investment; we cannot build everything, so how do we pick which patterns justify the expense? Develop criteria and mechanisms that can be used to help decide and direct investments.

Pattern Description

Summary: How do we capture a sufficient level of detail about a pattern to support evaluation and feed into design activities without overinvesting in these efforts? Create a pattern description to capture initial details of a pattern that can be used to evaluate the pattern and then as a starting point for designing the pattern.

Pattern Harvest

Summary: How do we capture and elicit best practices, in a more consumable form, from completed and proven projects? Use harvesting to capture the details of the best practice and put them into a pattern.

Update Existing Patterns
Summary: Best practices are evolving as the technology and the practices get spread out. How do we ensure that the collection of patterns within our organization continues to represent best practices? Update existing patterns as necessary to adapt to new technology or to evolving practices.

Chapter 12: Designing Patterns

This chapter focuses on the patterns and guidelines that assist in designing patterns.

Patterns

Compound Pattern
Problem: In situations where we have a number of patterns that work together to solve a related set of problems, how do we simplify the user experience and increase the value and power of the patterns? How do we ensure that related patterns are used together consistently and correctly?

Solution: Create a pattern that is a composite of other patterns. Combine patterns into a larger-grained unit that can easily be consumed by the Pattern User. As a result, the Pattern User needs to know only how to apply the compound pattern rather than the set of patterns encapsulated within.

Exemplar Analysis
Problem: How do we go from an exemplar to a pattern?

Solution: Perform an analysis of the exemplar. Identify the key entities involved in the pattern, the points of variability, a definition of the information that needs to be provided by a user of the pattern, the rules to be used to calculate any additional information needed by the pattern, and the aspects of the pattern that stay the same across applications of the pattern.

Meet-in-the-Middle Pattern Design
Problem: How do we successfully transition from the point where we have identified a pattern to where we have produced a usable pattern?

Solution: Follow a meet-in-the-middle approach to produce the pattern. Such an approach is pragmatic and practical and encourages focusing on the details of the solution as well as the higher-level issues, such as how the pattern should be written up, how it is consumed, and so forth.

Pattern Implementation
Problem: How do we speed up the use of a pattern in a solution, while ensuring that it is applied correctly and consistently?

Solution: Automate the pattern via the creation of a pattern implementation. In contrast to a pattern specification, which captures a pattern as formal written documentation, an implementation codifies a pattern in tooling, automating the use of the pattern.

Guidelines

Limited Points of Variability
Summary: When creating a pattern, how do we ensure that the user of the pattern is not overwhelmed and confused by the configuration and customization options for the pattern? Limit the number and types of points of variability. Ensure that the pattern provides the most important points of variability and then uses calculations and assumptions to leverage the user-provided information.

Pattern Creation Lifecycle
Summary: There is a flow in which we use existing patterns to help us build a solution that will serve as an exemplar. With an exemplar in hand, we can use abstraction and analysis to create a set of one or more patterns. We then use those patterns in the creation of future models that will serve as the basis for future patterns.

Pattern Implementation Extensibility
Summary: How can we facilitate the use of a pattern implementation in situations for which it was not originally intended? When designing a pattern implementation, ensure that the tooling used provides support for extensibility. Then, as part of the design, consider how and where to enable others to extend the solution.

Team Pattern Implementation Use
Summary: Software development is a team sport, requiring the efforts of many to succeed. How do we design pattern implementations to support team development scenarios? Consider the reapplication strategy, management of user-provided content, model structuring and merging support, and the languages that will be used.

Chapter 13: Creating Patterns

This chapter presents a set of patterns and guidelines that focus on providing guidance for creating patterns.

Patterns

Model-to-Model Pattern Implementation
Problem: When using models at multiple levels of abstraction, how do we support the transition between the different models while following best practices?

Solution: Create model-to-model pattern implementations that automate the transformation of a model at one level of abstraction to a model at another level of abstraction.

Model-to-Text Pattern Implementation

Problem: How can we transition from representations in models to text-based artifacts that directly represent the solution while following best practices?

Solution: Create model-to-text pattern implementations that take a model as input and then generate a set of text-based artifacts. These text-based artifacts can include code, documentation, scripts, and other elements.

UML Pattern Implementation

Problem: When using patterns within a UML model, we run into a number of challenges. How do we accelerate the application of patterns and ensure that they are applied correctly and consistently?

Solution: Create a UML pattern, that is, a pattern implementation that is specialized for use within UML models.

Guidelines

Automate Creation of Pattern Implementations

Summary: How can we reduce the amount of time it takes to build high-quality pattern implementations? Create and use pattern implementations to automate the creation of pattern implementations.

Pattern Specification

Summary: How can we quickly and efficiently document and communicate a pattern so that it can be reused? Write a pattern specification detailing the pattern name, context, problem, forces, solution, examples, related patterns, and other information.

Pattern Testing

Summary: How do we ensure that a pattern is consumable and of high quality? The simple answer is to test the pattern to ensure that it is consumable, meets quality expectations, and satisfies requirements.

Chapter 14: Packaging Patterns

This chapter presents a set of patterns and guidelines that provide guidance on how to package patterns to ensure that patterns can be found and consumed.

Patterns

Embedded Pattern Implementation Guidance

Problem: How can we eliminate hurdles and friction (and excuses) related to not following documented guidance and best practices?

Solution: Embed guidance on how to use the pattern into the tooling that hosts the pattern.

Provisionable Pattern Implementation

Problem: How do we support the deployment and provisioning of patterns to the Pattern User's work environment?

Solution: Leverage the capabilities of the tooling to create manageable units for the patterns and their associated artifacts.

Guidelines

Document Pattern

Summary: How do we ensure that the Pattern User is able to understand the details associated with how to install, configure, use, and uninstall a pattern? Document the pattern, providing the Pattern User with details on how to work with the pattern.

Document Pattern Relationships

Summary: How do we communicate which patterns should or should not be used with one another? Document the relationships between patterns, including dependencies, hierarchy, and cases where patterns are mutually exclusive.

Make Pattern Documentation Easily Accessible

Summary: How do we make a pattern easy for others to understand and work with? Make the pattern documentation that supports the pattern easy to find and access.

Package Related Patterns Together

Summary: How do we help Pattern Users to succeed in consuming multiple related patterns? Simplify how people find, consume, and work with related patterns by packaging them together.

Pattern Packaging

Summary: How can we share patterns in such a way that they are easy for others to consume? Package patterns so that they bring together the appropriate set of artifacts needed for consuming the pattern.

Pattern Version
Summary: How do we succeed in an environment where multiple versions of patterns exist? Use version numbers and a versioning strategy to organize and support the various instances.

Use Models in Documenting Patterns
Summary: How can we improve and simplify the documentation regarding the details about the design and use of a pattern? Provide visual models that show the details of a pattern and how to use it.

Chapter 15: Using Domain-Specific Languages with Patterns

This chapter focuses on patterns and guidelines to help in creating a simplified modeling experience for those using the patterns.

Patterns

DSL Model Template
Problem: How should models using a DSL be structured?

Solution: Provide the users of the modeling language with a model template to supply a starting structure and guidance.

Integrated Patterns and DSLs
Problem: How can we raise the level of abstraction and have the team focus on the problems to be solved while preventing them from getting lost in the details of the development languages?

Solution: Use DSLs within a PBE approach to enable working at higher levels of abstraction, a level closer to the solution space, while also leveraging best practices in the form of patterns.

Guidelines

Create a DSL
Summary: How do we take a design as input and create a DSL? Use a framework to help build the implementation, using either a specialized language creation framework or a general-purpose language that has extension capabilities.

Design a DSL
Summary: How do we design a consumable and high-quality DSL? Use a meet-in-the-middle approach to building the DSL that accounts for language scope, granularity, semantic completeness, user friendliness, and tool friendliness.

Meaningful Icons in a DSL
Summary: How do we make the DSL more intuitive, user-friendly, and easy to work with? Use meaningful and easy-to-understand icons to provide visual cues to those using the DSL.

Chapter 16: Consuming Patterns

This chapter focuses on a set of guidelines to help get the most out of using patterns. We change our focus to look at how the Pattern User role can succeed in using patterns.

Guidelines

Communicate Design with Patterns
Summary: How do we describe and communicate key aspects of a design to others? Use patterns to describe and communicate key design aspects of a solution.

Design Solutions with Patterns
Summary: How can we improve the delivery and the quality of applications while leveraging best practices? A key and traditional approach is to use patterns in designing the solution.

Pattern Density
Summary: How many patterns should be used in creating a solution? Manage the density of patterns that are used within a solution as a means to using the correct number of patterns.

Pattern Selection Driven by Requirements
Summary: How do we determine what patterns should be selected and used on a project? Use a combination of functional and nonfunctional requirements as a guide in selecting the patterns to use.

Refactor with Patterns
Summary: How do we improve an existing solution to align with best practices? Refactor the existing solution using patterns as the means and endpoint for the updated solution.

Select Large-Scope Patterns First
Summary: When it appears that it is possible that many patterns could/should be used in a solution, where should pattern selection start? Start with the patterns that have the largest impact or scope and then use smaller-scope patterns to embellish the details.

Use an Asset Repository

Summary: How do we quickly and easily find the patterns that are available for reuse within the organization? Use an asset repository to manage the patterns like any other reusable asset.

Use Pattern Definitions to Understand Existing Solutions

Summary: How do we quickly understand an existing solution? Is it well built? Has it stayed true to the design? Using a set of known pattern definitions, search the solution for occurrences of the patterns.

Use Patterns to Find Patterns

Summary: How do we find new patterns in existing solutions? Using the collection of known pattern definitions, analyze the existing solutions to find occurrences of new patterns.

Summary

We can use the PBE Patterns and Guidelines to help us identify, produce, consume, and manage patterns. This chapter has provided an overview of all of the PBE Patterns and Guidelines. When we initially review the list, it serves as an introduction to the set and the support provided for our PBE efforts. Once we've gained some familiarity with the patterns and guidelines, we can use this chapter as a reference that can quickly and easily be consulted.

Chapter 10

Foundational Patterns and Guidelines

If we could have only a small set of patterns and guidelines to use in helping us with our PBE efforts, which would they be? What would be the most important things to do and remember? Could such a set provide us with a foundation that we could then build upon as we use the other PBE Patterns and Guidelines?

This chapter provides such a set of PBE Patterns and Guidelines, a set that focuses on a range of topics that are core to the PBE discussion. Although the set is small, we will touch upon pattern identification, pattern production, pattern consumption, and pattern management. These foundational patterns will play a key role in our success in adopting and following PBE, reinforcing a disciplined, systematic, and quantifiable approach. This set of patterns helps us to answer questions such as these:

- When looking at the development lifecycle, where should we use patterns?

- Where can we find patterns?

- What type of patterns should we look for?

- How should we use patterns?

- What approach should we take when building patterns?

- How do we support the consumption of patterns?

- Last but not least, what are some of the factors that we should consider as we calculate the impact of our patterns?

> **Note**
>
> This chapter and those that follow in this part of the book are formatted for easy reference. There are two major sections within each chapter, one that lists the relevant patterns and another that lists the relevant guidelines. Within each of these sections the elements are listed alphabetically to support easy lookup.

Patterns

The patterns discussed in this section focus on a number of topics, ranging from where in the development effort we should use patterns to how we create patterns and then simplify consumption. The tie that binds them is their importance in providing a foundation for our PBE efforts.

End-to-End Pattern Use

Context

The organization recognizes that there are multiple stages and disciplines within the software development lifecycle. There is also recognition that there is a range of skills and capabilities across the team. And there is a need to increase productivity, improve quality, and better govern the software delivery effort.

Problem

Many aspects of the SDLC are tedious and error-prone. Efforts are further complicated by best practices that are not recorded adequately, communicated, understood, or followed. How do we get the organization to follow best practices in a consistent and enforced manner? How can we do so while also accelerating the speed of the project and improving overall quality?

Forces

- The entire development organization needs to be involved in adopting and using PBE.

- A separation of roles can ease the rollout of the PBE effort.

- We must ensure that we are keeping patterns up to date and reflective of current best practices.

- We must recognize that patterns do not exist in isolation. There are numerous roles, tools, and tasks within the SDLC.

- Culture increases in importance as we expand the scope of pattern impact.

- We need to make sure that there is the capability to author, update, and distribute process knowledge.

Solution

Use patterns with an end-to-end focus across the entire SDLC. We should not artificially restrict the areas where we use patterns.

Why would we use patterns for only a single aspect of the SDLC? No matter how efficient we become in using patterns for design, we still have a limited impact on the overall success of the project. Consider, as shown in Figure 10.1,[1] that the design discipline is just 15% of the overall effort of building a software solution. Perhaps we could have a greater impact with the implementation discipline, which accounts for 25% of project effort. However, "[c]oding is only the fourth most expensive activity when building large software applications. Maintenance, testing, and defect repair, documentation, and even meetings and communication can be more expensive."[2]

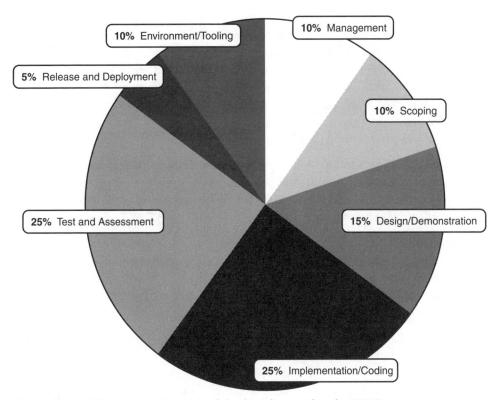

Figure 10.1 *Effort allocated to each of the disciplines within the SDLC*

1. Data used to generate the figure was sourced from Royce (2009).

2. Jacobson et al. (1997).

We need to broaden our scope and look beyond a single discipline as we adopt PBE. We should build and use patterns across as many of the disciplines of the lifecycle as possible. Why limit ourselves to one narrow slice of the overall effort? That sounds reasonable, but the question is, how do we make this happen?

The first obvious step is to consider as wide a scope as possible. As we look at each of the disciplines, we need to consider where patterns could be used and where new patterns may exist. However, we cannot force all of the roles, tasks, work products, and tools to revolve around patterns. Rather, we need to find ways to fit patterns into these elements—enhancing them, supporting them, and improving them. Here are some strategies that we can apply:

- **Skills and expectations.** Be aware of the skills and expectations of the target Pattern User community.

- **Pattern implementations and specifications.** Within PBE we use pattern specifications and pattern implementations. Where possible, we use automation, so there is a preference for pattern implementations, but there is great value in both types of patterns. We need to focus on capturing the patterns of value and then determine the best approach to building and using them. For instance, some roles and tasks may not be well suited to automation. In such cases it would make sense to focus on pattern specifications.

- **Culture.** Create a culture not only of pattern production but also of pattern consumption. Even if we create the best patterns in the world, if no one uses them, we have failed. We need to ensure that this culture is nurtured beyond just the people involved in design.

- **Development process authoring.** The organization's software development process should define the roles, work products, and tasks that detail how software will be delivered *and* call out the patterns to use. The set of patterns will change over time, so we need to update the process to account for the latest set. In addition, the use of patterns may lead to a reduction in process tasks and steps.

- **Tooling.** Each of the disciplines has tools that are specialized for certain tasks. For instance, the testing team has a set of tools that enable them to create and manage test cases, test the software, and manage defects as well as the associated patterns. We need to be aware of the artifacts that these tools work with, as there are many cases where we can use patterns to consume or generate them.

Example

In the case study, Oslec creates a pattern that starts with a focus on design, then increases in scope to include implementation and assessment. More specifically, as they create the Subsystem Façade pattern implementation, they increase the scope of the pattern to include the following:

- **Design.** The pattern brings together a number of design patterns, including the Session Façade and the Data Access Object patterns.

- **Implementation.** The pattern is enhanced to support the implementation of JPA code generation.

- **Assessment.** In addition to creating the design and implementation, the pattern generates a set of test cases.

In future iterations they could also use patterns to support the deployment of the LogoAuction application, further impacting the overall SDLC. In addition to having coverage across 70% of the SDLC, they would find that the use of patterns helps reduce defects, improve communication, and make maintenance easier.

Related Patterns and Guidelines

Determine Business Impact (Chapter 11), Pattern Opportunity (Chapter 11), Piecemeal Pattern Creation*[3]

Piecemeal Pattern Creation

Context

The organization plans to create and use patterns. There is time pressure on the project, and the organization is hesitant to make investments in reusable assets.

Problem

It can be difficult to figure out all aspects of a pattern during its initial design and creation. In addition, the scope of the pattern can be quite large. How can we deliver an effective pattern in a timely manner and positively impact our project?

Forces

- Not all patterns can be found, designed, built, and delivered within a single iteration.

- Risk is an issue when we do not use patterns or if we select patterns that end up not delivering the expected results.

---

3. In this and the following chapters, an asterisk after the pattern or guideline name indicates that the pattern or guideline is discussed in the current chapter.

- Increasing the scope of a pattern to touch upon a greater portion of the SDLC can have a positive impact on a project.

Solution

Take a piecemeal approach to creating patterns. We analyze and prioritize the development of the pattern features. We then map that prioritized effort across a set of iterations and incrementally deliver the needed pattern functionality. Such an approach allows us to deliver value to the project sooner; we are able to grow the scope of the pattern, easily adapt to changing requirements, incorporate lessons learned, and minimize the risk associated with the overall project. To guide our efforts, we can ask these questions:

- What are the most important aspects of the pattern that need to be delivered? What aspects can show up later? When does the pattern need to be used? How can we best minimize risk while delivering the most benefit?

- What areas of the pattern would provide the most significant portion of the ROI[4]? As a rough guideline, consider the 80/20 rule. Often we spend 80% of the effort on the last 20% of the functionality. Do we get the ROI we need from that remaining 20%? Where does the true value of the pattern come from? Can we focus on those areas first, release the pattern, and then use feedback and real-world experience to determine when and if further investments should be made?

- Consider the target audience that will be working with the pattern. What are their requirements for the pattern, and how do they prioritize those requirements? Taking things a step further, how will the pattern impact the solution being built? How does the pattern impact the key requirements and deliverables for the project where it will be used?

- What are the Pattern Users' current skill levels in comparison to the skill level needed to work with the pattern? If training is needed for using the pattern, when will the training occur? How does such a training plan align with the timing of feature delivery for the pattern?

- Are there related patterns? How will this pattern interact with those other patterns? Are the related patterns already built? If not, what is their delivery schedule and how does that impact the delivery of the pattern that is currently being analyzed?

---

4. For additional guidance on calculating ROI, asset value, and associated checklists, refer to Chapter 6 of DeCarlo et al. (2008).

We use the answers to these questions to guide us in creating a plan for building the pattern. We want to ensure that the early iterations provide us with a usable and useful pattern that delivers an appropriate ROI within the current project. In addition, we want to ensure that we are aware of how the pattern could be enhanced for use in later iterations or even future projects. The decision on when and where to build the enhancements can be made at another time that is convenient and logical.

For the Pattern User role, we need to keep in mind that the catalog of available patterns is updated continuously. As a result, the supply of patterns continues to evolve, be enhanced, and grow. Ideally, our projects will leverage an iterative and incremental cycle so that we can take advantage of the most recent pattern versions.

Example

An example of using this pattern appears in the case study when Jordan implements the Subsystem Façade pattern implementation in two steps. First he implements the JET component, which can be made available for reuse. Then he implements the model-mapping component, in which he could incorporate feedback received from those using the JET component.

Jordan also focuses on current requirements and core capabilities of the pattern, for instance, in Chapter 5 when he looks to a future version of the pattern to incorporate Gwen's enhancement request to generate the exposed business methods from the domain model. An additional requirement that surfaces in Chapter 7 is a request to support SOA-based services. This requirement is also set aside for a future release of the pattern.

Related Patterns and Guidelines

Determine Business Impact (Chapter 11), Pattern Creation Lifecycle (Chapter 12), Pattern Search*, Update Existing Patterns (Chapter 11)

Simple Solution Space

Context

We build solutions using multiple models and levels of abstraction. The development process is too complex, and skilled resources are at a premium.

Problem

Productivity is not high enough and the quality of the resulting solutions is insufficient. How can we leverage models, abstractions, and best practices without overwhelming the team?

Forces

- We need an expert-level understanding of the solution space, including the business and technical domains.

- We need to have an understanding of the skill level of the development team.

- Pressure can surface to get the project done by any means necessary.

- A holistic view of the development approach, domain, skills, and best practices is needed.

Solution

Simplify. Reduce the number of moving parts. Review and reduce models, DSLs, diagrams, and elements within diagrams. To assist and accelerate the effort, ensure that you are finding, creating, and applying the correct set of patterns.

As shown in Figure 10.2, if we look at a typical solution space, we use many models, and then within a model we use multiple DSLs and numerous types of diagrams. Digging a level deeper, we also see that within a DSL we use many language elements. There are too many moving parts, too many things to keep synchronized, and too many things to learn and remember.

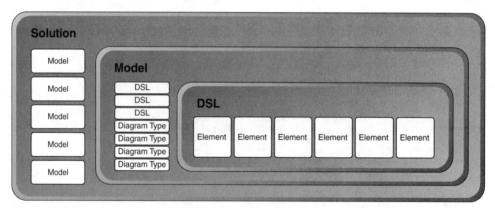

Figure 10.2 *Solution space and the many elements needed within to represent the solution*

Figure 10.3 displays a simpler solution space. In this case we've reduced the number of models. In addition, as we look within the model, we see that there are fewer DSLs and we use fewer diagram types, and within the DSLs there are fewer elements. To reach this point we need more than just intent. To help us reach this simpler state, we incorporate patterns, both specifications and implementations.

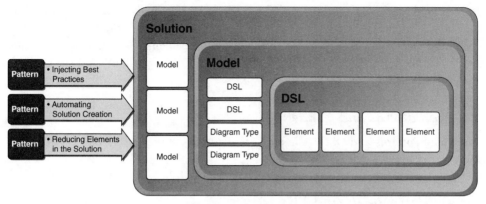

Figure 10.3 *Simplified solution space highlighting the role that patterns can play*

Patterns help us to simplify the solution space in three key ways:

- We are able to use both pattern specifications and implementations to help us inject best practices into our solution. We are able to create solutions that are based on best practices, eliminating incorrect and extraneous elements. We are creating a solution that is as concise and correct as possible.

- Pattern implementations can be used to automate the creation of the solution. Yes, we are automating the application of the best practice, but we are also encapsulating details, rules, and assumptions within the pattern implementation. The net result is that we are able to reduce the amount of modeling that we perform, leading to fewer elements in the solution space.

- In general we can use patterns to reduce the elements in the solution space. We do not need to show all details and aspects of a pattern in the solution; the pattern, being a known element, allows us to abstract away details.

Example

As we follow Oslec in the case study, we see that they are looking for ways to create a simple solution space. They want to identify and then use patterns, from both external and internal sources. When using pattern specifications, they are mindful of how much detail needs to be modeled and how much is implicit because of the use of the pattern.

In the case of pattern implementations, we see that the Oslec team identifies, creates, and then applies the Subsystem Façade pattern. By using this pattern, the Pattern User is able to define a solution for a subsystem with a simple DSL and a domain model. In their efforts to simplify the solution space, the project team has been able to remove the need for a more detailed model, such as an analysis or design model. In addition, although UML provides many elements and diagrams, they are able to direct the team to stick to a subset of the available elements. With this simpler solution space the team is better able to focus on the task at hand and meet the needs of the business.

Related Patterns and Guidelines

Integrated Patterns and DSLs (Chapter 15), Pattern Creation Lifecycle (Chapter 12), Piecemeal Pattern Creation*

Single Pattern–Varied Use Cases

Context

Patterns from a number of sources are available within the organization. We currently use patterns to help us create artifacts and deliverables.

Problem

How do we maximize the investment made in a pattern? How do we maximize the impact of our patterns?

Forces

- We need to measure and track the pattern investment and impact.

- Tooling limitations and a lack of standards can limit pattern ROI and impact.

Solution

There are a variety of use cases for how we use patterns. We need to consider the many ways in which we can use a pattern to support our development efforts. To maximize the ROI and impact of a pattern, we want to use it as often and in as many ways as possible.

In the discussion of the End-to-End Pattern Use pattern, we mentioned using patterns across the disciplines within the SDLC. However, what does it mean to use the pattern within a discipline? Do we apply the pattern only to solve a known problem? That's a common approach, but it should not be the only approach. Figure 10.4[5] highlights a number of different pattern use cases, that is, the different ways in which we can leverage patterns.

---

5. Based on information in Schneider and Lexvold (2008).

	Summary	Pattern(s) as Input	Pattern(s) as Output
Visualize	Represent pattern occurrences visually	✔	
Detect	Discover occurrences of known patterns	✔	
Refactor	Refactor artifacts to match a pattern	✔	
Apply	Impose a known pattern on artifacts	✔	
Harvest	Mine and codify new patterns from occurrences		✔
Create	Create new patterns or compound patterns		✔

Figure 10.4   *Examples of some of the ways in which we can use patterns in our development efforts*

In delivering a software solution, we can use patterns in many ways, including these:

- **Apply.** Starting with the most familiar approach, we can apply a known pattern to artifacts. The pattern helps us to solve a known problem and leads to a set of artifacts or deliverables that adhere to the pattern.

- **Detect.** Using definitions of known patterns, we can analyze a solution and discover occurrences of the patterns. We can use such information to help us with Pattern Density (Chapter 16).

- **Refactor.** We can refactor existing solutions using known pattern definitions as a guide and end point.

- **Visualize.** Using definitions of known patterns, we can analyze a solution and visualize instantiations of the patterns. Such an approach can help us to better understand the solution. We are able to rise above the details and view higher-order concepts.

- **Harvest.** We mine and codify new patterns from occurrences, using the existing collection of patterns to help in the discovery of potential uncharted patterns. In analyzing existing solutions, we can use known pattern definitions to highlight whitespace areas in the solution as well as possible compound patterns (Chapter 12).

- **Create.** We can create new patterns from scratch or create new compound patterns.

Example

Consider the case study of Oslec's LogoAuction application. Once the application is completed, it still needs to be maintained and supported by Oslec. The development team based in Boston, led by John, has been asked to create a fix pack to address a number of defects for the currently released version. John and his team now need to understand and work with the entirety of the code base. They could spend time reviewing the design documents and the code base. However, this would be time-consuming. Instead, they can use known pattern definitions to analyze and visualize the code base. In this way they can learn what patterns were used and generate diagrams that show where and how the patterns were used. With such information they are able to quickly understand the code and start on the bug fixes.

Related Patterns and Guidelines

Design Solutions with Patterns, Refactor with Patterns, Use Pattern Definitions to Understand Existing Solutions, Use Patterns to Find Patterns (all discussed in Chapter 16)

Guidelines

The following guidelines provide advice regarding the domains that we should consider as we identify patterns to build, as well as how we support the management and then consumption of patterns.

Domain-Driven Patterns

Summary

Create, acquire, and use patterns focused on meeting the needs of a domain as well as providing a bridge between domains. Typically, we would look to patterns in the business domain, technology domain, and crossing between these domains.

Introduction

As we develop solutions, we are usually provided with a set of functional requirements, that is, requirements stated from the point of view of the business, not in
terms of technology. How do we ensure the use of best practices when dealing with
issues and challenges related to the business domain? How does this fit with the
needs of the technology domain? How do the two come together? Considerations to
keep in mind include these:

- Although nonfunctional requirements are important, if the solution does not
  meet the needs of the business, the project has failed.

- We need to effectively and efficiently use the technology at hand.

- A well-built solution is able to support the business needs today and provide the
  flexibility for future requirements.

- We need to involve business representatives in the building of the solution, while
  not overwhelming them with technical details.

Explanation

With a technical background and focus, we can get caught up in looking for best
practices only within the technical domain. However, it is important (perhaps more
important) to look for best practices that allow us to solve the problems of the business. To do so, we need to use the PBE Core Values, Patterns, Guidelines, and Practice
to ensure that we are creating, acquiring, and using patterns that have a business focus.

We also need to ensure that we are looking at how business-focused patterns are
related to and can be used in combination with technically focused patterns. A successful project requires us to think in terms of the technology used to deliver the solution;
but what is the value if the solution does not meet the needs of the business? And
conversely, what is the value of producing a solution that adheres to the needs of the
business but cannot scale, is not stable or flexible?

Business patterns may have less reusability. At a minimum, they are usually limited
to the organization as they are seen as a competitive differentiator. We may also find
cases where patterns are applicable only to a specific project. We'll need to keep this
in mind as we consider investments in business patterns. Also, this limited reusability
may limit the opportunities to acquire business-focused patterns from outside
sources. The situation will have a different outcome depending on the role of your
organization. In a business organization, the reuse opportunities are limited to the
organization. However, for a systems integrator, a software vendor, or a trade organization, a business-specific pattern may apply to a group of businesses—across an

industry or possibly across a set of industries. In such cases the dynamics of the decision and associated ROI calculations will change.

Technology patterns can address a range of problems such as providing support for deployment descriptors, caching approaches, or even object creation. Each of these is key to how the solution is built, but it is not necessarily derived from a business's functional requirements.

In contrast to business patterns, technical patterns are easily transferable to other projects. Thus, the investment that we make in specifying and/or implementing a pattern can be recouped both on the current project as well as on other projects. In addition, external sources often provide an abundance of technology-focused patterns.

Usage of this guideline is shown in the case study as Oslec determines which patterns to build, acquire, and use in building the LogoAuction application. Some patterns, such as the DAO or the Subsystem Façade pattern, are too technical in nature to use in discussions with business stakeholders. In addition, these patterns, while useful in creating the solution, are not tied directly to a business requirement.

In contrast, patterns such as the Self-Service[6] pattern, which focuses on user interaction and reducing time to market, are more business-relevant. Additional examples include the Role and Quantity patterns,[7] as they map primarily to business concerns.

Related Patterns and Guidelines

Determine Business Impact (Chapter 11), Pattern Selection Driven by Requirements (Chapter 16)

Pattern Search

Summary

We know that we should be using patterns as we build our solutions. However, it is hard to find patterns to address a problem. Where and how do we find the patterns that we should be using? The short and simple answer is that we need to search for patterns.

Introduction

Finding patterns to address a problem can be difficult. Where and how do you find the patterns that you should be using? As we attempt to answer this question, consider the following:

---

6. Koushik et al. (2001).

7. Fowler (1997).

- We need to ensure that the organization has governance in place to support the patterns available. Pattern Users will assume that any pattern returned from a search is valid for use.

- Different roles and situations dictate which sources we consult as we search for patterns.

- We can find ourselves overwhelmed as a large number of patterns are available. It would be difficult and time-consuming to browse all the existing patterns to find the one(s) addressing a particular concern.

Explanation

Consider the effort saved when we can select from known problem/solution pairs rather than experimenting with numerous different solutions. However, this approach assumes that we have a catalog of patterns and are able to find the patterns that we need. Experience has shown that we are able to produce patterns (we only have to look at the impressive number of books about patterns), but so far we're not that good at consuming them. This is partly because of some cultural challenges, like the "not invented here" syndrome. But perhaps the primary difficulty is finding our way through the thousands of existing patterns. How can we easily identify the right patterns to solve our problems in our context?

A first step is to identify a collection of patterns and make them easily accessible. We can then build on this foundation by providing a way to guide project members through the pattern selection process. This could be achieved by using metadata to

- Describe the pattern, including details about the problem, solution, and context

- Link the pattern to all of the elements that constitute the pattern, such as the specification, implementation, DSL, model template, and documentation

- Link the pattern to related patterns

- Connect the pattern to typical requirements that the pattern can address

Team members should be able to search and then retrieve a set of patterns corresponding to a specific, defined context, simplifying decision making and pattern acquisition. Using visualization techniques to display the information can further facilitate this search and selection process.[8]

---

8. For a more detailed description please see Gonzalez and Lane (2008).

For patterns that have been published externally—from vendors and the community—we can look to outside sources. Searching the web is one option; however, a general search engine usually leads to general results. You need to consult sources that are specific to patterns; some to consider include

- Hillside.net pattern collection[9]

- *Handbook of Software Architecture* website and its patterns catalog[10]

- *The Pattern Almanac*[11]

- Sites dedicated to the domain on which we are focused (Java, .NET, UI, etc.) and the patterns that are discussed there

- Sites that are dedicated to the frameworks that we are leveraging

- Vendor websites

We can also simplify the search for external sources by taking time early in the project to identify a subset of external sources to leverage on the project. Based on experience and an initial understanding of project requirements, we can compile a list of sources that may prove useful. This list then serves as the starting point for external pattern searches. The list may change over the project lifetime. In addition, we can go beyond the list as needed. The goal is to produce a best-effort list that serves as a starting point for external searches.

When it comes to finding patterns that our own organization has built, there are two main sources to consult. The first is the organization's development process. The process should detail the tasks, roles, and work products needed to successfully complete the project. In detailing the tasks, the process should provide guidance and pointers to relevant patterns. The second source to consult is an asset repository. Additional advice for working with a repository is provided in the Use an Asset Repository guideline (Chapter 16).

Technical approaches to driving pattern consumption are successful only if we also address cultural issues. The entire team needs to be made aware of the need to search for patterns and be enabled and encouraged to do so.

---

9. Hillside pattern catalog: www.hillside.net/patterns/onlinepatterncatalog.htm.

10. Grady Booch's pattern catalog: www.handbookofsoftwarearchitecture.com/index.jsp?page= Patterns. To access this section you need to be registered. Registration is free.

11. Rising (2000).

Chapter 4 of the case study shows Oslec following Pattern Search as they create a list of external pattern sources to be consulted for building the LogoAuction application. In addition, Chapter 7 shows one of the development team members searching for the Subsystem Façade pattern implementation.

Related Patterns and Guidelines

Pattern Packaging (Chapter 14), Use an Asset Repository (Chapter 16)

Summary

The patterns and guidelines in this chapter focus on how we can identify, produce, consume, and manage patterns in building a foundation for our PBE initiative. We've touched upon the scope of our PBE efforts, looking at the relationship to the SDLC as well as how patterns come into play for business and technology domains. We can connect these ideas about scope with a piecemeal approach to building our patterns. It's one thing to have the right ideas and requirements for a pattern; it's another to ensure that the right aspects of the pattern are delivered. In addition, we looked at how we can improve the productivity of the team by creating a simple solution space, one that better leverages automation and abstraction. And all of this would be for naught if we ignored the topic of finding patterns. Pattern consumption is a topic that is frequently overlooked, and that ends up hurting our PBE efforts.

Chapter 11

Discovering Patterns

How do we discover and identify patterns? We can gather patterns from external sources such as vendors and the community easily enough. However, things get more complex when we seek to discover and identify the patterns that are unique to our organization. We also need to keep in mind that these two aspects—internal and external sourcing—do not happen in isolation. We strive to create a set of patterns that draws upon both sources and delivers a mix that is unique and tailored to the needs of our organization. The goal is to define a set that delivers a competitive advantage to the organization.

To succeed in discovering the patterns that we need, we can use the patterns and guidelines in this chapter to help us answer questions such as these:

- Patterns come from multiple sources; how do we find them?

- What are the best practices associated with finding patterns?

- Who should be involved? What should they do? When should they do it?

- Although numerous pattern opportunities can and will be identified, not all will be developed. How do we determine which patterns need to progress beyond just possibilities? Where do we make the investment? How do we decide?

- In the search for patterns, we don't always start from scratch. How can we leverage existing patterns as we try to identify and discover new ones?

> **Note**
>
> Creating our own patterns is a key step in rounding out other development processes such as MDD, Model-Driven Architecture (MDA), software factories, and others.[1] These approaches often depend on the ability of practitioners to use patterns that are unique to their situation but provide little guidance on how to discover those patterns. The patterns and guidelines in this chapter and those that follow address this gap.

---

1. See Appendix B for a discussion of the relationship between PBE and other software development approaches.

Patterns

In this section we look at the patterns that help us to figure out which patterns should be created. We examine how to identify opportunities for using and creating patterns. We also need to consider solutions that may serve as the basis for patterns, ideally best practices but possibly also worst practices.

Antipatterns

Context

The organization struggles to ensure that the entire team is following best practices consistently. In addition, testing and code reviews reveal that common mistakes are occurring.

Problem

How do we capture and then share common worst practices with the team? How do we ensure that the team is aware of and then avoids repeating these worst practices?

Forces

- A cultural change is needed that values the identification of worst practices. Time is spent on identifying, detailing, and then communicating worst practices. This may seem counterintuitive, since we expect investments to be made only in positive practices.

- Investment in antipatterns is similar to that made in patterns. A successful effort requires training, tooling, and time.

- Efforts related to antipatterns are usually more effective when linked with patterns that would help mitigate the antipatterns.

Solution

As a parallel effort to using patterns, we also need to identify, detail, and communicate antipatterns. An **antipattern** is a proven worst-practice solution applied within a given context.

There are a number of different approaches to identifying antipatterns: leveraging experience, harvesting from existing solutions, code reviews, and so on. As we identify antipatterns, we need to look at the ROI for creating the specification associated with the antipattern. For those antipatterns that justify the investment, we should create a specification and then make it available to the team via the asset repository, just as we do with pattern specifications.

In addition, as we document our development process, we should be certain to update the process to highlight cases where certain antipatterns may occur or are prevalent. We should also identify and document the patterns and guidelines that help mitigate or correct these antipatterns. Identifying an antipattern may be a good indication that there is a need for a pattern.

We can develop antipattern implementations that allow us to automatically detect the use of antipatterns. These can be useful for supporting automated reviews as part of a continuous integration effort.

Example

Within PBE there are a number of antipatterns:

- **Perfect Pattern.** Pattern producers spend a great deal of time accounting for all possibilities and points of variability as they create a pattern. As a result, the time frame to deliver the pattern is much longer than necessary (and sometimes the pattern is never released). This is similar to the "analysis paralysis" antipattern that can happen in software development projects. To counteract this antipattern, consider using the Piecemeal Pattern Creation pattern (Chapter 10) and the Update Existing Patterns guideline.

- **Generic DSL.** Software engineers spend a great deal of time and effort in making a DSL as generic as possible. Their logic is that doing so insulates them from changes in the underlying layers of the solution and is an investment in the future. However, this greatly diminishes the value of the DSL as it no longer is specific to the domain. If a general-purpose language is needed, it is best to use a generic language. To counteract this antipattern, consider using the Integrated Patterns and DSLs pattern and the Design a DSL guideline (Chapter 15).

- **Top-Down DSL Creation.** In designing a DSL that is directly tied to the domain, little consideration is given to how the language will be used. When we use models for design, communication, and generation, we need to be aware of how they will be consumed and leveraged. To that end, as we design the DSL, we need to ensure that we consider bottom-up constraints. To counteract this antipattern, consider using the Meet-in-the-Middle Pattern Creation pattern (Chapter 12) and the Design a DSL guideline (Chapter 15).

Related Patterns and Guidelines

Determine Business Impact*, Pattern Opportunity*, Single Pattern–Varied Use Cases (Chapter 10)

Pattern Opportunity

Context

A software project is under way for which requirements (use cases, user stories, etc.) have already been identified. The team is working through the current iteration.

Problem

Although we want to use patterns on a project, we are not sure what patterns to use. Perhaps the patterns we are aware of are either too generic or not the right fit for the current project. Overall, there is a lack of awareness regarding the solution being built and opportunities for creating and using new patterns. As a result, it looks as if similar and repetitive work will be performed manually, and likely not using best practices. How do we identify the opportunities for using patterns on our project?

Forces

- We need to spend time evaluating which patterns are worth pursuing, as we will likely identify more patterns than it makes sense to invest in.

- We will have to spend time analyzing the solution we are building.

- A cultural change accompanies PBE, whereby the team becomes conditioned to look for pattern opportunities.

Solution

As we start a project or iteration, we include time to consider how patterns could be used to help in creating the solution. Opportunity identification is all about looking for and finding opportunities where we can use patterns. We need to tune our creativity and sleuthing skills to hunt for pattern opportunities. These opportunities may involve patterns from external sources, those already created internally, or patterns that need to be built.

We need to look for situations where the same solution is used multiple times. We need to be able to use abstraction and simplification to see the true solution in situations, rather than just the details associated with each separate situation. We need to be able to uncover patterns that provide the best solution for the problem and context.

To start, we should be armed with the right questions:

- Have we already solved this problem?

- Will this solution need to be reused elsewhere? Which iteration of the project? Which project?

- Has someone else on the team already solved this problem?

- Does my work on this use case relate to the work that others are doing on their use cases?

- Are there common aspects of a solution that would apply across a number of use cases?

- Are there best practices associated with the frameworks that we're working with?

- In bringing together a number of frameworks, will any best practices emerge?

- Are there rules, assumptions, and constraints that would limit the amount of information that actually needs to be provided here?

- Do we have guidance on how to solve problems captured only as documentation? Do people follow the documentation?

This pattern provides a key mechanism for leveraging and engaging the team, providing them with an opportunity to be creative problem solvers. It will challenge them and require them to be creative, insightful, and innovative, always on the lookout for a better way of getting things done. Adopting such a culture makes for a much more enjoyable working environment. As we adopt and roll out PBE within our organization, it is important to make this clear to the team and to emphasize the importance of their role in making the program a success. In addition, as we work with them to find patterns, we also ensure that those who use the patterns will apply the solution consistently and rapidly. Ideally, everyone on the team contributes to this effort. Anyone can spot an opportunity, even if he or she doesn't know how to create or detail the pattern.

Note that this pattern is focused on finding the opportunity where a pattern may be applicable. We're not yet worried about how to write up the pattern as a specification or codifying the pattern in an implementation. Really, we are looking for candidate patterns. We've done some initial vetting of a pattern, but a full analysis of its impact and how to create it is not yet done at this point. We capture each opportunity that is identified in a candidate pattern list. As the project progresses, we will evaluate the candidate patterns and determine which warrant investment and should be developed.

This is a lightweight pattern that can easily be incorporated into our existing development process. The goal here is not to seek out all answers or perfect patterns. As the name of the pattern suggests, we are looking for opportunities. This pattern needs to become ingrained in the culture of the team and organization.

Common Pitfalls

A number of common pitfalls arise when following this pattern:

- **Abstraction blinders.** When creating a solution, we fail to recognize situations where we should be using patterns. We're so focused on what's directly in front of us that we fail to see what else is possible.

- **Waterfall pattern use.** We take some time early in the project to identify a set of existing patterns to use through the duration of the project. All of the pattern identification work is done at the beginning of the project. This inappropriately limits the patterns that we can use on the project.

- **Get 'em next time.** In some cases we wait until the end of the project to review and then try to harvest a set of patterns based on recurring solutions that occurred during development. This approach eliminates the benefits that can be achieved from the patterns on the current project. In addition, the harvesting approach is likely to fail in getting the assets built, because after the project the team members will be moving to new projects and tasks.

Example

In Chapter 4 we follow Oslec's efforts to identify pattern opportunities. The identification of the candidate patterns is a team effort, and many people and roles are involved. Although they have some specific meetings early in their efforts that focus on pattern opportunity identification, the team remains on alert for pattern opportunities throughout the project.

A number of candidate patterns are identified and captured in a candidate pattern list. The team reviews the list, evaluates the candidate patterns, and determines that the Subsystem Façade pattern is most important and should be developed.

Related Patterns and Guidelines

Antipatterns*, Determine Business Impact*, Recurring Solution*

Recurring Solution

Context

We have decided that we would like to find, build, and use patterns on our projects.

Problem

Although we want to use patterns that are specific to our situation and are looking for them, we are not sure when and where the best opportunities to create patterns exist. Where do we find patterns?

Forces

- The team must communicate and be looking at how to produce higher-order solutions.

- Expertise, creativity, and problem-solving skills are more valuable than ever.

- Traditional efforts such as documentation and code reviews increase in importance.

Solution

Looking for recurring implementations of solutions is an important mechanism for creating patterns. We can use a number of approaches:

- **Rule of Three.** In applying the Rule of Three, we are looking for situations where the same problem/solution set has occurred in three unique instances or situations. The logic behind the Rule of Three is that ". . . the first occurrence shows the design can work, the second occurrence is interesting, and the third occurrence suggests that the design might be worthy of being a pattern because it appears to have a wider applicability."[2]

- **Déjà vu.** Less formal than the Rule of Three, a sense of déjà vu may alert us to a possible pattern. Do we sense that we've seen this solution before? Does it seem that the work we are doing is similar to something that we've done in the past? Does it sound like something that someone else has been working on? Whether we call it an instinct, déjà vu, or a sixth sense, we need to be aware of when we sense that a solution has already appeared for the current problem.

- **Experience.** As we work on more projects and encounter more situations and solutions, we carry with us our own inventory of proven solutions. Over time, we will start to see some of those solutions reappearing. A brief journal, log, or other similar mechanism is useful for keeping track of solutions that we think have the potential to reappear. Again, we want to keep things as lightweight and simple as possible.

---

2. www.antipatterns.com/whatisapattern/.

- **Abstraction and simplification.** Being able to see beyond the details of the current problem and its solution and recognize higher-order elements at play is a key capability. In addition, we need to be able to simplify the solutions that we plan to build.

In reality, we will likely use a number of these approaches as we start to train ourselves to look for patterns. There is no single approach to finding patterns; however, having an open mind and the right attitude and culture can take us a long way.

Regardless of the approach that we take, a key aspect to keep in mind is that communication among the team members is more important than ever. Whether we have daily Scrums, frequent design reviews, study groups, or presentations on designs, we will want to encourage and support the team's discussion and sharing of ideas about work that they have under way. Without such communication, how will the team start to spot recurring solutions beyond the scope of their immediate deliverables?

Example

We see an example of using this pattern in the case study when the team elaborates the Subsystem Façade pattern based on the realization that in the past they have often used the Session Façade pattern along with the Data Access Object pattern.

Related Patterns and Guidelines

Antipatterns*, Pattern Creation Lifecycle (Chapter 12), Pattern Opportunity*

Guidelines

In the following guidelines we focus on advice to help determine which candidate patterns warrant an investment. We also discuss how we should capture sufficient details about the candidate pattern to support further investigation and development while not burdening the effort with too much formality. And last but not least, not all pattern investments need to be made in new patterns. We also need to consider how and when we should evolve and update existing patterns.

Determine Business Impact

Summary

Creating patterns for reuse requires an investment; how do we pick which patterns justify the expense? How do we decide which patterns transition from being candidate patterns to patterns that we will invest in and develop? Organizations have limited resources, so we can never build everything; we need to pick the right patterns to build. We need criteria and mechanisms that can help us decide and direct our investments.

Introduction

In following patterns such as Pattern Opportunity, we will find that the effort leads to the identification of a number of candidate patterns. Limited time and resources mean that not every candidate pattern can be developed. Here are some considerations to keep in mind for deciding which patterns warrant an investment:

- Much as for other development tools, we will come to see patterns as an investment that needs to be justified.

- Pattern identification and valuation efforts will start to show up on project plans.

- Regardless of whether a pattern is classified as related to the business domain or the technical domain, it will need to have a positive impact on the business.

- Pattern quality becomes valued higher than pattern quantity.

Explanation

We cannot build all of the patterns that we identify, so we need to use criteria and mechanisms to direct our investments.

A first step to consider is that when building a pattern, we need to tie it to key business efforts and results; our effort should be business-driven. Even patterns that have a technical impact need to be traceable to the impact that they will have on the project and the business. We need to be able to draw a connection from that pattern to the positive impact it will have on the business. Note that improving the time to market and increasing productivity are legitimate business goals. If we cannot determine that the pattern positively impacts the project, it is not worth pursuing any further. As discussed in the context of the Pattern Opportunity pattern, we want to be innovative. However, that innovation needs to matter and add value to the business.

So if we can trace the pattern to the areas where it will impact the business, we can move forward and start to further detail the value and ROI for the pattern. A key input into this step is to figure the pattern's cost; considerations include the following:

- How long will it take to build the pattern? In addition to looking at building the pattern specification or implementation, we also need to look at any efforts associated with truly defining the best-practice solution that will serve as the exemplar for the pattern. We may have to spend time completing the solution, refactoring the existing solution, or expanding the scope of the existing solution.

- Does the team have the skills needed to create the pattern? If not, how much training will they need? Will they need new and additional tooling?

- Will people need to be trained in using the pattern? If so, how many? Could the pattern be made more consumable? If so, what is the trade-off in costs between training and improving consumability?

- Will the team's development process need to be updated because of the pattern? What is the expected cost of that effort?

- Are any new tools needed to leverage the pattern? Could this expense be avoided if the pattern is not created?

- What costs are needed to deploy, manage, and support the pattern? The costs associated with the pattern go beyond just the initial development. Although these costs are often relatively fixed, we still need to account for them.

- What does past experience tell us about building patterns of similar size and complexity?

We also need to consider the other side of the ledger. Considerations related to determining the expected benefits of using the pattern include these:

- How many times will the pattern be used on the current project?

- Is it likely that the pattern will be used on future projects? If so, how many times could it be used in the future? Do we need to discount this benefit?

- What requirements will be addressed (even partially) by the use of the pattern? How important are these requirements? What is the likelihood that these requirements will change?

- Can the investment in the pattern be recouped on the current project?

As we look at the ROI, we also need to keep in mind the funding structure for the organization that is building the patterns. Will the pattern producers be part of the overall project team? Or will they be a separate team that supports all of the other development teams? Will they be seen as a profit center or a cost center? How will teams fund the development, maintenance, and support of the patterns once they are built?

An example of using this guideline is provided in Chapter 4, where the Oslec team reviews their candidate pattern list and evaluates the Subsystem Façade pattern. They give consideration to the impact the patterns identified will have on their project as well as the cost that will be associated with developing the pattern(s).

Related Patterns and Guidelines

Pattern Opportunity*, Update Existing Patterns*

Pattern Description

Summary

How do we capture a sufficient level of detail about a candidate pattern to support evaluation and feed into design activities without overinvesting in these efforts? Create a pattern description to capture initial details about a pattern that can be used to evaluate the pattern and then serve as a starting point for designing the pattern.

Introduction

In identifying candidate patterns we have started to recognize and find details about the potential pattern. We also know that as the patterns move along the workflow from candidate patterns and then into design and development, we will have to capture details about them. However, a balancing act is required. We need to capture these details while not overinvesting or making the effort overly formal.

How can we collect enough information about a pattern to evaluate it and support design activities without spending too much time on these efforts? As we attempt to answer this question, there are a number of considerations:

- We need a standard approach to capturing details for candidate patterns.

- Defining an approach to pattern descriptions increases the formality of how we identify and evaluate candidate patterns. Thus, we are increasing the investment in the PBE effort.

Explanation

The pattern description has a few fields that are similar to those found in a pattern specification. However, the pattern description is a much less formal, precise, and complete artifact. The description is used only as a starting point for creating complete and formal representations of the pattern.

A typical pattern description includes the following information:

- **Pattern name.** A name for the pattern.

- **Summary of the context.** In what contexts should we consider using the pattern?

- **Summary of the problem.** What problem is the pattern expected to solve?

- **Summary of the solution.** How does the pattern solve the problem?

- **Name(s) of the SME(s).** Who are the experts who can explain the pattern and assist in its creation?

- **List of related patterns.** What other patterns are expected to work with this pattern?

- **Areas of applicability.** Where in the current project do we expect the pattern to be used? What about in other projects?

This artifact is used early in the process. We want to balance the effort so that we are providing sufficient detail to help with the evaluation process while not over-investing. For those candidate patterns that get approved for further development, we will have a good place to start. We also need to remember that the content listed in the description will change and evolve.

Starting in Chapter 4, the Oslec team follows this guideline to create a pattern description for the Subsystem Façade pattern. The pattern description is completed in Chapter 5, and then it's used as an input when they design the Subsystem Façade pattern.

Related Patterns and Guidelines

Determine Business Impact*, Pattern Creation Lifecycle (Chapter 12), Pattern Opportunity*

Pattern Harvest

Summary

How do we capture and elicit best practices, in a more consumable form, from completed and proven projects? Use harvesting to capture the details of the best practice and put them into a pattern.

Introduction

The organization has already completed numerous projects, and we are certain that there are best practices within the code. We want to use these proven best practices in future projects. How do we capture them, in a more consumable form, from those projects? Considerations to keep in mind include these:

- Capturing best practices requires seeing beyond the specifics of a particular solution.

- We must view an existing code base as both an asset for the deployed system it represents and an asset for future patterns and systems.

Explanation

Harvest the details of the best practice and create a pattern with them. With harvesting, we consult existing, completed artifacts as sources for building out our library of patterns. As we look at the existing solution, we need to keep the following in mind:

- Is this truly the best-practice solution?

- In what situations would this solution be applicable? Does this situation occur often?

- What are the points of variability that need to be added to the solution as it moves from an instantiation of a solution to a pattern?

- What is the scope of the best-practice solution? What/where are the boundaries?

- Is this truly a single best-practice solution? Or have multiple best-practice solutions been used together to create a larger solution? If there are multiple best practices, do they have value individually? Would it make sense to use them individually?

- How common is it for this solution to be used?

We can use a number of approaches to figure out what needs to be put into the harvested pattern (specifications or implementations):

- **Documentation.** Consult the documentation for the solution. This should provide additional insights into the context in which it was used and why it was built the way it was. This can help guide others in successfully using a pattern based on such a solution in the future.

- **Automation.** Use known pattern definitions to feed into automation to find occurrences of those patterns within previously built solutions. Note that this may also lead to identification of compound patterns as well as adjacent patterns. It can also lead to a deeper understanding of the solution and support us as we create new patterns.

- **Visualization.** Looking at the code for past solutions can be quite time-consuming. In addition, the models and design specifications for a solution often are not updated as the project evolves. In such cases the artifacts are not the true source of information for a project once it concludes. Using visualization, where we create simple visual representations with UML, allows us to get a higher-level perspective on the elements in the project and how they relate. Visualization can often be done in an automated fashion, as there is a very direct mapping between the underlying element and its visual representation. Visualization helps to hide some of the details and lets us focus on more important aspects of the solution. This can improve the productivity and quality of the work that is done in harvesting patterns. Ideally, the visualization mechanism understands definitions of existing patterns.

- **Code reviews and inspections.** Part of the time spent in code review and inspections should be used to find, discuss, and then document the best practices that are present in the code. Leverage this effort and ensure that this knowledge is captured for use in the possible creation of a pattern from the solution. We are particularly interested in the rationale that goes along with the solution; for instance: Why and when should it be used? What are the implications of using it? Are there other related solutions (either complementary or mutually exclusive)?

Note that there is a momentum aspect to using Harvest Patterns. As we become more adept at identifying, documenting, and harvesting patterns, we will pick up speed. For instance, as we define a larger set of patterns, it will become quicker, easier, and more productive to run those definitions through pattern detection engines.

Related Patterns and Guidelines

Determine Business Impact*, Exemplar Analysis (Chapter 12), Recurring Solution*, Use Patterns to Find Patterns (Chapter 16)

Update Existing Patterns

Summary

Best practices evolve over time as technology and approaches mature and new innovations are introduced. How do we ensure that the collection of patterns within our organization continues to represent best practices? We need to keep in mind that creating new patterns is only one approach. Another approach is to update existing patterns.

Introduction

We have a collection of patterns that we use within the organization. We want to keep them up to date and valid. Best practices evolve over time because of changes in technology and new innovations. How do we ensure that our patterns continue to represent best practices? Some considerations include the following:

- We need to continue to evaluate which patterns warrant investment and support over time.

- Not all situations call for the development of a new pattern.

Explanation

As we look to enhance the collection of patterns we have available within the organization, it is important to keep in mind that creating new patterns is only one approach. Another approach is to update existing patterns as necessary to adapt to new technology or to evolving practices. In this way we leverage the investment that has already been made in the pattern and extend the time frame over which this investment pays off. Recognizing and planning for updates to existing patterns also helps us to avoid antipatterns such as Perfect Pattern.

Update Existing Patterns is related to the PBE Core Value of make your patterns live. A pattern is not created and then left alone, never revisited, fixed, or enhanced. After we make the pattern available, we need to continue to monitor the use of the pattern, best practices, and the associated technologies related to the pattern. Over time, one or more of these aspects (and likely others) will change and have an impact on the value and importance of the pattern. As the aspects and conditions surrounding the pattern change, we need to monitor the situation and update the pattern as appropriate.

The main focus of the effort is ensuring that the pattern is up to date, supporting the current best practices of the organization. Why and when should we update? Some scenarios include

- To address defects/bugs

- To address enhancement requests

- Changes to best practices

- Changes to associated technology

- To improve the design of the pattern

- To increase the scope of the pattern

As always, we need to ensure that the investment made in the update effort is justified, based on the value provided by the pattern.

Related Patterns and Guidelines

Determine Business Impact*, Piecemeal Pattern Creation (Chapter 10)

Summary

In this chapter we've focused on the efforts associated with determining the patterns we should use and build within our projects. This has included a look at how we figure out what patterns we can use, as well as how we can analyze the list of candidate patterns to figure out which patterns truly add value and contribute to the success of the business.

The patterns and guidelines in this chapter play a critical role in making PBE a systematic and disciplined approach to using patterns. Taking an ad hoc approach to finding, building, and using patterns is a sure way for a patterns initiative to fail. Without a clear analysis of what patterns are needed and the supporting ROI justifications, how can we support the claims that an investment is needed?

Most organizations already have accumulated numerous artifacts that can serve as the basis of patterns. We can leverage the expertise that exists in our personnel, existing solutions, and documentation to create patterns. In addition, we can take the opposite approach: What are the current worst practices? We need to be aware of these antipatterns as well, making sure that the team avoids them and their associated results.

Ultimately, business impact is critical. As we evaluate patterns and antipatterns, we need to focus on how these assets help us deliver the solutions needed by the business, and how they can help us do so better than other available alternatives.

Chapter 12

Designing Patterns

The patterns we design should already have been vetted and deemed worthy of investment. We need to come up with solid designs to make sure that these patterns deliver on their potential and meet the expectations of the organization. A poor design will flow into later stages, reducing the quality of the pattern and negatively impacting the ROI of the pattern and the overall PBE effort. We can have all the best intentions and a great infrastructure in place to support the use of patterns, but without properly designed patterns, the PBE effort will be unsuccessful.

The traditional skills used in designing software solutions are still relevant and help us in our pattern design efforts. For instance, when designing patterns, we need to ensure that we accurately interpret the underlying best practice. In cases where we are designing a pattern implementation, we are also concerned with usability, reliability, and performance. These aspects of pattern design can easily be mapped to those that we focus on for the design of traditional software solutions. However, there are unique details and areas specific to designing patterns. The patterns and guidelines in this chapter address these unique aspects of pattern design.

Patterns

In the following discussion we look at patterns to help us design patterns, with special consideration of the use of encapsulation and composition to create compound patterns. We also look at how we can leverage exemplars and a meet-in-the-middle approach in our design efforts.

Compound Pattern[1]

Context

A collection of patterns is available within the organization. The patterns vary in scope and purpose. Some of the patterns apply to related problems; others support different problem sets.

Problem

In situations where we have a number of patterns that work together to solve a related set of problems, how do we simplify the user experience and increase the value and power of the patterns? How do we ensure that related patterns are used together consistently and correctly?

Forces

- Patterns are used in combination without the flexibility of using them individually.

- We need to account for update cycles for all the individual elements that make up the composite solution.

- In supporting the compound pattern, it can be more difficult to determine the source of defects.

Solution

We create a pattern that is a composite of other patterns. We combine patterns into a larger-grained unit of reuse that can easily be consumed by the Pattern User. As a result, the Pattern User needs to know only how to apply the compound pattern rather than the set of patterns encapsulated within. Compound Pattern supports and builds upon two PBE Core Values:

1. Patterns are best used in combination, rather than in isolation.

2. Focus on making patterns consumable.

   Not only do we want to use patterns in combination, but we also want to simplify the experience in terms of both how the pattern is used and how it is produced.

   Looking at the situation from a Pattern User point of view, it is easier to understand a black box that encapsulates a number of patterns than to learn the details of

---

1. For additional background on compound patterns, consult Riehle (1997) and Buschmann et al. (2007).

each of the constituent patterns. We are able to focus only on the details that are publicly exposed by the compound. Private details that are encapsulated by the compound reduce the amount of comprehension that is needed.

From a pattern production point of view, rather than looking at producing a large-scope pattern as a large single entity, increasing risk and complexity, we can put together such a pattern by using pattern building blocks, each of which is a pattern. This approach allows us to easily test and work with the smaller components and work our way up to a larger solution. This maps quite directly to the idea of component-based development, with the qualification that our components are patterns.

Original references to this concept labeled compound patterns as composites. However, this led to confusion between this concept and the already existing Composite[2] pattern. To avoid confusion, the terminology was adjusted to use the term *compound*. With that in mind, we can refer to the following for additional guidance on compound patterns:

> In a composite pattern, the constituting patterns integrate with each other to achieve a synergy that gives the composite pattern its own identity beyond being just the sum of some patterns. This distinguishes a composite pattern from an arbitrary pattern composition, which may be a suitable solution for a specific design problem, but which does not recur as a pattern of its own.[3]

Example

The Subsystem Façade pattern described in the case study is a compound pattern that brings together a number of patterns, including the Session Façade, Data Access Object, Role, Money, Embedded Value, and Class Table Inheritance patterns, as shown in Figure 12.1.

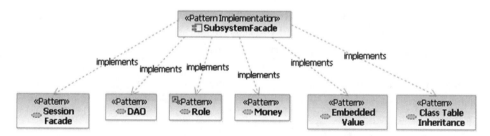

Figure 12.1   *Overview of the patterns encapsulated within the Subsystem Façade pattern*

---

2. Gamma et al. (1995).

3. Riehle (1997).

Related Patterns and Guidelines

Limited Points of Variability*, Pattern Implementation Extensibility*

Exemplar Analysis

Context

We have adopted PBE and want to create our own patterns and make them available to others. We also have one or more exemplars.

Problem

How do we go from an exemplar to a pattern?

Forces

- A quality exemplar is imperative to success. We need to invest in high-quality exemplars before performing any analysis or pattern creation. Performing an analysis on a low-quality exemplar is a wasted effort.

- If issues are found with the exemplar, the exemplar (and possibly the associated "best practice") needs to be corrected before proceeding with the analysis.

- Transitioning an exemplar to a pattern requires the involvement of multiple roles, including a Pattern Author/SME, Pattern Implementation Author, and Pattern Specification Author.

Solution

To design a pattern we need to analyze the associated exemplar. In exemplar analysis we identify the key entities involved in the pattern, specify the points of variability, define the information that the Pattern User provides, recognize the rules we can use to derive any additional information needed by the pattern, and identify the aspects of the pattern that stay the same across applications of the pattern. We work to ensure that we create a pattern that enables us to apply best practices, while supporting many users so that they can create a customized solution in their context.

As we perform exemplar analysis, we use some of the same tools and techniques that we would use in designing any software solution. We have many options available: pen and paper, whiteboards, and modeling tools. The key is that we want to think through the analysis of the exemplar and the resulting design and ensure that we can communicate that design to those creating the pattern.

Let's take a more detailed look at the tasks and considerations that come into play within exemplar analysis:

- **Type of pattern.** We need to determine the type of pattern that we are going to create. Looking at the exemplar, we can ascertain when and where the pattern applies. Does it apply within a model? Does it result in a model? Or does it result in the creation of a set of text-based artifacts? Is this a pattern that we should automate, or will it only be a specification?

- **Domain of the pattern.** We need to recognize the domain to which the pattern will apply. To design the pattern properly, we need to ensure that the team working on the design has an understanding of the pattern's domain. Without this understanding it is impossible to truly understand the nuances of the pattern, and we are likely to produce an ineffective solution.

- **Design roles involved in exemplar analysis.** When designing the pattern, a number of roles will be involved: a Pattern Author/SME, a Pattern Specification Author, and a Pattern Implementation Author. It may turn out that one person fills all three of these roles; however, usually multiple people are involved.

- **Scope of the exemplar.** As part of the analysis we need to gain an understanding of the scope of the exemplar. For instance, if we are looking at developing a pattern implementation and using this implementation to create a set of text-based artifacts, we need to understand the set of artifacts. How many files are in the set? What is in each of the files within the set? We can also look at whether the scope of the exemplar is too broad or too narrow. What is the essence of the exemplar? What additional elements have been or could be added? What is the value of having these additional elements? Does it make sense to enhance and broaden the scope at this time, or should that be postponed until a later version of the pattern?

- **Points of variability.** A point of variability is an aspect of the solution that is provided to the user to allow for changes in how the solution is applied. A point of variability enables users of the asset to provide information specific to their situation and have the result of using the asset reflect that input. This is a key aspect of working with a pattern: each time we use the pattern we are able to provide information specific to our content and have the output of the pattern be shaped and influenced by that input. As we identify and think through the points of variability associated with the pattern, we will also see that many parts of the solution will remain static across applications of the pattern. We can think of the pattern as providing us with a solution that brings together user input and static aspects of the pattern to produce a solution that is unique to the situation, while doing so according to best practices.

- **Roles, relationships, and multiplicity.** We've already determined the scope of the exemplar; now we need to give thought to the purpose of each the elements within it. Why is each element in the exemplar? Are there relationships between the elements? Is there a hierarchy among the elements in the solution? In recognizing the relationships, are there cases where multiplicity comes into play?

- **Artifact significance.** We need to consider the significance of each element in the exemplar. We need to train ourselves to look at the details and start to recognize higher-order elements and relationships. For instance, if we treat each line of code as a separate and unique aspect of a file, we will get lost in irrelevant details, miss higher-order relationships, and essentially won't be able to see the forest for the trees. In addition, some of the elements within will be static and other parts will be dynamic. When we look at content that is meant to be dynamic, there will be cases where input is required from the Pattern User. In other cases calculations can be made based on information provided by the Pattern User for some other requirement.

- **Input model.** Once we understand the scope of the exemplar, the points of variability, and the roles, relationships, and multiplicity, we need to give consideration to the information that we require the user of the pattern to provide. We call this information the input model. The input model leverages the roles, relationships, and multiplicity. In the case of a pattern specification, things are relatively simple and straightforward. We look to determine the roles in the pattern that need to be provided by the Pattern User. Things get more involved as we create and support pattern implementations.

- **Related patterns.** As we design the pattern, we also need to keep in mind that it may be related to other patterns. In some cases we may want to encapsulate the pattern in a compound pattern. In other cases we may find that it makes more sense to keep the pattern as an independent unit but ensure that it can easily be used with related patterns. We also need to understand situations where two or more patterns are mutually exclusive.

An exemplar is required input for designing a pattern. Patterns capture real-world, proven solutions. We do not want to get into situations where we are inventing the aspects of the pattern. We will run into issues with our patterns if they are not based on exemplars, including these:

- **Difficult to complete the pattern.** If we are not working toward a target, how do we know when we are done?

- **End user issues in applying the pattern.** If the solution is not based on a real-world, proven solution, it's likely that the pattern will have issues when it is applied. Such issues will negatively impact the motivation of the participants in a reuse program and lead the users to question the value of patterns.

- **Reduced pattern testability.** The exemplar becomes the first (and primary) test case for the pattern. We should be able to take a set of inputs that map to the exemplar and re-create the exemplar.

- **Decreased pattern adoption.** Without an exemplar it is difficult to convince others to use the pattern because there will be uncertainty regarding its origins.

Example

The Oslec team uses Exemplar Analysis as they design the Subsystem Façade pattern in Chapter 5. In this effort they identify an exemplar—a best-practice representation of the solution that should exist for subsystem façades within Oslec. They confirm with their SME that the exemplar is truly representative of best practices, is of sufficient scope, and contains sufficient variability. They then proceed to analyze the elements within the exemplar. In this analysis they determine the roles that each file plays and then dig further into the solution to identify the areas of variability within the files. In performing this analysis, they detail the elements, their roles, and how the variability points will map to information provided by the user of the pattern.

Related Patterns and Guidelines

Limited Points of Variability*, Pattern Creation Lifecycle*

Meet-in-the-Middle Pattern Design

Context

We have identified a candidate pattern and determined that it has appropriate potential and ROI.

Problem

How do we design a pattern that accurately codifies best practices while also being consumable?

Forces

- We need to recognize that multiple perspectives are needed as we design a pattern.

- We need to ensure that there is a balance among the perspectives.

Solution

Three approaches to design that are often discussed include top-down, bottom-up, and meet-in-the-middle. The approaches are common and the names self-explanatory, so we'll review them quite quickly. In top-down design, we start with high-level artifacts and work our way down to more detailed artifacts. In bottom-up, we start with detailed artifacts and work our way up to high-level artifacts. In the meet-in-the-middle approach, we compromise and incorporate both top-down and bottom-up approaches, meeting in the middle.

If we work in only a top-down fashion, we risk delivering a pattern that ends up not being true to the underlying best practice. If we focus on the design of the pattern only from a top-down perspective, we will not sufficiently leverage the exemplar and risk diverging from it. If we work only from a bottom-up perspective, we stay true to the exemplar, but we risk producing a pattern that is difficult to understand and work with. We risk losing sight of the bigger picture and can end up with a pattern that is not as simple, abstract, or consumable as it should be.

A meet-in-the-middle approach forces us to focus on the details of the solution as well as the higher-level issues, such as how the pattern should be written up and how it is consumed. When we look at things from a higher-level perspective, we can start to think about the rules, constraints, and assumptions that can assist us with consumability. How can they be used to simplify how the pattern will be consumed? How can we use them to increase the scope and impact of the pattern? We can also start to think about how the user should interact with the pattern. Should the pattern be just a specification? Would a pattern implementation also make sense? What tooling would be impacted by the use of the pattern? How will the pattern fit in with the development process? How will the introduction of the pattern impact the development process?

We then connect these ideas and aspects of the design with the details that we find and understand as we work with the exemplar. As we apply exemplar analysis, we see the different roles, artifacts, and the associated input information that are needed for the pattern. However, we recognize, based on our top-down efforts, that the input model to the pattern is not necessarily the model that the Pattern User will see. We can simplify the user model and how that model is represented to the user and connect that user model to the input model that the pattern requires.

We balance the two perspectives and need to approach the effort iteratively and incrementally. Alternating between the two perspectives will help us align the design of our pattern.

Example

In the case study the Oslec team uses this pattern when they build the Subsystem Façade pattern implementation. The Subsystem Façade is based on an exemplar coming from an existing solution, providing a bottom-up perspective on the pattern implementation. From a top-down perspective, they have a domain model that is to be used as a representation of the input model. The team then works to bring these two perspectives together to create a pattern that is true to the solution but is also consumable by the Pattern Users.

Related Patterns and Guidelines

Exemplar Analysis*, Pattern Creation Lifecycle*

Pattern Implementation

Context

The organization has adopted PBE and wants to move beyond just documenting best practices and following them manually.

Problem

Having pattern specifications is useful, but they can be tedious to apply (many steps, human error, etc.). And if we need to make changes to how the pattern is applied, we find that the reapplication of the pattern is tedious. We may also find that we still require a significant amount of expertise to apply a pattern specification. Last but not least, it is difficult to enforce governance of the pattern when the team is just using pattern specifications. How do we speed up the use of a pattern in a solution while ensuring that it is applied correctly and consistently?

Forces

- We require tooling that supports the creation and use of pattern implementations. We also need to ensure that the team is equipped to succeed with these tools.

- Quality and testing efforts typically associated with software deliverables need to be updated to support pattern implementations.

Solution

Automate the pattern by creating a pattern implementation. In contrast to a pattern specification, which captures a pattern as formal written documentation, an implementation codifies a pattern in tooling, automating the use of the pattern.

So the question we have to ask is, how is a pattern implementation surfaced in tooling? There's actually not a single simple answer to the question. We can automate a pattern in tooling a number of different ways. Some of the possibilities include the use of a wizard, plug-in, model-to-model pattern implementation, UML pattern implementation, or model-to-text pattern implementation. The key is to understand each of these approaches and choose the right one for the situation. Some of the things that we want to consider as we decide how we wish to create an implementation include these:

- Where and when should the pattern be used?

- What does it take as input?

- What does it generate as output?

- Are we working with models?

- Are we generating text-based artifacts?

- How should the Pattern User work with the pattern implementation?

Based on the answers to these questions, we select one or more types of pattern implementations. We say "one or more," as it is possible and common to use several types of pattern implementations in combination. For instance, we can use a UML pattern implementation to help us create an input model that is then consumed by a model-to-model pattern implementation.

We also need to consider the trade-off between intelligence in the pattern implementation and the level of detail required in the input model. We may find that we want to keep the input model as simple as possible. In that case the pattern implementation needs to be more intelligent, using rules and assumptions to help interpret the model. If we go to the extreme and have all details in the model, we would likely use a code generator that is able to do a simple and direct mapping from the input model to the output model.

As patterns are used in combination and do not exist in isolation, we should also watch for other pattern implementations that we can leverage in building our pattern implementation. Often a pattern implementation is a compound pattern, so we will want to incorporate other patterns into our efforts. In addition, as we build our pattern implementation, we will need to look at proper componentization to enable others to reuse portions of our pattern implementation as they build their own pattern implementations.

Example

A selection of pattern implementation examples is covered in Chapter 2. Additional model-to-model and model-to-text pattern implementations are identified, designed, built, and used in the case study.

Related Patterns and Guidelines

Compound Pattern*, Exemplar Analysis*, Model-to-Model Pattern Implementation (Chapter 13), Model-to-Text Pattern Implementation (Chapter 13), Pattern Creation Lifecycle*, Pattern Implementation Extensibility (Chapter 13), Pattern Specification (Chapter 13), UML Pattern Implementation (Chapter 13)

Guidelines

The following guidelines provide further advice on how to design patterns. In particular, we look at the overall lifecycle that brings together the solutions, exemplars, and patterns. We also consider how we can use patterns in team settings; after all, development is rarely an individual effort. The discussion also looks at variability points and extension points as two mechanisms to help with pattern customization.

Limited Points of Variability

Summary

When creating a pattern, how do we ensure that Pattern Users are able to customize the application of the pattern to suit the specifics of their situation? While doing so, how do we ensure that Pattern Users are not overwhelmed and confused by the configuration and customization options for the pattern? We need to limit the number and types of points of variability to ensure that the pattern provides the most important ones and then uses calculations and assumptions to leverage the input information provided by the Pattern User.

Introduction

A key aspect of a pattern is that it provides points of variability. These enable Pattern Users to customize the pattern and ensure that the pattern can be applied in the context in which they are operating. As the designers of the pattern, we face a balancing act. We want to provide Pattern Users with flexibility and configurability so that the pattern can be used in their situation. As we want to support a range of Pattern Users in a number of situations, the usual outcome is that as the number of Pattern Users grows, the requirements for configurability increase. However, the more flexible and configurable the pattern becomes, the more difficult it is to use. How do we ensure that the user of the pattern is not overwhelmed and confused by the configuration and customization options for the pattern? How do we ensure that the pattern is flexible and configurable and can be widely used? As we try to answer these questions, there are a number of considerations to keep in mind:

- We need to recognize and consider the pattern as well as related artifacts such as other pattern implementations, model templates, and DSLs.

- We need to pay attention to user feedback and adjust the points of variability as necessary to support usability.

- Simpler does not mean simplistic. We need to identify as few variability points as possible, but it is most important that we have all the necessary points of variability.

Explanation

Patterns by definition are reusable assets that are meant to be customizable. Recall from Chapter 1 where we highlighted that a pattern

> . . . describes a problem which occurs over and over again in our environment, and then describes the core of the solution to that problem, in such a way that you can use this solution a million times over, without ever doing it the same way twice.[4]

To allow a pattern to be used "a million times over, without ever doing it the same way twice," we need variability points. However, the situation is not so simple as to just use variability points; there is a balancing act between consumability and customizability. On the one hand, if we create a pattern with too many points of variability, the pattern becomes too complex to use, requiring that the Pattern User spend a great deal of time in not only learning the pattern, but also figuring out how it can be configured for their situation. On the other hand, a pattern with too few or no points of variability is no longer a pattern. In the case of too few points of variability, Pattern Users are unable to make the pattern specific to the needs of their situation; context no longer really comes into play when applying the pattern.

As we design the pattern and consider the points of variability, we have a number of options:

- **Use assumptions and derivations.** In designing a pattern we need to ensure that the pattern provides the most important points of variability and then uses derivations and assumptions to leverage the user-provided information. In the case of a derivation, we are able to deduce some of the pattern parameters based on other information provided by the Pattern User. Much like the effort that goes

---

4. Alexander (1977).

into database normalization, why ask the Pattern User to provide information that can be calculated? Adding assumptions to the pattern can help us reduce the number of points of variability.

- **Split the pattern into multiple patterns.** Does the existence of many points of variability indicate that we are trying to capture more than one pattern? Have we gone overboard in trying to apply the Compound Pattern pattern?

- **Create a larger pattern.** Is there a larger-order pattern that we can use to customize the inner pattern according to best practices, while limiting the amount of input required from the user of the pattern?

- **Use related patterns.** Are there existing patterns that could be used in conjunction with the pattern? Do they help eliminate the amount of variability needed for this pattern?

- **Validate the pattern with actual users.** Test the pattern with end users. Do they find it overly complex? What flexibility do they say they need in the pattern? Which variability points do they use as they apply the pattern in real-world situations?

As we determine the points of variability for a pattern, it is important to make sure that we are capturing this information as part of the specification and related documentation. In the case of the pattern implementation, we will also use the associated pattern documentation to further detail the points of variability.

In Chapter 5 of the case study, while describing exemplar analysis for the Subsystem Façade pattern, we see how the Oslec team follows this guideline to analyze the exemplar to identify the points of variability and how they try to maximize the use of derivation to minimize the input information needed. More specifically, they first identify those aspects that do indeed vary, as opposed to those that remain static. As they analyze the elements that vary, they recognize that there are cases where a number of elements are related. Based on the relationship, they could reduce the amount of information provided by the Pattern User and then use calculations to populate the set of related elements. The Oslec team also creates a compound pattern and shares information among the set of patterns, again limiting the amount of detail required in the input model. In Chapter 6 they wrap up development of the pattern and move forward, working with a Pattern User to test the pattern and ensure that it both works and provides the correct level of variability.

Related Patterns and Guidelines

Exemplar Analysis*, Pattern Implementation Extensibility*

Pattern Creation Lifecycle

Summary

There is a flow in which we use existing patterns to help us build solutions that will serve as exemplars, which in turn lead to the creation of new patterns. With an exemplar in hand, we can use abstraction and analysis to create a set of one or more new patterns. We then use those patterns in the creation of future models that will serve as the basis for future patterns.

Introduction

As we begin to create patterns, we may find that it seems daunting. Where do our exemplars come from? How do we progress from exemplars to new patterns? What role do patterns play in the creation of exemplars? How can we then leverage patterns in the creation of additional patterns? How do these patterns fit into our development efforts? To find answers to these questions, there are a number of considerations to keep in mind:

- Mass-market tooling generates generic aspects of a solution. Most aspects of the solution that are unique and specific to an organization are created manually.

- The team needs to have abstraction and simplification skills while also being able to see the bigger picture of how elements relate and can come together.

- Exemplars need to be proven, best-practice solutions. They will serve as the basis for a pattern. As such, they are incredibly important.

Explanation

To design the pattern we need to recognize, understand, and follow the pattern creation lifecycle. Figure 12.2 illustrates this lifecycle, which shows how we use existing patterns to help build solutions that will serve as exemplars. Once an exemplar has been created, we use abstraction and analysis to create a set of one or more patterns. The lifecycle then continues as we use those patterns in the creation of future models that will serve as the basis for future exemplars and in turn patterns, and so on.

When we consider the models that we create in crafting an exemplar, our focus is usually on depth rather than breadth. We want to create the best-practice approach to some slice of the solution that can then be reused many times in building the rest of the solution. We are looking for situations where it is difficult or impractical for others to re-create instantiations of the exemplar for their specific situation. We often find that expertise is limited and therefore a valuable resource, so we want to leverage that expertise as widely across the organization as possible. To that end, we want

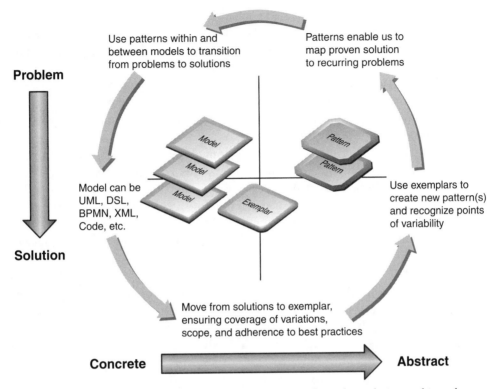

Use patterns within and between models to transition from problems to solutions
Patterns enable us to map proven solution to recurring problems
Problem
Solution
Model
Model
Model
Pattern
Pattern
Exemplar
Model can be UML, DSL, BPMN, XML, Code, etc.
Use exemplars to create new pattern(s) and recognize points of variability
Move from solutions to exemplar, ensuring coverage of variations, scope, and adherence to best practices
Concrete
Abstract

Figure 12.2 *An overview of the flow from requirements through a solution and into the creation of a pattern*

to create the best-practice solution, and then find a way to make that solution available for others to use in building out the breadth of the solution. We replicate the use of the exemplar, but with the use of variability points we make each instantiation unique to the context of the situation. In other words, we provide a pattern to the organization to help us build out the complete solution that is needed.

This guideline is an important mind shift in how we use modern tooling. Rather than using tools as is to create a solution, we need instead to look at these tools as mechanisms that we can use to help us build our own tools—more specifically, our exemplars and patterns. A mainstream product will always have gaps and shortcomings with respect to problems that are specific to an organization. If the tools were tailored to a particular environment, the vendor would have much too small a market and would not make any money on its investment.[5] So the vendor creates tools that solve a wide range of problems for a wide range of customers.

5. The idea of the Long Tail comes into play here. For more discussion on the Long Tail, refer to Anderson (2006) and Kraus (2005).

When we create our exemplar, we leverage the features of the tooling we have purchased or already created. Generic wizards and automations in tools can be used to form the foundation of the exemplars. We then use this output as the starting point for crafting the solution that is unique to our situation. We use automation provided by the tool as strategically as possible. We leverage its strengths in using it to build out the generic aspects of the exemplar. The work that we put into customizing and enhancing the output is work that we want others to be able to avoid. Of course, we are also aided in this effort by the use of existing patterns.

In the case of an MDD approach, we usually think through the design as we work through multiple models, with each model being used at a specific level of abstraction. As seen in Figure 12.2, as we create our exemplar, we can follow a similar approach. A benefit of building the exemplar and then in turn the pattern is that once the pattern has been built, we don't require all those who wish to replicate the solution to use numerous models. We can avoid having to keep all of the models in sync as well as avoid the tasks associated with such efforts (reverse engineering, model reconciliation, etc.).

As we look at Figure 12.2, we can see that we are operating on two axes. The first axis is related to where we stand in relation to the problem versus the solution. We are driven by the problem as we work toward creating a solution that becomes an exemplar. This is straightforward, as we use the details of the problem to guide us in creating our exemplar, which includes selecting the appropriate existing patterns to use. The other axis is related to how concrete or abstract the element is. As we build out the exemplar, we extend its scope to account for variability and variations that might not exist in any one instance of the solution but would show up in an analysis of a range of instantiations of solutions based on the best-practice approaches that are embodied by the exemplar. In this way we start to move from a very concrete and specific representation of the solution to something that is a little more abstract. As we continue to increase the level of abstraction and work toward the problem space, we start to approach the definition of the pattern. The pattern allows us to handle variability by providing points of variability that allow Pattern Users to influence the pattern output.

To summarize, we use one or more models to work from a problem and move into the solution space. We then move from this concrete representation of the solution to one that is more abstract, which we call an exemplar. Once we have an exemplar in hand, we increase the amount of abstraction and start to think about how this relates to the problem space, which ends up being represented as a pattern. With completed patterns available, we can then continue the cycle.

The case study provides an example of the full pattern creation lifecycle, from the use of patterns in defining a solution, transitioning the solution to an exemplar, using that exemplar to create a pattern, and then using that pattern in creating the solution.

Related Patterns and Guidelines

Design Solutions with Patterns (Chapter 16), Piecemeal Pattern Creation (Chapter 10), Simple Solution Space (Chapter 10)

Pattern Implementation Extensibility

Summary

How can we facilitate the use of a pattern implementation in situations for which it was not originally intended? As part of the design, consider how and where we want to enable others to extend the pattern implementation.

Introduction

As we design our patterns, we cannot account for all possible future uses. If we do so, we will either overengineer the pattern or find ourselves in a situation where we are never able to finish the pattern. However, we'd still like to make our patterns flexible and adaptable to unforeseen situations. How can we do so without overengineering the solution? How can we do so while still delivering a completed pattern within reasonable and expected timelines? Consider:

- There is a balancing act between increasing reuse potential and increasing complexity.

- Documentation and packaging associated with the pattern must detail and support extensibility. The documentation needs to be thorough enough to detail the extension points as well as how to use them to extend the pattern.

- The pattern implementation platform we are using must provide a mechanism for extensibility.

Explanation

As discussed in relation to the Limited Points of Variability guideline, we want to design a solution that provides a balance between usability and configurability. In that case much of our focus was on how we can consume a pattern as is. However, we also need to look at the design from the point of view of others who may want to build a new pattern. In such a situation those building the new pattern may find that our pattern provides them with a significant portion of the solution needed for their pattern. One approach to adding capabilities to such a pattern is to use Compound Pattern. Another approach, which we discuss in this guideline, is to provide extension points, which allow for extending the pattern.

An extension point is a formally defined construct associated with the pattern implementation that allows others to add to or alter the pattern. For example, in using a model-to-text pattern implementation we may use an extension point to change the way code is generated for certain situations.

When looking at how to design a pattern so that it is extensible, we need to keep the following in mind:

- **Balance continues to be important.** We want to ensure that we have the right balance between producing a pattern for our current needs and providing support for future unknown needs.

- **Targeted extensibility.** As we define the extension point, we identify where it makes sense for the pattern to be extended. It is a way for the pattern author to ensure that the pattern essence is preserved even when extended. What are the most important and critical aspects and elements of the pattern that we are designing? What elements of the pattern would provide the most value to someone looking to reuse these elements via extensibility? We want to focus the limited time and effort we have for extensibility on those areas we see as providing the most value to future pattern implementations.

- **Platform capabilities.** When designing a pattern implementation, we need to ensure that the tooling that we are using for the implementation provides support for extensibility. Also, different platforms have different mechanisms in place for supporting extensibility. As part of the design, we need to consider how and where we want to enable others to extend the solution.

The Eclipse platform provides an example of this approach through its mechanism for Extension Points.[6] Pattern implementations built on the Eclipse platform are typically developed and then delivered as Eclipse plug-ins, so we are able to use the standard Eclipse Extension Point mechanism for our patterns. With the extension points in place, we can modify the behavior of the pattern, the output of the pattern, or calculations that are performed upon elements from the input model. The Pattern Implementation Author needs to be aware of this capability and use it judiciously, as we want to avoid overinvesting in flexibility and meeting future unknown needs.

Related Patterns and Guidelines

Plug-in pattern,[7] Limited Points of Variability*

---

6. Details on extending Eclipse and working with Extension Points can be found in D'Anjou et al. (2004).

7. Marquardt (2006).

Team Pattern Implementation Use

Summary

Software development is a team sport, requiring the efforts of many to succeed. Thus, the patterns that are built need to support a team environment. How do we design patterns to support team development scenarios?

When we design patterns for a team environment, we need to consider the reapplication strategy, management of user-provided content, model structuring and merging support, and the languages that will be used.

Introduction

We want to use a number of pattern implementations across our development team, including multiple levels of abstraction. How do we design our patterns to support team development scenarios? For instance, when the team is using our patterns in building their solution, how do they share models? How do they add code to the solution? How do they modify code that was generated by the pattern? How are round-trip scenarios supported? As we attempt to answer these questions, there are a number of considerations to keep in mind:

- Testing efforts associated with the resulting pattern need to account for team and reapplication scenarios.

- We need to ensure that the artifacts that are generated by the pattern stay true once they are generated. If Pattern Users need to change the output from the pattern, perhaps they need to revisit whether they are using the correct pattern.

- We need to plan how we want to support the customization of output from the pattern.

Explanation

Designing patterns for use in a team environment requires that we consider the reapplication strategy, management of user-provided content, model structuring and merging support, and the languages that will be used.

Let's start by considering ownership of the artifacts that are generated by a pattern. This particularly applies when looking at model-to-text pattern implementations; that is, we are at the point where we are moving from some higher level of abstraction to where we are working with code, configuration files, and other text-based artifacts. Usually we find that the pattern we are using will not lead to 100% content generation, so we have a situation where some percentage of the solution is generated by the pattern and the rest needs to be created by the user. However, what happens when we need to update the model? What happens to user-created code when requirements change? Designs are updated? Defects are identified?

When looking at the ownership of the output, we can see that there are four possibilities:

1. **Pattern-implementation-owned.** The pattern implementation owns the output and expects that the user will not touch or update this output. No user modification is allowed.

2. **User-modifiable.** In this situation the pattern implementation will write default values to the output unless the user specifies custom output.

3. **Seeded.** A pattern implementation will write this element only once. After the content has been seeded, users are free to do as they desire.

4. **Other.** The pattern implementation may encounter output that exists in the target output that is none of these other options. It could be content that is user-generated or possibly generated by another pattern implementation.

We need to make sure that the user of the transformation is aware of the owner of the content and how it can be updated. Therefore, we need to identify the owner of the output in some way, either by annotation or by putting the output in a specific location. A best practice is to keep output that is transformation-owned separate from other elements.

As we design our pattern, we need to keep each of the four ownership scenarios in mind and set up our pattern accordingly. Recognizing the content owner and clearly identifying how code is owned become important when it comes time to reapply a pattern. When the pattern is reapplied, we need to be able to determine its behavior. Should it overwrite the content that is already in the target? Should it leave it as is? Are there situations where the files are shared between the user and the pattern? Should it try to merge the new and the old? As we design our pattern, we need to keep these questions in mind and determine a reapply contract that will work for our pattern and the expected Pattern Users. Once we define this contract, we need to ensure that it is documented and published.

As we work with code that is user-modifiable, we need to ensure that our design identifies how we want to handle this scenario. We can use special tags or instructions in our pattern output to indicate the behavior that is supported when the pattern is reapplied. For instance, we can use a tag to denote where a user can add content to the output without concern that the pattern will overwrite the content when the pattern is reapplied. As we design, we want to be strategic in terms of where and how we provide user-modifiable regions.

We want user-modifiable regions only in places where we truly need the user to provide content. We do not want to use them just to take shortcuts in figuring out what the pattern should be creating for us. Overuse of user-modifiable regions leads to situations where we undercut the best practices in the pattern, as the Pattern User can essentially change the pattern solution, reducing our adherence to best practices and consistency. We also need to make sure that we are not underusing such annotations, because this may lead to user frustration with the pattern. There will be times and places that users need to customize; they should not have to change the pattern to get the output that is needed.

As we grasp how the pattern works with individual users and an iterative process, we need to expand the scope and complexity and start to think about what happens when there are multiple people working in this situation. For example, the user model may be created, populated, and maintained by multiple users; how are we supporting these users? Ideally, the modeling language and tooling that we select will support model fragments and model merging. In this way we can isolate the changes that are made, and in cases where multiple people are working in the same fragment, we can merge the changes.

At a design level, we're not overly concerned with all of the details of the tag, or the code in the templates, but we do need to understand when and where such functionality will need to be used. In addition, we need to understand the capabilities and support provided by the tooling and languages that we have selected. For instance, many UML tools provide out-of-the-box support for model merge and working with model fragments. So, if we build a DSL on top of UML using a profile, we will benefit from being able to reuse these features.

A simple example can be seen in the way compilers work. They often support the use of src and bin directories. The compiler will use the src directory as input and will overwrite any and all contents in the bin directory, as it is compiler-owned.

When working with JET in creating templates to support such a scenario, we can direct those building the pattern to use the <c:userRegion> tag. In the case of working with Java, we can leverage the <java:merge> tag within JET. This tag will cause the generated contents to be merged with the content already found in an output file. We provide such an example while developing the Subsystem Façade pattern in the case study.

Related Patterns and Guidelines

Integrated Patterns and DSLs (Chapter 15), Simple Solution Space (Chapter 10)

Summary

There are a number of skills and considerations that come into play as we design patterns. For instance, we need to understand the pattern creation lifecycle and the relationship among solutions, exemplars, and patterns. We also need to give thought to how patterns will be consumed, supporting ease of use as well as team scenarios. The design also needs to account for how the pattern will be customizable. The pattern output needs to be customizable to the specific context of the Pattern User. However, there is a balancing act between customization and ease of use. Overall, much as in designing any solution, we need to consider our requirements and options and select the trade-offs that make the most sense for the situation.

Chapter 13

Creating Patterns

With a design in hand, we now move forward to create the pattern. However, how do we ensure that we will successfully implement that design? What are the best practices to follow when creating a model-to-model pattern implementation? How do we write up a pattern specification? As we build the pattern, how do we ensure that we are meeting quality goals? What do we do to test a pattern? The patterns and guidelines in this chapter will help answer these questions.

Patterns

In this section we discuss patterns to help us create model-to-model, model-to-text, and UML pattern implementations.

Model-to-Model Pattern Implementation

Context

We plan on integrating abstraction in our design efforts while using models at each level of abstraction.

Problem

When using models at multiple levels of abstraction, how do we support the transition between the different models while following best practices? At the same time, how do we also improve quality, support governance, and optimize the skills of the team?

Forces

- We need to be able to think about and understand models at the meta level.

- We are making investments in artifacts that support the creation of interim deliverables. Our stakeholders are expecting software that meets their requirements, not pattern implementations. We need to ensure that the investment in creating these patterns is warranted and supports us in meeting the needs of the project.

Solution

A key aspect of working with model-driven development (MDD) is that we leverage models at multiple levels of abstraction. However, we also need to have support for automating how we move between these levels of abstraction. To that end, a pattern implementation that can work with an input or source model and then generate elements in an output or target model is needed. This type of pattern implementation is called a model-to-model pattern implementation, and it automates the transformation of a model at one level of abstraction to a model at another level of abstraction.

It's important at this point to emphasize that we need a solid understanding of metamodels, both in general and the specific metamodels that we will be working with. A metamodel is a model that describes another model at one level of description higher. Another way of saying this is that a metamodel is a model that describes a modeling language. When we are building a model-to-model pattern implementation, we work at the metamodel level, with the definition of modeling languages.

Figure 13.1 provides a high-level, conceptual overview of a model-to-model pattern implementation. As seen in the diagram, we have two metamodels: an input metamodel and an output metamodel. We then create a series of mappings to define the relationship between these elements. Once we have defined the mappings, we generate the pattern implementation that is able to automate the application of the pattern.

A metamodel foundation makes it possible to create model-to-model pattern implementations. With a metamodel in place, we are able to make rules and act upon known types, which in turn consume the elements created by the modeler.

Moving forward from the work performed in exemplar analysis, and with a design in hand, we need to keep in mind the following:

- What are the metamodels that need to be used in this pattern? Note that although Figure 13.1 shows a single metamodel at the input and output levels, multiple metamodels can be mapped to each of these levels.

- What is the mapping between the metamodel elements? Is a flow or hierarchy needed as we navigate between elements that participate in the mapping?

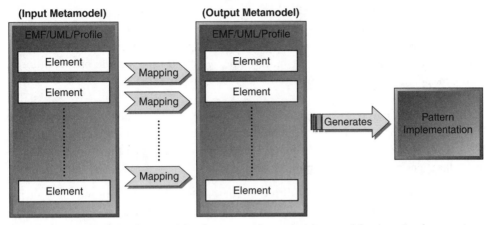

(Input Metamodel) **(Output Metamodel)**

Figure 13.1 *A high-level view of the elements within a model-to-model pattern implementation*

- As we map between metamodel elements, are any additional calculations, filtering, or other special steps needed?

Example[1]

One way in which we can create model-to-model pattern implementations is with the model-mapping capabilities within Rational Software Architect (RSA). The model-mapping capabilities allow us to define the relationship between the metamodel elements that support two models: a source model and a target model. Based on the relationship that is defined by a set of mappings, along with a set of rules and filters, we can create a pattern implementation that will support moving between any two models. Within RSA, the main language that is used for defining metamodels is the Eclipse Modeling Framework (EMF). Even the UML metamodel that is used in RSA is defined using EMF.

In building the pattern implementation, we need to understand the EMF API and the elements that it provides. Where we go from there depends on the languages that we are using for our source and target models. If we are just using plain old UML, we will need to learn the UML metamodel. If we have extended UML by using profiles to create our own language, we need to invest additional time in learning the details of those metamodels. In cases where we have created a custom DSL with EMF, we will need to take the time to learn the specifics of those metamodels.

---

1. Full tutorials describing how to create model-to-model pattern implementations are available via Ackerman, Portier, and Gerken (2008b) and DeCarlo et al. (2008).

With RSA we can use a number of different kinds of mappings to connect model elements between the input model and the output model. The types of mappings include move, submap, custom, and inherited maps. Each pattern implementation that we create will include one or more maps, which in turn include one or more of these mappings.

- The move mapping is quite simple. We're telling the transformation that we want to copy the information from the source element to the target element. This does require compatibility between the two elements; they must have similar types and one-to-one multiplicity.

- If the types of the elements differ, or they do not have one-to-one multiplicity, we have to use one of the other mapping types, either custom or submap. Submap is an indication that we are going to provide more details via another map (and set of mappings). The other map usually takes us a step deeper into the input object so that we can see the elements within that object. Then within the submap we can create mappings between the subelements with elements in the target model. A custom mapping provides us with a less constrained environment to work in; we use code to work with the API and detail the mapping.

- Within each of the mappings we have options to introduce some snippets of code to customize how the mapping will work. Regardless of the mapping that is used, the goal is to minimize the amount of code used. We want to leverage the drag-and-drop interface to specify the mappings and then use the tooling to generate the transformation code.

Figure 13.2 provides an overview of the specialized editor that is used for creating model-to-model pattern implementations in RSA. For each of the models used in the pattern implementation, we are provided with a view of the underlying metamodel so we can see an input metamodel and an output metamodel. For each metamodel there exist one or more elements. Each element can have a set of properties (essentially these are subelements). As we build the pattern implementation, we create one or more mappings between elements in the input metamodel and elements in the output metamodel. After we create the complete set of mappings, the tooling generates the code necessary to support the pattern implementation.

Related Patterns and Guidelines

Exemplar Analysis (Chapter 12), Integrated Patterns and DSLs (Chapter 15), Model-to-Text Pattern Implementation*, Pattern Implementation (Chapter 12)

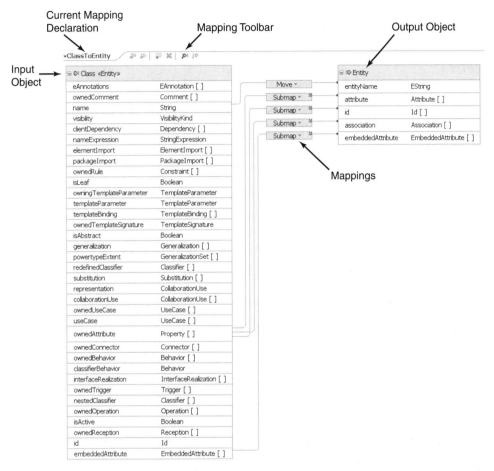

Figure 13.2 *An example of the model-mapping capabilities within Rational Software Architect*

Model-to-Text Pattern Implementation

Context

The project will result in the creation of many text-based artifacts, including code, scripts, and configuration files.

Problem

When creating a solution, we use models as part of our design efforts. However, how can we transition from representations in models to text-based artifacts while following best practices? And how can we do so while improving productivity, increasing the quality of the solution, supporting governance, and optimizing the skills within the organization?

Forces

- We need to consider how the input model will be created, managed, and surfaced to the user. Working with an XML file is sufficient for testing but is not a good choice to roll out to a team for general use.

- In iterative projects we need to think about what will happen when the pattern implementation is reapplied.

Solution

Create model-to-text pattern implementations, which take a model as input and then generate a set of text-based artifacts. These text-based artifacts can include code, documentation, scripts, configuration files, and so on.

Typically a template-based approach is used to support the creation of a model-to-text pattern implementation. A template is used to represent the artifact that is to be generated. Within the template we will find a combination of static text and code or script that allows us to dynamically alter the text that is generated, leveraging user-provided content.

In creating the template, we usually start with a file provided by the exemplar. The exemplar project may have multiple instances of a file that plays a single role in the solution. For instance, if our exemplar is for generating JavaBeans, we will often see that an exemplar has more than one Bean in the project. We do not create a template for each Bean. Although there are multiple files, there is only one Bean role. As we create our template, we usually select a single instance of the Bean that is most representative of what we need to generate. If necessary, we can augment the content of the file by borrowing from the other files as needed to ensure that we account for the full range of output possibilities.

In parallel to the effort associated with the templates, we need to create an input model. The input model defines the metamodel that will constrain the information that is accepted by the pattern. In this metamodel we define the entities, their relationships, and their properties. When Pattern Users work with the pattern, the information that they provide will need to adhere to the structure defined by the metamodel.

When the pattern is applied, the input model is "merged" with the templates; that is, each template evaluates the input model using the code or script in the template. Information is retrieved from the input model and combined with the static portion of the template, and then a new file is created.

Building on the design work that has been done in exemplar analysis, we can keep the following in mind as we start to create model-to-text pattern implementations:

- Ensure that the team working on the pattern implementation includes both a Pattern Author/SME role and a Pattern Implementation Author. These roles need to work together to build the pattern.

- What should the input model be? What is the relationship between the entities? What attributes need to be captured? What attributes can be calculated?

- Which files in the exemplar should serve as templates?

- What aspects of the template need to be customized to support dynamicity? How does this relate to the input model?

Example

One way in which we can build model-to-text pattern implementations is through the use of JET,[2] which is available in Eclipse-based products. JET has been a boon in creating model-to-text pattern implementations because it enables us to quickly create pattern implementations that are easy to use, powerful, and generate a significant amount of content for our project. This is in contrast to UML pattern implementations, where there is more effort involved in the development and a more limited scope. A UML pattern implementation has value, but when we are looking at where and when to make an investment, JET-based patterns are a better place to start.

Figure 13.3 provides a high-level view of the way that JET works. JET follows a Model-View-Controller[3] pattern. The model in this case is the input model—the information that the Pattern User provides. The input model is typically provided as XML or as an EMF-based model. The control and view aspects of the pattern are both filled by templates. In the case of the control role, usually a small set of templates is used to control the execution of the pattern. The control template is aware of the input model, the calculations for information needed by other templates, and the other templates that participate in the pattern. The view templates are representations of the elements that need to be generated. They contain a combination of static text along with XPath code that allows for adding dynamicity.

---

2. We can also use platforms other than JET to build model-to-text pattern implementations. Additional related platforms that can be used include AndroMDA, XPand, and RSA's API-based transformation engine.

3. Buschmann et al. (1996).

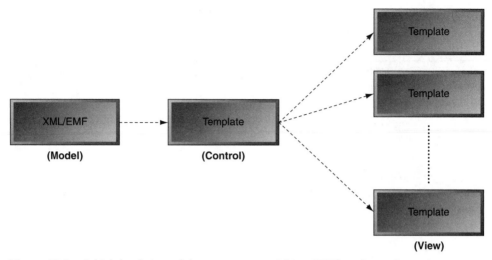

Figure 13.3 *A high-level view of the components within a JET-based transformation*

So how do we build a model-to-text pattern implementation? If we follow through on looking at JET as an example, the answer depends on the product that we are using. Eclipse as a stand-alone product provides only the JET runtime and basic text editors. If we use RSA, there are specialized editors that can be used. Let's take a closer look at what we can do with the specialized editors in RSA.

Within RSA, we find that we build on exemplar analysis with a set of steps and tooling known as Exemplar Authoring:

- Launch the JET wizard and specify the scope of the exemplar projects. These are the exemplars that will be used as the basis for building the pattern implementation. The Pattern Author/SME and the Pattern Implementation Author will figure out the artifacts that belong in the exemplar. One or more Eclipse projects will serve as the basis of the exemplar.

- As shown in Figure 13.4, once we have settled on the scope of the exemplar, we focus on the input schema and associated output actions. The input schema is used to define the elements, attributes, and calculations that work with data associated with the pattern. The output actions handle tasks such as creating required projects and files.

- Once we have settled on the input schema and output actions, we turn our focus to the templates associated with the pattern. For each type of artifact that we need to create, there is one associated template. Within the template there is a combination of static and dynamic elements. The static elements are those things that remain the same each and every time we apply the pattern. The dynamic elements will change based on the input model provided by the Pattern User. With JET, we use XPath to access and manipulate information from the input model.

At this point, however, we will only have created a pattern implementation that accepts a text-based input model. We can write XML files by hand, but that doesn't seem to fit the goal of boosting productivity. One approach we could take is to build a wizard or form in Eclipse to capture the input model.

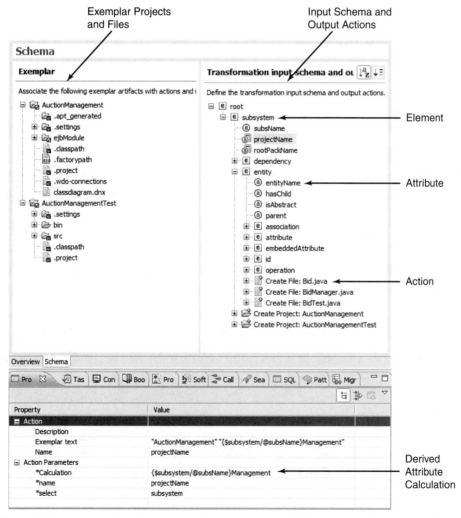

Figure 13.4 *Exemplar authoring in action in creating a JET-based model-to-text pattern implementation*

Another option is a visual model using UML or a DSL. If we go down this path, we can connect the visual model to JET using model mapping. To do so, we use our DSL/UML as the metamodel for the input model in the mapping, and we use the JET input model as the output model for the model mapping.[4]

Related Patterns and Guidelines

Exemplar Analysis (Chapter 12), Model-to-Model Pattern Implementation*, Pattern Creation Lifecycle (Chapter 12), Pattern Implementation (Chapter 12), UML Pattern Implementation*

UML Pattern Implementation

Context

We are working with UML to architect and design our PBE solutions. We need to incorporate best practices in our efforts.

Problem

When using patterns within a UML model, we run into a number of challenges. How do we accelerate the application of patterns and ensure that they are applied correctly and consistently?

Forces

- Code can be generated from the model using a code generator or other pattern implementations, but they need to be able to interpret the results of the UML pattern implementation.

- Communication is supported by recording pattern instances in the model.

- Although we are using best practices in creating the solution, the impact is limited by the narrow scope of UML pattern implementations.

Solution

Create a UML pattern implementation, that is, a pattern implementation that is specialized for use within UML models. Rather than looking at ways in which we can move between levels of abstraction, we use UML pattern implementations within a model to ensure that we are structuring the elements within the model according to

---

4. Examples of this approach are provided in Chapters 2 and 5.

best practices. As can be expected, since we are working within a UML model, the input and output for the pattern are UML elements.

Building on the design work that has been done in exemplar analysis, we can keep the following in mind as we start to create UML pattern implementations:

- What are the roles involved in the pattern?

- What UML elements (metamodel elements) should map to those roles?

- What diagrams should the pattern work with?

- What happens as instances of UML elements are bound to the roles that participate in the pattern? Are there any dependencies between elements? What happens when elements are unbound?

- Should the pattern leverage other patterns, either as parameters or encapsulated within the pattern?

- What assumptions can be made about the pattern? What information is truly needed as input? What can be derived? What can be assumed?

- What information is needed above and beyond what is captured in UML? Are there existing profiles that can be used?

Example

For example, using products such as Rational Software Architect, we can create UML pattern implementations. In the case of RSA, a UML pattern implementation is built as an Eclipse plug-in. It is primarily built to work with structural elements such as class diagrams. When building the pattern, there is a wizard that will walk us through the creation of the structure of the pattern (i.e., the roles, rules, and dependencies). Once the wizard has generated the skeleton of the pattern, it is up to us to code the behavior of the pattern using the available APIs from Eclipse, Rational Modeling Platform APIs, and other related APIs such as UML2 API and EMF.[5]

Figure 13.5 shows a UML pattern implementation for the application of a Session Façade. As shown in the image, the Pattern User is able to bind elements to the pattern instance, which then updates the model elements.

This perspective is different from what we work with as we create the pattern. However, to create a UML pattern implementation we need to be familiar with the representation and the elements associated with a finished UML pattern implementation.

---

5. A full tutorial describing how to create a UML pattern implementation is available in Ackerman and Portier (2007b).

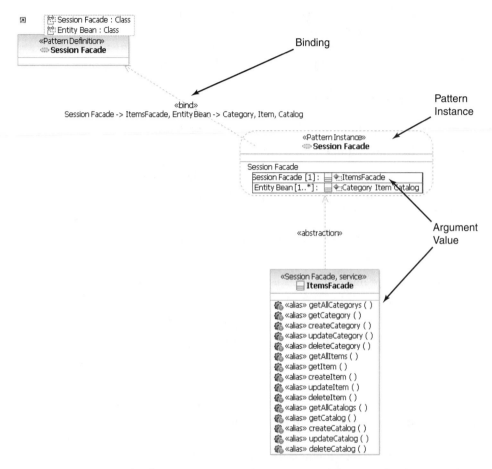

Figure 13.5   *An example of a UML pattern implementation within Rational Software Architect*

The behavior of binding roles to the pattern instance plays a key role in how we define pattern behavior.

Figure 13.6 depicts the key classes and relationships of the elements involved as we create a UML pattern implementation; in this case we'll take a look at the Master-Detail pattern that was introduced in Chapter 2. Starting at the top of the diagram, we see that there is a PatternLibrary class. Each UML pattern implementation that we create within RSA belongs to a pattern library, which is just a collection of related patterns. We specify the name of the library and which patterns belong to the library. The concept of a pattern library is important in helping with the consumability of UML pattern implementations. It allows the Pattern Implementation Author to group related patterns together to simplify how a Pattern User finds and works with patterns.

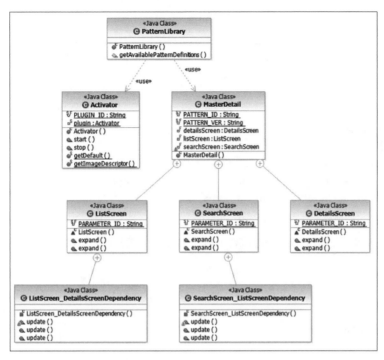

Figure 13.6 *An overview of the elements that constitute the Master-Detail pattern*

Moving to the next-lower level of elements in the diagram, we see an Activator class and a MasterDetail class. The Activator class is found in all plug-in projects and is used by Eclipse as it launches a plug-in. We do not have to add any code to this class. The MasterDetail class is the high-level representation of our pattern. There is one such pattern class for each pattern in the pattern library.

At the third layer of the diagram we see three classes: ListScreen, SearchScreen, and DetailsScreen. These classes map directly to the parameters associated with the pattern. We end up performing most of our coding effort in these classes. The code we write will go into methods associated with the actions related to the Pattern User binding and unbinding parameters to the pattern instance. The code that we add to these expand() methods is limited by the UML2 API, RSA API, and our imagination. Typically we add code to these methods to update the model, updating existing elements or working with new elements.

The final layer of elements in the diagram, ListScreen_DetailsScreenDependency and SearchScreen_ListScreenDependency, represent situations where we recognize that there are dependencies between some of the pattern parameters. In such situations we want to perform actions on the model based on Pattern User activity related to a set of dependent parameters.

Related Patterns and Guidelines

Exemplar Analysis (Chapter 12), Model-to-Model Pattern Implementation*, Model-to-Text Pattern Implementation*, Pattern Implementation (Chapter 12), Pattern Implementation Extensibility (Chapter 12)

Guidelines

In the following guidelines we discuss the creation of pattern specifications, automating pattern creation, and testing patterns.

Automate Creation of Pattern Implementations

Summary

How can we reduce the amount of time it takes to build high-quality pattern implementations? Create and use pattern implementations to automate the creation of pattern implementations.

Introduction

The team has adopted PBE and is creating pattern implementations that are unique to the organization. As with other initiatives, there is pressure to produce better results, more quickly.

How can we build high-quality pattern implementations in less time? Pattern implementations can be used to automate the creation of pattern implementations. Keep in mind:

- We need to be able to apply our pattern discovery and creation skills at an even more abstract level, using them to create patterns for patterns. In cases where an organization is getting started with PBE and creating patterns, it can be quite a leap to consider patterns to automate the creation of patterns.

- As the target patterns evolve over time, the metapatterns will need to be updated as well.

Explanation

As we've seen with the general use of pattern implementations, they can support us in building solutions more quickly and with higher quality than if we tried to perform the same work manually. We are able to use best practices and automation to ensure that those patterns are applied consistently and quickly. We can apply the same thinking to how we build pattern implementations. We can think of these as being metapatterns, that is, patterns for patterns. We can create and use pattern implementations to automate the creation of pattern implementations.

As we become experienced and familiar with creating patterns, we may find that there are cases where we are performing repetitive steps. At this point we should be conditioned to always be on the lookout for opportunities for creating patterns. We want to look at recurring solutions and see if it makes sense to not only capture them as a pattern, but to create a pattern implementation that will assist us in creating other pattern implementations.

For example, we may decide to use Eclipse-based wizards as the front end to our model-to-text pattern implementations rather than XML or UML. Thus, for each pattern implementation we build, we would also create an associated Eclipse-based wizard. Each wizard would be its own Eclipse plug-in project—a project that would need to be aware of the model-to-text pattern implementation as well as the metamodel that is associated with the pattern. Rather than going through all of the manual steps in re-creating this best-practice solution, we can recognize it as a pattern and create a supporting pattern implementation as a way to advance our efforts in building pattern implementations.

Related Patterns and Guidelines

Determine Business Impact (Chapter 11), Pattern Implementation (Chapter 12), Pattern Opportunity (Chapter 11)

Pattern Specification

Summary

How do we define and document a pattern so that it can be understood and reused? Write a pattern specification detailing the pattern name, context, problem, forces, solution, examples, related patterns, and so forth.

Introduction

We have identified a pattern and we want to define and document it so that it can be reused. Here are some considerations to keep in mind:

- Using a standardized format for recording best practices improves communication.

- A pattern specification can be used to help support the reuse of pattern implementations.

Explanation

To successfully define and document patterns, we write pattern specifications detailing the pattern name, context, problem, forces, solution, examples, related patterns, and other information about it. Without a specification, the pattern doesn't really exist for use and reuse. Pattern specifications can also be used in conjunction with a pattern implementation, providing further support for how, when, and where the pattern implementation should be used.

In writing the pattern specification, there are a number of things to keep in mind:

- Use a standard format. A number of formats are available for pattern specifications. We need to take the time to evaluate and select a format that works for our situation.

- Gather and incorporate feedback. Get people involved in reading and reviewing the pattern before it is "released." Note that this process needs to be only as formal as we require it to be.

- Patterns will evolve and mature over time; no one expects a perfect pattern specification upon its initial release. Resist the urge to overengineer.

- Leverage patterns that detail how to create patterns. In addition to the patterns captured in this book, there are other patterns that can be leveraged. For instance, Figure 13.7 illustrates the Pattern Language for Pattern Writing.

The patterns referenced in Figure 13.7, such as Single-Pass Readable, Skippable Sections, Findable Sections, Evocative Name, Terminology Tailored to Audience, and others, help us to successfully write a pattern specification. This book uses the Mandatory Elements Present pattern as the basis for pattern specifications. In following this pattern, the pattern specifications include these sections:

- **Pattern name:** the name of the pattern, allowing others to easily reference it.

- **Context:** the circumstances in which we would use the pattern. These circumstances place constraints on how the problem can be solved. There are times when the context is described in terms of patterns that have already been applied.

- **Problem:** a description of the problem that the pattern will address.

- **Forces:** the considerations that must be taken into account when applying a pattern. These considerations may at times be contradictory, so we leverage the context to help us prioritize the forces.

- **Solution:** the solution to the problem.

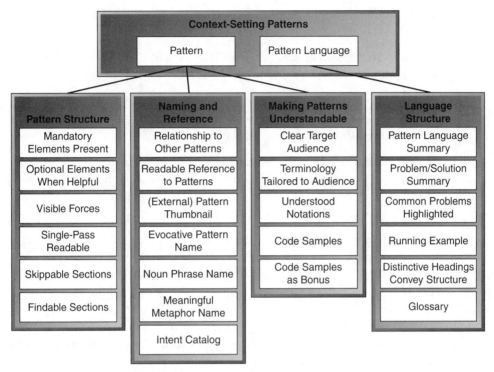

Figure 13.7 *A graphical view of the Pattern Language for Pattern Writing pattern*
This figure is a reproduction of Figure 29-1 from page 531 of Martin, R. C., D. Riehle, and F. Buschmann. 1998. "Context-Setting Patterns." In Pattern Languages of Program Design 3. Boston: Addison-Wesley. Reproduced by permission of Pearson Education.

A few other sections of the PBE pattern specifications are based on the Optional Elements When Helpful pattern, including these:

- **Example:** an example of the pattern being applied.

- **Related patterns:** a list of patterns that are in some way related to the pattern being discussed. These may include patterns that offer alternate solutions, patterns that could/should be used along with the pattern under discussion, and patterns that may solve similar problems in a more generic or more specific approach.

Some of the additional patterns used in creating the PBE Patterns include

- **Visible Forces pattern.** Following on the Mandatory Elements Present pattern, we ensure that forces that are associated with the pattern are highly visible.

- **Findable Sections pattern.** This pattern ensures quick and easy navigation through the sections within the pattern specification.

- **Relationship to Other Patterns pattern.** This pattern details the relationships between patterns.

- **Readable References to Patterns pattern.** Many pattern descriptions reference other patterns. We have used those pattern names within the write-up and have ensured that the formatting highlights the references.

- **(External) Pattern Thumbnail pattern.** This pattern references patterns from external sources and summarizes their details. The case study in Part II also uses this pattern.

- **Evocative Pattern Name pattern.** In a catalog of many patterns, remembering and locating them are difficult if the patterns have poor or nondescriptive names. This pattern provides guidance for robust pattern names.

In addition to using patterns to write our specifications, additional support is available in the form of specification templates. Rather than starting from scratch, we can use specification templates to give us a head start. A number of templates are available for us to use as inspiration for our own templates. These templates have been used in other books and reference websites and within many companies. If we need to, we can tweak the templates to improve the fit for our organization, but they should provide us with a high percentage of the solution that we need. In addition, the templates can be used in conjunction with the patterns discussed previously; and as we review the templates, we'll see that they align with and have already used some of the patterns. Some of the templates to consider include the following:

- **GoF Pattern Specification Template.** The fields in this template[6] include Pattern Name, Intent, Also Known As, Motivation, Applicability, Structure, Participants, Participant Name, Collaborations, Consequences, Implementation, Sample Code and Usage, Program Listing, Known Uses, Related Patterns.

  One issue that we may run into with the GoF template is that it is tailored specifically to design patterns. What if we want to capture other types of patterns? In that case we would need to either tailor the template to the type of pattern that we are using, or else look for other templates that are better suited to the type of pattern that we are detailing.

---

6. The GoF template is explained and used in Gamma et al. (1995).

- **Microsoft Pattern Specification Templates.**[7] Microsoft has made two templates available; one template is used for architecture and design patterns, and the other template is used for implementation patterns. This highlights the fact that we can use different templates not only based on the preference of the organization, but also based on the type of pattern that we are creating. We don't need to settle for a one-size-fits-all solution. The Architecture and Design Patterns Template includes the following fields: Pattern Name, Context, Problem, Forces, Solution, Example, Resulting Context, Aliases*, Testing Considerations*, Security Considerations*, Operational Considerations*, Known Uses*, Variants*, Related Patterns*, Acknowledgments*.

  The Implementation Patterns Template includes the following fields: Pattern Name, Context, Implementation Strategy, Resulting Context, Background*, Example*, Tests*, Testing Considerations*, Security Considerations*, Operational Considerations*, Known Uses*, Variants*, Related Patterns*, Acknowledgments*.

  The fields with an asterisk are optional elements. The template uses the Optional Elements When Helpful pattern. In this way we keep the number of fields to only those that are important to the pattern and those using the patterns. If an optional field/element is not needed, it is excluded from the pattern specification.

We can see from this list that although there are some variations, there is overlap, with some elements appearing consistently across the templates.

When selecting or creating a template, we should keep in mind that some fields should be captured as metadata in an asset repository, rather than just within the pattern specification itself. For instance, the author of the pattern, when the pattern was last updated, contact information, and similar details, while important, should be provided only where needed to avoid cluttering the specification.

Participating in a pattern writers' workshop[8] can be helpful in creating pattern specifications. In such a workshop, peers read and evaluate each other's patterns and then provide suggestions for how to improve them. Although some workshops are held formally in a conference-like setting, we can use the same approach within our organization as a way to validate and improve the quality of our own patterns.

There's even a set of patterns associated with the writers' workshop. These patterns include Safe Setting, Authors Are Experts, Workshop Comprises Authors, Community of Trust, Moderator Guides the Workshop, Sitting in a Circle, Authors Circle,

---

7. Al-Sabt et al. (2003).

8. Guidance on pattern writers' workshops can be found at www.cs.wustl.edu/~schmidt/writersworkshop.html.

Reading Just Before Reviewing, Author Reads the Work, Fly on the Wall, Volunteer Summarizes the Work, Positive Feedback First, Suggestions for Improvement, Author Asks for Clarification, Thank the Author, Selective Changes, Clearing the Palate.[9]

The specifications for the PBE Patterns discussed in Chapters 10 through 16 serve as examples to support this guideline. An additional example is in Appendix D with the specification of the Subsystem Façade pattern.

Related Patterns and Guidelines

Exemplar Analysis (Chapter 12), Pattern Description (Chapter 11), Pattern Language for Pattern Writing[10]

Pattern Testing

Summary

How do we ensure that a pattern has sufficient quality and is consumable? The simple answer is to test the pattern.

Introduction

Quality and consumability are critical aspects of PBE. Regardless of the importance of a best practice, if the resulting pattern is not consumable or lacks quality, it will not be used. An unused pattern is a wasted investment and will lead to a failed PBE initiative. Considerations to keep in mind include these:

- Multiple roles need to come together to support the testing effort, including a Pattern Author/SME, Pattern Specification Author, Pattern Implementation Author, Asset Librarian, and Pattern Tester.

- Automating the test in the context of a pattern implementation could significantly improve the productivity and reduce the delivery time for a new pattern implementation.

Explanation

To ensure that we produce consumable and high-quality patterns we need to effectively test them. But what does it mean to test a pattern? And how do we do so effectively?

---

9. http://c2.com/cgi/wiki?WritersWorkshopPatterns and http://users.rcn.com/jcoplien/Patterns/WritersWorkshop/.

10. Meszaros and Doble (1998).

Do we just reread the pattern specification? Do we check the grammar? For a pattern implementation, is it enough that the code compiles and runs?

As we get started, let's consider the different aspects of quality that we can evaluate. First, let's take a look at criteria that apply to both pattern specifications and pattern implementations:

- Is this truly the best practice?

- Have we accurately captured the best practice?

- Is the pattern consumable? Can a Pattern User understand and work with the pattern?

- Have we successfully provided the correct points of variability that would allow others to apply these best practices to their situation?

Here are some additional criteria specific to pattern implementations:

- Is the pattern reliable?

- Does the pattern run without error?

- Can the pattern recover from situations where invalid input is provided?

- Does it fail gracefully when it encounters an exception that it can't handle?

- Does the pattern meet performance expectations?

- Is the pattern packaged and documented correctly to support reuse?

With these perspectives and questions in mind, it should be apparent that pattern testing represents many considerations and will impact many of the PBE roles, including Asset Librarian, Pattern Author/SME, Pattern Implementation Author, Pattern Specification Author, and Pattern Tester. All of these roles come into play as we test our patterns; each role works through the considerations that best align with his or her area(s) of specialization. The Pattern Tester is the primary participant in working through this pattern, but this role will leverage the entire set of roles in successfully testing a pattern. With this in mind, let's take a more detailed look at how we can test patterns.

A good place to start is to ensure that the exemplar on which we are basing the pattern is of sufficient quality. Early in our pattern development efforts, we want to review the exemplar with the Pattern Author/SME. At a minimum, an exemplar should run. That's a good start, but that doesn't mean that it is a quality solution. We need to follow through with other normal quality-measuring steps: reviews, inspections, and testing. The exemplar is a key artifact in many ways; the first and most obvious way is as the basis of the pattern. The exemplar can also represent our first test case. We should be able to take the completed pattern and re-create instances of the exemplar.

Once we have a quality exemplar in place, we can move forward and take other steps to ensure the quality of the pattern. We can double-check the patterns that we followed in writing the pattern, as discussed in the Pattern Specification guideline.

Microsoft's "Testing Software Patterns" publication proposes a five-part testing strategy,[11] which includes

- **Literature comparison.** Compare the pattern specification to other already written pattern specifications. We want to ensure that the specification is well formed and that the guidance that is provided aligns with already created patterns.

- **Solution comparison.** Ensure that the solution, as guided by the pattern, is a good solution in comparison to solutions described by other patterns.

- **Solution testing.** Ensure that the solution itself is of high quality. This step is close to traditional testing—we need to make sure that the solution that the pattern leads to is of high quality. Because we are building our pattern based on an exemplar, we already have a good start on this effort.

- **Technical writing clarity.** Look at how consumable the writing is for the pattern specification and any other documentation that supports the pattern implementation. The directions associated with the pattern should be clear, and the flow through the pattern should be self-evident.

- **Brainstorming and proof by contradiction.** Ensure that the pattern is correct and behaves gracefully when exception conditions arise.

We can also use the following Pattern Writing Checklist[12] as a guide for checking the quality of a pattern. The checklist includes the following tips:

A Pattern . . .
- Describes a single kind of problem.
- Describes the context in which the problem occurs.
- Describes the solution as a constructable software entity.
- Describes design steps or rules for constructing the solution.
- Describes the forces leading to the solution.
- Describes evidence that the solution optimally resolves forces.

---

11. Al-Sabt et al. (2003).

12. http://hillside.net/index.php/pattern-writing-checklist.

- Describes details that are allowed to vary, and those that are not.
- Describes at least one actual instance of use.
- Describes evidence of generality across different instances.
- Describes or refers to variants and subpatterns.
- Describes or refers to other patterns that it relies upon.
- Describes or refers to other patterns that rely upon this pattern.
- Relates to other patterns with similar contexts, problems, or solutions.

Recall that pattern implementations built on the Eclipse platform are created as plug-ins. Thus, we can leverage the tooling and best practices associated with testing plug-ins. To test a plug-in we can launch an instance of Eclipse from our development instance; this is called a runtime instance of the Workbench. We can then inspect, set break points, and walk through the code.

We also need to make sure that we are managing the test effort, the results from the tests, and the versions of the patterns.

Related Patterns and Guidelines

Pattern Implementation (Chapter 12), Pattern Specification*, Pattern Version (Chapter 14), Update Existing Patterns (Chapter 11), Use an Asset Repository (Chapter 16)

Summary

We've looked at how we can create the two key types of patterns: pattern specifications and pattern implementations. Approaches to building a pattern implementation include UML pattern implementations, model-to-model pattern implementations, and model-to-text pattern implementations. This chapter discusses patterns for creating these types of patterns, as well as considerations to keep in mind as we do so. Model-to-text patterns provide a great way to get started in building our own pattern implementations. They are easy to learn and quick to build and can impact a significant portion of a project.

Pattern specifications are also a key part of our toolkit, helping us in detailing and communicating our patterns. A number of templates are available to help us in detailing our own pattern specifications. We want to standardize on a template for the organization as a way to simplify the authoring effort and also make the resulting patterns more consumable. Templates also can be used in conjunction with a pattern implementation, providing further support for how, when, and where the pattern implementation should be used.

Perhaps most important of all, we need to ensure that we are producing high-quality patterns. A focus on best practices in designing and then creating patterns is very important. But we still need to ensure that we understand how to test the patterns that we create. Regardless of the importance of the proven solution within the pattern, if the pattern has poor quality, it will not get used and our reuse efforts will fail.

Chapter 14

Packaging Patterns

Successfully implementing PBE and an associated reuse effort is about more than just identifying and building patterns. We need to eliminate friction and hurdles that prevent patterns from being consumed effectively and efficiently. In eliminating these hurdles, some of the questions that we need to answer include these:

- How do we package patterns to support consumption and reuse?

- How do we make the patterns available to others so that they are easy to find and work with?

- How do we make the patterns available in such a way that they are easy to support when new versions need to be made available?

- What if searching for a pattern fails to turn up relevant results or turns up irrelevant ones?

- Once a pattern is found, how do we make sure that people will succeed in using it?

The patterns and guidelines in this chapter will help us in ensuring that Pattern Users can easily find the right version of the right pattern and use it successfully.

Patterns

In this section we look at a couple of patterns for packaging patterns. These patterns provide guidance on how we can package documentation and how we can make patterns provisionable.

Embedded Pattern Implementation Guidance

Context

We have completed the work involved in creating a pattern implementation and want to support its reuse by making it as consumable as possible.

Problem

The likelihood of written documentation being ignored increases as the effort required to find and leverage the documentation increases. How can we eliminate hurdles related to following documented guidance and best practices?

Forces

- We need to understand how to surface guidance and documentation within selected tooling environments.

- Even if documentation is easy to find, it still needs to be well written.

- If the underlying pattern implementation is updated, we need to revisit and then redeploy the associated guidance.

- If the tooling selection changes, pattern implementation guidance will have to be migrated to the new platform.

Solution

There is a two-step approach to simplifying access to pattern implementation guidance. The first step is related to how and where the Pattern User finds and interacts with the guidance. A simple and immediate step is to embed documentation within the help system of the tooling platform. As Pattern Users attempt to apply the pattern implementation, they can quickly and easily find the documentation that supports the use of the pattern. Such an approach is successful, as it provides

- **Consistency.** Pattern Users are able to find guidance to support the pattern implementation in a manner that is consistent with finding guidance for any other aspect of the tooling.

- **Context.** Pattern Users are able to see, review, and follow the guidance within the context in which they are working. They do not have to switch focus from the tooling that hosts the pattern implementation.

The second step we can take is to investigate and then leverage mechanisms that go beyond static documentation. Being able to find guidance in a location that is consistent within the platform and to be able to review that guidance within the context of the tool is a strong first step. However, if we stop there, we're still just giving the Pattern User a document to read. With a little effort, we can go beyond the results that can be achieved with just static documentation.

Many modern development tools, such as Eclipse, provide mechanisms that we can leverage. Some possibilities to consider include

- **Automation.** There are often cases where a number of steps need to be performed in sequence as we build a solution. We can use automation to guide us through the application of the pattern in a step-by-step fashion.

- **Interactive examples.** Use built-in web browser capabilities to include interactive guidance on succeeding with the pattern implementation. This can include videos, animations, and simulations.

- **Linking to supporting materials.** A pattern rarely exists in isolation, so we can provide links to related materials in the pattern implementation guidance. These can include materials related to the domain and the development process, as well as additional and related patterns.

We want to be practical and provide as much guidance as is needed. And we want to make it as easy and simple as possible for the Pattern User to consume that information and be productive in doing so.

Example

With the Eclipse platform we can include documentation within the pattern plug-in. The documentation can be integrated with the Eclipse help system so that the Pattern User can easily access it. However, we can take things a step further and provide a more interactive and automated experience. To do so with Eclipse we can use the Composite Cheat Sheet[1] mechanism to lead Pattern Users through a series of steps. Composite Cheat Sheets provide the benefit of being able to automate steps, so they enable us to document and automate the workflow. This automation can consist of launching a wizard, creating a diagram, or other user actions. We can also instruct the Composite Cheat Sheet to leverage Eclipse's built-in web browser to display

---

1. More details on the features provided by Composite Cheat Sheets as well as guidance on how to construct them are provided in Tiedt (2006).

images that provide further guidance on how to succeed in using the pattern implementation.

When using a Composite Cheat Sheet, we can automate steps of

- Building the input model

- Configuring the pattern

- Running the pattern

- Evaluating the output from the pattern

- Reapplying the pattern

Composite Cheat Sheets can work well with patterns, since we can guide users in how they can apply a pattern or even groups of patterns. Although our focus in this example is on using Composite Cheat Sheets in support of pattern implementations, we could also use them with pattern specifications. In addition, Composite Cheat Sheets are able to support us in consuming patterns for different purposes such as design, pattern detection, and pattern harvesting.

We can also use Composite Cheat Sheets to provide domain guidance when using more generic patterns. Thus, we can provide details and examples that relate to the domain to simplify any translation that is needed when applying the pattern within a domain.

Related Patterns and Guidelines

Document Pattern*, Make Pattern Documentation Easily Accessible*

Provisionable Pattern Implementation

Context

As the team works through one or more projects that leverage PBE, they will use a number of different pattern implementations.

Problem

As the team works with many patterns, they will need to be able to deploy those patterns and associated artifacts into their work environment. Over time and as projects change, they will need to update pattern implementations with new versions or uninstall some patterns and replace them with others. How do we support the deployment and provisioning of patterns to the Pattern User's work environment?

Forces

- We need to understand the provisioning options for our selected tooling.

- We need to ensure that we have appropriate governance measures in place.

- If the underlying tooling changes, the provisioning approach will need to be revisited.

Solution

Change is inevitable. Project requirements will change. Patterns are living and will change. Thus, it is clear that we will be dealing with installation, licensing, versioning, and removal issues. We need to make this as simple and manageable for the Pattern User as possible. We leverage the capabilities of our tooling to create provisionable units for our patterns and their associated artifacts. Typically we determine if the target platform for our pattern implementations has the following:

- **Extension management.** The platform should provide a mechanism for managing extensions to the platform. This mechanism should support Pattern Users as they install, update, and uninstall pattern implementations. In addition, Pattern Users should be able to quickly ascertain which versions of which patterns are currently available.

- **Packaging support.** The tooling should support the packaging of our pattern implementations. Ideally, the tooling enables us to capture the metadata associated with a specific pattern implementation. Some of the metadata that we need to capture for a pattern implementation includes version, license, keywords, and support details.

- **Asset repository integration.** The platform should provide integration with the asset repository that the organization uses. In other words, are we able to search the asset repository from the target platform? If so, once we find a pattern implementation, is it easy to install?

- **Cardinality.** The platform should provide support for packaging sets of patterns together. There are cases where we want to treat a set of patterns as a single entity. The set should be installed as a single unit, updated as a single unit, and removed as a single unit.

Example

When working with the Eclipse platform, we can use its packaging mechanisms. At a minimum we can use plug-ins, the standard Eclipse extension mechanism, to contain a set of patterns. We can include some version information and other related information in this package. The Pattern User is able to see which plug-ins are installed and the version of each plug-in and can disable, uninstall, or update the plug-ins. Typically we package our plug-ins by using a mechanism called a feature. A feature provides a way for us to include licensing information, version information, and better integration with the platform than publishing as just a plug-in. It also allows us to bring a set of plug-ins together as one deployable unit.

Related Patterns and Guidelines

Make Pattern Documentation Easily Accessible*

Guidelines

These guidelines provide advice on how we document patterns, package patterns, and handle versioning.

Document Pattern

Summary

How do we ensure that the Pattern User is able to understand how to install, configure, use, and uninstall a pattern? We create and provide documentation that details the pattern, providing the Pattern User with support for installation, configuration, use, updating, and removal.

Introduction

Ideally, we find ourselves in a situation where we have created a number of patterns that are specific to the organization, and we want to make them consumable and support reuse. How do we ensure that the Pattern User is able to understand the details about installing, configuring, using, updating, and uninstalling the pattern? As we try to answer these questions, consider the following:

- We need to be able to look at working with the pattern implementation from the Pattern User point of view.

- A number of roles need to come together to support this effort, including the Pattern Author/SME, the Pattern Specification Author, and the Pattern Implementation Author.

Explanation

Document the pattern to provide the Pattern User with details on how to succeed in working with the pattern. At a minimum, details should include how to install, configure, use, update, and uninstall the pattern.

We need to consider whether the documentation is going to support a pattern implementation or a pattern specification. In the case of a pattern specification, there is a much lower requirement for additional documentation because the specification itself is a formally written document. Also, there is little to worry about in regard to installation, updates, and removal of the pattern. We can focus our efforts solely on writing the best pattern specification possible.

The need for providing supporting documentation is much higher with a pattern implementation as we are essentially deploying a piece of software. When documenting a pattern implementation, we seek to provide answers to the following questions:

- How do we install the pattern?

- How do we specify the input model? Note that it can be very helpful to provide a sample input model.

- How do we apply the pattern?

- How do elements in the input model map to elements in the output model? A table that lists each of the elements that are interpreted and how they are translated can be a useful way to answer this question.

- How can the pattern be configured?

- What is the reapply behavior?

- What are the extension points and how can the pattern be extended? There will be cases where the pattern is not quite a perfect fit, but it could serve as the basis for a new pattern that is more specific to the situation.

- Are there additional related patterns that need to be considered?

- What DSLs should be used with the pattern?

Keep in mind that there are multiple audiences for the pattern; documentation should be tailored to each of the audiences and clearly labeled to indicate which aspects of the documentation apply to which audience. Audiences to consider as we create the documentation include these:

- **Pattern Users.** They need to know the background of the pattern: What is it? When should it be used? They also need to know how to use the pattern: How should it be applied? How should it be configured? How can it be unapplied? Also, they need to know how to install and uninstall the pattern.

- **Pattern producers.** Pattern producers may attempt to leverage our pattern in future development, either through extension or creation of a compound pattern. They need to understand the pattern's intended use, how it is implemented and designed. However, their focus is from a black-box point of view; they are not concerned about the code.

- **Maintenance team.** The pattern implementation, like other software deliverables, often has a longer-than-anticipated lifetime and will go through multiple releases. We need to provide support for the team that will be performing this maintenance work. Currently the maintenance team may be the team that did the original development, but as we've seen with other software, things change. The maintenance team will need to have a white-box view of the pattern, allowing them to understand the details behind its design and implementation. This audience needs to leverage the materials provided to the other audiences as well, so they will also have a black-box view of the pattern.

The goal is to make the pattern as consumable as possible, providing the user of the pattern with the information needed to succeed.

Related Patterns and Guidelines

Communicate Design with Patterns (Chapter 16), Document Pattern Relationships*, Embedded Pattern Implementation Guidance*, Make Pattern Documentation Easily Accessible*, Use Models in Documenting Patterns*

Document Pattern Relationships

Summary

How do we communicate which patterns should or should not be used with one another? Document the relationships between patterns, including dependencies, hierarchy, and cases where patterns are mutually exclusive.

Introduction

The team is following PBE and a set of patterns has been made available, including those acquired and those created. In following PBE, the team is aware that patterns should be used in combination. However, which patterns should be used together? Which patterns should not be used together? As we package our patterns, how do we communicate pattern relationships to the Pattern User? Considerations to keep in mind include these:

- In crafting a solution we need to recognize that multiple patterns will come together and interact.

- Ideally an asset repository is used for capturing pattern relationship information. Such an approach allows for the information to be easily updated after the pattern has been released for use, without requiring a rerelease of the pattern.

Explanation

The relationships between patterns, including dependencies, hierarchy, and cases where patterns are mutually exclusive, should be documented. As discussed earlier, when following PBE, we look to use patterns in combination, rather than in isolation. Relationships exist among patterns. In some cases a pair of patterns may be mutually exclusive; that is, the selection of one pattern may preclude the use of another pattern. In other cases there may be a hierarchy among a set of patterns such that the selection of one pattern leads to using one or more patterns that are supportive of that higher-level pattern.

A Pattern User should be able to quickly ascertain which patterns can be used together and how. This is important from both a pattern packaging point of view as well as from a pattern design point of view.

When designing a pattern, we need to be aware of its possible relationships. We want to document and detail any dependencies between the pattern and other patterns. It may be that we create a pattern catalog that defines a set of patterns and possibly some of the relationships. Or we may take things even further and define a pattern language that defines a set of patterns, their relationships, and an order in which the patterns should be used.[2]

As the pattern is completed, packaged, and deployed, we can leverage an asset repository to manage the pattern and to detail dependencies between the pattern and other patterns. An asset repository also provides support for Pattern Users to add feedback and detail relationships.

Figure 14.1 shows a diagram created to provide an overview of a set of SOA architectural patterns. As part of the overview the diagram indicates the relationships between the patterns within the set. The relationships that are denoted include those patterns that should be used together as well as those that are mutually exclusive. The diagram is simple and high-level and provides Pattern Users with an excellent resource to consult as they try to understand the set of patterns and how they should be used.

---

2. Further information about pattern catalogs and pattern languages is provided in Appendix A.

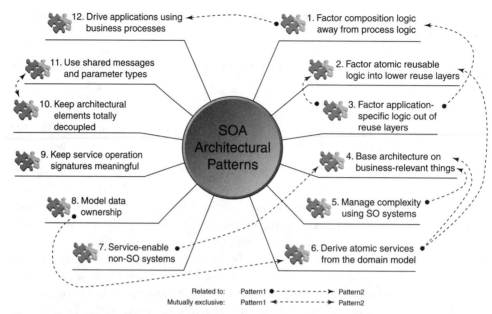

Figure 14.1 *Simple diagram to highlight a set of SOA architectural patterns and their relationships*

Related Patterns and Guidelines

Document Pattern*, Pattern Search (Chapter 10), Use an Asset Repository (Chapter 16)

Make Pattern Documentation Easily Accessible

Summary

How do we make a pattern easy for others to understand and work with? Make the pattern documentation easily accessible. The documentation should be easy to find and consume, supporting the Pattern User in the task at hand.

Introduction

The potential of a pattern will never be realized if Pattern Users cannot understand how to work with the pattern. How do we make it easy for Pattern Users to find and consume a pattern? Here are some considerations to keep in mind:

- We need to think about and understand the different ways in which a pattern can be consumed.

- We need to consider the lifecycle stages associated with a pattern, including locating, installing, using, updating, and uninstalling.

Explanation

Make the pattern documentation easily accessible. Finding the documentation and searching it for necessary information should be straightforward for Pattern Users.

In documenting a pattern, we need to think about the different scenarios in which someone would want guidance for the pattern and how that impacts the way we make documentation available. Some typical scenarios include

- **Pattern selection.** We should strive to make all documentation regarding the pattern available outside of the pattern packaging, allowing others to learn about the pattern (from either a design or a usage point of view) so that they can do so without having to first install the pattern. One scenario in which this is useful is assisting Pattern Users as they determine which pattern should be used. Metadata and summaries are useful in narrowing down the list of patterns to use, but to make a final selection, more details on how to use the pattern are needed.

- **Pattern installation.** Special instructions for installing a pattern implementation may be captured as documentation. When we provide a pattern to others for use, we put the pattern in a package, but installation documentation should be available outside of the package. What use is the documentation if it can be accessed only once the pattern has been installed?

- **Creating compound patterns.** Another scenario arises for those building new compound patterns. Again, metadata and summaries are useful for filtering the field of patterns, but more information is needed for making a final decision regarding which pattern to include in a compound.

A proper asset management strategy and associated governance policy are needed. When some documentation is outside of the pattern package, there are multiple related assets to manage. In addition, we should ensure that relationships between the assets are properly documented and detailed in the asset repository. This will enable anyone who finds the pattern in the repository to follow the relationships to the relevant and related assets.

Related Patterns and Guidelines

Communicate Design with Patterns (Chapter 16), Design Solutions with Patterns (Chapter 16), Embedded Pattern Implementation Documentation*, Refactor with

Patterns (Chapter 16), Use Pattern Definitions to Understand Existing Solutions (Chapter 16), Use Patterns to Find Patterns (Chapter 16)

Package Related Patterns Together

Summary

How do we help Pattern Users to succeed in consuming multiple related patterns? Simplify how people find, consume, and work with related patterns by packaging them together.

Introduction

A number of related patterns have been created and need to be made available for reuse. How do we help Pattern Users succeed in consuming such a set of patterns? As we try to answer this question, consider these factors:

- We need to see patterns as a set of elements that work together and support one another in crafting a solution.

- We need to ensure that Pattern Users understand that although a set of patterns is packaged together, they are not forced to use all of the patterns in the set. We still need to ensure that we are using the right patterns in the right situations.

- We need to detail the relationships among the patterns packaged together.

- Capturing metrics and feedback can be more difficult for a specific, individual pattern within a set of patterns.

Explanation

Package related patterns together to simplify how people find, consume, and work with them. When we create a package, we can put multiple patterns together within it. However, we need to create the package with the right set of patterns within. We can't haphazardly put together a random collection of patterns that don't fit well together. Such an approach provides no value to the person who wants to use the patterns. There are multiple considerations that we need to keep in mind as we create the set, including

- **Set size.** Limit the size of the set by adding only those patterns that make the most sense. Consider whether we have too many packages with too few patterns in each. Too many patterns and associated packages can seem cluttered and be difficult to manage.

- **Relationships.** Ideally, we are building a collection that is highly cohesive. We can also look at the coupling between the patterns in the set. Does the use of one pattern require the use of another pattern?

- **Simplification.** We want to encapsulate a number of patterns within a compound pattern. To the Pattern User, the resulting package should appear as a single pattern rather than a collection of individual patterns.

- **Expected usage.** When and how will the patterns be used? Will the typical user consume all of the patterns on the same project? If not all, then what percentage would get used? Is there a clear delineation between groups of patterns and their usage profile? Would it make sense to subdivide the set of patterns into smaller packages?

- **Update cycle.** Because patterns are living, it's likely that they will need to be updated over time. Are all of the patterns on the same update cycle? If not, how close are they in their update cycles? Can the ones more frequently updated wait to be released until those on longer update cycles are released? Or do we perform more updates? How mature are the patterns? How likely are the patterns to change?

- **Pattern types.** What types of patterns are in the set? Are they pattern specifications? Pattern implementations? Both?

- **Versioning.** Keep in mind that we will have to apply a version number to the artifacts. A decision has to be made about how we will version the elements that constitute this component. Do we version each element separately? Do we apply the same version number to all of the artifacts? For example, when using the Eclipse platform, we do have some flexibility in this area because each plug-in can have its own version number, and a feature used to package the set of plug-ins can be given its own version number. Take advantage of this capability; end users only ever see the version number from the feature. From a development and maintenance point of view, this extra level of granularity provides us with additional manageability. A modern and capable software configuration management and build system will help us to manage the versioning.

- **Source.** When we receive a package of patterns from outside the organization, what will we do if they are all packaged as individual patterns? Will we group and repackage them?

Take the time to think through and analyze what is the right decision for the situation. Would it make more sense to put a set of patterns together as a single package? Or is there more value in making them available individually? How will this decision impact those who will work with the package and the patterns within? Will the resulting asset simplify their use of the patterns or introduce unnecessary complexity into their workflow?

Related Patterns and Guidelines

Compound Pattern (Chapter 12), Pattern Packaging*, Pattern Search (Chapter 10), Update Existing Patterns (Chapter 11)

Pattern Packaging

Summary

How can we share patterns in such a way that they are easy for others to consume? Package patterns, bringing together the appropriate set of artifacts needed for successfully consuming the patterns. The user only needs to grab the package, rather than searching for all of the constituent parts.

Introduction

Patterns have been created within the organization or acquired from an outside source. Pattern Users get frustrated if it is too difficult to consume a pattern. How can we share patterns in such a way that they are easy for Pattern Users to consume? Keep in mind that

- Cultural changes can be difficult.

- Reusable assets that are difficult to find won't be reused. Also, we need to find the right solution to our problem in the current context.

- Reusable assets that are difficult to reuse, won't be reused.

Explanation

Package patterns so that they can easily be shared and consumed by Pattern Users. The package should bring together the appropriate set of artifacts[3] needed for consuming the pattern, so the Pattern User can grab a single package, rather than find all of the individual parts. Forcing the Pattern User to fabricate the pattern from a loosely associated set of composite parts is a sure way to cause a pattern initiative to

---

3. Numerous different types of artifacts could be included in the package, such as pattern implementations, pattern specifications, documentation, installation instructions, samples, DSLs, templates, licenses, and source files.

fail. As we design and build the pattern, we have great insight into the pattern and its related elements. Using this insight, we can package the pattern so that it is easy for Pattern Users to consume.

Overall the focus is on keeping things as simple as possible for the Pattern User. This is a good thought to start with, but it's not very specific about how we can succeed with our packaging efforts. More detailed considerations for packaging a pattern include these:

- How will patterns be stored, searched, and then used?

- In the case of pattern implementations, how does the pattern install into the host environment? Can the packaging support how the pattern works with tooling?

- A pattern implementation can have an associated pattern specification. How do we make both the specification and the implementation available to Pattern Users?

- What is the relationship between source artifacts and binaries? Can our software configuration management and build system support us in building pattern packages?

- What asset repository solution will we use? How does it support the packaging of patterns? How does it impact how we will package patterns?

- How will the packaged asset be tested? Of course, we've already tested the pattern itself, but we also need to ensure that we have thoroughly tested the packaging of the pattern and how the pattern will be consumed. Deploying an asset that fails on installation by the end user will have negative consequences both for that asset as well as for our patterns initiative.

- The pattern should be packaged in such a way that it can be easily managed.

- How does packaging support reuse of the pattern by other Pattern Authors as they look to build compound patterns?

- What is the relationship between the pattern itself and its supporting artifacts? How do they get packaged?

- When do we release and package a pattern? When should it be rereleased/ updated?

- What do we do when patterns from other sources do not have direct alignment with our own pattern packaging? Do we repackage? Allow the variation? Request new packaging from the supplier? What if the packaging does not include all of the supporting artifacts that we require from internal assets? Do we augment those packages?

The key point is that we need to plan and implement carefully how we package a pattern and make it available. We've already made an investment in identifying, designing, and building the pattern. All of that effort goes to waste if that's where we stop. We're close to the finish; however, there's still work to be done.

Related Patterns and Guidelines

Compound Pattern (Chapter 12), Embedded Pattern Implementation Documentation*, Integrated Patterns and DSLs (Chapter 15), Make Pattern Documentation Easily Accessible*, Pattern Implementation Extensibility (Chapter 12), Use an Asset Repository (Chapter 16)

Pattern Version

Summary

How do we succeed in an environment where multiple versions of patterns exist? Use version numbers and a versioning strategy to manage and support the various instances.

Introduction

How can we tell which version is which when there are multiple versions of a pattern? Which one should we use? How do we communicate this information to Pattern Users? Considerations include these:

- Pattern producers and Pattern Users need to be aware of the pattern version in use.

- Pattern producers and Pattern Users need to understand where and how they can determine the currently supported version.

- Pattern producers and Pattern Users need to understand where and how to access version numbers for a specific pattern.

Explanation

Use version numbers and a versioning strategy to organize and support the various versions of a pattern. The key is to recognize that patterns are living, evolve over time, and are in many ways similar to other software deliverables. For this reason we need to leverage some of the best practices from other, traditional software deliverables. In this case we want to leverage a sound approach to how we version and communicate versions to the consumers and maintainers of patterns.

We'll end up having versions of our patterns in both a software configuration management system and an asset repository. The important thing to keep in mind is that these two repositories serve different purposes and have separate lifecycles that happen to intersect at points in time. The software configuration management solution is used to provide team and versioning support for the pattern as it is being created. This applies whether we are working with specifications or implementations, and also to the associated and supporting artifacts that are related to the pattern. The list of artifacts includes documentation, samples, installation instructions, and other elements. The asset repository is used to manage and make available the assets that are to be reused by the Pattern Users. We put our final, packaged version of the asset in the asset repository. An asset repository is responsible for supporting and managing the consumption of completed patterns.

The version number should be clearly displayed in relevant places such as the packaging, the documentation (documentation that discusses installation as well as the documentation that covers usage), as well as the code and templates. A modern software configuration management and build system should be able to provide assistance in maintaining this information.

Related Patterns and Guidelines

Package Related Patterns Together*, Pattern Packaging*, Provisionable Pattern Implementation*, Use an Asset Repository (Chapter 16)

Use Models in Documenting Patterns

Summary

How can we improve and simplify the documentation regarding the details about the design and use of a pattern? Provide visual models that detail a pattern and how to use it. As we've seen in the creation of other software solutions, the use of visual models is a proven and effective mechanism for communication and education.

Introduction

A number of groups within the organization need to understand details about patterns. These needs range from simple to complex and cover the design, implementation, and use of patterns. How can we improve and simplify pattern documentation? As we attempt to answer this question, there are a number of considerations to keep in mind:

- We need to understand how to create models and diagrams effectively. There are many options for diagram types and the information that we include.

- Not everyone prefers visual communication.

- Consistency in modeling languages reduces learning requirements and can make communication easier.

Explanation

Create visual models that provide details on a pattern and how to use it. As we've seen in other software solutions, visual models are a proven and effective communication mechanism.

Because we need to support multiple audiences with documentation, we need to keep these audiences in mind as we create visual models. Each audience will be looking for different information. We can create a single model with multiple perspectives and then publish as appropriate to the specific audiences.

In addition to targeting our diagrams to the audience, we also need to target diagrams based on the best way to represent the pattern. When it comes to visual representations, there is no one-size-fits-all solution. For instance, with UML we see that there are many diagrams, each with a specific purpose. Is our goal to convey information about the structure of the pattern? Are we looking to provide details on the behavior of the pattern? As we answer these questions, we can continue to dive deeper into specific types of diagrams that highlight some important aspect of the pattern.

There are a number of approaches that we can take to model pattern definitions and pattern instantiations. Samples of these approaches are provided in the Communicate Design with Patterns guideline.

Related Patterns and Guidelines

Communicate Design with Patterns (Chapter 16), Document Pattern*

Summary

The focus of pattern packaging is taking the steps necessary to make the pattern as easy to find, install, use, and update as possible. We need to ensure that we are reducing or eliminating as many hurdles as possible for those who wish to reuse the pattern. Old habits and culture tend to guide people toward reinventing solutions rather than reusing existing solutions. We need to remove as many excuses as possible for not working with these reusable assets. We need to support the pattern as a reusable asset. We might create the world's best and most important pattern, but it has no value if we don't support its consumption by others; it may as well have never been created. This is part of the discipline of PBE; we need to follow through and go beyond just creating a technical solution.

We also need to recognize that a pattern does not exist unto itself; it's related to other artifacts. Patterns do not exist in isolation; they are related to requirements, other patterns, DSLs, profiles, and model templates. As part of the effort to support reuse, we need to be aware of these relationships and make the user community aware of them.

All in all, we need to ensure that we are making it as simple as possible for Pattern Users to find, access, and install the patterns. The challenge that should be left for users is figuring out how to apply the solution in their situation. Anything that distracts from that focus is a shortfall in our efforts in building and providing the pattern.

Chapter 15

Using Domain-Specific Languages with Patterns

Domain-specific languages (DSLs) and patterns can each boost productivity, simplify how we represent solutions, and support the use of automation. With such capabilities they can improve the quality of solutions, reduce time to market, and help us to leverage skills within the organization. Fortunately, DSLs and patterns are complementary topics. There is a synergy between them that allows us to further boost productivity, quality, and how we leverage expertise beyond what can be achieved by using them in isolation. This chapter will look at patterns and guidelines that support DSLs and patterns.

In addition to looking at how we can best use patterns and DSLs together, we will also look at guidelines to use in designing and creating DSLs.

Patterns

The following patterns provide guidance on how we can use model templates to support the consumption of DSLs and how patterns and DSLs can be used together.

DSL Model Template

Context

A DSL has been created and we want others to succeed in working with the DSL.

Problem

From a user perspective, when modeling with a DSL it is unclear how to get started. Starting with a blank screen can be intimidating and disorienting. How should models be structured? What diagrams should be created? What language elements should be used together?

Forces

- Often a model can be structured in multiple valid ways. Some users might think that the template provides the only valid approach.

- Model templates need to be updated as the language and best practices evolve.

- By default, nothing realigns the model with the template. So if deviation from the template occurs, the model may need to be realigned manually.

Solution

For many, it can be quite intimidating to start a project with a blank screen. What do I need to create? Where should it be put? How do the elements relate to one another? Even in cases where we have provided the user with patterns to be used within the model, it can be confusing and intimidating to try to figure out where those patterns should be used.

To assist in creating models based on a DSL, provide a model template. A model template provides a default structure with which to get started using the elements provided by the DSL. This includes guidance on the packages to use and what goes in the packages, as well as guidance on elements that are used together, default diagrams, viewpoints/perspectives, and documentation.

A model template should be created as the DSL starts to solidify, and it can be used to test out the DSL. Some questions to ask in building the template include these:

- What are the different diagrams that the language supports?

- What are the relationships between the diagrams?

- Are there timing considerations in regard to when each of the diagrams should be created?

- Of the available language elements, which are the most common? Which are the least common?

- What are the expected user roles that will need to work in creating models using the language? What are the expected user roles that will need information from the model? How do the needs of these roles align? Differ?

- How will models feed into other work products? Are there associated model-to-model or model-to-text pattern implementations that the models will need to work with? Do they have requirements for how input models need to be structured?

- Are there patterns that should be used within the models? What diagrams do they relate to? Are there any timing or ordering issues related to the use of patterns and the DSL elements?

Example

When working with Rational Software Architect (RSA) to create SOA-based solutions, you can use the Software Services Profile[1] to create models of your solution. The DSL contains the elements shown in Figure 15.1. As expected, when working within the SOA domain, we see model elements such as Service, ServiceProvider, ServiceConsumer, Message, and other domain-specific terms.

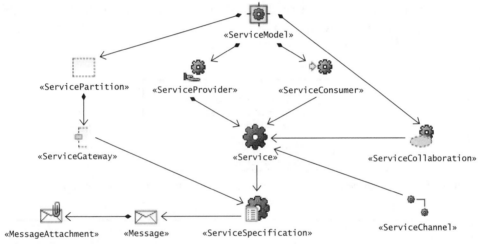

Figure 15.1 *Graphical view of the Software Services Profile*

However, for the user it can be confusing to figure out when and where to use these elements. How should you structure the model? Are there recurring ways in which the elements should be used together? Are there different viewpoints/perspectives that should be supported? Looking at the elements and basic relationships is a difficult way to figure out answers to these questions. Documentation and tutorials offer some assistance, but they require us to remember the details rather than guiding us toward a solution.

Figures 15.2, 15.3, and 15.4 are views of a template providing guidance on how the model should be structured, covering the following:

---

1. Johnston (2005).

- **Perspectives.** As shown in Figure 15.2, there are three suggested perspectives to use: Collaboration, Message, and Service, marked with the «perspective» keyword.

- **Grouping elements.** As shown in Figure 15.3, the template, via a set of Reusable Design Elements, provides guidance to the user regarding how elements should be used together. For instance, there is a set of elements that come together to create a «serviceProvider». The set will change depending on whether it is a complex service, a legacy provider, or just a simple provider.

- **Naming guidance.** Figures 15.3 and 15.4 show how the template provides a set of parameterized names for the different types of model elements and diagrams. The idea is that the user of the template can copy and paste elements from this package and use them elsewhere in the model. Each of the reusable elements has a parameterized name indicated with ${} characters. Typically the name is composed of a static portion and a dynamic portion, enabling the user to create a meaningful name that follows convention.

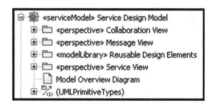

Figure 15.2 *An overview of a model template for use with modeling SOA solutions*

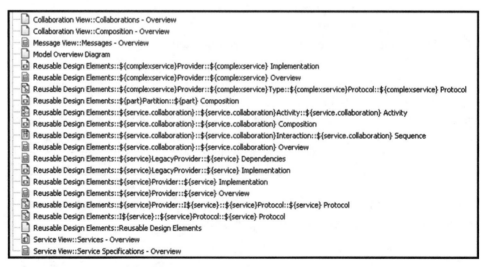

Figure 15.3 *A view of the diagrams provided by the SOA model template*

Figure 15.4 *A view of the structural elements provided by the SOA model template*

Related Patterns and Guidelines

Integrated Patterns and DSLs*

Integrated Patterns and DSLs

Context

When building a software solution, we need to simplify the development effort with the goals of boosting productivity, increasing quality, and improving governance of the effort. The members of the team have varying skill levels and areas of expertise in both the business and technical domains.

Problem

How can we provide the team with an environment that assists them in building solutions specific to the domain? More specifically, how can we raise the level of abstraction and have the team focus on the problems to be solved while preventing them from getting lost in the details of the development languages? And how can they do so in a way that leverages proven best practices?

Forces

- Languages that are specific to a domain, as the name suggests, are specific to a certain situation. This limits the transferability of skills because the domain is narrower. With a narrower domain we find that there is less availability of training, documentation, support, and skilled people. In contrast, a generic language and associated tooling are easily transferable and widely supported (tooling, education, books, etc.).

- Time is needed to find exemplars and best practices before patterns can be created for use with the DSL.

- Tooling to support the language needs to be created. The amount of investment will vary depending on the capabilities of the underlying platform and the complexity of the domain.

Solution

Use a DSL—a language that captures information for a specific problem domain— and patterns in combination so that we can work at a level closer to the solution space, while also leveraging best practices in the form of patterns. Such a language can be graphical or textual. The key point is that it is targeted to a specific area and is not meant to be used generally across a range of problem spaces. This is in contrast to a general-purpose language, which is used to solve problems across many domains.

As discussed with regard to the Simple Solution Space pattern (Chapter 10), we aim to boost productivity and improve quality and governance by simplifying the working environment. One way to accomplish this simplification is to get closer to the problem space by focusing on the domain. The domain could be related to technology or business, but typically we are trying to solve the problems of the business, and it benefits us to be able to think in those terms. This allows us to more easily discuss the solution with our business counterparts, confirm requirements, and build a solution that meets their needs.

As shown in Figure 15.5, there is an overlapping relationship between a domain, a DSL, and patterns. The DSL is entirely contained within the domain, whereas patterns partially overlap. Patterns provide us with support in the domain but also assist us as we make the transition from a domain into other domains such as a technology-specifc representation.

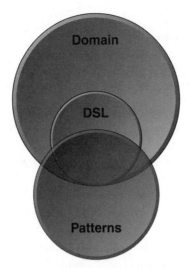

Figure 15.5 *Abstract view of the relationship between a domain, patterns, and a DSL*

When we look at general-purpose tools, we find that they present a number of challenges. That a general-purpose tool can apply to any situation is both its greatest strength and greatest weakness. Having general-purpose tools allows us to find many resources that can help us solve problems. Support for general-purpose tooling is widely available via training and documentation, and it is relatively easy to find skilled practitioners. However, generality is also a weakness, because the tooling is not targeted at any specific situation. We need to understand how to map between general concepts and the needs and demands of our problem space. So now not only do we need to figure out the solution, but we also need to figure out how to map between concepts in the problem space and the generic concepts we have available in our tooling.

As seen in Figure 15.6, there are a number of ways in which DSLs and patterns support and work with one another. Let's take a more detailed look at each of the interconnections:

- **Guide model structure.** Regardless of the language that we use in creating a model, our goals are always the same. We want to leverage best practices in capturing a representation of the solution. We can use patterns and DSLs to help us achieve these goals. The DSL narrows the solution space and can also provide rules, constraints, and validations to help specify the solution. An associated model template can provide guidance on how to create the model. However, we can take things even further by using patterns. One or more patterns can be used within a model to guide us in constructing portions of the model.

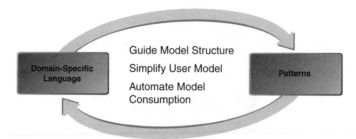

Figure 15.6 *Patterns and DSLs leverage and support one another.*

- **Simplify user model.** A user model provides input into a pattern. However, we want to make the use of the pattern, and in turn the creation of the user model, as simple as possible. To do so, we can use a DSL that provides us with a narrow solution space, a set of constraints and rules, and support for validating the correctness of the user model. In combination, these elements make it easier for a Pattern User to create a correct user model.

- **Automate model consumption.** Ideally, a model should be used for communication, design, and generation. A DSL alone can certainly address the first two aspects: communication and design. However, pattern implementations play a key role in assisting us in working with a DSL and generating aspects of our solution. When we look at generating output from a model, we find that we can generate a higher percentage of the solution when we narrow the domain space. As we narrow that space, we are able to make more assumptions and leverage rules and constraints to help us in mapping elements from a modeling representation to output elements.

In summary, use patterns and DSLs in combination. Together they enable us to boost productivity and improve quality and governance by guiding us in structuring our models, simplifying the creation of user models, and automating model consumption. And although DSLs and patterns can be used in isolation, higher value is achieved by using them together.

Example

In Chapter 5 we see the Oslec team create the Subsystem Façade profile to be used with the Subsystem Façade pattern. They use a name specific to the pattern, as for now the goal is to use the DSL specifically with this pattern. If, at a later time, they determine that there is wider applicability for the DSL, they can consider a new name or enhancements as needed.

Related Patterns and Guidelines

Pattern Implementation (Chapter 12), Simple Solution Space (Chapter 10)

Guidelines

These guidelines focus on advice for how to design and create DSLs.

Create a DSL

Summary

How do we take a design as input and create a DSL? Typically we build an implementation of the DSL using either a specialized language creation framework or a general-purpose language that has extension capabilities.

Introduction

We have determined that a DSL is needed because generic modeling languages do not meet the needs of our situation. We've already invested time in creating a design for the DSL. How do we use that design to create a DSL? Considerations to keep in mind include these:

- As the underlying platform evolves, we will likely have to update the DSL and its supporting elements.

- As the target domain changes, we will likely have to update the DSL and its supporting elements.

Explanation

By formalizing the language, in terms of specification as well as implementation, we support our PBE efforts. By putting the DSL into tooling, we further automate our design efforts and provide users with familiar domain terms and concepts in their design environment. Automation of model consumption is not possible with an informal language.

To create the DSL in tooling we use a framework to help build the implementation. We either use a specialized language creation framework or a general-purpose language that has extension capabilities.

We have a number of choices in building tooling support for DSLs. To keep things simple, we'll look at two examples, one from a specialized language creation framework and another from a general-purpose language that has extension capabilities. When working with Eclipse, the Eclipse Modeling Framework (EMF) fills the role of language creation framework, and UML fills the role of a general-purpose language that has extension capabilities.

UML is a general-purpose modeling language and can be used to model any type of software solution. However, because it is general-purpose, we end up using constructs and language elements that are generic; they are not specialized for any specific domain. Even as a general-purpose language, though, its supporting specification is lengthy. To be targeted and specific to many domains, the language would be unwieldy and no one would be able to use it. To address this issue, the creators of the language supplied it with an extension mechanism, known as Profiles, which allows the language to be customized and made specific to a domain.

EMF is an interesting language in that its domain is related to creating other languages. With respect to Eclipse-based tools, the UML2 API is actually built using EMF.

When looking at these two options, there are a number of considerations to keep in mind:

- **Freedom versus reuse.** When choosing between UML and EMF, we need to weigh the trade-offs between how much freedom is provided by the framework and how much preexisting content and support we can reuse. If we choose freedom, via EMF, we will essentially be starting from scratch. If we choose reuse, via UML, we become constrained in our implementation. With UML we also have to take time to simplify the user experience. Ideally, our tooling is able to hide diagrams and model elements that are not relevant to our domain.

- **Simplicity.** When using UML, the extension mechanism is simple and much of the work can be done without writing any code. In addition, many preexisting facilities are available to work with UML-based languages and support merging, creating subunits, and team model use. EMF is a more involved effort and takes longer to implement.

- **User education.** UML is a widely known and supported language. If we build our DSL using UML, we are able to leverage this supporting infrastructure and draw upon a large pool of talent that is already familiar with the base of our DSL. In the case of an EMF-based language, we have fewer constraints in our implementation; however, the more we deviate from standard languages, the less likely we are to find individuals who have relevant experience.

Related Patterns and Guidelines

Design a DSL*, Integrated Patterns and DSLs*, Simple Solution Space (Chapter 10)

Design a DSL

Summary

How do we design a consumable and high-quality DSL? When building a DSL, we need to use a meet-in-the-middle approach that accounts for language scope, granularity, semantic completeness, user friendliness, and tool friendliness.

Introduction

We have determined that a DSL is needed because generic modeling languages do not meet our needs. How do we design a consumable and high-quality DSL? Keep in mind:

- We must understand the other assets that we have available, or could have available, to help us in creating a useful and productive work environment. These could include, but are not limited to, patterns, model templates, UI customization, documentation, and wizards.

- We should use both high- and low-fidelity approaches to representing the solutions we are creating. Low-fidelity approaches can be used to quickly and inexpensively determine whether solutions will work with the expected consumers of the resulting deliverables.

Explanation

When designing a consumable and high-quality DSL, some key considerations to keep in mind include the following:

- Is the language easy to understand?

- Is it complete?

- Does it avoid redundancies?

- Does it avoid asking the user to provide information that could be calculated?

- Does the language limit the number of elements that are used?

- Do the language and associated modeling environment guide the user to successful use of the language?

To design a DSL that meets such requirements we need to consider the right aspects and use the right approaches. First let's take a look at some of the aspects that we need to consider:

- **Scope.** As we look at the elements that form the basis of our language, we want to ensure that the language has the right scope. We don't want too many elements, but only those elements that are truly needed for our practitioners to successfully use the DSL.

- **Granularity.** We want to ensure not only that we have a full vocabulary, but also that the elements have the correct granularity. Are we putting the correct level of detail in the model and its elements, and then using assumptions, rules, and configuration options to capture other details as appropriate?

- **Semantic completeness.** Do the language elements selected allow us to describe solutions in the problem space? Are all the elements in the language useful and purposeful? Do all of the arrangements and uses of elements make sense?

- **User friendliness.** The language needs to be user-friendly. Those who work with the solution need to be able to understand and work with the language.

- **Tool friendliness.** We also need to look at how we can implement the language in tooling. As we look at the design, are there aspects of the language that would be difficult to implement in tooling? Are there ways in which we could alter the design to make it easier to put into tooling? Are there aspects of the tooling that we can leverage to help simplify the use of the language? For instance, can the tooling platform assist in creating palettes? Hide unnecessary views, diagrams, and elements, especially those not related to the DSL?

- **Implementation considerations.** As part of the design we also need to consider how the design will be realized in an implementation. The tooling and language that we use to realize the design will have an impact on the choices that we make as part of the design. Two common approaches to building the DSL are to use a specialized language creation framework (for example, EMF) or a general-purpose language that has extension capabilities (for example, UML).

With these aspects in mind, let's take a look at the approaches we can use to design a DSL:

- **Meet in the middle.** Use a meet-in-the-middle approach that combines aspects of top-down and bottom-up design.

  From a top-down point of view, we are looking at things from the perspective of the domain and the end user. What is the vocabulary of the domain? What are the key concepts? How do they relate? What skills do the users of the language possess? Do rules and best practices exist in the domain? Some details may be captured in documentation, but others may exist only as tribal knowledge. We can also look at other languages for ideas about what is needed in our new language. In particular, what elements and diagrams exist in other languages?

From a bottom-up point of view, we are looking at things from the perspective of how we are going to consume the language and use it to generate other aspects of the solution. Are there patterns that need the DSL support? What do the patterns expect for their input models? How does this reconcile with the details that are emerging from the top-down perspective? We end up with a balancing act where we need to be aware of the elements at the lower level of abstraction, but we also don't want to overly influence the language in the DSL, which is supposed to be at a higher level of abstraction.

- **Balance.** We need to balance these characteristics. We can't have a language that is focused on user friendliness to the exclusion of being tool-friendly. We cannot have a solution that focuses on scope to the exclusion of granularity and semantic completeness.

- **Sketching.** Do not rush into implementation and use of tooling in the design of the language. As we begin our design efforts, we can take advantage of simple tools such as pen and paper or whiteboards to sketch out the language. What are the elements within the language? What properties are associated with the elements? What are the relationships between the elements? Once we feel that we have a good start in describing the language, we can begin to create draft storyboards for some of the use cases associated with the domain we are attempting to model. How well does the language help us to describe the solution? We may also want to include experts from the domain in these sessions to help us in both the design and use of the language.

- **Storyboards.** Work with users and discuss different scenarios where the language will be used. Then use storyboards to detail the solution using the language. Will the language allow us to describe solutions? Are our users able to create storyboards successfully with the current design? What feedback do they have? How can we incorporate this feedback into our design?

- **Model.** Create a model to visualize the language elements, their properties, and their relationships. This can help to further refine the language and also serve to communicate details of the language to those implementing aspects of the tooling and related patterns.

- **Review existing languages.** Last, but not least, we can take time to look at other existing languages, whether it's UML or an existing DSL. As we examine the existing artifact, we can give thought to how that language serves the needs of its audience.

Related Patterns and Guidelines

Create a DSL*, Integrated Patterns and DSLs*, Simple Solution Space (Chapter 10)

Meaningful Icons in a DSL

Summary

How do we make the DSL more intuitive, user-friendly, and easy to work with? Use meaningful and easy-to-understand icons to provide visual cues to those using the DSL.

Introduction

We have determined that a DSL is needed because generic modeling languages do not meet the needs of our situation. We've already invested time in creating a design for the DSL and are working on the implementation of the DSL.

It can be difficult to understand what certain aspects of a DSL are intended to mean. For example, generic lines, boxes, and shapes do not convey enough information and guidance to the user of the language. We want to ensure that communication with the DSL is as straightforward as possible. What can we do to make the DSL easier to work with? Considerations to keep in mind include these:

- We need to be able to produce or procure a set of icons that are meaningful within the domain.

- Graphical representations can be open to multiple interpretations. Consultation with the expected user base is essential to ensure that they interpret the icons as anticipated.

Explanation

We should use meaningful and easy-to-understand icons to provide visual cues to those using the DSL. Just using a generic box leaves the user guessing and leads to misinterpretation. With training, the user will learn the meaning of such elements, but the burden of remembering the meaning is on the user.

Instead, we work to use useful and meaningful icons within the DSL for each of the graphical elements within the language. The icons should be related to the domain and clearly communicate the meaning of the language element.

As shown in Figure 15.7, when working with RSA to create SOA-based solutions, we can use the Software Services Profile. In contrast, Figure 15.8[2] provides an overview of the language using just lines and boxes. The lack of meaningful icons makes the language much less intuitive.

Related Patterns and Guidelines

Create a DSL*, Design a DSL*

---

2. Ibid.

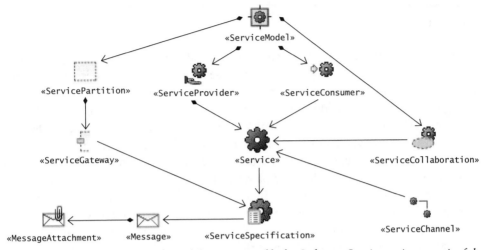

Figure 15.7 *Graphical overview of the UML Profile for Software Services using meaningful icons*

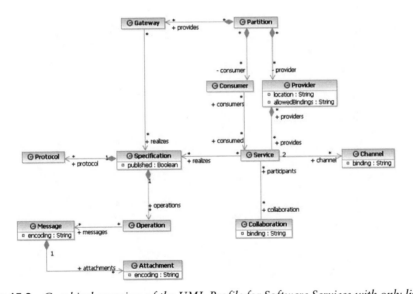

Figure 15.8 *Graphical overview of the UML Profile for Software Services with only lines and boxes*

Copyright IBM developerWorks, www.ibm.com/developerworks. Reused with permission.

Summary

Using DSLs and patterns together allows us to boost productivity, quality, and how we leverage expertise beyond what can be achieved by using them in isolation. However, it is not as simple as just saying, "Use DSLs and patterns." We need to give thought to how they should be used together and how we can design and implement a quality DSL, one that works well with patterns. In addition, we can look at how to drive consumability via the use of model templates and meaningful icons.

In Chapter 1 we discussed the importance of creativity and the freedom to be creative. As we create a set of DSLs and patterns that work together, we are indeed placing constraints on how the team will build the solution. However, we have not eliminated creativity or the freedom to create. Rather, we have moved the target to channel creativity into areas of higher value. We need to be creative in figuring out the DSLs and patterns that will be used to deliver a solution.

Chapter 16

Consuming Patterns

In earlier chapters we've looked at supporting pattern consumption via the creation of the right patterns, designing and creating patterns according to best practices, packaging patterns to support reuse, and improving consumability with the use of DSLs. As important as it is to build the right patterns in the right ways, value disappears if we fail to follow through and use these important assets. We now need to look at things from the Pattern User's perspective. This chapter discusses a set of guidelines supporting how an organization can succeed in consuming patterns.

As Pattern Users, we look at how we leverage pattern specifications and pattern implementations to improve the way we build software solutions. We need to understand how to decide which patterns to use. Also, having the wrong focus or too narrow a focus when picking patterns may lead us into situations where we will later have to come back and redo the effort, as other patterns and aspects of the solution could impact and invalidate the work that has already been done. Last, but not least, we need to keep in mind that there are a number of ways in which we can use patterns, some of which are summarized in Figure 16.1.[1]

Guidelines

The following guidelines provide advice on how we can find the right number of patterns to use in a solution, the many ways we can use patterns, and how to select the patterns that we use.

---

1. Based on information in Schneider and Lexvold (2008).

	Summary	Pattern(s) as Input	Pattern(s) as Output
Visualize	Represent pattern occurrences visually	✔	
Detect	Discover occurrences of known patterns	✔	
Refactor	Refactor artifacts to match a pattern	✔	
Apply	Impose a known pattern on artifacts	✔	
Harvest	Mine and codify new patterns from occurrences		✔
Create	Create new patterns or compound patterns		✔

Figure 16.1 *Some of the ways in which we can use patterns*

Communicate Design with Patterns

Summary

How do we communicate key aspects of a design to others? In addition to using patterns to improve our design, we also use patterns as a means to describe that design.

Introduction

When working in a team environment, we need a way to communicate the design of the solution to others on the team. How do we describe and communicate key aspects of a design to others, and in a way that minimizes the amount of effort while still being clear? Considerations to keep in mind include these:

- We need to recognize that creating a software solution is rarely, if ever, an individual accomplishment. We work with many others in designing, implementing, and maintaining the solution. Enabling others to comprehend the solution is paramount to the team's success.

- We need to see beyond the individual details that constitute a solution.

- We need to recognize that the team comprises many roles and that each of these roles has different information requirements.

Explanation

Patterns can be used as a means to communicate a design in addition to improving a design. This allows us to simplify the solution vocabulary. We can focus on the patterns rather than all of the details that go into the solution.

If we accept that we can use patterns to communicate the design, we then need to think about what needs to be captured. How do we model the patterns that are used? How do we ensure that we are providing sufficient detail while avoiding being too low-level and overwhelming? What about patterns that exist across models? What about pattern instances?

When modeling, we focus on what information we are trying to capture and how we will use that information. This applies to modeling software solutions in general and can also be applied to how we model patterns. If we start with the information we are trying to capture, the modeling of patterns falls into two different cases: modeling pattern definitions and modeling pattern instantiations. We can relate this back to the idea of a class and an object within object-oriented analysis and design. The pattern definition is similar to the concept of a class, and a pattern instantiation is similar to the concept of an object.

In the case of a pattern definition, we are focused on clearly explaining to others what the pattern is, how it works, points of variability (also called roles), structure, behavior, and other aspects. However, a pattern definition is not connected, or bound, to any specific solution. In the case of a pattern instantiation, our focus is on how a specific pattern is used within a solution. More specifically, how is that pattern bound to the solution? What are the elements from the solution that are bound to the roles provided by the pattern? We want to detail each instance of the pattern that is bound to elements and has been applied within our solution. We do not need to communicate all of the details related to the pattern, but only those that best help us to understand how the pattern is being used in the solution; our focus is on the interaction between the solution and a specific instance of the pattern. If we require more details on the specifics of the pattern itself, we can always refer to the pattern definition.

In documenting pattern definitions and pattern instantiations, we can vary the amount of detail that we include in diagrams. The level of detail is highly dependent on the intent of the modeling. For example, if the model will be used as a sketch, we don't need as much detail as if we plan to generate code from the model.

In the following sections we'll look at how we can model pattern definitions and pattern instantiations. We'll start with modeling pattern instantiations because it is a little simpler to see the pattern from more of a black-box perspective. We are not concerned with all of the details related to the pattern, just those aspects needed to connect the pattern into the solution. We use UML, but we could also use any visual modeling technique that allows us to create similar constructs.

Modeling Pattern Instantiations

> **Note**
>
> In modeling pattern instantiations our approach and level of detail will vary depending on the platform and pattern implementations that are used. In some cases our pattern implementations will create a pattern instantiation and we won't have to spend time on modeling the details. In other cases we will want a pattern implementation to consume a pattern instantiation. In such cases the level of detail recorded for the instantiation will depend on the "intelligence" of the consuming pattern implementation. Some pattern implementations are able to succeed with a minimal amount of detail provided as input.

Starting with a simplified approach, pattern instantiations can be represented as collaborations with directed associations pointing to the elements fulfilling the parameters of the pattern. An example of a pattern instantiation is shown in Figure 16.2.

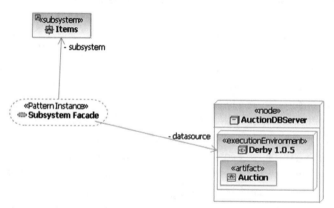

Figure 16.2   *Model of a simplified pattern instantiation*

More specifically, Figure 16.2 shows an instantiation of the Subsystem Façade pattern. The figure shows that the pattern has two parameters. The first one, subsystem, is fulfilled by the Items subsystem; the second one, datasource, is fulfilled by the Auction database. This is very much a black-box view, as the pattern consumer is shown only the pattern and those elements that are bound to the pattern. The pattern definition, which isn't shown, describes how the parameters relate to each other as well as the details

of the pattern. This is a more informal approach to modeling the pattern instantiation. A simple code generator would be unable to do much with this pattern instantiation.
A pattern implementation that understands the stereotypes may be able to interpret
the elements and successfully work with the representation.

If we want to use pattern instantiations with a simple code generator, just showing
the pattern occurrence is not sufficient. Instead, we need to more formally instantiate
the pattern, creating or modifying the participant elements. The code generator is
then able to act upon the pattern instantiation without needing to understand the
pattern. To that end, we create diagrams in our model that contain more detailed pattern instantiations. As an example, Figure 16.3 shows a more detailed pattern instantiation for the Item entity. Although we keep the diagram simple by focusing on just
this one entity, there's still a lot of detail.

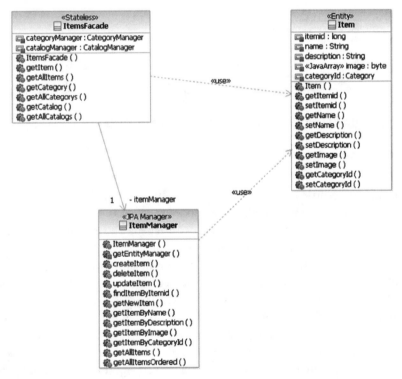

Figure 16.3 *Subsystem Façade participants for the* Item *entity*

We can also create higher-level, summary diagrams to list the patterns that are
used and the relationships between these instances. This may be as simple as pulling

together the elements (for example, collaborations) that have been stereotyped as «Pattern Instance» and putting them into a perspective. Figure 16.4 shows a set of pattern occurrences within a single diagram. We can store them in multiple diagrams as needed to manage a large set of patterns or to communicate with different audiences. The perspective can include diagrams that show the patterns used and those that interact with one another. We can use abstraction as appropriate to hide and show details related to the pattern to highlight how they are used within the solution.

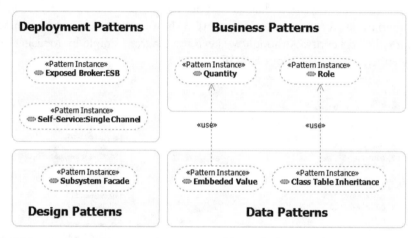

Figure 16.4   *A view of the pattern instances used in a solution*

Things become a little more complex as we begin working across levels of abstraction. To date, tools have provided little support in terms of creating and supporting diagrams that detail the use of patterns across levels of abstraction. For many tools, we are able to see configuration files that provide details on the use of patterns in this situation. These configuration files denote the input and output models as well as points of variability that allow us to further customize how the pattern will be applied. However, we cannot let tool deficiencies deter us from effectively modeling our solutions. A simple addition to our efforts is to create a high-level diagram that illustrates the use of the pattern along with the input and output models that are bound to the pattern. We can add such diagrams to the source model, the target model, or else a separate model that is focused on keeping track of such information. As an example, Figure 16.5 shows that an instance of the Subsystem Façade pattern implementation uses the User subsystem package as input and generates two Java projects, UserManagement and UserManagementTest.

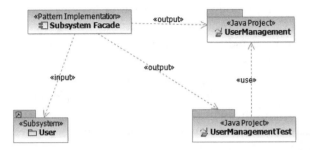

Figure 16.5   *Modeling pattern instantiations that operate across levels of abstraction*

Modeling Pattern Definitions

> **Note**
>
> Modeling pattern definitions using the approaches discussed here is useful as we look to communicate or think through a design. However, if we wish to support automation, the pattern needs to be defined via the use of a pattern implementation.

Modeling pattern definitions is similar to modeling pattern instantiations in many ways. For example, we can adjust the level of detail depending on the purposes of the diagrams and models. To that end, Figure 16.6 provides a view that shows the participating classes for the Subsystem Façade pattern defined in the case study.

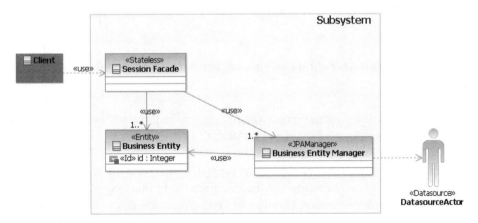

Figure 16.6   *Subsystem Façade pattern participant classes*

Modeling pattern definitions is the way that we document the details of the pattern in a visual manner. We are able to communicate the key elements of the pattern, their roles, relationships, and how they can be bound to elements from the problem/solution space. We can use these models/diagrams of pattern definitions to further describe pattern specifications or pattern implementations. Regardless of whether the pattern definition is documenting a specification or an implementation, it is harmless in regard to the overall model and how other artifacts (model- or code-based) are generated. A pattern definition supports blueprints and documentation only, not the generation of artifacts.

We can use a composite structure diagram to precisely model how the different participants interact, particularly when modeling a compound pattern (Chapter 12). Figure 16.7 illustrates one view of such a diagram. In this case we are providing an external view that only relates the pattern to the elements that can be bound.

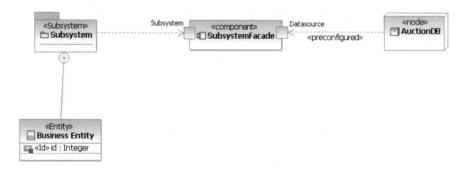

Figure 16.7   *External view of the composite structure representation of the Subsystem Façade pattern*

In contrast, Figure 16.8 shows another approach where we expose the internals of the pattern:

- External ports are used to represent the pattern parameters. Subsystem Façade has two parameters: Subsystem and Datasource.

- Boxes inside the structure diagram represent the patterns that are brought together to define the Subsystem Façade pattern. In this case we have encapsulated two patterns: Session Façade and Data Access Object.

- Session Façade and Data Access Object have ports to represent the parameters that they accept. However, these ports are internal and not visible to the Pattern User. Input is mapped to these internal ports by the Subsystem Façade.

- The ownedEntities connector between Subsystem and BusinessObject represents the set of Entities within a subsystem. To be considered a valid Entity, a class needs to have the Entity stereotype applied to it.

- The Session Façade pattern has two parameters: Facade and BusinessObject. The BusinessObject parameter is bound to information provided by the Pattern User via the Subsystem parameter. The Facade parameter is bound to an element created internally by the Subsystem Façade pattern.

- The multiplicity [1..*] after the BusinessObject parameter indicates that for each Session Façade we can have one or more Business Objects.

- The Data Access Object pattern has two parameters: BusinessObject and Datasource. Datasource is provided by the user of Subsystem Façade. BusinessObject is driven by the set of Business Objects provided to the Session Façade pattern.

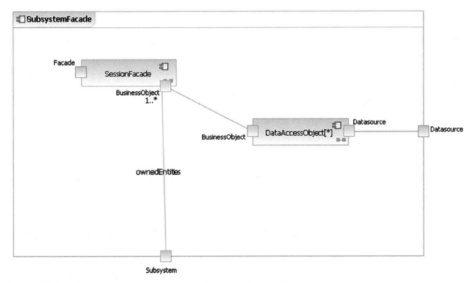

Figure 16.8 *Composite structure providing an internal view of a compound pattern*

Related Patterns and Guidelines

Document Pattern (Chapter 14), Use Pattern Definitions to Understand Existing Solutions*

Design Solutions with Patterns

Summary

How can we improve the delivery and the quality of applications while leveraging best practices? A key and traditional approach is to use patterns in designing the solution.

Introduction

How can we improve the delivery and the quality of our applications and ensure that the team is adhering to the organization's best practices? Using patterns to design the solution is a key, traditional approach. Some considerations to keep in mind are these:

- The team needs to understand patterns in general and how they can be used in creating solutions.

- We need to be comfortable with the concepts of abstraction, best practices, and simplification.

- We need to understand when and how we should use pattern specifications versus pattern implementations.

Explanation

Much as we use subsystems, components, and mechanisms in designing our solution, we should include patterns in our toolkit of design constructs. Using patterns in our design can assist us in many ways, such as these:

- **Improving the design.** Patterns provide us with a set of proven approaches that we can use in our design.

- **Communicating the design.** Patterns provide us with a vocabulary that can be used in describing the solution to others.

- **Generating a solution.** Pattern implementations and code generators can interpret pattern instances in our design and generate portions of the solution.

- **Accelerating the design effort.** Using patterns, we are able to avoid rework, reduce defects, and reduce the amount of time taken to find the right solution.

- **Leveraging skills.** As our patterns codify the best practices of the organization, others can benefit from this investment.

As we design a solution, we consider the problem and the context in which it exists and use that information as a guide to selecting patterns. We use patterns throughout our efforts in designing the solution, within and across multiple levels of abstraction. We also use a number of different types of patterns, such as architectural patterns, design patterns, and idioms.

From a cultural point of view, we need to ensure that the team is aware of the patterns that are available and that there is an expectation that they will use patterns in their work. If we do not stress the importance of patterns in design, we risk that they will be ignored or used in a nonstrategic manner. Last, but not least, as we design with patterns, we can use both pattern specifications and pattern implementations.

Chapter 4 of the case study provides examples of building a deployment architecture using patterns as well as data and business design with patterns. Chapter 7 shows how to design a component using the Subsystem Façade pattern.

Related Patterns and Guidelines

Communicate Design with Patterns*, Compound Pattern (Chapter 12), Pattern Opportunity (Chapter 11)

Pattern Density

Summary

How many patterns should be used in creating a solution? Manage the density of patterns that are used within a solution as a means to using the correct number of patterns.

Introduction

When creating a solution, we want to use patterns where and as often as it makes sense. However, how can we determine how many patterns should be used? Here are some considerations to keep in mind:

- We need to consider whether we have used patterns effectively across the scope of the entire solution.

- As in art, music, or even cooking, our completed solution needs to be more than the sum of its parts.

Explanation

Manage the density of patterns that are used within a solution. The goal of following this guideline is to ensure that we are using neither too many patterns nor too few.

"Analysis of 'good' software architecture tends to reveal a high density of tightly integrated patterns."[2]

Keep in mind that it is not as simple as counting the number of patterns that are used. As we attempt to determine the density, we need to remember that there are factors beyond just the total count. We need to look at the category of the pattern, the impact of the pattern within its scope, and the importance of the pattern to the overall solution. For instance, is a solution that uses 36 instances of the Singleton pattern better than a solution that uses only the Layers pattern? Probably not; the Layers pattern is an architectural pattern and has an impact across the solution, whereas each of the Singleton pattern instances has a very narrow scope.

In addition to scope, we are looking for "a high density of tightly integrated patterns."[3] As Alexander adds:

> It is possible to make buildings by stringing together patterns in a rather loose way. A building made like this, is an assembly of patterns. It is not dense. It is not profound. But it is also possible to put patterns together in such a way that many patterns overlap in the same physical space: the building is very dense; it has many meanings captured in a small space; and through this density, it becomes profound.[4]

So in addition to the total number of patterns, we are also interested in whether they are tightly integrated—how we use the patterns in combination. When we look at using patterns in combination, we need to consider that there are a number of different ways in which patterns can be combined. Some possibilities include these:

- Shared input parameters can connect patterns.

- The output of one pattern can serve as the input to another pattern.

- We can have compound patterns.

Although we can make our solutions more profound and elegant with a density of patterns within, we should be careful not to put patterns in the solution and build up density just for the sake of doing so. "However, achieving higher pattern density is not simply a matter of arbitrarily throwing together as many patterns as possible in as few classes as possible . . ."[5] As discussed throughout this book, we need to be systematic and disciplined, ensuring that the patterns we use are valuable to the solution.

When designing the solution, we need to be conscious of which areas within the solution use patterns and which do not, and how pattern density varies across the

---

2. Buschmann et al. (2007).

3. Ibid.

4. Alexander (1977).

5. Buschmann et al. (2007).

solution. A specific area may not use any patterns at all for a variety of reasons, some of which could be these:

- The person who created the solution might not be aware of any patterns that apply. This may be a result of failing to search, a search that is unsuccessful, or an inability to connect the problem with a pattern that would provide a solution.

- It is a new domain or technology, and no patterns have yet been identified.

- The solution is sufficiently saturated with patterns, and we want to highlight a specific area of the solution as being unique.

The final item listed is interesting in that there are times and places where we will not want to use patterns. As with most architecture and design decisions, there is some gray area when deciding whether to use patterns. Generally it is a good idea to use them. However, not using patterns can be a way to highlight an aspect of the system that requires special attention or that is unique to the project. As the architects/designers we need to find the right balance.

This can be related to jazz music, where a musician uses silence to emphasize part of the composition and to contrast the other non-silent parts of the performance:

> Silence isn't just the canvas upon which music is painted. It's one of the colors on the composer's palette. What sets jazz apart from other music forms is that each musician (through improvisation) is also a composer and needs to know how to use silence effectively. I've often thought that a master class should be taught on the role of silence in music because measures of silence are not waiting periods. These are times of active listening, much like a good conversation.
>
> Technique in jazz is paramount, and utilizing silence is part of technique. Knowing when to play notes and fill a void or when to lay back is just as important as playing the right notes. Utilizing silence for very brief (less than a few beats) or for longer periods (measure after measure) creates an impact on the listener. It can add emphasis to what other instruments are playing because the notes stand out more. When one band member pulls back from playing, the passages played by the others move forward in the listener's ears.[6]

We should be aware of the cases where patterns are not used and the reasons why. Just as important as finding and detailing where patterns are used, we should take time to look at the system in places where patterns are not used. Silence is telling us something; we need to be aware of the silence and then interpret it. Imagine a solution that has no patterns, or one that has no silence—both are likely to have major issues.

---

6. Neftzger, T. (2005). "The role of silence in music: All about jazz." February. www.allaboutjazz .com/php/article.php?id=16481.

Related Patterns and Guidelines

Design Solutions with Patterns*, Pattern Selection Driven by Requirements*, Select Large-Scope Patterns First*

Pattern Selection Driven by Requirements

Summary

How do we determine which patterns should be selected and used on a project? Use a combination of functional and nonfunctional requirements as a guide in selecting the patterns to use.

Introduction

Is there a way to determine what patterns should be chosen to use in a project? Here are some considerations to keep in mind:

- As project requirements change, we need to recognize that this will have an impact on the selected patterns.

- Asset repositories can be helpful in connecting patterns and requirements.

- Pattern forces and considerations can be used to help evaluate the requirement quality. Do not see the pattern selection process as a one-way street. The guidance and expertise codified in the pattern can be used to help us gather better requirements.

Explanation

Use the project requirements, including functional and nonfunctional requirements, to guide pattern selection. We need to ensure that the selected patterns add value to our project and to the overall business, that we are using the right patterns in the right spots. The selected patterns should align with the requirements of the project, ensuring that we deliver the solution that the business needs.

A positive aspect to such a focus is that it helps drive us to our patterns based on what we actually need the system to do. We avoid getting lost in the details of the system and using patterns just for the sake of using patterns.

An asset repository is a key mechanism that comes into play here. The team needs to be aware of where to look for patterns and understand how to search that repository. In addition, when we populate the repository, we need to attach proper metadata and classifications to the patterns so that they are found when searches are performed based on requirements. This is a critical link; without such a mapping, how can we move from requirements to patterns?

Not only do we consume patterns, but we want to support future pattern consumption. As we use patterns, we will find out more about situations in which the pattern applies, which requirements the pattern maps to, which patterns are related, and the contexts in which the pattern can be used. We need to provide this information to others who will use the patterns as well as to those who build and maintain the patterns. This helps others to find patterns and also leads to higher-quality patterns.

In Chapter 4 of the case study the Oslec team follows this guideline to identify the IBM e-business deployment patterns that fit the application's functional and nonfunctional requirements.

Related Patterns and Guidelines

Determine Business Impact (Chapter 11), Domain-Driven Patterns (Chapter 10), Pattern Search (Chapter 10), Use an Asset Repository*

Refactor with Patterns

Summary

How do we improve an existing solution to align with best practices? Refactor the solution using patterns as the means and end point for the updated solution.

Introduction

A solution, or part of one, has already been built. However, the solution is not quite right; the quality of the implementation needs to be improved without changing the functional aspect of the solution. How do we improve the solution to align with best practices? Some considerations to keep in mind are these:

- We need to understand the patterns that are available within the organization. Some we will know and remember from previous experience; in other cases we need to be able to quickly search and access documentation that explains the pattern.

- We are taking the time and effort to locate code and aspects of the solution that are not quite right. This could be through code inspections and testing or via the use of automated quality measurements.

- We need to ensure that we are able to test our solution and the elements within before, during, and after refactoring.

- Our tooling and process must support an iterative and incremental approach that allows us to adjust and update the solution.

Explanation

Recall that refactoring is "a change made to the internal structure of software to make it easier to understand and cheaper to modify without changing its observable behavior."[7] From a black-box perspective we have a solution that works (or seems to), but when we take a white-box perspective, we find that the quality and actual implementation of the solution are not sufficient. The solution may have bugs or perhaps it's just too difficult to understand and maintain. We want to improve the quality of how the solution is built, without changing the outside view of it.

Refactoring is typically the way that such work is done; however, how do we know what the new and improved solution should look like? Just saying that we need to modify and improve the solution leaves quite a few possibilities. If we ask the same team or individual to redo the work, it's likely that we won't like the new solution either. So how do we provide further input into the refactoring effort and improve our chance of success?

Patterns can and should play a key role in our refactoring efforts. One approach is to refactor the existing solution using patterns as an end point for the updated solution. "There is a natural relation between patterns and refactorings. Patterns are where we want to be; refactorings are ways to get there from somewhere else."[8] A second approach is to use patterns not as the end point but as input to reach a new end point. The resulting end point incorporates the use of one or more patterns but in its result does not resemble just a single pattern.

Keep in mind that by using patterns proactively, we can produce better solutions in the first place and reduce the amount of refactoring that needs to be done.

Related Patterns and Guidelines

Antipatterns (Chapter 11), Compound Pattern (Chapter 12), Design Solutions with Patterns*

Select Large-Scope Patterns First

Summary

When it appears that it is possible that many patterns could be used in a solution, where should pattern selection start? Start with the largest-scope patterns and then use smaller-scope patterns to embellish the details.

---

7. Fowler (1999).

8. Ibid.

Introduction

The organization has a set of patterns collected from multiple sources. The patterns vary in terms of their purpose, scope, and level of abstraction. It appears that many patterns could and should be used in a solution. Where should pattern selection start? For instance, worrying about selecting a pattern such as Singleton early in a project makes little sense as it has limited scope and impact. Also, as we progress through the project, it may turn out that we don't even need to use that pattern. How do we avoid focusing on patterns that have a limited impact on the project? Keep in mind the following:

- We need to understand the purpose, scope, and level of abstraction of the patterns.

- We need to understand the relationships that exist between the patterns.

- Asset repositories and pattern documentation can assist us in understanding the patterns and their characteristics.

Explanation

Start with the largest-scope patterns and then embellish the details with smaller-scope patterns. If we do identify some smaller-scope patterns first, we briefly note them and where we think they fit. However, we don't get carried away in figuring out all the details about using them until we are sure that we have the larger-scope patterns in place. The larger-scope patterns will have a significant impact on the solution and will in part determine which smaller-scope patterns we select.

This approach aligns with how we manage our project and the design of the overall solution: looking at the larger subsystems, higher-risk items, and those items that are more architecturally significant. The same approach applies as we work with patterns. Small-scope, limited-impact patterns usually have little to no architectural significance. We first want to find architecturally significant patterns and then select additional patterns.

Focusing on the larger-scale patterns first will help us find and pick the smaller-scale patterns. Once we have selected some larger-scope patterns, we have constrained the solution space in which we can pick other patterns. This is a process that will repeat itself as we go from a larger scope to a narrower and narrower one.

A good place to start is to look at the architectural style that we are using for the application that we are creating. An architectural style includes a set of guiding principles along with a set of architectural patterns. Selecting the architectural style sets us on a path where we are looking at using the architectural patterns associated with the style. Once we have settled on our architectural patterns, we can start to look at patterns that will work with and embellish the solution.

The size, scope, and relationships of the patterns cannot be overlooked as we work with them. As Alexander states in *A Pattern Language*:

> In short, no pattern is an isolated entity. Each pattern can exist in the world, only to the extent that it is supported by other patterns; the larger patterns in which it is embedded, the patterns of the same size that surround it, and the smaller patterns which are embedded in it.[9]

We need to have a proper repository, including classifications and documentation for our patterns. Patterns need to be easy to find, and we need to be able to search on appropriate criteria. In this case we want to understand the relationships among the patterns.

In general, we can look at the levels associated with pattern categories, such as architectural patterns, design patterns, and idioms.[10] Each of these types of patterns has a specific scope and level of abstraction at which they apply. Selection of an architectural pattern will guide and restrict the design patterns that we use. In turn, the selection of a design pattern will guide and restrict the idioms that we use.

As a specific example, we can examine the IBM Patterns for e-Business.[11] As shown in Figure 16.9,[12] when working through this catalog of patterns via its website, we are guided through the patterns from business scope, to application, down to runtime. Changing the business focus leads to a different set of patterns being selected.

Related Patterns and Guidelines

Design Solutions with Patterns*, Pattern Selection Driven by Requirements*, Use an Asset Repository*

---

9. Alexander (1977).

10. Additional details regarding pattern categories are found in Appendix A

11. Koushik et al. (2001).

12. Ibid.

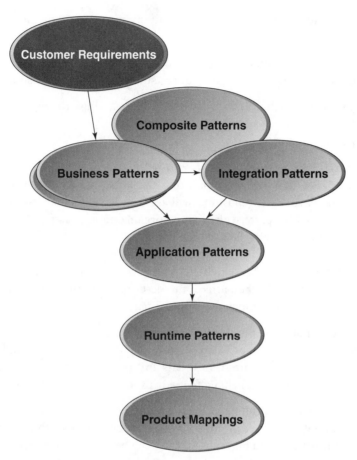

Figure 16.9 *View of the pattern categories within the IBM Patterns for e-Business*
Copyright IBM developerWorks, www.ibm.com/developerworks. Reused with permission.

Use an Asset Repository

Summary

How do we quickly and easily find the patterns that are available for reuse within the organization? Use an asset repository to manage the patterns, as we would any other reusable asset.

Introduction

With a set of patterns available for reuse within the organization, how do we easily and quickly find the patterns we need? Considerations to keep in mind include these:

- Investment in acquiring, installing, maintaining, and using the repository is needed.

- The repository is valuable only if used by the team. They must deploy, search for, and then access the patterns that are stored within the repository.

- We must give thought to how we will configure and use the repository.

Explanation

Like any other reusable asset, patterns can be managed in an asset repository. We want to make sure that we are supporting the reuse of our patterns; their value derives from reuse. An asset repository will assist us in finding, accessing, discussing, and managing the use of patterns within the organization. Let's take a more in-depth look at how we interact with the asset repository:

- **Search for patterns.** We search for patterns based on a number of aspects, including the name of the pattern, the description of the pattern, and even the requirements that are associated with the pattern.

- **Find related patterns.** Because we use patterns in combination and recognize that there are relationships between patterns, it's not enough to find just single, isolated patterns. The pattern metadata in the repository provides us with this relationship information, helping to guide us in selecting the right patterns to use.

- **Review feedback and ratings provided by other users.** Patterns are about benefiting from the experience of others. We can extend this idea to the way we interact with the patterns and the repository. We can benefit from the experience of those who created the pattern, as well as those who have already used it. In this way we can gain further understanding of pattern usability, quality, and flexibility.

- **Allow us to leave feedback and ratings.** The pattern is living, so our input and feedback help to ensure that the pattern continues to evolve and improve as necessary.

- **Support the organization's governance efforts.** Using patterns only from the asset repository will help ensure that we are using patterns that have gone through the organization's review process.

Asset repositories are typically user-friendly and provide a number of interfaces through which to access assets, including web and development tool integrations. The other benefit of working with the repository is that we support the organization's need to find details regarding reuse metrics. Which patterns are most often found in searches? Which are most often downloaded and used? Which patterns have the highest ratings? Which have the most complaints? Which patterns were used within which projects?

Chapter 7 describes an example of the usage of this guideline as Rajesh's team searches for the Subsystem Façade pattern implementation in the Oslec asset repository.

Related Patterns and Guidelines

Pattern Packaging (Chapter 14), Pattern Search (Chapter 10), Update Existing Patterns (Chapter 11)

Use Pattern Definitions to Understand Existing Solutions

Introduction

How do we quickly gain an understanding of an existing solution? Is it well built? Has it stayed true to the design? Using a set of known pattern definitions, search the solution for occurrences of the patterns.

Summary

There are multiple projects under way within the organization, at varying stages of completion. Some of the solutions have been built without following a PBE approach. Some patterns may have been used, but not in a systematic and disciplined way. In many cases, when we gain access to an existing software solution, we find that we struggle to comprehend it. The documentation is poor or nonexistent, and it is unclear what the major design elements are within the solution. How do we understand the solution and determine if it is well built and true to the design? Here are some considerations to keep in mind:

- An organization requires a set of meaningful patterns. Having access to a limited and generic set of patterns will reduce the effectiveness of applying this guideline.

- Despite best intentions, documentation for a system usually leaves much to be desired.

Explanation

Using a set of known pattern definitions, search the solution for occurrences of the patterns. In this way we can use the pattern definitions to quickly gain an understanding of the solution. Using the patterns as a higher-level abstraction of the solution elements allows us to more productively analyze and understand the solution.

Looking at the solution without having the pattern definitions can be frustrating, as it is difficult to ascertain how elements are related, their purpose, and how they work. It can also be overwhelming, as there are many elements within the solution; it can be difficult to see the forest for the trees.

Such an effort can also be performed manually with the use of pattern specifications, but this method generally takes more time. When performing the work manually, it is a good idea to document the results, preferably visually. This provides a record of pattern use for any others who later need to learn, work with, and possibly support the solution.

The search method for patterns that are used should also support the use and recognition of antipatterns. Not only do we want to see what has been done well in creating the solution; we want to see what has been done according to worst practices. By using both patterns and antipatterns in analyzing the solution, we gain an understanding of the solution's strengths and weaknesses.

The Architectural Discovery feature in Rational Software Architect is an example of automated pattern instance detection. This feature enables a user to take a set of predefined patterns, custom patterns, and antipatterns as input in determining where and how patterns are used in the solution. The System for Pattern Query and Recognition[13] (SPQR) is another example of automated detection of pattern instances from source code.

Related Patterns and Guidelines

Antipatterns (Chapter 11), Communicate Design with Patterns*, Refactor with Patterns*

Use Patterns to Find Patterns

Summary

How do we find new patterns in existing solutions? Using a collection of known pattern definitions, analyze solutions to find occurrences of new patterns.

Introduction

The team has created or partially created one or more solutions. The organization also has acquired a catalog of pattern definitions, from multiple sources (internal, vendor, and/or community). How do we find new patterns in existing solutions? Considerations to keep in mind include these:

---

13. For an overview of SPQR you can read Smith and Stotts (2003). See also www.cs.unc.edu/~smithja/SPQR.html.

- As the collection of patterns grows and becomes more specific to the needs of the organization, we will become more adept at finding valuable patterns.

- We need to see patterns as key architectural elements of our solutions.

Explanation

Using the collection of known pattern definitions, analyze the existing solutions to find occurrences of new patterns. At first this might seem a little counterintuitive; how can existing patterns help us to find new patterns?

The first thing that we can do, keeping in mind that patterns are used in combination, is to look for new compound patterns. We can use existing pattern definitions to examine existing solutions, looking for recurring cases where already known patterns are used together. Rather than always trying to remember how this set of patterns fits together, we can create a compound pattern.

We can also extend this scenario and consider cases where not only is there a recurring set of patterns, but there are also additional nonclassified elements participating. So not only have we found patterns that work together; we've possibly found a new pattern that joins with the set of known patterns.

We can also examine the pattern density within the solution and identify areas where not many existing patterns have been used. Are there some elements in that area of the solution that are used repeatedly and consistently? So rather than analyzing the entire solution, we are able to reduce the scope of the search space and more productively look for new patterns.

Related Patterns and Guidelines

Compound Pattern (Chapter 12), Pattern Density*

Summary

Consuming patterns is an important aspect of PBE. What is the value of producing patterns if no one is reusing them?

We need to be able to find the patterns that fit and work within our context. The requirements specified by those who will use the solution are a driving force in this effort. The requirements direct us toward patterns, which in turn steer us toward additional patterns. The scope and impact of patterns motivate us to use them throughout and across the solution.

The guidelines in this chapter illustrate a number of ways in which we can use patterns: design, communication, refactoring, pattern identification, and as a way to understand existing solutions. As we calculate the ROI of the patterns we have within the organization, we need to look at the many ways in which we can use patterns.

Part III

Additional Topics

This part of the book covers a set of additional topics to further our understanding of PBE. We start by taking a deeper look at some of the PBE benefits (Chapter 17). We then discuss some of the economic considerations of PBE (Chapter 18) and finish by looking at some of the PBE misconceptions (Chapter 19) that may need to be overcome as we adopt and roll out PBE.

Chapter 17

Benefits of PBE

This chapter discusses the benefits of adopting PBE and its Core Values, Patterns, Guidelines, and Practice. We will also touch upon some of the associated PBE Patterns and Guidelines that can help achieve those benefits. Details for the Patterns and Guidelines were provided in Part II, starting in Chapter 9.

The following sections discuss the benefits of PBE according to the area that they impact, starting with the benefits commonly associated with patterns and automation, namely, productivity, quality, and communication. Later sections look at the benefits of PBE with respect to leveraging skills and expertise and improved governance.

Keep in mind that these benefits do not exist in isolation. They can impact and reinforce one another and lead to an upward spiral of success. For example, productivity enhancements from using and applying the patterns can free up time for other efforts. The team can focus on the specifics of the domain and unique aspects of the problem they are working on while leveraging patterns from already solved problems. This leads to more interest in the project—more creative and interesting solutions, better quality, and yet higher productivity.

Increased Productivity

In this section we'll look at how the adoption of PBE increases productivity and enables us to develop and deliver software solutions more quickly and efficiently.

Reuse

A good place to start discussing increased productivity is the concept of reuse. Why would we want to repeat work and effort that's already been done?

Patterns and Reuse

Patterns allow us to codify our best practices and to reuse them (manually or via automation) on different applications. We are able to invest once in the creation of the pattern and then use that solution many times over; we avoid effort associated with reinventing the solution. In addition, with patterns we look to reuse the design, allowing us to apply the best practice many times over while tailoring the solution to our context. Design reuse allows us to work at a higher level of abstraction, providing a further boost to productivity.[1] PBE Patterns and Guidelines that assist us in supporting patterns and reuse include Limited Points of Variability (Chapter 12), Pattern Implementation (Chapter 12), Pattern Implementation Extensibility (Chapter 12), and Pattern Specification (Chapter 13).

Timing of Reuse

Historically, reusable assets were often created at the end of a project. The goal was to then use those assets on future projects. This practice led to criticism that the benefits of reuse are always seen on the next project. It's like investing for the future, the first project "paying the price" of the reuse. However, we are able to create and use patterns within the same project, and so the productivity benefits of using a pattern specification or a pattern implementation can be achieved in the same project in which the pattern was created.

Consider a project that involves persisting business entities using Hibernate. We could develop the Hibernate-related elements for the business entities that are within the scope of the current iteration. Alternatively, we could write a Hibernate persistence pattern specification or, even better, develop the related pattern implementation, so all the other developers who have to persist a business entity would apply our pattern. Note that we are not trying to build out for some potential but unknown reuse. When we create the pattern, we know how many times it will be used and where. The pattern approach would definitely be a huge timesaver if there were a large number of entities to persist on our project. And as the architects, we spend significantly less time answering the same questions over and over again, such as "How should I persist my business entity?" or "How do we implement a Hibernate-based solution?" Such a scenario does, however, place an onus on the developers within the organization to be familiar with PBE Patterns and Guidelines such as Communicate Design with Patterns (Chapter 16), End-to-End Pattern Use (Chapter 10), Pattern Opportunity (Chapter 11), Pattern Search (Chapter 10), and Single Pattern–Varied Use Cases (Chapter 10).

---

1. For a more detailed discussion about the benefits of design reuse over code reuse, please see Biggerstaff and Richter (1987).

Systematic, Disciplined, and Quantifiable Nature of PBE

An important part of PBE is to be systematic, disciplined, and quantifiable. As we plan our projects, we analyze the possibilities and potential for patterns. Once a list of candidate patterns has been identified, we review and evaluate each of the patterns to determine and ensure that an appropriate ROI can be achieved. We recognize that we have limited resources, time, and expertise; we need to invest these resources in the areas where they make sense for the organization. Over time, we will identify many more patterns than those that will actually be acquired or built; however, we build only those that make sense based on our analysis. Productivity can be negatively impacted if we lack discipline and build any and every pattern that is possible. And as we move forward in consuming and working with our patterns, we capture metrics related to the impact of the patterns. We can leverage PBE Patterns such as Determine Business Impact (Chapter 11), Pattern Opportunity (Chapter 11), and Pattern Selection Driven by Requirements (Chapter 16) to help us focus on achieving success with patterns and reuse.

Patterns in Combination

We can boost productivity by using patterns in combination. This can be accomplished by recognizing and leveraging pattern categories, or through the creation and use of compound patterns.

Pattern Categories

A pattern captures the best available solution to a given problem in a specific context. This applies whether we are looking at a pattern with as small a scope as the Singleton[2] pattern or a larger-scale pattern that impacts the architecture of an application, like the Broker[3] pattern. In itself each of these examples provides a productivity boost, but we certainly expect the Broker pattern to more significantly impact the application than the Singleton pattern. Some of the common pattern categories, as seen in Figure 17.1, reflect the different levels of scope, impact, and abstraction that patterns support. Larger-scale patterns, such as an architectural pattern, have a greater impact on the project, as they directly drive a greater proportion of the overall solution.

We can leverage pattern categories systematically so that we consider and select our larger-scale patterns in advance of those of smaller scope. Such an approach

---

2. Gamma et al. (1995).

3. Buschmann et al. (1996).

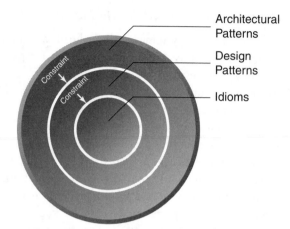

Architectural
Patterns

Design
Patterns

Idioms

Figure 17.1 *Leverage patterns systematically, selecting large-scope patterns first, followed by patterns successively addressing smaller scope.*

improves our productivity because the selection of larger-scale patterns will influence and constrain our choice of smaller-scale patterns. In contrast, not following any approach and selecting an assortment of patterns in an ad hoc fashion could lead to pattern mismatches, rework, and a longer path to a solution.

Compound Patterns

The true productivity multiplier comes not only from the use of larger-scope patterns but also from the use of compound patterns. Recall that in a compound pattern we encapsulate a number of patterns that work together inside a larger pattern. A synergy is provided by the patterns working together within the compound. In addition, Pattern Users are able to more easily and quickly use the combined set of patterns. Patterns such as Compound Pattern (Chapter 12), Pattern Selection Driven by Requirements (Chapter 16), and Select Large-Scope Patterns First (Chapter 16) help ensure that we are systematic and following best practices in regard to pattern scope and pattern compositions.

Pattern Implementations

Using automation in the form of pattern implementations can significantly boost productivity. It is not necessary for each member of the team to internalize a pattern specification and then apply it (ideally, consistently with how the rest of the team will use it); a pattern implementation reduces the amount of knowledge needed to successfully apply the pattern. And the pattern implementation will apply the pattern consistently for each user in the organization.

This could become even more critical in the context of compound patterns. The pattern implementation is able to use encapsulation to hide the details (as necessary and desired) of the patterns within the compound pattern. Thus, the user of the pattern need only be concerned with the exposed, simplified interface of the compound pattern.

Last, but certainly not least, a pattern can be both applied and reapplied much faster with automation than manually. A pattern implementation can generate hundreds of elements in seconds, all according to best practice. Performing the same work manually is time-consuming and likely to lead to the introduction of errors. PBE Patterns such as Compound Pattern (Chapter 12), Model-to-Model Pattern Implementation (Chapter 12), Model-to-Text Pattern Implementation (Chapter 13), Pattern Implementation (Chapter 12), and Simple Solution Space (Chapter 10) help guide us in creating effective pattern implementations.

Increased Quality

By definition, a pattern represents a proven best-practice solution to a recurring problem. Given that, by getting our team to adopt and use patterns, we will end up with higher-quality solutions. Such higher-quality solutions are easier to understand, support, and test. In cases where we can create a pattern implementation, we can take this even further and aim to eliminate human error with an automated application of the pattern. Automation will apply the pattern exactly the same way it did in all previous instantiations (except allowing for the pattern's points of variability). If we discover an issue with a pattern implementation, reapplication is much quicker than manually updating multiple applications of a pattern specification.

Consistency is another facet of quality; the greater the consistency in the system, the easier it is to understand and maintain. In the case of patterns, we are not just consistently applying any solution; we are consistently applying the best practices codified by the pattern.

These benefits can be realized only if the use of the pattern is systematic and disciplined. Consistency will not be realized if only a small number of people in the company are using the patterns. The PBE Practice helps in tackling the adoption issue by defining the roles, tasks, and work products associated with PBE, and it does so in a format that can be integrated with other process components. Additional support for quality is provided via PBE Patterns and Guidelines, including Design Solutions with Patterns (Chapter 16), Integrated Patterns and DSLs (Chapter 15), Pattern Testing (Chapter 13), Refactor with Patterns (Chapter 16), and Use Pattern Definitions to Understand Existing Solutions (Chapter 16).

Beauty of Software Architecture

Another more fundamental and subtle aspect of quality that we want to impact is referred to as the "beauty of software" or the "beauty of (software) architecture." To explain it, let's take a quick detour through the civil engineering domain. We have all probably experienced the feeling of beauty of architecture while looking at a building, a cathedral, or a bridge. Christopher Alexander[4] explains this feeling by referring to the perception of the "quality without a name." For him the beauty of architecture is more a mix of color and form, fitness to purpose as well as fitness to the environment, elegance, and simplicity—the little something that makes the building "alive." It's close to what mathematics teachers used to call the beauty of a demonstration: simple, clear, fit to the purpose.

According to Grady Booch[5] and others, this same definition of beauty can be applied to software systems and their architecture. Patterns, particularly patterns used in combination, are an important factor contributing to that beauty. Their organization as a cohesive set makes the overall system glow and live; or, as Christopher Alexander writes, "The more living patterns there are in a thing—a room, a building, or a town—the more it comes to life as an entirety, the more it glows, the more it has this self-maintaining fire, which is the quality without a name."[6]

When creating software solutions, we strive toward results that are fit to their purpose and environment, that have a sense of simplicity and elegance. Patterns, whether in civil architecture or software, increase our odds of attaining these goals. PBE Patterns and Guidelines such as Compound Pattern (Chapter 12), Pattern Density (Chapter 16), and Pattern Implementation (Chapter 12) help us to work toward beauty in software architecture.

Improved Communication

We have seen in the previous sections that patterns positively impact productivity and quality because they codify, and, in the case of pattern implementations, automate, best practices. Patterns can be seen as an abstraction of the design as they can summarize a complex set of design and architecture elements and interactions. In the context of communication, we leverage the capability of patterns to provide useful abstractions and a simple and meaningful vocabulary for working with those

---

4. Alexander (1979).

5. Booch (2007).

6. Alexander (1979).

abstractions. Tens of pages of description can be replaced with the names of two or three patterns, considerably reducing the size of the solution documentation. This reduces the volume of the information that needs to be exchanged, while still maintaining its integrity and comprehensibility, improving the communication between the project members as well as with stakeholders.

A benefit of using pattern specifications is that they document design decisions in a clear and well-defined format, making these decisions easier to communicate. The pattern specification describes the problem, context, and the corresponding solution. Someone reading the pattern specification can easily understand the design decisions and the rationale behind those decisions. This improves communication among project members both during and after the project.

This last aspect, documentation of the application at the end of the project, is growing in importance as more and more systems are getting older and the people who developed them are retiring. A quote from Galileo comes to mind: "All truths are easy to understand once they are discovered; the point is to discover them." When we are given an existing application to learn and support, it can be difficult to learn its intricacies. The code describes *what* the application really is, but not *why* it is what it is; it is therefore difficult (sometimes impossible) to answer questions such as "What are the design decisions that led to the actual architecture and design?" The challenge is to discover the truths behind the system; once discovered, they are usually easy to understand.

Modeling is a good way to capture design information, but we often find it challenging to keep the model and code synchronized. In those situations it's always the code that wins out. In some cases we find that if we'd like to see the model maintained, we need to keep the modeling simple and to a minimum. The bigger and more complex the model, the more likely it is that it will quickly get out of sync. Patterns can help summarize some of these design and architecture decisions, reducing the amount of model elements to maintain. In addition, as tooling continues to advance, we will see additional support for patterns to be understood by the platform. Thus we will be able to examine existing code bases and have our tools recognize and record instances of pattern instantiations.

Using well-known patterns (public or internal) also simplifies design and architecture discussions. Rather than spending time drawing a complex diagram or describing details of the element design, referring to a pattern helps each project participant understand the related design or architecture. This fact highlights another characteristic of patterns: they need to be publicized. To obtain this kind of benefit, we need to make our patterns known and easily accessible so that designers and architects can familiarize themselves with them and use them in their discussions as easily as we use metaphors in our day-to-day life.

A number of PBE Patterns and Guidelines can be used to achieve improved communication, including Communicate Design with Patterns (Chapter 16), Embedded Pattern Implementation Guidance (Chapter 14), Integrated Patterns and DSLs (Chapter 15), Simple Solution Space (Chapter 10), and Use an Asset Repository (Chapter 16).

Better Leveraging of Skills and Expertise

The benefits we have considered so far are commonly associated with patterns usage, with the exception perhaps of the notion of beauty of architecture. The next benefit, leveraging of skills and expertise, although an important benefit, is often overlooked.

When looking at the current configuration of our software delivery organizations, we can relate them to the effort and support needed to build a human pyramid. When the pyramid is only 10 feet high, probably four or five people would be enough to build it. However, looking at Figure 17.2, we see that when building a pyramid that reaches 20 to 30 feet, we start to face some significant challenges in terms of the huge number of people needed to support the pyramid.

Figure 17.2   *A mass of support is needed to reach the goal of the team.*
Photo by Alex Castella. Reused under the Creative Commons license.

Similarly, in today's software delivery organizations, in order to help the business reach new heights we need a large number of experts. However, that is one of the key resources that most teams and organizations lack. Experts are usually shared among projects, often generating contention and sometimes even bottlenecks. As a result, we struggle to find our way to successful project results. We certainly have tried a number of approaches to help us along, such as better tools and better documentation and communication. However, we still manage to come up short because of the lack of availability of these critical resources. What we really need to do is find ways to invert the pyramid, as shown in Figure 17.3, and have a small number of experts at the bottom who in turn are able to support a large number of other members of the organization (business and IT alike).

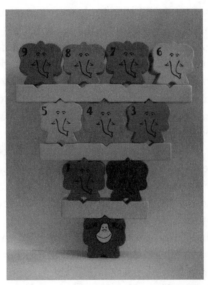

Figure 17.3 *With patterns we invert the pyramid in order to better leverage available expertise.*

Patterns help by enabling experts to codify their experiences and solutions in a manner that is easy to consume and leverage by others. Pattern Users need to know only how to use the pattern, not all of the details that went into its creation. They also get to bypass all of the trial and error that went into determining the best-practice solution. So, even though we have a small set of experts, the rest of the team is able to more efficiently leverage them and their knowledge by using patterns to solve common problems while calling upon the experts to help with new or more complex problems.

We also need to consider cases where a number of patterns are composed together; it may turn out that Pattern Users are not even aware that some of the patterns (and solutions) exist, never mind that they can be used together. In contrast, the expert can better determine that a composition of patterns is indeed the solution. An expert can fast-forward the effort in using these patterns by packaging them all together as a compound pattern. PBE Patterns and Guidelines that help us to better leverage expertise include Compound Pattern (Chapter 12), Integrated Patterns and DSLs (Chapter 15), Package Related Patterns Together (Chapter 14), Pattern Creation Lifecycle (Chapter 12), Pattern Implementation (Chapter 12), and Simple Solution Space (Chapter 10).

Improved Governance

Earlier in this chapter we considered a simple example of using a Hibernate-based solution for implementing object-relational mapping for a solution. In that case the architect chose this mechanism and the best-practice approach for using the mechanism.

When building a solution, how do we ensure that it is built according to design and that the selected patterns, best practices, frameworks, and standards are used? In addition, once such constructs are used, how do we ensure that the instantiations stay true to their original specification? For instance, if a pattern implementation is used to generate some portion of the solution, how do we ensure that the generated content is not changed? How do we prevent "undesirable creativity"? Clearly, we want our teams to be creative, but we also want them to channel those creative energies into the appropriate areas of the solution.

Pattern implementations can help by automating the initial application of best practices. However, as noted previously, this doesn't solve all the problems we run into. The variability points provided by a pattern help in that they allow us to customize the solution that is generated, so that the solution fits our context. We can take things a step further by having "user-modifiable" regions that specify where in a generated solution the Pattern User can augment the solution.

There are two additional ways in which we can leverage automation. The first is through integration with an automated build system. Each time we build the application we can have the build system invoke the pattern implementation, ensuring that the generated portions stay true to the best practice. In such a situation all generated output is overwritten except for that which is located in "user-modifiable" regions. A second approach that we can use is automated pattern detection solutions, which verify that certain patterns are used in the solution and that the instantiations are true to form.

The use of PBE and an asset repository also help us govern our pattern catalog and guide investment in the right patterns, maintaining only the ones that are used, giving us more time to invest in discovering and codifying new patterns, and validating the patterns that are made available. PBE Patterns and Guidelines that support governance efforts include Antipatterns (Chapter 11), End-to-End Pattern Use (Chapter 10), Limited Points of Variability (Chapter 12), Pattern Implementation (Chapter 12), Update Existing Patterns (Chapter 11), and Use an Asset Repository (Chapter 16).

Support for Globally Distributed Development

Another dimension that increases the complexity of governing the software delivery effort is when we have a globally distributed team. Ensuring that all the members of a team are headed in the same (and correct) direction can be challenging enough when everyone is in the same building. Things become even more daunting if the team members are distributed throughout the world, across multiple time zones, and we're dealing with multiple cultures and languages.

All the benefits of PBE mentioned earlier in this chapter are also applicable to this kind of development, but the following benefits are specific to this situation:

- **Communication.** In some cases not every member of the team has a common first language. There can be challenges in communication, based on both understanding the language as well as cultural references. Patterns help to address these challenges by providing a common vocabulary that is documented according to well-known principles.

- **Automation.** Providing all team members with a relevant set of pattern implementations ensures that best practices are consistently applied by all the team members, wherever they are located. This will increase the cohesion and maintainability of the application.

- **Detection.** Using patterns as input into software analysis and detection tools can ensure that deliverables adhere to and leverage the correct set of patterns and best practices. This is particularly applicable when the application is architected in one location and then implemented elsewhere. Detection for pattern use and adherence can be integrated into an automated build process.

PBE Patterns and Guidelines that support globally distributed development include Communicate Design with Patterns (Chapter 16), Design Solutions with Patterns (Chapter 16), and Use Pattern Definitions to Understand Existing Solutions (Chapter 16).

Summary

In this chapter we looked at the benefits of adopting PBE, where we use both pattern specifications and pattern implementations in a systematic, disciplined, and quantifiable manner. We looked at some of the more obvious benefits, such as increased productivity, improved quality, and improved communication. These are benefits that are often mentioned in other literature that discusses patterns. However, this is not the full extent of the benefits that can be achieved through the use of patterns. Three additional benefits need to be considered as we seek to leverage patterns within our projects. These benefits include support for governance, support for globally distributed development, and increased leveraging of available expertise.

The chapter highlighted how some of the PBE Patterns and Guidelines can help us achieve the benefits associated with PBE. Full coverage of these patterns and guidelines begins in Chapter 9.

It is also important to note that PBE can provide us these benefits, whatever development process we are using. Chapter 8 describes how to adopt PBE into an organization and highlights the relationship of PBE to some well-known processes and process frameworks.

Chapter 18

Economic Considerations of PBE

So far we have been looking at PBE from a technical perspective, which is an important perspective for a technical book. But writing software is not only about technical information and discussions. The cliché "Build a better mousetrap and the world will beat a path to your door" is not entirely true. Patterns and PBE provide us with a great mousetrap, but we need to look at and understand the economic considerations of these approaches if we aim to be truly successful.

Key Economic Aspects of PBE

As we start this chapter, it's fair to ask, "Why should we look at the economics of patterns? Patterns are only a technical concern." As we work through this chapter, we will see that while patterns are part of the technical domain, they have an economic impact on projects and the companies that use them.

We begin examining the economic considerations of PBE with a definition of economics: "Economics is the study of the use of scarce resources which have alternative uses."[1] This definition is a nice fit as we look at the enterprise. We have limited time, skills, resources, and money, and often there are many alternatives available to us. We need to be able to understand the options available and the impact of our choices as we decide which alternatives to pursue. Knowing how PBE can impact the economics of a project, we will be better armed to get the most from pattern adoption and application.

---

1. Sowell, Thomas (2007). *Basic Economics: A Common Sense Guide to the Economy, Third Edition* (New York: Basic Books).

The economic considerations that we discuss are organized according to the following PBE aspects:

- **Pattern sources.** Where should the patterns that we use come from?

- **PBE adoption.** What needs to be considered when we adopt a PBE approach?

- **Pattern implementations.** What needs to be considered when creating pattern implementations?

- **PBE projects.** How does PBE impact our projects?

Each of these aspects will be discussed further in the following sections.

Pattern Sources

Many developers consider the *Design Patterns*[2] book to be *the* source of patterns available to use. The book provides a set of patterns that are well known, proven, and easy to follow. However, this set of patterns is just the tip of the iceberg. If we search the web or online booksellers, we find numerous books and articles describing the many patterns that are available. There are thousands of patterns that we can use within our projects. Having a large number of patterns available from a variety of sources is a good thing.

However, we should not be content knowing that there are a lot of patterns out there that we might be able to use. In order to fully benefit from PBE, both from a deliverable and an economic point of view, we need to focus on the sources of the patterns and establish that we are leveraging the correct sources and the correct patterns. To simplify our thinking about the sources of patterns, we can group them into three main types, as shown in Figure 18.1:

- **Vendor.** When building our own solutions, we typically use runtimes, languages, and code libraries provided by a set of vendors. Each vendor leverages experiences in building and supporting its products. Typically, a vendor makes a set of patterns available that codifies these experiences. As customers, we benefit from a vendor's expertise and experience with a wide-ranging set of projects. However, the patterns produced are still quite generic, as the vendor works to support a wide variety of customers. The goal of the vendor is to provide best practices to as wide an audience as possible.

---

2. Gamma et al. (1995).

Figure 18.1 *The three sources of patterns*

- **Community.** The community, whether an open-source community, a user group, or individuals, is another external source of patterns. The community comes together based on a shared interest and discusses successes, failures, and challenges; over time a set of patterns and best practices emerges. Usually the patterns that emerge from such a community, while useful, tend to be more general. The community realizes that there is a benefit in coming together to identify and codify best practices. However, there needs to be a level of generality in the patterns; otherwise they would not be applicable across the community. In addition, the community can include people who are from rival organizations. They benefit from sharing some knowledge, but they also have best practices that provide a competitive advantage and are kept private.

- **Our own organization.** Although we are using tools from vendors and the community, some aspects of the project and approach are unique to our organization. Over time, the organization (whether it is our team, our division, or the whole company) develops its own best practices and patterns. In many cases these represent key intellectual assets that provide the organization with a competitive advantage. The patterns developed by an organization can vary in terms of whether they are generic or very specific. If they are general, it can be beneficial to find ways to publish and share the results of the work; the community can then work with you to increase the quality and usefulness of the patterns.

Patterns that are specific to the organization and provide a competitive advantage usually are not disclosed to outside parties.

Selecting the right patterns from the right sources is one of the keys to increasing a project's ROI.

Pattern Selection Criteria

Regardless of the source of patterns, we cannot look at just the total quantity. A focus solely on quantity can lead us down a path where we believe that a large selection of patterns means that they've all been identified and we just need to pick the ones for our project. We need the right patterns for the work we are doing. So the question we need to ask is, how do we find the right pattern(s)? There are a number of attributes and characteristics that we should consider as we begin to select our patterns. As with other architectural discussions and decisions, there isn't a single right answer. We need to review the different considerations and determine which are most important. We can then use the selected criteria to help us decide on the patterns to select. Often we find that this is a balancing act—the importance of one criterion will impact the selection of another. Some of the pattern selection criteria to consider include these:

- **Maturity.** Is the pattern stable and mature enough that we can predict productivity and quality benefits? Have related antipatterns been identified?

- **Support.** Is there any support available to help deal with issues that could arise while using the pattern, especially with pattern implementations, or must we rely only on our own resources for assistance?

- **Education.** Are there educational resources available to assist in learning how to properly identify opportunities for using the pattern? Do the materials explain how to apply the pattern properly?

- **Cardinality.** Is the pattern part of a set? Or does it exist unto itself?

- **Relationships.** Have relationships with other patterns been identified and documented?

- **Category.** At what level is the pattern applicable? For example, is it an architectural pattern? Design pattern? Idiom?

- **Strategic impact.** How does the use of the pattern align with business goals? How important is the pattern to overall success?

- **Vendor dependence.** Is the pattern dependent on a specific vendor or is it vendor-independent?

- **Fit.** How closely does the pattern fit our context? If the pattern does not have 100% alignment, how much effort will it take to improve the fit? What is an acceptable level of fit?

- **Cost.** What is the cost to obtain and use the pattern? In addition to any acquisition costs, we should also assign a cost to the other criteria.

Table 18.1 examines the three main pattern sources, using some of the criteria just described, and lists some of the advantages and disadvantages of each. The goal is to help us define the mix of patterns from the different sources. Successful projects focus on finding the right mix; success is unlikely if we focus on only a single source.

Table 18.1   *Pattern Sources Comparison*

Pattern Source	Advantages	Disadvantages
Vendor	Reduces the cost of ownership of the vendor's product as using patterns abstracts some of the lower-level details.	Increases reliance on the vendor and possible vendor lock-in.
	Lowers the risk of adoption as the patterns have been proven.	Competitors have access to the same pool of best practices. How do we differentiate?
	Cost-effective, as the patterns are developed by the vendor and are usually included in the vendor's product at no extra cost.	Patterns are limited to the scope of the vendor's product and might not be specific to the details of a heterogeneous environment.
	New hires are more likely to be familiar with and have experience with the patterns. There is a larger pool of experienced hires to draw upon and less need to train new hires on the use of the patterns.	Patterns are likely narrower in scope and at a lower level. They are also usually more generic as they are intended for a wide audience.
	Documentation and support are provided by the vendor (likely to also include internationalization), so less expensive than having internal support.	Patterns are restricted to supported product scenarios and directions.
	Quality assurance is provided by the vendor as well as a collection of customers.	

(continues)

Table 18.1 *Pattern Sources Comparison (Continued)*

Pattern Source	Advantages	Disadvantages
Community	Not tied to a specific vendor. Prevents vendor lock-in.	May not be as reliable and precise as patterns provided by a vendor.
	Lowers the risk of adoption as the patterns have been proven and are widely accepted and validated by many people.	Competitors have access to the same pool of best practices. How do we differentiate?
	Cost-effective, as others contribute to the development of the patterns.	Patterns may not be specific to the details of an environment.
	New hires are likely to be familiar with and have experience with the patterns, so there is less need to train new hires on their use.	
	Documentation and support are provided by the community, so less expensive than having internal support.	Support is usually less "reliable" than vendor support, and the extent of the documentation depends on what the community provides.
	Patterns from the community are usually of broader scope than vendor ones.	Patterns are likely more generic as they are intended for a broader audience.
	Patterns developed internally can be taken to the community for validation and enhancement.	
Our organization	We are able to differentiate, as the intellectual capital captured in the pattern is unique to the organization.	It's difficult to ascertain that this is indeed a best practice.
	Team is focused on looking for and using patterns.	More costly as we have to develop and maintain it internally. Can be expensive and time-consuming to build. Is there an ROI for the asset?
	Not tied to a specific vendor. Prevents vendor lock-in.	If we are building a pattern implementation, we may find ourselves tied to a specific vendor's pattern platform technology.
	Documentation and support are adapted to the context, vocabulary, and practices of the organization.	More costly, as we need to internally build the documentation and provide support.
	May be more reliable and precise than patterns from external sources. We know our domain and goals better than any external source.	May not be as reliable and precise as patterns provided by a vendor, as a vendor has greater insight into product internals.
		New hires will need to be trained on patterns specific to our organization.

Pattern Source Recommendation

As shown in Table 18.1, each source has advantages and disadvantages. So as is the case with many other decisions, the source we select for our patterns will depend on the circumstances surrounding the decision. In general, the best advice regarding the correct source is "It depends." The selection criteria provided in previous sections should help us evaluate both the pattern and its source.

Depending on the project and even the stage of the project in the lifecycle, we will choose patterns from different sources. For example, architectural patterns are often abstract enough that we can receive positive benefits by taking them from the community. In contrast, when we get into the design of components, we would probably mix vendor patterns with our own patterns, or refine vendor patterns to adapt them to our specific context. A little more specific than "It depends" is a view that we should strike a balance among the three sources, leveraging community and vendor patterns as much as we can and developing patterns where it is necessary. As shown in Figure 18.2, successful PBE projects find that their patterns overlap the three sources; the degree of overlapping, as we might expect, "depends."

Figure 18.2   *Balancing sources in pattern selection*

PBE Adoption

When looking to adopt a PBE approach, we also need to give some thought to the resources required to adopt and implement it. As shown in Figure 18.3, to successfully adopt PBE we need to consider issues such as tooling, methodology enhancements, training, cultural changes, pattern acquisition costs, and time and effort associated with pattern development and support.

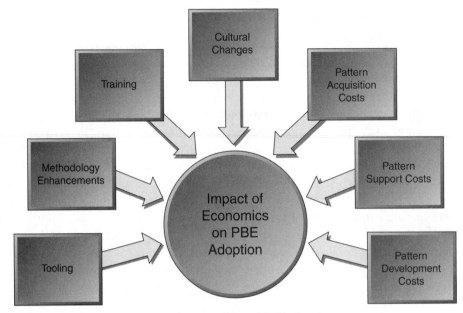

Figure 18.3   *Elements impacting the economics of PBE adoption*

Tooling[3]

With respect to tooling, we need to consider both the production and the consumption of patterns. For consumption, we want to make it as simple as possible for those within our teams to be able to find and leverage the patterns that are available.[4] Helping to fill this need is a category of tools known as asset repositories. If we have only a few patterns, we can likely skip a productized repository and use simple tools such as a web server or a wiki. We do need to ensure that the simple tools allow us to share information about the pattern. However, if there is a large number of patterns, as well as other assets to use, we will need more sophisticated tooling.

When looking for a repository, some features to consider include the following:

- **Asset search and discovery.** Pattern users should be able to quickly and accurately find patterns. Ideally, ease of searching supports us in relating patterns to one another as well as to requirements.

- **Feedback and usage information.** We should be able to see feedback provided by Pattern Users as well as details on pattern usage. We should also be able to track who has downloaded which pattern.

3. Coverage of PBE tooling options is provided in Appendix C.

4. For a more detailed description please see Gonzalez and Lane (2008).

- **Governance support.** The repository should assist us in enforcing our pattern governance policies. The repository should not be a free-for-all or a dumping ground. We need to be able to manage how patterns get put into the repository and how they are made available for use.

On the production side, we need to find and leverage tools that support capturing pattern specifications and, where appropriate, building pattern implementations. In capturing a pattern specification, our tool needs are quite simple; we can use an editor or word processor along with a standard template to ensure that we capture the specification consistently.

Things become more interesting when we address creating pattern implementations. At this point we require development tooling, preferably tooling that provides a platform for working with models and using those models to drive automation via patterns. There are multiple tools available in this space, some from commercial vendors as well as some open-source alternatives. Here are some tooling capabilities to consider:

- **Exemplar support.** Does the tooling under evaluation help with the analysis of exemplars? Does it help to automate the work as it progresses from an exemplar to a pattern?

- **Packaging.** Does the tooling provide support for packaging the patterns that we create?

- **Pattern implementation types.** What types of pattern implementations does the tooling support? Model-to-model? Model-to-text? UML patterns?

- **Compound patterns.** Does the tooling support the creation of compound patterns?

And on the pattern consumption side, we need to think about the related runtime tooling for our pattern implementations. Some capabilities of the runtime tooling to consider include these:

- **Input model.** What mechanisms does the platform provide for creating input models for the pattern implementation?

- **Pattern documentation and guidance.** How does the tooling support Pattern Users and guide them to the correct application of the pattern? Is the pattern documentation easily accessible? Are there additional capabilities provided to help guide the Pattern Users?

- **Install, update, uninstall.** How simple is it for the Pattern User to install, update, and uninstall the pattern?

- **Indicating pattern use.** As the Pattern User creates solutions with patterns, how does the platform record and indicate the use of those patterns?

- **Exemplar creation.** Can the tooling be used to help create exemplars?

- **Patterns in combination.** When Pattern Users create solutions, they will use multiple patterns in combination. Does the platform support the use of multiple patterns within a single solution? Can the patterns share parameters? Can the output of one pattern serve as the input for another pattern?

Methodology Enhancements

As discussed in Chapter 8 and Appendix F, PBE is a software development practice, not a process unto itself. As such, the PBE Practice is combined with other practices to form a complete process solution. As we look to adopt PBE, we need to keep in mind that we will need to incorporate the PBE Practice into our existing development process. This is a straightforward cost that we incur as we enhance our development process.

An aspect that is new when incorporating PBE is that we need to continuously monitor and adjust our process as we build our pattern collection. Typically a pattern will automate one or more steps related to the process, and in doing so it might impact roles, workflows, or artifacts. Based on the pattern and its impact, we will then need to update and republish the process.

Training

Regarding the costs associated with training, there are a number of perspectives to keep in mind. The following are some of the key skills that we need to develop:

- **Identify patterns.** We expect that the entire team will be able to identify patterns related to their domains of expertise. Everyone on the team should be contributing to the effort and supporting this creative and valuable aspect of the PBE effort.

- **Write pattern specifications.** A subset of the team will need to develop specialized skills that support the creation of pattern specifications. They will also need to be able to apply these skills in reviewing pattern specifications that others create.

- **Create pattern implementations.** A small subset of the team will need to develop skills related to creating pattern implementations for the selected tooling platform. This includes learning how to create one or more of model-to-model pattern implementations, model-to-text patterns implementations, and UML pattern implementations.

- **Manage pattern assets.** A small subset of the team will need to learn how to set up governance policies for the pattern assets and enforce the policies via practices and automation.

- **Apply patterns.** The team should be taught how to use the development tool to apply pattern specifications and pattern implementations.

Cultural Changes

Chapter 19 discusses the challenges and misconceptions that need to be addressed when looking to adopt PBE. A number of these issues are related to the cultural challenges associated with PBE. Thus, we need to influence and change the culture of the adopting organization so that we

- Encourage creative thinking to solve recurring problems. Channel creativity and problem solving into solving the right set of problems.

- Continuously look for new patterns. Recognize recurring and proven solutions and ensure that they are codified as patterns.

- Seek opportunities to use patterns. Reuse proven solutions instead of reinventing the wheel.

Pattern Acquisition Costs

There are usually costs associated with acquiring a pattern from an external source such as a vendor. The obvious cost is the purchase price of the pattern. However, there may be additional costs in terms of professional services support, maintenance contracts, training, and associated tooling.

Pattern Support Costs

Regardless of the sources of our patterns, there will be support costs. Obviously, each of the patterns will require documentation and support. However, there are relationships between patterns and we use them in combination. We need to recognize that there can be costs associated with supporting patterns used in combination.

Pattern Development Costs

In cases where we determine that it is in our best interests to build a pattern ourselves, we need to recognize that there will be costs. If our current tooling does not support PBE, we need to look at the costs associated with acquiring any necessary tooling. The tooling may be used for pattern development, testing, or deployment. We also need to recognize the costs associated with designing, developing, testing, deploying, managing, and maintaining the pattern.

Pattern Implementations

When should we create an implementation? The answer to this question is not a set time in the project lifecycle. Rather, we need criteria to help us judge when we should build a pattern implementation. Recall from the definition of economics that we have limited resources and alternatives available in regard to how we use those resources.

Let's start by reviewing a few of the PBE Core Values:

- Always identify and build new patterns.

- Patterns can be built and used within the same project.

- Make your patterns live.

If we accept and work according to these values, will we find ourselves building every pattern that we discover? Will we spend all our time enhancing and embellishing the existing patterns? Of course not; our goal is to ship software that meets our business needs, not to specialize in pattern creation. To make the right decisions, we need criteria that we can use in applying these core values. Some relevant criteria include these:

- **Expected cost of the pattern.** What is the cost for the initial development? What is the cost for validating that the pattern is indeed a best practice? What is the cost for consuming the pattern? How much will it cost to maintain and support the pattern?

- **Expected benefit from using the pattern.** How many times will it be used? How much effort will be saved each time the pattern is used? How long will it take to successfully learn to use the pattern? Is there an expectation that the pattern can be reused in other instances? Other projects? If so, is it quantifiable?

- **Project-specific factors.** What other work will not get done if we develop this pattern? What impact will this have on our overall project deadlines? How will it impact the intermediate milestone deliverables?

We can use these questions (and the associated answers) as a guide in determining when it makes sense to develop a pattern implementation and when it makes sense to defer. As with most other development discussions, there is no simple answer, and it will depend on the specifics of the situation.

PBE Projects

When looking at the economics of software projects and the impact of patterns on those projects, we need to consider the type of organization that is building the patterns. For example, a systems integrator (SI) will have some considerations and factors that differ from those of an internal IT organization. Then, depending on the organization, a number of different situations and scenarios need to be analyzed, including the status of the project, the type of project, and other factors.

Systems Integrators

SIs face a number of challenges when it comes to their projects and PBE. However, they also have a chance to reap the greatest rewards from adopting PBE.

In regard to challenges, there are two main perspectives that we need to examine. The first pertains to how the organization bills for its work. Traditionally, an SI adopts one of two models for projects, either to bill per hour or to bill on a fixed-price basis for project completion. In the case where the organization is billing per hour, there is a great deal of pressure to ensure that the number of billable hours is maintained. Adopting PBE and seeing a significant reduction in time to completion is in direct conflict with this pressure. In the case of per-project, fixed-rate compensation, there is a strong incentive for the SI to adopt a PBE approach.

Other considerations besides billing rates come into play when considering whether to adopt PBE. SIs, like other organizations, are also concerned with quality, skill shortages, and governance. A decision on when, where, and how to adopt PBE needs to take each of these aspects into account.

Another perspective that needs to be considered when looking at SIs and PBE surfaces in situations where an SI builds a pattern based on consulting efforts. This makes a great deal of sense, as a pattern is supposed to be based on experience. However, an SI needs to consider how it manages its customer relationships and the contracts it uses for its engagements. In these discussions and negotiations, consideration must be given to who will be the owner of intellectual capital (such as patterns) that is developed during the engagement. In addition, for the organization that brings in an SI, how will the access to proprietary company patterns be handled?

IT Organization

Shifting our focus to an IT organization, the issues are much simpler than those for an SI. The biggest consideration (aside from those discussed earlier in this chapter) is that of project estimation.

As we start out in adopting PBE and building out our catalog of patterns, there can be great uncertainty about the impact patterns will have on our project plans. However, as our collection and experience with patterns mature, we can act with much higher confidence about which patterns to use, the likelihood of new patterns being discovered, and the impact any new patterns will have on project timelines.

When getting started with PBE, we should ensure that an iterative and incremental approach is adopted. Within each iteration we need to consider the patterns that may be available and what their impact will be for the current iteration. In addition, we need to be conservative in the way that we incorporate this analysis into our estimating.

As we estimate the project, we need to look broadly in terms of the activities and roles that are impacted. We may find that new tasks are introduced while other tasks can be minimized or eliminated. For example, we may have an opportunity to add new tasks such as further requirements validation due to the use of DSLs and patterns related to the business domain. Or we may see trade-offs when looking at the underlying code quality. For example, we need to ensure exemplar quality while recognizing that this can reduce efforts needed in testing the resulting solution.

Independent Software Vendor

An independent software vendor (ISV) needs to calculate the value of candidate patterns. What is the value to the organization? Customers? Partners? In performing these calculations, the ISV will examine the impact patterns could have on professional services, customer adoption rates, product pull-through, customer satisfaction, and competitive differentiation. The answers to these questions will help an ISV determine whether to create the pattern, how much to charge, and when to make the pattern available.

Summary

Leveraging and succeeding with PBE is not just a technical concern; economic considerations also come into play. We have limited resources and many choices as to how we can use those resources. We need to make sure that we are aware of the implications of PBE activities and how they can impact our projects and organizations. We need to consider pattern sources, PBE adoption, pattern implementations, and PBE projects. Each of these presents factors that can impact our success. We need to take a disciplined and systematic approach to leveraging patterns, bearing these considerations in mind as we quantify the impact of our choices and the steps we take.

Chapter 19

PBE Misconceptions

As we come to the end, we reflect on the journey. With new ideas, skills, and approaches, it's exciting to think of the impact we can have on our projects. However, taking the next steps is never as easy or straightforward as we hope it will be. It's with a dash of reality and tempered enthusiasm that we reflect. Will everyone on the team automatically pick up PBE? Can we just flip a switch and have a team that shares a culture, skills, and view of the right path forward? Adopting a new approach becomes much more difficult as we scale across multiple teams and the entire organization. There are challenges in navigating the road ahead. To help us forge ahead we can look at misconceptions and roadblocks that may arise. As they say, "Knowledge is power."

PBE Eliminates Creativity

A good place to start is creativity. How will developers on the team react to PBE? Will people feel constrained and limited? Will adopting PBE stifle the creativity of the team? Will they become bored and unproductive and look elsewhere for better, more interesting opportunities? These fears and concerns are common and arise from PBE concepts such as the use of automation and reuse of solutions created by others.

Let's take a look at some ways in which we can address and counteract this misconception:

- **Pattern specifications and implementations.** We choose the balance of pattern specifications and implementations that we use in our projects. Adopting an approach that focuses on pattern specifications could help to alleviate concerns about creativity and automation by using patterns as guidance and blueprints. A trade-off with this approach is that we miss out on the benefits of automation. The best approach is to find a balance between pattern specifications and pattern implementations.

- **Reinventing the wheel.** PBE does not look to automate all tasks, but to focus on common and recurring tasks—specifically those that have a proven, best-practice solution. Do pattern implementations really reduce the creativity of our teams? How much creativity is there in creating the same solution over and over again? Pattern implementations automate the repetitive and mundane tasks, allowing team members to spend more time on interesting and creative ones.

- **Pattern production and application.** PBE also encourages us to continuously look for and apply patterns. This is highly creative and challenging, whether we are trying to identify and codify a new pattern or apply an existing pattern (specifications or implementations) to a specific problem.

PBE Patterns and Guidelines such as Antipatterns (Chapter 11), Pattern Opportunity (Chapter 11), and Simple Solution Space (Chapter 10) are some examples of the opportunities provided to exercise creativity.

PBE Introduces Project Risk

Another misconception is that PBE will introduce unnecessary risk into a project. Project leadership needs to manage project risk and a usual suspect is new approaches. They'll request that the transition to the new approach be done later, on another project.

A good way to start dispelling this misconception is to cite the PBE Core Values. In such a review and discussion, there are some key ideas that should surface:

- **Iterative and incremental.** PBE is not a one-time effort, nor is it a waterfall approach to solving all the problems associated with a project. In each of our iterations we attempt to figure out how best to leverage patterns. In addition, even with the patterns we create, we apply similar thinking. Within each iteration we evaluate the value and completeness of the patterns, with a focus on adding value to the patterns and the projects that consume those patterns.

- **Creativity and best practices.** We want to leverage the creativity and best practices of the team. We want to communicate the best practices in a standard format and ideally automate their use.

- **Process integration.** We seek to integrate PBE into our software development process. We do not throw away the previous investments made in defining and refining our software development process.

- **Project recovery.** In some cases we may not be able to convince leadership that PBE has a role in our current project. In such cases we need to keep in mind that PBE can also serve an important role in project recovery. Pattern implementations can provide a significant boost to team productivity and the quality of the resulting solution.

PBE Patterns such as Determine Business Impact (Chapter 11), Meet-in-the-Middle Pattern Creation (Chapter 12), Pattern Creation Lifecycle (Chapter 12), and Piecemeal Pattern Creation (Chapter 10) are some examples of patterns that you can use to manage risk.

Pattern Identification Is Not for Everybody

In some cases people will develop a belief that only a few select people can define patterns. They see patterns as being invented by others—the top performers, industry thought leaders, and software vendors.

However, patterns are not invented but discovered. And there are a number of skills and traits that come into play. For instance, observational skills are important, as pattern discovery comes from observing different projects and being able to make a pairing between a recurring problem and a given solution. There are also cultural aspects that come into play; we need to create a culture that looks for and values patterns.

Once we've identified the essence of a pattern (the problem/solution pair), there are resources available that we can consult to help us write the pattern. These resources include books and pattern-writing conferences, as well as other Pattern Specification Authors. Pattern-writing conferences are organized as workshops where participants submit their pattern(s), which are then discussed with the goal of improving their descriptions. Pattern Languages of Programs (PLoP) conferences are probably the best-known pattern-writing conferences. Books such as *Patterns Hatching*[1] by John Vlissides provide tips on how to write patterns. This book also provides an interesting insight into how the GoF patterns were identified, captured, and disseminated. It is interesting to see that quite a few discussions and iterations went into how the GoF patterns were developed. In the end, those of us consuming the patterns just see a finished book with a great set of patterns. Viewing the finished product without an understanding of the effort, iterations, and debate that went into the patterns can make pattern authoring seem intimidating.

---

1. Vlissides (1998).

We also need to know some of the signs that alert us to potential patterns. As we work on our projects, do we

- Keep solving the same problem?

- Reuse existing solutions via copy and paste?

- Keep answering the same questions?

- Encounter a sense of déjà vu?

If we answer yes to any of these questions, we should consider that we might be dealing with a pattern. We can't be afraid to get started; all pattern authors start with a first pattern. To help in this effort, we can consider PBE Patterns and Guidelines, including Domain-Driven Patterns (Chapter 10), Pattern Opportunity (Chapter 11), Recurring Solution (Chapter 11), and Use Patterns to Find Patterns (Chapter 16).

Patterns Need to Be Used Everywhere, All the Time

Sometimes people get a little too enthusiastic about using patterns. Every problem needs to have a pattern that is used to solve it. Every solution where a pattern is not yet used needs to become a pattern. All patterns, all the time, everywhere and anywhere.

To address this misconception, we need to be systematic, disciplined, and quantifiable in how we use patterns. We do not use patterns everywhere and for any reason. We do not create patterns out of any and all solutions.

In adopting PBE, we analyze the problems that we have to address. In some cases we will find that the requirements, content, and situation make it ideal for us to apply an existing pattern. In some cases we will find that a pattern does not exist; however, the opportunity to create one for the situation is appealing. In further analyzing the situation, we find that we can achieve a positive ROI on the pattern, using it in multiple situations on the current project and others.

In some cases, however, we will find that patterns do not exist in an area for a reason. Perhaps the situation is so unique that it does not make sense to capture the solution as a pattern. In some cases it may be that we have a solution for the problem, but we would not consider it a best-practice solution. It works, but we wouldn't want anyone else to reuse it.

As much as we need to be open to creative solutions and on the lookout for patterns, we also need a critical and discerning eye. We do not want to end up creating a junkyard in our pattern repository, whereby we create large numbers of meaningless patterns that make it difficult to find patterns that truly add value. To help address this misconception, consider PBE Patterns and Guidelines, including Determine Business Impact (Chapter 11), Pattern Density (Chapter 16), Pattern Selection Driven by Requirements (Chapter 16), Pattern Testing (Chapter 13), and Select Large-Scope Patterns First (Chapter 16).

PBE Is Overly Formal

Some see PBE as too formal—too many steps, roles, work products, and generally just too many things to do and remember.

The PBE Core Values can be a great way to dispel this misconception. They provide a short, simple, easy-to-remember set of ideas that serve as a foundation to help in succeeding with PBE. Some additional considerations to keep in mind:

- **Pattern consumption.** We can think of patterns as another tool in our toolbox, to be used when needed. We don't need to put patterns everywhere or make the solution fit the pattern. We use them when and where they make sense; we need to be practical and pragmatic.

- **Pattern production.** Being practical and pragmatic carries over to the production side as well. We evaluate which patterns should be created and how much investment we put into the creation effort. Such evaluation can be as formal as needed. The actual creation of the pattern can be done using many of the skills, steps, and roles that we traditionally use in our other projects. Changing focus, we also see that we can make Pattern Users more productive by creating pattern implementations that automate steps and work product generation. Less to remember, less to do.

- **Pattern practice and process customization.** The PBE Practice should be used along with other practices in creating a development process that suits the needs of the team and development organization. We need to ensure that the process provides the correct level of formality as desired and needed. More details regarding the PBE Practice are provided in Chapter 8, "PBE and the Software Development Process," and Appendix F.

Some of the PBE Patterns and Guidelines to consider in managing overhead and formality in your development efforts include Determine Business Impact (Chapter 11), Integrated Patterns and DSLs (Chapter 15), Pattern Density (Chapter 16), Pattern Packaging (Chapter 14), and Use an Asset Repository (Chapter 16).

PBE Is Only for Design

In some cases people consider patterns only for design. Figure 19.1[2] shows the distribution of project effort by development discipline.[3] If we look at all of the work that needs to get done in defining, designing, implementing, testing, deploying, and maintaining a software application, it is very clear that only a fraction of the time is spent in design; as shown in the figure, design represents only 15% of the overall project effort.

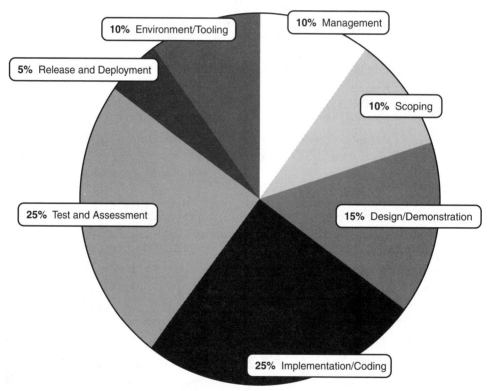

Figure 19.1   *Effort allocated to each of the disciplines within the SDLC*

PBE is about patterns, and patterns can exist across the SDLC. PBE applies to the core development activities of software development covering requirements, architecture,

---

2. Data used to generate the figure was sourced from Royce (2009).

3. Note that assessment is roughly equivalent to testing and that the environment encompasses configuration and change management.

design, implementation, assessment, environments, and deployment, which, according to Figure 19.1, represent 80% of a project. Taking a holistic view of the project and where we can use patterns is more interesting and will have a much greater impact than unnecessarily restricting ourselves to just the 15% devoted to design.

We can also embrace the PBE Core Value "Make your patterns live" as we create patterns. We may start out with a specific aspect of the design or the code. However, we don't want to stop at this point. Once we have built the initial pattern, we need to put thought and effort into figuring out how we can add more responsibility and "scope." In the case of a code pattern, we can start to think about generating related test cases, associated documentation, deployment scripts, and so on. In this way we start to address the other tasks that we need to accomplish when we deliver a software application.

Some of the PBE Patterns and Guidelines that can help you get beyond a design-only mind-set include Antipatterns (Chapter 11), Determine Business Impact (Chapter 11), Domain-Driven Patterns (Chapter 10), End-to-End Pattern Use (Chapter 10), Refactor with Patterns (Chapter 16), and Use Pattern Definitions to Understand Existing Solutions (Chapter 16).

PBE Is Only for Forward Engineering

Related to the previous misconception, we find that some will use patterns only for forward-engineering a solution. As Figure 19.2 illustrates, there are a number of different pattern use cases[4] that we can leverage within PBE. Patterns can be applied as in the common forward-engineering approach, but they can also be harvested from existing applications. Other uses include detecting pattern occurrences within existing code and using patterns in refactoring.[5]

Ideally, we would like to use a single pattern definition to drive each of the use cases, allowing us to get a better return on investing in a pattern. While this is possible for pattern specifications, unfortunately today's tooling is not quite at the point of making it possible for us to develop a pattern implementation and use it as input for these different use cases. However, the good news is that with the extensibility of modern IDEs, Eclipse particularly, we can still leverage these use cases, at the cost of creating different pattern implementations. For example, we can use the Architectural Discovery feature of IBM Rational Software Architecture to analyze a model or code base and identify occurrences of patterns.

---

4. Information for the figure is from Schneider and Lexvold (2008).

5. Kerievsky (2004).

	Summary	Pattern(s) as Input	Pattern(s) as Output
Visualize	Represent pattern occurrences visually	✔	
Detect	Discover occurrences of known patterns	✔	
Refactor	Refactor artifacts to match a pattern	✔	
Apply	Impose a known pattern on artifacts	✔	
Harvest	Mine and codify new patterns from occurrences		✔
Create	Create new patterns or compound patterns		✔

Figure 19.2 *A single pattern definition supports multiple use cases.*

Some of the PBE Patterns and Guidelines that can help you get more from your patterns include Antipatterns (Chapter 11), Refactor with Patterns (Chapter 16), and Use Pattern Definitions to Understand Existing Solutions (Chapter 16).

Guilty by Association

Some still question the value of using models and modeling languages to simplify development. They are comfortable and familiar with code and prefer to continue just using code, not trusting modeling and any associated generation capabilities.[6] PBE and MDD are complementary but are not coupled. The choice of one does not automatically require the use of the other. We can adopt an MDD approach without using PBE and vice versa. For example, we can use pattern specifications as blueprints to help us design solutions.

---

6. A debate about the value of UML modeling is outside the scope of this book; this section touches upon the subject as some associate pattern usage with UML modeling approaches.

When using pattern implementations, we don't necessarily need to use UML or even visual models. We definitely need to develop an input model that will allow us to apply the pattern and generate output, but this model can be represented using a DSL or something as simple as an XML file. Remember, a model is just an abstraction of reality, where we hide unnecessary details. We can represent such a model in many different ways.

Some PBE Patterns and Guidelines to consider include Integrated Patterns and DSLs (Chapter 15), Model-to-Text Pattern Implementation (Chapter 13), and Simple Solution Space (Chapter 10).

PBE Requires Tools from a Specific Vendor

A final misconception is related to tooling and vendors. Some come to believe that following PBE requires tools from a specific vendor.

A first step in addressing this misconception is recognizing that we can leverage PBE without using any tools. We can receive many benefits from following PBE, even if we are not using automation via pattern implementations. If we want to use pattern implementations, a number of different options are available, from the open-source community as well as commercially from software vendors. Appendix C provides an overview of some of the different tooling options.

One issue that does arise is that pattern implementations have not yet reached the stage of open standards and specifications. A pattern implementation that is created in one tool cannot be used directly in another tool. Of course, pattern specifications are tool-agnostic, but implementations, once built, are connected to a tool.

Some PBE Patterns and Guidelines to consider include Antipatterns (Chapter 11), Communicate Design with Patterns (Chapter 16), Pattern Specification (Chapter 13), Refactor with Patterns (Chapter 16), and Use Pattern Definitions to Understand Existing Solutions (Chapter 16).

Summary

PBE is practical and pragmatic and can be adapted to the level of formality and automation you need. It is not only about design and automation; we can use patterns (specifications and implementations) to help with assessment, environments, and deployments. We can foster creativity while taking on risk and tackling troubled projects. And last but not least, PBE is not restricted to an elite set of users. Anyone with the ability to observe, identify, and synthesize while working with recurring problems and common solutions possesses the fundamental skills to practice PBE.

With PBE skills and knowledge, an awareness of misconceptions, and how we can remedy these issues, we are ready to move forward. We can successfully adopt and grow PBE within our team and organization.

Part IV

Appendices

Part IV includes a set of appendices that provide support for the main body of the book. Here we include coverage of related definitions (Appendix A), comparisons to other software development approaches (Appendix B), PBE tooling options (Appendix C), a visual view of the PBE Patterns and Guidelines (Appendix D), a pattern specification for the Subsystem Façade pattern (Appendix E), and a more in-depth look at the PBE Practice (Appendix F).

Appendix A

PBE Definitions

The goal of this appendix is to provide additional support for understanding a number of the concepts associated with PBE.

Code Generators

A code generator is a program that writes other programs. Although *code* is a part of the name, the code generator can also generate other types of artifacts. For example, a code generator could also generate documentation or deployment descriptors. Many of the benefits that code generators offer, such as productivity and quality improvements, are also offered by pattern implementations.

So at this point we have to ask, "Is a pattern implementation, specifically one that focuses on generating text-based artifacts, just a code generator?" There are definitely similarities between the two concepts. However, there are differences as well, some minor and some more substantial. The largest differences are a matter of focus and scope; a pattern implementation associated with PBE has a larger scope aimed at leveraging multiple levels of abstraction. In addition, we look at a pattern implementation as a composition of patterns, whereas code generators generally are not discussed in this way. Last, but not least, with PBE we focus on capturing and working with best-practice-based solutions. The pattern implementation codifies a set of best practices; it is not just a translation of the model into code.

▼

Pattern Implementations versus Transformations

Model transformation is another term closely related to code generator. "Model transformation is the process of converting one model to another model of the same system."[1] A transformation

---

1. Miller and Mukerji (2003).

may contain many patterns as part of its workings. However, it may also be the case that a transformation is a very literal translation between elements in the source model and elements in the target model. For instance, if we look at a UML-to-Java transformation, there is a direct mapping between elements in UML such as a class, operations, and attributes and their counterparts in the Java language. Would it be accurate to call such a transformation a pattern implementation? Where is the best practice?

Typically we should, even if it is mostly an academic exercise, draw a line between simple transformations and pattern implementations. The two elements can share the same tooling, platform, and APIs yet be considered different things. There can be some imprecision in making a distinction in some cases, but most often it should be clear whether we are dealing with a pattern implementation or a transformation (or a simple code generator). We can refer back to our definition of a pattern to assist us in making the determination.

Domain-Specific Languages

The patterns that we build will accept a set of input elements, often captured in a model. To support the processing of the model by computers in an automated fashion we use a formal language, leveraging a metamodel, to define the elements that can appear in the model. Building on that understanding, we can start to discuss the language that we use for the model. We could use a general-purpose language such as UML as the basis for the input model to the pattern. However, with a general-purpose language we may end up with ambiguity and an associated gap between our problem space and how we will describe the solution. One way in which people have dealt with this gap is to model at a level that is very close to what they want to implement. In these cases the implementation technology dictates how the modeling should be handled.

Another approach to dealing with this issue is to use a language that is better aligned with the problem space or domain. We refer to a language that is aligned with the problem domain as a domain-specific language (DSL). More specifically, a domain-specific language is "a programming language or specification language dedicated to a particular problem domain, a particular problem representation technique, and/or a particular solution technique."[2] As such, a DSL provides "concepts and rules within a language that represent things in the application domain, rather than concepts of a given programming language."[3] The DSL enables us to use a

---

2. http://en.wikipedia.org/wiki/Domain-specific_language.

3. Kelly and Tolvanen (2008).

higher level of abstraction and thereby both speak about and focus on the problem at hand rather than the underlying implementation. This simplifies the consumption and use of the language because the users are familiar with the vocabulary of the domain, and therefore they are also familiar with the DSL.

Tools that can be used to implement a DSL include the Eclipse Modeling Framework (EMF)[4]/Graphical Modeling Framework (GMF)[5] from the Eclipse platform, UML Profiles to extend UML, and tools from other vendors such as Microsoft or MetaEdit.

Some of the benefits of using a DSL include these:

- **Support for automation.** A DSL written as a formal language is suitable for automation and can be translated into other artifacts. Also, a DSL can often include assumptions and constraints that support a higher percentage of artifact generation compared to general-purpose languages.

- **Support for people.** A DSL can improve communication between roles, utilization of team member skills, and governance. With respect to governance, a DSL constrains and focuses the solution and hides unnecessary elements. When combined with appropriate automations, a DSL can enforce architectural approaches and best practices.

- **Support for business/domain.** The DSL uses terms and concepts that map directly to the problem space. It simplifies communication between business and technical project participants, hides irrelevant technical details, and provides a more precise validation of requirements to the design team.

Exemplar

When we build a new pattern (whether a specification or an implementation), we need to keep in mind that patterns are discovered rather than invented. To this end, we often look for representative reference solutions that we can analyze and use as the basis for the pattern. We call this reference solution an exemplar.

According to the *American Heritage Dictionary*, an exemplar is defined as follows:

1. One that is worthy of imitation; a model.

2. One that is typical or representative; an example.

---

4. Additional information on EMF can be found at www.eclipse.org/modeling/emf/.

5. Additional information on GMF can be found at www.eclipse.org/modeling/gmf/.

3. An ideal that serves as a pattern; an archetype.

4. A copy, as of a book.[6]

So the question arises, "What exemplars do we need to consider for possible input into the pattern creation process?" When we look to identify a possible pattern, we are on the lookout for exemplars as well as for situations where the "Rule of Three" applies. The Rule of Three is used for judging where a possible pattern may exist; in this case we are looking for situations where the same problem/solution set has occurred in three unique instances/situations.

> RULE OF THREE: A software pattern documents a recurring solution. The pattern solution abstracts three or more experiences. The solution is something which is regularly applied or practiced by some community(s) of sophisticated developers and architects. The logical basis for the rule of three is: the first occurrence shows the design can work, the second occurrence is interesting, and the third occurrence suggests that the design *might* be worthy of being a pattern because it appears to have a wider applicability. *Non-normative comment:* The informal concept behind the rule-of-three is: the first occurrence is an event, the second occurrence is a coincidence, and the third occurrence may be a pattern.[7]

A good exemplar has the following characteristics:

- It works. As a representation of a best-practice-based solution, it should by definition be a solution that works.

- It exhibits the necessary variability and flexibility that will be required of the resulting pattern.

- It has a Pattern Author/Subject Matter Expert (SME) who understands the exemplar and can support others in gaining an understanding of it.

Metamodel

A metamodel is a model that describes another model at one level of description higher. Another way of saying this is that a metamodel is a model that describes another modeling language. This includes describing the semantics and notation of the language. For example, the UML metamodel describes in precise detail the meaning of the elements within the language such as a class, attribute, and operation. In

---

6. *American Heritage Dictionary of the English Language, Fourth Edition.* Retrieved June 30, 2008, from http://dictionary.reference.com/browse/exemplar.

7. www.antipatterns.com/whatisapattern/.

addition to defining the elements themselves, the metamodel describes the meaning of the relationships between these elements.

Figure A.1[8] provides an overview of the relationships between a metamodel, model, and the real-world artifacts that need to be modeled. The upper left-hand quadrant is the quickest and easiest to understand. In this case we are looking at the real-world instances of artifacts that we want to represent in a model such as customer, account, order, and employee.

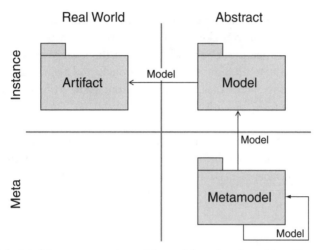

Figure A.1   *Relationships among metamodel, model, and real-world artifacts*
Copyright IBM developerWorks, www.ibm.com/developerworks. Reused with permission.

Moving to the upper right-hand quadrant, we can view a model as providing an abstract representation of instances. Here we can see the creation of model elements that represent those real-world instances mentioned previously. For example, we see model elements that can be used to represent customer, account, and order. Some familiar model elements from the UML realm include class, activity, and component. To that end we end up having a class named Customer.

Finishing up in the lower right-hand quadrant of the figure, we see that a metamodel exists at an abstract and meta level where we describe other abstract things. At this level we define the model elements that will be available to us when we create our model. If we relate this back to UML, it is at this level that we define the modeling elements such as class, activity, and component as well as their relationships. We will find a class named Class.

---

8. Kovari (2007).

By using a metamodel to describe and define the model language, we support two key communication needs:

- **Communication between people.** As there is a well-defined basis for the language, we can use our understanding of the language as the basis for interpreting models that use it. Referring again to UML, we can see that once someone understands UML, he or she can interpret models based on this language regardless of who created the model or when it was created.

- **Communication with machines.** If we want to use a model as an input into automation, we need to make sure that the model can be read and interpreted by a machine. A metamodel provides us with the level of precision needed by a computer to understand a model unambiguously and accurately. In turn, a computer can use associated rules, constraints, and assumptions to generate output artifacts based on the provided model.

Tools and frameworks are available to support the creation and use of both metamodels and models. The more difficult part of the work is the thought that goes into determining what concepts need to be represented and the relationships between them. The more mechanical aspects of creating and supporting the metamodel(s) are handled by tooling.

Model

Key to working with patterns is the use of models. A very general, high-level definition of a model is that it is an abstraction or a simplification of reality. A good model includes those elements that are relevant to the given level of abstraction, while hiding or ignoring those details/elements that are not relevant. A model may be structural, emphasizing the organization of the system, or behavioral, emphasizing the dynamics of the system.

The language used within the model can vary among formalized textual, formalized graphical, or natural language. A formal language exists when time and effort are taken to document the syntax and semantics of the language, typically accomplished via the use of a metamodel. UML is a formal language that can be used to capture a model. However, a model can also be captured in an informal language, such as when we draw a diagram with boxes, lines, and arrows but without explanations or definitions for those elements.

Pattern Catalog

"A Pattern Catalog is a collection of (possibly) related patterns. Patterns in a pattern catalog do not form a Pattern Language; that is, their contexts do not weave them together."[9] A pattern catalog can include details on the relationships between patterns. However, the depth of any details provided about the relationships is not to the same level found in a pattern language.

Pattern Categories

As we look at the set of available patterns, we can see that they vary in terms of the scope of solution impact and the level of abstraction in which they operate. If we compare the Façade pattern to the Layers pattern, it is quite clear that they are significantly different in terms of scope and abstraction. The Layers pattern impacts the overall architecture of the system, whereas we would see the Façade pattern have an impact at the design level of the solution. When determining which patterns to use, it is helpful to categorize the available patterns, using their scope and abstraction characteristics to classify them.

In categorizing patterns, as shown in Figure A.2, three common categories are used: architectural patterns, design patterns, and idioms. Let's take a look at a definition for each of these categories:

- "An architectural pattern expresses a fundamental structural organization schema for software systems. It provides a set of predefined subsystems, specifies their relationships, and includes rules and guidelines for organizing the relationships between them."[10]

- "A design pattern systematically names, motivates, and explains a general design that addresses a recurring design problem in object-oriented systems. It describes the problem, the solution, when to apply the solution, and its consequences. It also gives implementation hints and examples. The solution is a general arrangement of objects and classes that solve the problem. The solution is customized and implemented to solve the problem in a particular context."[11]

---

9. http://c2.com/cgi/wiki?PatternCatalog.

10. Buschmann et al. (1996).

11. Gamma et al. (1995).

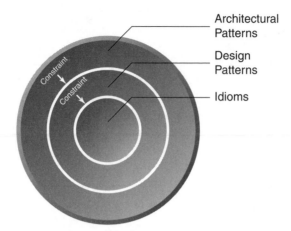

Architectural
Patterns

Design
Patterns

Idioms

Figure A.2   *A common set of pattern categories*

- "An idiom is a low-level pattern specific to a programming language. An idiom describes how to implement particular aspects of components or the relationships between them using the features of the given language."[12]

Pattern Language

We've discussed how patterns are used in combination, and we expect that a solution will use numerous patterns. However, how do we know what patterns to use together? How do we know in what order we should use the patterns? One way in which we can gain some of this insight is through the use of a pattern language. A pattern language is "a network of interrelated patterns that define a process for resolving software development problems systematically."[13] There will be cases where we believe that we've found a pattern but upon further investigation determine that there are a number of "paths" through the pattern or that the pattern has a large number of steps. In such cases it may make sense to refactor the pattern into a set of patterns and distribute them as a pattern language.

Pattern languages can be used to solve many types of problems, just like a pattern. As a matter of fact, we can even use pattern languages to help us in building our own patterns. For example, a key aspect of PBE is that we should both produce and con-

12. Buschmann et al. (1996).

13. Buschmann et al. (2007).

sume patterns. Since we will create our own patterns, including specifications and implementations, it makes sense to use patterns to help create patterns. We can think of these as metapatterns or pattern patterns. A pattern language for creating patterns is illustrated in Figure A.3.

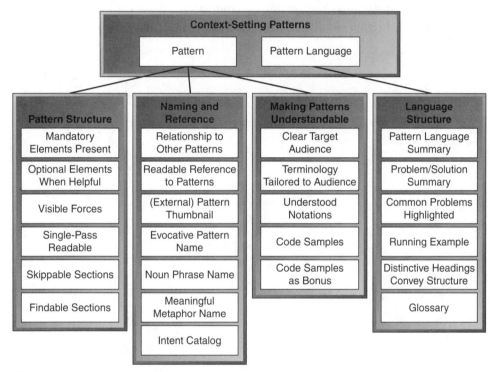

Figure A.3   *A set of metapatterns or pattern patterns*
This figure is a reproduction of Figure 29-1 from page 531 of Martin, R. C., D. Riehle, and F. Buschmann. 1998. "Context-Setting Patterns." In Pattern Languages of Program Design *3. Boston: Addison-Wesley. Reproduced by permission of Pearson Education.*

In this pattern language there exists a set of patterns that provide guidance for building patterns and pattern languages. Trying to fit all of these best practices and guidance into a single pattern would result in a pattern that would be unusable. We can even relate the construction of the language to what we see when we develop our software solutions. We don't just build a single monolithic class, component, or service. Instead we break the solution into smaller, meaningful pieces, leveraging encapsulation, separation of concerns, and abstraction.

Reusable Asset

An asset is ". . . a collection of artifacts that provides a solution to a problem. The asset has instructions on how it should be used and is reusable in one or more contexts, such as a development or a runtime context. The asset may also be extended and customized through variability points."[14]

---

14. Larsen (2006).

Appendix B

PBE and Other Development Approaches

This appendix discusses how PBE relates to other available development practices, including asset-based development, model-driven development, Model-Driven Architecture, and software factories.

Asset-Based Development

As introduced in Chapter 1, there is a strong connection between PBE and asset-based development (ABD). ABD is focused on how to leverage investments made in software artifacts in future projects. These investments cover a wide range of artifacts, from requirements, to models, code, tests, even deployment scripts. ABD includes four major areas—process, standards, tooling, and assets—all of which are focused on how you can successfully reuse and benefit from the investments that are made in your software projects.

We can say that a pattern is a type of asset, and we can see PBE as a specific type of implementation of an ABD program. The difference is that although we consider a wide range of artifacts and aspects of development in PBE, we look at these as exemplars for use in creating patterns. In PBE, the primary assets that are distributed and reused are patterns.

A key standard available in support of ABD is the Reusable Asset Specification (RAS) from the Object Management Group (OMG). RAS is used to package an asset to support the consumption of assets by tools and people. Typically the RAS-packaged asset contains a set of artifacts as well as a manifest that describes the asset.[1]

---

1. Additional details regarding assets and the Reusable Asset Specification are available via Reusable Asset Specification, OMG Available Specification Version 2.2 formal/05-11-02, Object Management Group. November 2005. www.omg.org/cgi-bin/doc?formal/2005-11-02.

Model-Driven Development (MDD)

Generally when we discuss MDD, we are referring to an approach to software development whereby we leverage models at multiple levels of abstraction. The elements that exist within a model at a certain level of abstraction are in turn related to elements at the next level of abstraction. This view of MDD can be seen in the following definition for model-driven: ". . . meaning that the system developed is organized in terms of different models with specific purposes and whose elements relate (trace) to each other."[2]

In recent years more focus has been placed on using automation and thereby using the elements found in one model to generate the elements of a model found at another level of abstraction. "Truly model-driven development uses automated transformations in a manner similar to the way a pure coding approach uses compilers."[3]

Regardless of whether the migration between levels of abstraction is something that happens manually or through automation, we still need some guidance as to how the migration should be performed. Sometimes this transformation is very direct and quite simple. For instance, if we are moving from a detailed design document, it is quite easy to figure out how to transform the elements in the model into code elements. This transformation capability has been available in modeling tools for a number of years now. Although it enables us to generate a great deal of code, have we really added much value to the development process? Yes, the code is generated faster than a human can write it, but has the modeler ended up just drawing the code? The goal is to use models to abstract away details; however, we put so many details into the model that the generation of code is simple. As a result, the value we derive from using MDD transformations is limited (especially when compared to the potential). We are able to achieve all of our modeling-related goals, including design, communication, and generation, but we are designing at such a low level of abstraction that the model transformation provides little real value.

What if we want to simplify things for the modeler? What if we want to ensure that best practices are going into the design? To simplify things for the modeler and to truly bring value to our models we need to better leverage abstraction and best practices. Using patterns in and across models is a key step in doing so. We can take things even further with the use of DSLs (including the use of constraints, rules, and assumptions). Having patterns and DSLs enables us to simplify the solution so that we can reduce the number of levels of abstraction, and even within a level of abstraction we can reduce the amount of information that we need to capture from the modeler.

---

2. Jacobson et al. (1999).

3. Kelly and Tolvanen (2008).

PBE provides us with an approach to find patterns and the related and supporting DSLs. We can envision the relationship between MDD and PBE as shown in Figure B.1.

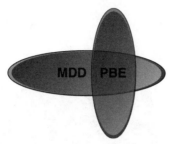

Figure B.1   *The relationship between MDD and PBE*

Clearly, there is overlap between MDD and PBE. MDD assumes developers will create models while incorporating best practices. Thus, there is the expectation that the solution that is modeled will use patterns. However, within MDD there is little to no guidance for how to find these patterns. In addition, MDD does not help us figure out how to start to compress the number of levels of abstraction that we need.

Model-Driven Architecture (MDA)

Model-Driven Architecture is a specific implementation of MDD that is being led by the OMG. According to the OMG:

> The Model-Driven Architecture starts with the well-known and long established idea of separating the specification of the operation of a system from the details of the way that system uses the capabilities of its platform.

> MDA provides an approach for, and enables tools to be provided for:
> - specifying a system independently of the platform that supports it,
> - specifying platforms,
> - choosing a particular platform for the system, and
> - transforming the system specification into one for a particular platform.

> The three primary goals of MDA are portability, interoperability and reusability through architectural separation of concerns.[4]

---

4. Miller and Mukerji (2003).

Like MDD, MDA recognizes that the transformations between levels of abstraction can be done either manually or in an automated fashion. However, those supporting and attempting MDA place much more focus on the idea of using automation.

As shown in Figure B.2, MDA is one possible approach to MDD.

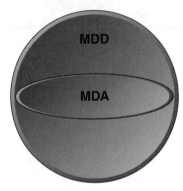

Figure B.2   *MDA is a subset of MDD.*

Specific to the MDA approach to MDD is a prescribed set of viewpoints that are represented in models. These viewpoints are

- Computation-Independent Model (CIM)

- Platform-Independent Model (PIM)

- Platform-Specific Model (PSM)

Most often you will find that the solution has one or more PSMs to support the generation of the solution. Patterns play a key role in supporting the transformation from one viewpoint to another.

Figure B.3 shows that the relationship between MDA and PBE is similar to the previously discussed relationship between MDD and PBE. There is definitely overlap and a connection between PBE and MDA. However, there exist ideas, guidance, and roles in PBE that do not exist in MDA.

Here are some of the differences between MDA and PBE:

- Very little guidance is provided on how to capture and create the patterns necessary to support you in MDA.

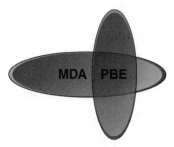

Figure B.3 *The relationship between MDA and PBE*

- There is little discussion in the MDA literature regarding the other pattern use cases that are possible. Within PBE we do not restrict our thinking to just using patterns for forward-engineering a solution. Patterns can and do support many use cases when we are building a solution; forward engineering is just one of many.

- MDA has more of a top-down focus than PBE.

- PBE is more explicit in calling out the idea that the transformations that are used between levels of abstraction are themselves pattern implementations.

Software Factories

A software factory (SF) is defined by Greenfield and Short as follows:

> A software factory is a software product line that configures extensible tools, processes, and content using a software factory template based on a software factory schema to automate the development and maintenance of variants of an archetypical product by adapting, assembling, and configuring framework based components.[5]

The terms *software factory schema* and *software factory template* in this definition merit further explanation:

> A SF Schema defines, categorizes and summarizes the artifacts and assets required to build a software product line. It can be seen as a recipe listing ingredients, tools and the application process. A SF Template is based on the SF Schema and represents the implementation of the SF Schema that means that all defined assets and artifacts have to be built and made available. The implementation comprises among others developing DSLs. The SF Template can be seen as a bag of groceries containing the ingredients listed in the recipe (SF Schema).[6]

---

5. Greenfield and Short (2004).

6. Demir (2004).

And related to the concept of an exemplar, we see within software factories the concept of an archetype. It is defined as follows:

archetype: An ideal example of a type after which other similar things are patterned[7]

It is important to note that while modeling and automation are key elements in software factories, there is also an emphasis on ensuring that the right process is built to support the factory. Figure B.4 depicts the relationship between software factories and MDD.

Figure B.4   *Overview of the relationship between software factories and MDD*

In this relationship there are certainly aspects of software factories that are contained within MDD. However, software factories are much broader in scope as they deal not only with how your application would be generated from your model(s) but also with all of the supporting tools that would be involved in making your development easier.

Just as with MDD, there is a strong and important role for patterns in software factories. To automate and support the production lines we need to find the correct set of patterns. However, the software factory approach and related literature provide little or no guidance on how to create and use patterns together such as is detailed in PBE. Thus, we can view the relationship between software factories and PBE as shown in Figure B.5.

As seen in the diagram, PBE is narrower in scope than both MDD and software factories. There is a great deal of overlap and synergy between these approaches. However, PBE provides content that is unique and exists outside of either of these

---

7. *American Heritage Dictionary of the English Language, Fourth Edition.* Retrieved July 2, 2008, from http://dictionary.reference.com/browse/archetype.

Figure B.5 *Overview of the relationship between software factories and PBE*

approaches. PBE provides a set of tasks, roles, and work products that we can bring to bear in our MDD and software factory projects. For example, PBE provides guidance in terms of the roles that are needed for creating and managing a set of patterns. In addition, PBE provides guidance on when, where, and how to build the patterns you will use.

Keep in mind that PBE is not limited to just supporting software factories and MDD. PBE is a software development practice that can be applied and used within other practices and approaches.

Appendix C

PBE Tooling Options

This appendix provides an overview of some of the tooling that can be used when following PBE. The list of tools is not exhaustive but will give you a head start in understanding some of the options available. Throughout the book we have looked at the use of Rational Software Architect (RSA) in supporting PBE. RSA is an excellent choice of product to use, but it is not the only choice.

When reviewing the tools available, it is worthwhile to keep in mind the relationship between PBE and other software development approaches such as MDA, MDD, and software factories. With each of these approaches you will often find one or more tools available to assist you. As PBE is compatible with these approaches, it is also compatible with the associated tooling.

Eclipse Modeling Project

The Eclipse Modeling Project[1] serves as the home to numerous technologies that can support a PBE approach. Specific technologies include EMF, Xpand, JET, and UML. In combination they provide support for model-to-model pattern implementations, model-to-text pattern implementations, and DSLs.

IBM Rational Software Modeling Platform

Throughout the book we discussed many examples leveraging capabilities from IBM Rational Software Architect.[2] With an Eclipse heritage, it leverages the

---

1. More information is available at the Eclipse Modeling Project home page: www.eclipse.org/modeling/.

2. More information is available at the Rational Software Architect home page: www-01.ibm.com/software/awdtools/swarchitect/websphere/.

capabilities provided by the Eclipse Modeling Framework and provides rich support for PBE.

AndroMDA

AndroMDA[3] is an open-source MDA platform that enables the creation and use of cartridges to deliver automation in transforming models into text-based artifacts. In addition to supporting the creation of cartridges, AndroMDA has a number of cartridges already made and available for use. The premade cartridges support several popular platforms and frameworks such as Spring, Hibernate, and .NET.

Microsoft Visual Studio

Microsoft Visual Studio[4] is an option for those looking to apply PBE in creating .NET-based solutions. The platform has support for creating and working with best practices and patterns,[5] DSLs,[6] model-to-text pattern implementations,[7] and software factories.[8]

Sparx Enterprise Architect

Sparx Enterprise Architect[9] is a modeling and MDA tool. It provides support for a set of prebuilt MDA transformations and allows for the creation and customization of

---

3. More information can be found at the AndroMDA homepage: www.andromda.org/.

4. The home page for Visual Studio is www.microsoft.com/visualstudio/en-us/default.mspx.

5. Microsoft MSDN (2009). "Microsoft patterns & practices: Proven practices for predictable results." http://msdn.microsoft.com/en-us/library/ms998572.aspx.

6. Microsoft MSDN (2008). "Domain-specific languages." July. http://msdn.microsoft.com/en-us/library/bb126259.aspx.

7. Microsoft MSDN (2007). "Generating artifacts by using text templates." November. http://msdn.microsoft.com/en-us/library/bb126445.aspx.

8. For an introduction to software factories, consult Greenfield and Short (2004).

9. The home page for Sparx Enterprise Architect is www.sparxsystems.com.au/.

such transformations. In addition, Enterprise Architect enables you to create your own DSLs via the use of UML Profiles.

Process Tooling and Framework

Eclipse Process Framework Composer

The Eclipse Process Framework (EPF) is, as the name implies, an element available from the Eclipse project. More specifically, it is a sub-project within Eclipse's Technology Project. As such, like Eclipse, EPF is an open-source project—you can contribute to the project, download the code, or download the binaries. Information, code, and downloads for Eclipse and EPF can be found at www.eclipse.org and www.eclipse.org/epf/, respectively.

There are two main goals for the EPF project:

1. To provide a framework and tooling for creating and working with software processes

2. To provide process content for a range of processes

So, in essence, the project provides a framework on which we can detail the specifics of a software development process, a metamodel. We end up using that metamodel to create models that detail a development process. There is also a tool that works with that metamodel, providing a user-friendly way in which to model a process. That tool is known as the Eclipse Process Framework Composer.

Process plug-ins are available for download from the EPF site, including OpenUP, XP, Scrum, and MAM. Additional details for these plug-ins are available from the EPF site. If you want to create your own process, in addition to leveraging existing content, you'll also want to take a look at MAM, the Method Authoring Method for Eclipse Practices. It provides guidance on how to author your own content.

IBM Rational Method Composer

There is also a commercial offering, known as IBM Rational Method Composer (RMC)[10] and IBM Rational Unified Process (RUP), which can assist you in creating and publishing your own process. RMC builds on top of EPF Composer, and plug-ins

---

10. More information about RMC can be found at www-01.ibm.com/software/awdtools/rup/.

built with EPF Composer can be used with RMC. IBM Rational published a number of process plug-ins that can be used with RMC, covering a range of topics such as SOA, asset-based development, portfolio management, maintenance projects, DoDAF (Department of Defense Architecture Framework), and others. Ideally, you will also use either EPF Composer or Rational Method Composer to leverage the PBE Practice content and insert it into your own custom process.

Appendix D

PBE Patterns and Guidelines

This appendix provides a graphical view of the PBE Patterns (Figure D.1 on page 370) and PBE Guidelines (Figure D.2 on page 371).

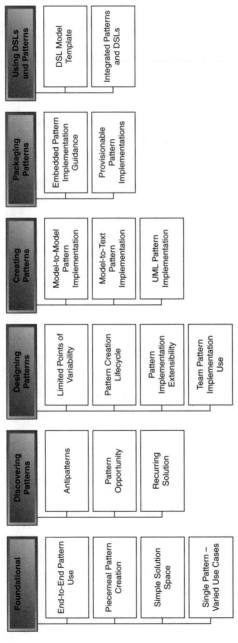

Figure D.1 *A view of the PBE Patterns sorted by category*

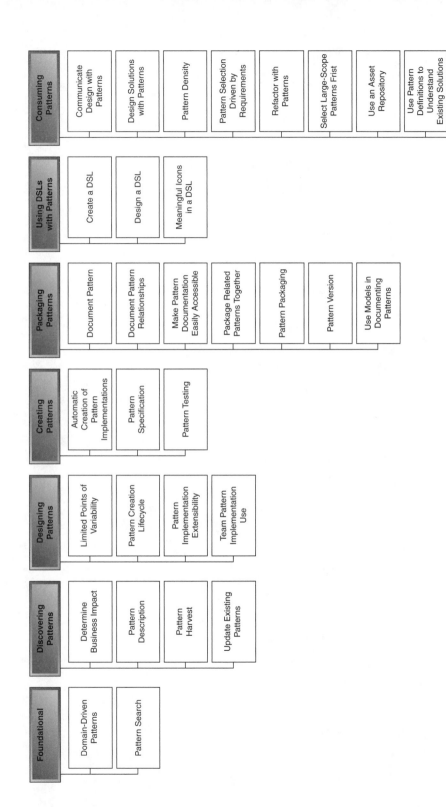

Figure D.2 *A view of the PBE Guidelines sorted by category*

Appendix E

Subsystem Façade Pattern Specification

Context

A set of database-stored business entities needs to be made accessible.

Problem

Database-stored business entities and services need to be exposed to remote clients. However, this could result in a tight coupling between the clients and the business entities, making maintenance or updates difficult. Also, having the database access code mixed with the business code would make the migration to a new database difficult.

Forces

- Simplify the interaction with clients external to the subsystem by hiding the complexity of the internal entities.

- Allow looser coupling with the database provider as data retrieval and updates are abstracted via JPA managers.

- Improve maintenance and portability by hiding subsystem internals and abstracting database access.

Solution

Group related business entities into a subsystem and use a Session Façade to encapsulate the business entities. Remote clients interact with the Session Façade via a coarse-grained service. Access to the database is abstracted away by the Business Entity Manager.

Figure E.1 shows the structural view of the participating elements.

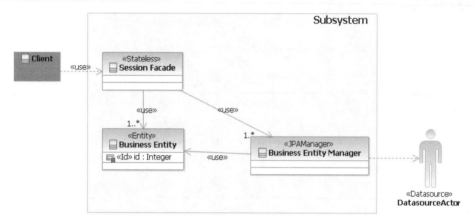

Figure E.1   *Static view of the Subsystem Façade participants*

The participants are as follows:

- **Subsystem.** The subsystem contains the business entities that the façade is shielding.

- **Session Façade.** The Session Façade is used to hide subsystem business entities and expose coarse-grained services. Some of the basic exposed services provide access to a subsystem entity based on its id as well as retrieving all entities of a given type.

- **Business Entity.** The Business Entity role is to carry data that is exchanged and manipulated by the Session Façade.

- **Business Entity Manager.** The Business Entity Manager is used to create, update, retrieve, and delete business entities from the data source.

- **Datasource:** The Datasource represents the connection to the database that is used to store the entities.

Figure E.2 shows a behavioral view of the participants. The client calls the createEntity() operation of the Session Façade. The Session Façade creates a new Business Entity and sets the entity's attributes. The Session Façade then creates a new Business Entity Manager and calls the create operation that inserts the new entity into the database via the Datasource.

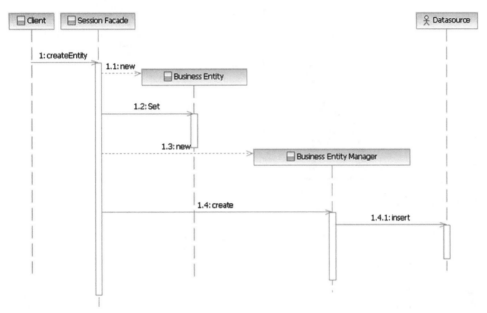

Figure E.2 *Behavioral view of the Subsystem Façade participants*

Sample Code

This section shows an example application of the pattern. Figure E.3 gives an overview of the different classes involved, and the listings that follow detail the associated code.

Listing E.1 shows an example of a Session Façade with the creation of a JPA manager (BidManager), the retrieval of a specific entity based on its id (getBid), and the retrieval of all entities (getAllBids).

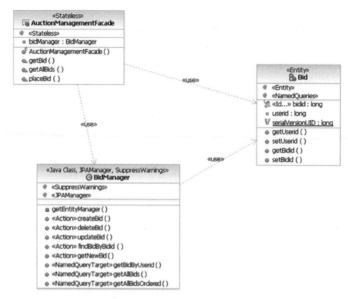

Figure E.3   *Overview of the sample participants*

Listing E.1   Session Façade *Example:* AuctionManagementFacade.java

```java
package auctionmanagement.facade;

import java.util.List;
import javax.ejb.Stateless;
import javax.persistence.PersistenceException;
import auctionmanagement.entities.Auction;
import auctionmanagement.entities.Bid;
import auctionmanagement.entities.Payment;
import auctionmanagement.entities.controller.AuctionManager;
import auctionmanagement.entities.controller.BidManager;
import auctionmanagement.entities.controller.PaymentManager;

/**
 * Session Bean implementation class AuctionManager
 */
@Stateless
public class AuctionManagementFacade implements AuctionFacadeInterface {
    private AuctionManager auctionManager = new AuctionManager();
    private BidManager bidManager = new BidManager();
    private PaymentManager paymentManager = new PaymentManager();

    /**
     * Default constructor.
     */
```

```
    public AuctionManagementFacade() {
        // TODO Auto-generated constructor stub
    }

    public Auction getAuction(long auctionId)
      throws PersistenceException {
        return auctionManager.findAuctionByAuctionId(auctionId);
    }

    public List<Auction> getAllAuctions()
      throws PersistenceException{
        return auctionManager.getAllAuctions();
    }
    public Bid getBid(long bidId) throws PersistenceException {
        return bidManager.findBidByBidId(bidId);
    }

    public List<Bid> getAllBids() throws PersistenceException {
        return bidManager.getAllBids();
    }

    public Payment getPayment(long paymentId)
      throws PersistenceException {
        return paymentManager.findPaymentByPaymentId(paymentId);
    }

    public List<Payment> getAllPayments()
      throws PersistenceException {
        return paymentManager.getAllPayments();
    }

    // Add your business methods here
}
```

Listing E.2 shows the details of the Bid.java JPA entity with declaration of JPA queries (getBidByUserid, getAllBids, getAllBidsOrdered), the entity ID (bidid), one attribute (userid), their getters and setters, as well as the entity serial ID (serialVersionUID).

Listing E.2 *Business Object Example:* Bid.java

```
package auctionmanagement.entities;

import java.io.Serializable;
import javax.persistence.Column;
import javax.persistence.Entity;
import javax.persistence.Id;
import javax.persistence.NamedQueries;
import javax.persistence.NamedQuery;
```

```
@Entity
@NamedQueries({
@NamedQuery(name="getBidByUserid",
   query = "SELECT b FROM Bid b WHERE b.userid = :userid"),
@NamedQuery(name="getAllBids", query = "SELECT b FROM Bid b"),
@NamedQuery(name="getAllBidsOrdered",
   query = "SELECT b FROM Bid b ORDER BY b.bid_id")})

public  class Bid implements Serializable {
   @Id
   @Column(name="BID_ID")
   private long bidid;
   private long userid;
   private static final long serialVersionUID = 1L;


   public long getBidid() {
      return this.bidid;
   }

   public long getUserid() {
      return userid;
   }

   public void setUserid(long userid) {
      this.userid = userid;
   }

   public void setBidid(long bidid) {
      this.bidid = bidid;
   }

}
```

Listing E.3 shows the details of the `BidManager.java` JPA manager with the retrieval of a JPA entity manager (`getEntityManager`), entity CRUD operations (`createBid`, `findBidByBidid`, `updateBid`, and `deleteBid`), attribute queries (`getBidByUserid`), and operations to retrieve the entities (`getAllBids`, `getAllBidsOrdered`).

Listing E.3   *Business Object Manager Example:* `BidManager.java`

```
package auctionmanagement.entities.controller;

import java.sql.Timestamp;
import users.entities.Bidder;
import auctionmanagement.entities.Auction;
import auctionmanagement.entities.Bid;
import com.ibm.jpa.web.JPAManager;
```

```java
import javax.persistence.EntityManager;
import javax.persistence.EntityManagerFactory;
import javax.persistence.PersistenceException;
import javax.persistence.RollbackException;
import com.ibm.jpa.web.NamedQueryTarget;
import com.ibm.jpa.web.Action;
import javax.persistence.Persistence;
import javax.persistence.Query;
import java.lang.String;
import java.util.List;

@JPAManager(targetEntity=auctionmanagement.entities.Bid.class)
@SuppressWarnings("unchecked")
public class BidManager {

    public BidManager() {

    }

    private EntityManager getEntityManager() {
        EntityManagerFactory emf = Persistence
          .createEntityManagerFactory("AuctionManagement");
           return emf.createEntityManager();
    }

    @Action(Action.ACTION_TYPE.CREATE)
    public String createBid(Bid bid) throws PersistenceException {
        EntityManager em = getEntityManager();
        try {
            em.getTransaction().begin();
            em.persist(bid);
            em.getTransaction().commit();
        } catch (PersistenceException  ex) {
            if (ex instanceof RollbackException){
                try {
                    if (em.getTransaction().isActive()) {
                        em.getTransaction().rollback();
                    }
                } catch (PersistenceException e) {
                    e.printStackTrace();
                    throw e;
                }
            } else {
                throw ex;
            }
        } finally {
            em.close();
        }
```

```java
        return "";
}

@Action(Action.ACTION_TYPE.DELETE)
public String deleteBid(Bid bid) throws PersistenceException {
    EntityManager em = getEntityManager();
    try {
        em.getTransaction().begin();
        bid = em.merge(bid);
        em.remove(bid);
        em.getTransaction().commit();
    } catch (PersistenceException  ex) {
        if (ex instanceof RollbackException){
            try {
                if (em.getTransaction().isActive()) {
                    em.getTransaction().rollback();
                }
            } catch (PersistenceException e) {
                e.printStackTrace();
                throw e;
            }
        } else {
            throw ex;
        }
    } finally {
        em.close();
    }
    return "";
}

@Action(Action.ACTION_TYPE.UPDATE)
public String updateBid(Bid bid) throws PersistenceException {
    EntityManager em = getEntityManager();
    try {
        em.getTransaction().begin();
        bid = em.merge(bid);
        em.getTransaction().commit();
    } catch (PersistenceException  ex) {
        if (ex instanceof RollbackException){
            try {
                if (em.getTransaction().isActive()) {
                    em.getTransaction().rollback();
                }
            } catch (PersistenceException e) {
                e.printStackTrace();
                throw e;
            }
```

```
        } else {
            throw ex;
        }
    } finally {
        em.close();
    }
    return "";
}


@Action(Action.ACTION_TYPE.FIND)
public Bid findBidByBidId(long bidId) {
    Bid bid = null;
    EntityManager em = getEntityManager();
    try {
        bid = (Bid) em.find(Bid.class, bidId);
    } finally {
        em.close();
    }
    return bid;
}


@Action(Action.ACTION_TYPE.NEW)
public Bid getNewBid() {
    Bid bid = new Bid();
    return bid;
}


@NamedQueryTarget("getBidByBidTime")
public List<Bid> getBidByBidTime(Timestamp bidTime) {
    EntityManager em = getEntityManager();
    List<Bid> results = null;
    try {
        Query query = em.createNamedQuery("getBidByBidTime");
        query.setParameter("bidTime", bidTime);
        results = (List<Bid>) query.getResultList();
    } finally {
        em.close();
    }
    return results;
}


@NamedQueryTarget("getBidByAuction")
public List<Bid> getBidByAuction(Auction auction) {
    EntityManager em = getEntityManager();
    List<Bid> results = null;
    try {
        Query query = em.createNamedQuery("getBidByAuction");
```

```java
            query.setParameter("auction", auction);
            results = (List<Bid>) query.getResultList();
        } finally {
            em.close();
        }
        return results;
    }

    @NamedQueryTarget("getBidByBidder")
    public List<Bid> getBidByBidder(Bidder bidder) {
        EntityManager em = getEntityManager();
        List<Bid> results = null;
        try {
            Query query = em.createNamedQuery("getBidByBidder");
            query.setParameter("bidder", bidder);
            results = (List<Bid>) query.getResultList();
        } finally {
            em.close();
        }
        return results;
    }

    @NamedQueryTarget("getAllBids")
    public List<Bid> getAllBids() {
        EntityManager em = getEntityManager();
        List<Bid> results = null;
        try {
            Query query = em.createNamedQuery("getAllBids");
            results = (List<Bid>) query.getResultList();
        } finally {
            em.close();
        }
        return results;
    }

    @NamedQueryTarget("getAllBidsOrdered")
    public List<Bid> getAllBidsOrdered() {
        EntityManager em = getEntityManager();
        List<Bid> results = null;
        try {
            Query query = em.createNamedQuery("getAllBidsOrdered");
            results = (List<Bid>) query.getResultList();
        } finally {
            em.close();
        }
        return results;
    }
}
```

Pattern Composition

The Subsystem Façade pattern is a compound pattern that is composed of the Session Façade and the Data Access Object patterns[1] as shown in Figure E.4.

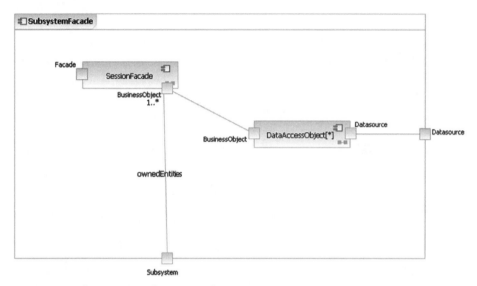

Figure E.4   *Subsystem Façade composed patterns*

In Figure E.4 we see that the two composed patterns are linked through the BusinessObject parameter. The SessionFaçade shields one or more (1..*) BusinessObjects. We also see that for each BusinessObject there is one corresponding DataAccessObject. The BusinessObjects bound to the SessionFaçade and DataAccessObject BusinessObject parameters are the entities owned by the subsystem.

---

1. For more details about the Session Façade and the Data Access Object patterns please refer to Alur et al. (2003).

Appendix F

Introduction to the PBE Practice

This appendix provides an overview of the PBE Practice, highlighting the main roles, work products, and tasks involved in PBE. The goal of this appendix is to provide additional details regarding the practice to assist in further understanding the case study and PBE in general. This material also serves as an introduction to the full PBE Practice, which is available for download as both an EPF Composer plug-in and a published process configuration.

PBE Roles

A good place to start in following a development process is to figure out the roles that are involved in the effort. When looking at the roles, it is important to keep in mind that a role does not necessarily map to a single person. A person may end up filling multiple roles, or a role may end up being filled by multiple people. So there can be a many-to-many relationship between people and roles. In a larger organization we may find that each role maps directly to one or more individuals. In smaller organizations the roles may be less formally recognized and an individual may fill more than one role.

Figure F.1 shows all the roles involved in PBE and maps them to the areas in which they perform tasks. Only the main roles are described in the remainder of the section; the others are more standard and are self-explanatory. Beneath each role there is a listing of the case study chapters where the role participates in the effort.

Asset Librarian

The Asset Librarian is responsible for managing reusable assets. Typically the person in the role works with an asset repository, making sure that the reusable assets are managed properly. Asset Librarians set up communities of interest and users, review

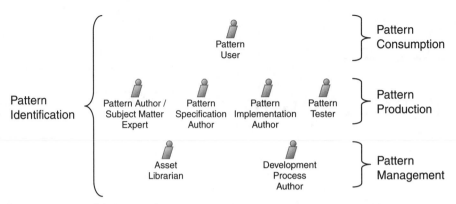

Figure F.1   *View of the PBE roles*

workflows, and facilitate the reuse program. As shown in Figure F.2, the Asset Librarian is the primary performer for the Deploy Pattern to Asset Repository task and is responsible for the reusable asset work product.

Figure F.2   *Overview of Asset Librarian role and associated tasks and work products*

Skills typically required to fill this role include

- Strong organizational skills

- Knowledge of the tools and practices related to managing reusable assets

Pattern Author/Subject Matter Expert (SME)

The Pattern Author/Subject Matter Expert (SME) is an expert within a business or technical domain. As shown in Figure F.3, Pattern Authors/SMEs are primary performers of a number of tasks, including Capture Reuse Metrics and Evaluate Candidate Patterns. They are experts in the domain associated with the pattern and partner with other roles in creating pattern specifications and implementations.

Figure F.3 *Overview of Pattern Author/SME role and associated tasks*

Skills typically required to fill this role include

- Expertise related to the targeted technology or business domain
- Intimate knowledge of the pattern and experience applying it successfully

Pattern Specification Author

The Pattern Specification Author is responsible for writing pattern specifications, that is, the formal written documentation that describes a pattern. This includes the description of the problem, solution, and consequences of use, as well as pointers to additional related patterns. The Pattern Specification Author does not necessarily need to be skilled in the domain related to the pattern and depends on the Pattern Author/SME to provide assistance and explanations as needed.

As shown in Figure F.4, the Pattern Specification Author participates in a number of tasks, including Create a Pattern Specification, Make Pattern Available for Reuse, and Review Feedback. The role is also responsible for the pattern specification work product.

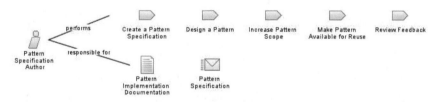

Figure F.4 *Overview of Pattern Specification Author role and associated tasks and work products*

Skills typically required to fill this role include

- Knowledge of the templates and practices of pattern specification
- Strong technical writing skills
- Knowledge of the targeted technology or business area (desirable)

Pattern Implementation Author

The Pattern Implementation Author is an expert in creating pattern implementations. This includes, but is not limited to, the creation of one or more of model-to-model pattern implementations, model-to-text pattern implementations, UML patterns, and DSLs. Like the Pattern Specification Author, the Pattern Implementation Author is not an expert in the domain of a specific pattern.

As shown in Figure F.5, the Pattern Implementation Author participates in a number of tasks, including Build a Pattern Implementation, Design a Pattern, Increase Pattern Scope, Make Pattern Available for Reuse, and Review Feedback. In addition, this role has responsibility for the pattern implementation and pattern implementation documentation work products.

Figure F.5   *Overview of Pattern Implementation Author role and associated tasks and work products*

Skills typically required to fill this role include

- Knowledge of the tools and practices used for creating a pattern implementation

- Knowledge of the targeted technology or business areas (desirable)

Pattern Tester

The Pattern Tester role is responsible for testing pattern specifications and implementations. The role collaborates with the Pattern Author/SME, the Pattern Implementation Author, and the Pattern Specification Author in testing the pattern. This role is responsible for the Test a Pattern task and will work with the defect artifact.

Skills typically required to fill this role include

- Knowledge of testing approaches and techniques

- Diagnostic and problem-solving skills

- Knowledge of the targeted technology or business area (desirable)

Pattern User

Everyone within the development organization fills the Pattern User role, as everyone should be looking to use patterns. This role focuses on the use of patterns in helping to create and deliver software. Keep in mind that patterns can be used for many things, including the creation of other patterns. As shown in Figure F.6, the Pattern User role participates in the following tasks: Capture Reuse Metrics, Locate a Pattern, Model Pattern Use, Provide Feedback on a Pattern, and Use a Pattern. Pattern Users are responsible for the pattern feedback and pattern metric work products.

Figure F.6 *Overview of the Pattern User role and associated tasks and work products*

Skills typically required to fill this role include

- Ability to recognize opportunities where a pattern could be used
- Ability to work with an asset repository to find and reuse patterns

PBE Main Work Products

In this section we discuss the work products associated with the PBE Practice. As the different roles work through their tasks, they will consume and produce different artifacts, called work products.

Figure F.7 shows the PBE work products as well as their relationships. The arrows show the work product flow and how those work products, in turn, influence other work products. Beneath each work product there is a listing of the case study chapters where the work product is involved.

The rest of this section describes the main work products, skipping those that are self-explanatory.

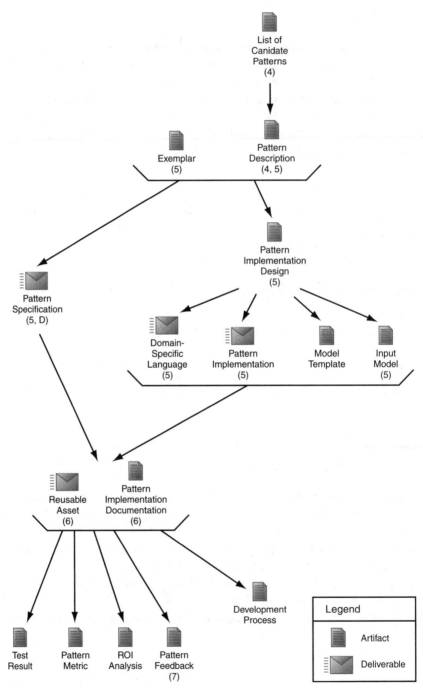

Figure F.7   *Overview of PBE work products and their relationships*

Domain-Specific Language

A domain-specific language (DSL) is a language used to capture information for a specific domain. Such a language can be graphical or textual. It is targeted to a specific area and should not be used generally across a range of problem spaces.

DSLs are often used in conjunction with patterns. Thus, DSLs are a common deliverable when following PBE.

Exemplar

An exemplar represents the results (or output) associated with the application of a best practice. This is the best-practice-based solution that will serve as the target reference as we design and create a pattern. This is a key artifact that serves as input into the pattern creation effort.

List of Candidate Patterns

As we identify candidate patterns, we add them to a list, recognizing that not all of them will end up being built. We evaluate the candidate patterns in the list and determine which make the most sense to create.

Pattern Description

A pattern description is an artifact that provides a high-level description of a pattern. This description is much less detailed than a pattern specification and will later serve as the input into the creation of patterns (including both specifications and implementations). The pattern description provides a lightweight and easy method for capturing initial details about the pattern that can be fleshed out as we progress through evaluation and design efforts.

Pattern Implementation

A pattern implementation automates the application of a pattern in a particular environment. The patterns become tools themselves, concrete artifacts within the development environment.

Pattern Implementation Design

This artifact details the design for a pattern implementation. The artifact will contain details regarding

- The major components that constitute the pattern and how those components fit together

- The expected behavior of each of the components

- Input expectations for each of the components

- Expected output from each of the components

- Diagrams as necessary to help others understand the design

- Documentation as necessary to help others understand the design

Pattern Implementation Documentation

This documentation describes a pattern implementation, how to use it, and how to install it and provides guidance and pointers to other related patterns. When creating this artifact, we reference the pattern design, description, and specification.

Input Model

An input model is used to provide input into a pattern implementation. Its content maps to the roles and points of variability associated with the pattern, allowing us to make the pattern unique to our specific context. The input model may take a number of different forms, including XML, UML, EMF, or even a 3GL such as Java. The actual representation of the model may be hidden from the user via the use of a wizard, form, or other view.

Pattern Specification

A pattern specification is the formal written documentation that describes a pattern. This documentation details the problem, solution, and consequences of a pattern along with guidance on related patterns.

Reusable Asset

An asset is ". . . a collection of artifacts that provides a solution to a problem. The asset has instructions on how it should be used and is reusable in one or more contexts, such as a development or a runtime context. The asset may also be extended and customized through variability points."[1]

Task Order

At this point we have an understanding of the roles and work products associated with a PBE effort. The next step is to look at the tasks defined within the PBE Practice. As part of this discussion we will take a high-level look at each task, the participating roles, and the work products that are consumed and produced.

Recall that within PBE we have four major focus areas: pattern identification, pattern production, pattern consumption, and pattern management. Figure F.8 shows how these different focus areas interact.

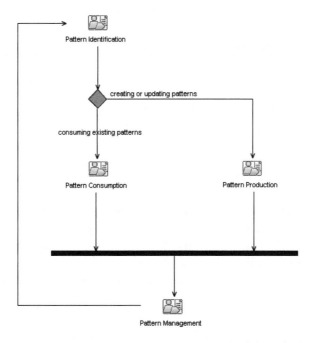

Figure F.8 *Overview of PBE focus areas and their relationships*

---

1. Larsen (2006).

With this view in mind, we can use Table F.1 to help us understand when each of the tasks from the PBE Practice should be considered for use. The chapter numbers shown in parenthesis following the task name are the case study chapters in which the tasks are used.

Table F.1   *Mapping of Tasks to Phases of PBE*

Pattern Identification	Pattern Production	Pattern Consumption	Pattern Management
Find Project Patterns (Chapter 4)	Design a Pattern (Chapter 5)	Locate a Pattern (Chapters 4, 5, 6, 7)	Deploy Pattern to Asset Repository (Chapter 6)
Evaluate Candidate Patterns (Chapter 4)	Create a Pattern Specification (Chapter 5)	Use a Pattern (Chapters 4, 5, 6, 7)	Review Feedback (Chapter 7)
Increase Pattern Scope (Chapters 4, 7)	Build a Pattern Implementation (Chapter 5)	Model Pattern Use (Chapters 4, 5, 6, 7)	Capture Reuse Metrics (Chapter 7)
	Make a Pattern Available for Reuse (Chapter 6)	Provide Feedback on a Pattern (Chapter 7)	Update Development Process (Chapter 4)
	Test a Pattern (Chapter 5)		

An additional aspect to consider in regard to the timing of the performance of the PBE tasks is the larger overall process and associated practices being used.

PBE Tasks

At this point we have an understanding of the roles and work products in the PBE Practice. However, what work must be done by these roles to create and consume these work products? In this section we work through the list of tasks associated with PBE. For each task a high-level overview is provided. More details about each task are available in the PBE Practice. The tasks are grouped and listed following the order in Table F.1.

Pattern Identification

Figure F.9 shows pattern identification tasks and workflows.

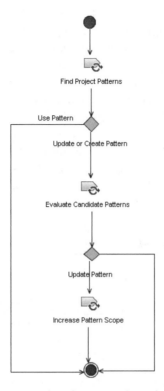

Figure F.9 *Overview of the pattern identification tasks and workflow*

Find Project Patterns

In this task we find the set of patterns that we want to consider using in our project(s). The patterns can be sourced via a number of different options and may also be at different levels of maturity or completeness.

In terms of sources, some of the options include

- Patterns from external sources such as vendors and the community

- Patterns from internal sources such as preexisting patterns and patterns that need to be created

Our focus is on figuring out the set of patterns that could have an impact on the project. We spend some time and effort in putting together a list of candidate patterns. We perform some analysis on the patterns and their possible impact. But our focus is on being thorough in terms of identifying and finding patterns, not the filtering. As a result of this task we produce a candidate pattern list.

Keep in mind that in an iterative and incremental approach to development we would revisit this task multiple times during the project. At the beginning of the project we are still learning about the requirements associated with the project. As time and the project progress, our understanding grows, and usually requirements and priorities change. Therefore, we do not want to overinvest time in this task at the beginning of the project or expect that all patterns will be identified up front.

As shown in Table F.2, this task is inclusive and meant to involve the entire team. Good ideas and input can come from any member of the team, and everyone should be encouraged to contribute to the effort. In terms of input to this task we need to look at the requirements related to the project. The functional and nonfunctional requirements will be used to help us determine when and where patterns may have an impact on the project.

Table F.2 *Summary of Relationships to Find Project Patterns Task*

Relationships		
Roles	Primary performer:	Additional performers:
	Architect	Pattern User
Inputs	Mandatory:	Optional:
	Requirements	None
Outputs	List of candidate patterns	
Patterns and Guidelines	Antipatterns (Chapter 11), Domain-Driven Patterns (Chapter 10), Pattern Opportunity (Chapter 11), Recurring Solution (Chapter 11), Use Patterns to Find Patterns (Chapter 16)	
Steps	Identify existing patterns that would be applicable.	
	Identify opportunities for patterns to be created.	
	Compile a list of candidate patterns.	

Evaluate Candidate Patterns

In this task we determine which of the candidate patterns should be invested in and created. With PBE, we want to be systematic and disciplined in how we use patterns. We need to have some rigor in place, guiding us as we figure out what patterns we should use, why they should be used, and the expected impact. This is especially important when we create our own patterns. It is not acceptable to deliver a pattern that has no value to the project.

It makes sense that we would evaluate our candidate patterns in much the same way as we perform similar work with other architecturally significant aspects of building a solution. For instance, we would typically answer the following questions:

- What architecturally significant elements should we use?

- What is the benefit of using those elements?

- What are the associated constraints and challenges?

Although the primary performer of this task is only the Pattern Author/SME, Table F.3 shows that many others in the organization assist in performing the task. When reviewing the list of candidate patterns, we seek assistance from those who will help to create the pattern as well as those who will use the pattern.

Table F.3 *Summary of Relationships to Evaluate Candidate Patterns Task*

Relationships		
Roles	Primary performer: Pattern Author/SME	Additional performers: Pattern Implementation Author Pattern Specification Author Pattern User
Inputs	Mandatory: List of candidate patterns Pattern description	Optional: None
Outputs	Pattern description List of candidate patterns ROI analysis	
Patterns and Guidelines	Determine Business Impact (Chapter 10), Pattern Description (Chapter 11), Piecemeal Pattern Creation (Chapter 10), Simple Solution Space (Chapter 10)	
Steps	Acquire a list of candidate patterns. Create initial pattern descriptions. Calculate the ROI for each pattern. Rank/select patterns based on ROI. Update pattern descriptions.	

Increase Pattern Scope

In the Increase Pattern Scope task we grow the scope of a pattern to drive generation of additional related artifacts. After we release the pattern, we will start to receive feedback from users regarding the pattern. They will tell us what works well and what doesn't work so well and will suggest areas for improvement. This becomes a source for determining how the pattern should evolve in future releases. However, this is not the only source of input on the future direction of the pattern. We also can work with the Pattern Author/SME to determine ways in which we can extend the scope of the pattern.

When looking at expanding the scope of the pattern, we want to find ways in which we can leverage as much of the existing infrastructure as possible and generate more value from the effort to date. For example, the pattern requires that users provide an input model with many details about their specific situations. We could use this information to generate code associated with a best practice. The information provided in the input model is valuable and is usually applicable to more than just code. We could start to think of all of the other things that are related: test cases, deployment scripts, database scripts, packaging, documentation, and so on. We could also look at other ways in which we can extend the usage scenario. Would the introduction of a graphical DSL help users more successfully use the pattern? Additional constraints? Additional assumptions? This is still adding scope, just in a different dimension.

When building out the scope of the pattern, we want to think about what extensions to the pattern will provide the most ROI. Much as we did when we evaluated which patterns we should build, we need to analyze which extensions should be made. Just because an extension can be made, doesn't mean that it should be.

As shown in Table F.4, the primary performer for this task is the Pattern Implementation Author since this task is applicable to the creation of pattern implementations.

Table F.4 *Summary of Relationships to Increase Pattern Scope Task*

Relationships		
Roles	Primary performer:	Additional performers:
	Pattern Implementation Author	Pattern Author/SME
	Pattern Specification Author	
Inputs	Mandatory:	Optional:
	Pattern feedback	Domain-specific language
		Pattern implementation
		Pattern specification
		ROI analysis
Outputs	Domain-specific language	
	Pattern implementation	
	Pattern specification	
Patterns and Guidelines	Determine Business Impact (Chapter 11), End-to-End Pattern Use (Chapter 10), Integrated Patterns and DSLs (Chapter 15), Piecemeal Pattern Creation (Chapter 10), Simple Solution Space (Chapter 10)	
Steps	Identify a pattern that has already been released.	
	Analyze user feedback.	
	Analyze the pattern and current scope.	
	Analyze candidate extensions.	
	Enhance the pattern to cover a larger scope.	

Pattern Production

Figure F.10 shows pattern production tasks and workflows.

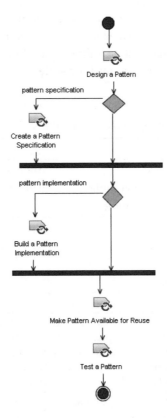

Figure F.10 *Overview of pattern production tasks and workflows*

Design a Pattern

Once we have decided that a pattern is to be built, we have to come up with a design for it. We need to ensure that a pattern description has been created. As we design the pattern, we use the PBE Core Values and PBE Patterns and Guidelines to guide the effort.

Recall from the PBE Core Values that when we design a pattern, it is important to remember that we usually use a number of patterns in combination. So we need to understand how the new pattern will be used in relation to other patterns. In addition, we need to consider whether we are going to target the creation of a pattern specification or a pattern implementation. An exemplar, as listed in Table F.5, is a key input to the efforts associated with this task, ensuring that the pattern is grounded in a proven best practice.

We also need to ensure that the exemplar that is used as the basis for the pattern is of high quality. We can start by using traditional testing approaches to ensure that the exemplar is indeed a representation of best practices and that it works. However, we also want to take things a step further and make sure that the exemplar is a good foundation for the patterns that will be built on top of it. For instance, does it exhibit the necessary variability to truly account for the flexibility that will be needed by the Pattern Users?

Table F.5 *Summary of Relationships to Design a Pattern Task*

Relationships		
Roles	**Primary performer:**	**Additional performers:**
	Pattern Implementation Author	Pattern Author/SME
	Pattern Specification Author	
Inputs	**Mandatory:**	**Optional:**
	List of candidate patterns	ROI analysis
	Exemplar	
	Pattern description	
Outputs	Pattern design	
Patterns and Guidelines	Compound Pattern (Chapter 12), Exemplar Analysis (Chapter 12), Limited Points of Variability (Chapter12), Meet-in-the-Middle Pattern Design (Chapter 12), Pattern Creation Lifecycle (Chapter 12), Pattern Harvest (Chapter 11), Pattern Implementation (Chapter 12), Pattern Implementation Extensibility (Chapter 12), Team Pattern Implementation Use (Chapter 12)	
Steps	Review the pattern description and evaluation.	
	Determine the type of pattern that needs to be created.	
	Select a pattern specification template.	
	Determine the composite parts of the pattern implementation.	
	Understand the architecture of the pattern implementation.	
	Determine the related artifacts to create.	
	Evaluate the exemplar.	
	Evaluate and manage abstractions.	

Create a Pattern Specification

Generally, patterns have been presented as formal written documentation that explains the pattern. We refer to these patterns as pattern specifications. In this task we build upon the effort from the Design a Pattern task. We want to embellish the design and capture the details in the pattern specification, using a pattern specification template. Usually, within an organization we try to use a standardized pattern specification template for capturing pattern specifications. This helps to ensure that the information that is most important to the organization is captured and that we can train people on a standard approach to creating pattern specifications, and it simplifies the effort needed to understand the pattern specification.

As shown in Table F.6, the primary performers of this task are the Pattern Author/SME and the Pattern Specification Author. In cases where a pattern implementation is also being created, they will interact with the Pattern Implementation Author. Inputs to this task include the exemplar and pattern description. We may also need to consider the related pattern implementation and associated DSL.

Table F.6 *Summary of Relationships to Create a Pattern Specification Task*

Relationships		
Roles	**Primary performer:**	**Additional performers:**
	Pattern Specification Author	Pattern Author/SME
Inputs	**Mandatory:**	**Optional:**
	Exemplar	Domain-specific language
	Pattern description	
Outputs	Pattern specification	
Patterns and Guidelines	Pattern Specification (Chapter 13)	
Steps	Select a pattern specification template.	
	Collaborate with related roles and leverage-related artifacts.	
	Write the pattern specification.	

Build a Pattern Implementation

In this task we create a pattern implementation that leverages the design that was created in the Design a Pattern task. Recall that there are a number of types of pattern implementations that can be used independently or in combination, including UML pattern implementations, model-to-text pattern implementations, and model-to-model pattern implementations. For examples of pattern implementations please refer to Chapter 2.

To make the pattern implementation easier to use, we can also develop a domain-specific language (DSL). Other artifacts and deliverables related to this task include

- Pattern input model
- Pattern description

Table F.7 provides a summary of the relationships of other process elements of this task. As mentioned in the role descriptions, it is unlikely that Pattern Implementation Authors have the domain knowledge to build the pattern on their own; they will collaborate with a Pattern Author/SME. If it is decided that a pattern specification is also needed, the Pattern Specification Author role will also join in the effort of completing this task.

Table F.7 *Summary of Relationships to Build a Pattern Implementation Task*

Relationships		
Roles	Primary performer: Pattern Implementation Author	Additional performers: Pattern Author/SME Pattern Specification Author
Inputs	Mandatory: Exemplar Pattern design	Optional: Pattern specification Pattern description
Outputs	Domain-specific language Pattern implementation Pattern input model	
Patterns and Guidelines	Automate Creation of Pattern Implementations (Chapter 13), Model-to-Model Pattern Implementation (Chapter 13), Model-to-Text Pattern Implementation (Chapter 13), UML Pattern Implementation (Chapter 13), Using DSLs with Patterns guidelines and patterns (Chapter 15)	
Steps	Create/select the domain-specific language. Create the pattern implementation components. Test the pattern implementation components. Integrate the components.	

Make Pattern Available for Reuse

In this task we take the patterns that we have created, along with associated artifacts, and package them for reuse. The focus here is on ensuring that the assets are as consumable as possible. Artifacts that usually get included within and alongside the patterns include the DSL, pattern implementation documentation (within the asset and alongside), sample models used for input/testing the pattern, and model templates to guide the user in creating an input model.

Here are some of the things that we need to consider in this task:

- How should the pattern be packaged?

- How are relationships between patterns handled?

- How are supporting artifacts made available?

- How can the user learn about and understand how to use the pattern?

As shown in Table F.8, the Pattern Implementation Author and Pattern Specification Author roles focus on making their respective assets available for reuse. They will look to the Asset Librarian role to provide assistance in regard to reusable assets in general.

Table F.8 *Summary of Relationships to Make Pattern Available for Reuse Task*

Relationships		
Roles	**Primary performer:**	**Additional performers:**
	Pattern Implementation Author	Asset Librarian
	Pattern Specification Author	
Inputs	**Mandatory:**	**Optional:**
	Pattern description	Domain-specific language
	Pattern implementation	Model template
	Pattern specification	
Outputs	Pattern implementation documentation	
	Reusable asset	
Patterns and Guidelines	Document Pattern, Document Pattern Relationships, Embedded Pattern Implementation Guidance, Make Pattern Documentation Easily Accessible, Package Related Patterns Together, Pattern Packaging, Pattern Version, Provisionable Pattern Implementation, Use Models in Documenting Patterns (all in Chapter 14)	
Steps	Document the pattern.	
	Find artifacts that need to be packaged alongside the asset.	
	Determine the set of artifacts that need to be packaged inside the asset.	
	Connect the documentation to the pattern asset.	
	Export the project as a reusable asset.	
	Test the asset.	

Test a Pattern

A product that lacks quality will not be used successfully. In the case of a pattern, this means that the investment in identifying, evaluating, designing, building, and deploying the pattern has been for naught.

As for any other development activity, testing is an important component of ensuring quality. In the context of patterns, they should be tested on multiple levels and in multiple ways. Developer testing is part of the pattern developer activities, whereas this task focuses more on the functional testing, also called "black-box" testing. The tester tests the reusable asset packaged by the pattern developer and validates that the pattern when applied produces the expected result.

As shown in Table F.9, we see that this kind of testing is mainly the responsibility of the Pattern Tester role, with other roles involved as necessary to support the effort.

Pattern implementation and pattern implementation documentation are mandatory only when testing a pattern implementation, while a pattern specification is mandatory when testing a pattern specification.

Table F.9 *Summary of Relationships to Test a Pattern Task*

Relationships		
Roles	Primary performer: Pattern Tester	Additional performers: Pattern Author/SME Pattern Implementation Author Pattern Specification Author
Inputs	Mandatory: Reusable asset	Optional: Domain-specific language
Outputs	Test result	
Patterns and Guidelines	Pattern Testing (Chapter 13)	
Steps	Identify test cases. Build the test cases. Test the pattern. Record the test results.	

Pattern Consumption

Figure F.11 shows pattern consumption tasks and workflows.

Locate a Pattern

As Pattern Users, we want to locate a pattern that can help to solve a recurring problem. In the Locate a Pattern task we conduct a search of the pattern repository (or a set of pattern repositories) to find the available patterns that fit our needs.

If we are unable to find a pattern that suits our requirements, we need to escalate the issue to the leadership team for the project. It may turn out that the pattern was considered during the Find Project Patterns task but was found to provide insufficient value; it may turn out that it was not considered, or that the pattern does exist but the search was not conducted properly.

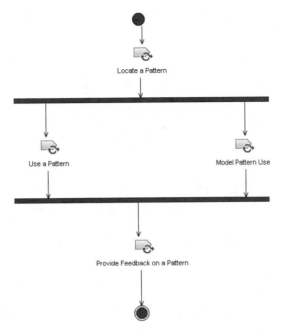

Figure F.11 *Overview of pattern consumption tasks and workflows*

When searching through the repository, we may find a number of patterns that potentially suit our requirements. At this point we will need to further evaluate the patterns and perhaps enter the Use a Pattern task with a set of patterns.

As shown in Table F.10, the primary performer of this task is the Pattern User role. Upon completion of this task we should have found a set of patterns that can assist us in our efforts, or else we will have raised a flag indicating that we have a recurring problem and are unable to locate a pattern.

Table F.10 *Summary of Relationships to Locate a Pattern Task*

Relationships		
Roles	Primary performer:	Additional performers:
	Pattern User	None
Inputs	Mandatory:	Optional:
	Requirements	None
	Problem	
Outputs	Reusable asset	

(continues)

Table F.10   *Summary of Relationships to Locate a Pattern Task (Continued)*

Relationships	
Patterns and Guidelines	Pattern Search (Chapter 10), Pattern Selection Driven by Requirements (Chapter 16), Select Large-Scope Patterns First (Chapter 16), Use an Asset Repository (Chapter 16)
Steps	Search the repository.
	Communicate that the pattern cannot be located.

Use a Pattern

At this point the Pattern User has found a pattern that can be applied to help solve a particular problem. This task focuses on helping the Pattern User successfully consume the pattern.

As we look to use the pattern, we want to document where and how the pattern is used. If we are leveraging modeling as we create the solution, it makes sense to document that the pattern is being used, where and how it is being used, and how it connects to other patterns.

At this point the steps that we have taken will be the same whether we are dealing with a pattern specification or a pattern implementation. However, moving forward, we find that the steps will diverge, as we need to work to the specifics of each type of pattern.

Note that when using a pattern the output can vary widely, as patterns can be used for many things and many situations. As a result, the output from this task will be some set of artifacts that are based on the pattern that is used. This may be a model, a portion of a model, or some text-based artifact such as code, configuration scripts, XML files, and so on.

Use a Pattern Specification

In terms of working with just a pattern specification, the path forward is quite simple. There should be a minimal amount of documentation that ships with the specification. To move forward and use the pattern, we first need to read and then comprehend the pattern specification itself. When reading the specification, we need to consider the following:

- Does the pattern address the problem?

- Can we live with the constraints associated with applying the pattern?

- Does the pattern have relationships with other patterns? What type of relationship(s)? Can the pattern be used in conjunction with other patterns, or are the relationships mutually exclusive? If there are relationships, have we already used some of those patterns? Would it make sense to look at applying those other patterns if they have not already been used?

Once we have a firm understanding of the pattern, we can then apply the pattern.

Use a Pattern Implementation

In terms of working with a pattern implementation, our next step after finding the pattern is consulting the more detailed pattern implementation documentation that is provided along with the pattern. We use this documentation to further understand the pattern, how the pattern is used, how it can be applied, and how we connect the details that are specific to our situation with the points of variability that are provided by the pattern. We will also find out how many patterns are in the package, how they are related, and any supporting DSL and customizations to the modeling environment. Once we feel comfortable with our understanding of the pattern, we need to install it. The documentation that ships alongside the pattern helps us to gain this understanding.

Once we have installed the pattern, we should check to make sure that the pattern works with provided samples and that documentation for the pattern is available within our work environment. In addition, we should check for supporting artifacts that could help us comprehend and use the pattern(s).

Then we can start working on defining an input model matching our context and applying the pattern as described in the supporting documentation.

As shown in Table F.11, the primary performer for this task is the Pattern User role. Note that the table does not explicitly call out a list of outputs as the list is unbounded, limited only by the needs of the project and the creativity of the Pattern Authors.

Table F.11 *Summary of Relationships to Use a Pattern Task*

Relationships		
Roles	**Primary performer:**	**Additional performers:**
	Pattern User	None
Inputs	**Mandatory:**	**Optional:**
	Pattern implementation	Domain-specific language
	Pattern implementation documentation	
	Pattern specification	
Outputs	Architecture	
	Design	
	Implementation	
	Test	

(*continues*)

Table F.11   *Summary of Relationships to Use a Pattern Task (Continued)*

Relationships	
Patterns and Guidelines	Single Pattern–Varied Use Cases (Chapter 10), Design Solutions with Patterns (Chapter 16), Refactor with Patterns (Chapter 16), Use Pattern Definitions to Understand Existing Solutions (Chapter 16), Use Patterns to Find Patterns (Chapter 16)
Steps	Review the documentation.
	Install the pattern.
	Create the input model.
	Apply the pattern.
	Review the output.

Model Pattern Use

In this task we focus on modeling the patterns that are used in a solution. Traditionally we have used modeling to capture details about the architecturally significant aspects of a solution; such thinking and effort also apply to the patterns used within a solution. Some of the reasons and benefits of modeling the patterns used include these:

- **Improved design.** It is clear and explicit where architecturally significant elements, such as patterns, have been used. Modeling also highlights where patterns have not been used, can alert us to areas where patterns are absent, and helps us as we review solutions.

- **Improved communication.** It becomes easier for others to understand the solution.

- **Education.** We can use such models to educate others on the design and the use of patterns.

Keep in mind that we are not looking at a one-size-fits-all approach to the use of modeling. We've seen that modeling can be used in many forms and at varying levels of detail and effort. We may use models to sketch out the design of the solution, or we may use models as a blueprint that details a majority of the aspects related to the solution. Regardless of the depth, we can stay consistent with our modeling preference and still include details about the patterns in use.

The Communicate Design with Patterns guideline provides examples of modeling pattern usage.

The primary performer for this task, as shown in Table F.12, is the Pattern User role.

Table F.12 *Summary of Relationships to Model Pattern Use Task*

Relationships		
Roles	**Primary performer:**	**Additional performers:**
	Pattern User	None
Inputs	**Mandatory:**	**Optional:**
	Pattern implementation	Pattern input model
	Pattern implementation documentation	
	Pattern specification	
Outputs	Design model	
Patterns and Guidelines	Communicate Design with Patterns (Chapter 16)	
Steps	Identify definitions that need to be modeled.	
	Identify instantiations that need to be modeled.	
	Create diagrams.	

Provide Feedback on a Pattern

When using a pattern, we should provide feedback to the pattern maintainers to improve the quality and increase the value of the pattern. This feedback can be used as input into the next iteration of pattern development as well as help to guide efforts in expanding the scope of the pattern. This feedback can also be used to help others determine if they should use the pattern.

The primary output of this task is pattern feedback, as shown in Table F.13, which is provided by the Pattern User.

Table F.13 *Summary of Relationships to Provide Feedback on a Pattern Task*

Relationships		
Roles	**Primary performer:**	**Additional performers:**
	Pattern User	None
Inputs	**Mandatory:**	**Optional:**
	Pattern implementation	None
	Pattern specification	
Outputs	Pattern feedback	
Patterns and Guidelines	Update Existing Patterns (Chapter 11)	
Steps	Find the asset in the asset repository.	
	Detail the feedback on the asset entry within the asset repository.	
	Provide additional details to the pattern maintainer (as needed).	

Pattern Management

Figure F.12 shows pattern management tasks and workflows.

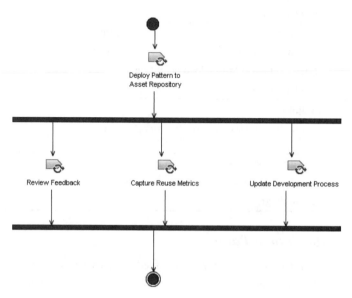

Figure F.12   *Overview of pattern management tasks and workflows*

Deploy Pattern to Asset Repository

Once the pattern has been documented and packaged, we have to make it available for reuse. The key mechanism that we use here is the asset repository. Depending on the needs of our ABD program, we can select from a range of different approaches for our repository. We may use a tool that is specifically focused on assets, one that is more general but focused on versioning, or we may use something as simple as a network folder or wiki. The key idea is that we have a known location that allows us to make assets available for reuse while managing versions and feedback. In addition, we want to be sure to use the correct level of tooling and support to meet the needs of our effort. As the scope of the reuse effort grows, we will want to ensure that our repository approach meets our needs in regard to aspects such as governance, collaboration, security, versioning, and availability.

We store the artifacts related to the pattern in the repository, including the pattern itself (pattern specifications and pattern implementation), the associated pattern implementation documentation, and DSLs. When we submit the asset to the repository, we may have to participate in an approval process. During that process the appropriate parties review the asset before making it widely available. When we create the record for the asset in the repository, we provide details on the pattern: What type of asset is it? What can it be used for? To whom should it be made available?

The primary performer for this task, as shown in Table F.14, is the Asset Librarian. Again, it is important to keep in mind that a person can take on multiple roles. Many organizations do not have a single person who is 100% dedicated to the Asset Librarian role. However, this does not mean that the work done by the role is not performed. It may be that the role is shared by a number of people or that one person takes on this role as one of many.

Table F.14 *Summary of Relationships to Deploy Pattern to Asset Repository Task*

Relationships		
Roles	Primary performer: Asset Librarian	Additional performers: Pattern Author/SME Pattern Implementation Author Pattern Specification Author
Inputs	Mandatory: Reusable asset Pattern implementation documentation	Optional: None
Outputs	Reusable asset	
Patterns and Guidelines	Pattern Packaging (Chapter 14), Use an Asset Repository (Chapter 16)	
Steps	Upload the asset to the asset repository and update the metadata. Validate the asset. Announce the update to the user community.	

Review Feedback

From a pattern creation, maintenance, and support point of view, we need to have a mind-set that we don't just create and release a single version of the pattern and never expect to see that asset again. Focusing on a big-bang approach that sees just one release that has everything the pattern could ever need is a path to failure. Focusing on the essence of the pattern and then augmenting future versions is the approach we need to adopt. Feedback from Pattern Users is an important input when determining how to prioritize enhancements to a pattern in future releases.

In this task we look at things from the point of view of the owner of the pattern, which is typically the Pattern Implementation Author or the Pattern Specification Author. We need to be diligent in ensuring that we are following up on feedback and improving the quality of our patterns. We cannot have a fire-and-forget mentality. The culture around the reuse program is very important, and having Pattern Users consume the pattern and then submit feedback is a key behavior that needs to be supported and reinforced. Ignoring the feedback, arguing with users, or not following through can have serious negative consequences on the reuse program.

We will review the feedback and discussions in the pattern repository to gain insights into how pattern users are faring in using patterns. How often are the patterns used? What positive suggestions are being made about improving them? What issues have users run into? What are the priorities associated with these issues? What is the value of the pattern that these feedback items are assigned to? How important is the underlying pattern to the organization?

When we originally created a pattern, we did not automatically build it just because potential had been identified. We performed an analysis and invested in only those patterns that were deemed to provide the appropriate ROI. As we anticipate releasing a new version of a pattern, one that incorporates user feedback, we will end up performing a similar analysis. It is therefore important that we have a good understanding of the outstanding issues, the impact that they would have on the pattern, the effort associated with implementing these changes, and the expected benefit from implementing them.

In addition to consulting the asset repository for user feedback, we should also take time to discuss and interact directly with those using the patterns. One approach is to follow up on comments and feedback that have been provided. Another option is to follow up based on those who have downloaded the artifact. In this case we leverage some of the capabilities of an asset repository, which tracks how many times each pattern is downloaded and who has obtained a copy of the pattern. Discussing the pattern with those who downloaded it but did not record feedback may provide some valuable insights. Perhaps they downloaded the pattern but found that it didn't meet their needs. Did they misunderstand the pattern description and metadata? Or is that information misleading?

As shown in Table F.15, the primary performers of this task are the Pattern Implementation Author and Pattern Specification Author roles. The Asset Librarian and the Pattern Author/SME assist them in reviewing the feedback. The Asset Librarian provides assistance in working with and capturing information from the asset repository. The Pattern Author/SME provides insights into the domain and the pattern, helping to validate and ascertain the value of the feedback.

Table F.15   *Summary of Relationships to Review Feedback Task*

Relationships		
Roles	Primary performer:	Additional performers:
	Pattern Implementation Author	Asset Librarian
	Pattern Specification Author	Pattern Author/SME
Inputs	Mandatory:	Optional:
	Pattern feedback	None

Table F.15 *Summary of Relationships to Review Feedback Task (Continued)*

Relationships	
Outputs	Candidate pattern list
Patterns and Guidelines	Determine Business Impact (Chapter 11), Pattern Version (Chapter 14), Update Existing Pattern (Chapter 11), Use an Asset Repository (Chapter 16)
Steps	Review feedback as posted to the asset repository.
	Follow up with Pattern Users regarding feedback.
	Follow up with users who have not provided feedback.
	Analyze and prioritize the feedback.
	Record actionable requests in the change management solution.

Capture Reuse Metrics

A key aspect of following a PBE approach is to be systematic and disciplined while also quantifying results. It is not sufficient to just use patterns because we expect it to be a good approach. We need numbers, metrics that detail the impact and support the decisions that are made. Anecdotal evidence can help but is not nearly as effective.

We attempt to capture metrics at a number of key points as we work through our PBE workflows; for instance, in the Evaluate Candidate Patterns task we can see that metrics play a key role in deciding which patterns we should initially invest in. However, a focus on metrics doesn't occur only within this one task. We also need to capture and leverage metrics as we support the Provide Feedback on a Pattern, Increase Pattern Scope, and Review Feedback tasks. When using a pattern, we need to understand its ROI. What was the investment made in acquiring the pattern, and then what was the return on that investment?

In Table F.16 we see that a number of roles are involved in supporting this task. They require the support of several artifacts, including the list of candidate patterns, pattern description, pattern feedback, and ROI analysis. Being able to quantify the results is a shared responsibility, and a focus on results cuts across many tasks.

Table F.16 *Summary of Relationships to Capture Reuse Metrics Task*

Relationships		
Roles	**Primary performer:**	**Additional performers:**
	Pattern Author/SME	Pattern Implementation Author
	Pattern User	Pattern Specification Author
Inputs	**Mandatory:**	**Optional:**
	List of candidate patterns	None
	Pattern description	
	Pattern feedback	
	ROI analysis	

(continues)

Table F.16 *Summary of Relationships to Capture Reuse Metrics Task (Continued)*

Relationships	
Outputs	List of candidate patterns
	Pattern metrics
Patterns and Guidelines	Determine Business Impact (Chapter 11), Use an Asset Repository (Chapter 16)
Steps	Review the pattern evaluation metrics.
	Analyze the relative costs and benefits.
	Capture actual reuse metrics.
	Record the metrics.
	Determine the business impact of the pattern.

Update Development Process

As we leverage other tasks such as Build a Pattern Implementation and Increase Pattern Scope, we find that the pattern implementations end up affecting aspects of the development process. For instance, a pattern implementation can automate the performance of many steps and generate many artifacts. Previously, these tasks would have been performed manually and would have required a number of roles to be involved and coordinated. If in our development efforts we adopt such a pattern implementation, we have to remove references to the performance of the manual steps and in their place discuss when, where, and how to use the automation as part of the process. Ideally, we end up simplifying the development process; a simpler process with fewer manual steps is easier to follow and leads to success.

A key idea to keep in mind in this task, as in most any software development process-related effort, is that the process being followed is not static. It does not occur in a vacuum, oblivious to any changes made in how we work and the tools that we use. Thus, we always need to keep an eye on how we've documented the process and be aware that it will need to be updated periodically to reflect the current practices of the team.

EPF Composer is an excellent tool to help in such efforts, as it allows for easy modification and publishing of process content. We do not need to manually update the files that detail the process. Rather we update the model that represents the process and then republish. Once it is republished, it's an easy task to push the documentation out to the team.

Knowing that this is a task we are going to have to do, and understanding the tools that will help us accomplish the task, let's take some time to discuss what needs to be considered.

A good place to start is to analyze the patterns that we are using. As there are a number of steps along the way where we have analyzed the patterns that we are going to acquire, build, and use, we know what patterns will be used before they are actually used.

In some cases, such as the use of a UML pattern, the impact is too narrow to be detailed in the development process. However, the guidance to use UML patterns, or even a set of patterns, would be a detail that is worth including.

As we get to patterns with a bigger scope, we need to start accounting for how these patterns will impact the development process. In addition, as we start to combine and encapsulate larger-scope patterns, we are able to compress the development process even more. The more we are able to compress and simplify the development process, the more pressing is the need to ensure that these changes are recorded and made available to the team.

In addition, we also need to account for how these larger-scope patterns impact additional ancillary tasks. For example, we would have tasks in the development process that relate to the deployment of the code, build, and testing efforts. Again, we have insight into the patterns in advance of them actually being used. In this case we are well aware of how far the scope of the pattern extends. We can ask ourselves, how does the scope of the pattern impact development tasks? Testing tasks? Deployment tasks? Requirements?

As shown in Table F.17, the primary performer for this task is the Development Process Author role. This role will consult with the Pattern Author/SME to provide guidance on the patterns that are used and their possible impact on the process.

Table F.17 *Summary of Relationships to Update Development Process Task*

Relationships		
Roles	**Primary performer:**	**Additional performers:**
	Development Process Author	Pattern Author/SME
		Pattern Implementation Author
Inputs	**Mandatory:**	**Optional:**
	Development process	None
	Pattern implementation	
	Pattern implementation documentation	
	Pattern specification	
Outputs	Development process	
Patterns and Guidelines	End-to-End Pattern Use (Chapter 10)	
Steps	Review the patterns.	
	Prioritize the patterns.	
	Update the process tasks, work products, and roles to account for the use of the pattern.	
	Republish the development process (as needed).	

References and Resources

References

Ackerman, L., and B. Portier. 2007a. "Using model-driven development and pattern-based engineering to design SOA: Part 1. Creating UML Profiles and model templates." *developerWorks* (April 17). www.ibm.com/developerworks/edu/dw-rt-umlprofiles.html.

———. 2007b. "Using model-driven development and pattern-based engineering to design SOA: Part 2. Patterns-based engineering." *developerWorks* (September 25). www.ibm.com/developerworks/edu/dw-rt-umlprofiles2.html.

Ackerman, L., B. Portier, and C. Gerken. 2008a. "Using model-driven development and pattern-based engineering to design SOA: Part 3. Eclipse Modeling Framework Technology Java Emitter Template transformations." *developerWorks* (June 10). www.ibm.com/developerworks/edu/dw-r-umlprofiles3.html.

———. 2008b. "Using model-driven development and pattern-based engineering to design SOA: Part 4. Model-to-model transformations and connecting models to EMFT JET transformations." *developerWorks* (June 17). www.ibm.com/developerworks/edu/dw-r-umlprofiles4.html.

Alexander, C. 1977. *A Pattern Language: Towns, Buildings, Construction*. New York: Oxford University Press.

———. 1979. *The Timeless Way of Building*. New York: Oxford University Press.

Al-Sabt, M., et al. 2003. "Testing software patterns." Microsoft. http://msdn.microsoft.com/en-us/library/ms979209.aspx.

Alur, D., J. Crupi, and D. Malks. 2003. *Core J2EE Patterns, Second Edition*. Upper Saddle River, NJ: Prentice Hall. Some content is also available at www.corej2eepatterns.com/Patterns2ndEd/index.htm.

Ambler, Scott, and Celso Gonzalez. 2008. "Agile model-driven development." *Better Software* (June). www.stickyminds.com/BetterSoftware/magazine.asp?fn=cifea&id=110.

Anderson, C. 2006. *The Long Tail*. New York: Hyperion.

Arsanjani, A., et al. 2007. "Design an SOA solution using a reference architecture: Improve your development process using the SOA solution stack." *developerWorks* (March 28). www.ibm.com/developerworks/library/ar-archtemp/.

Baumer, D., et al. 2000. "Role object." In *Pattern Languages of Program Design 4*, edited by N. Harrison, B. Foote, and H. Rohnert. Reading, MA: Addison-Wesley.

Beck, K. 2003. *Test-Driven Development: By Example*. Boston: Addison-Wesley.

Biggerstaff, T. J., and C. Richter. 1987. "Reusability framework, assessment, and directions." *IEEE Software* 4, no. 2 (March).

Booch, G. 2007. "The promise, the limits, and the beauty of software." Lecture presented to the British Computer Society, January 22, Manchester, UK. www.bcs.org/server.php?show=nav.9785.

Buschmann, F., K. Henney, and D. Schmidt. 2007. *Pattern-Oriented Software Architecture 5: On Patterns and Pattern Languages*. Indianapolis, IN: John Wiley & Sons.

Buschmann, F., R. Meunier, H. Rohnert, P. Somerlad, and M. Stal. 1996. *Pattern-Oriented Software Architecture: A System of Patterns, Vol. 1*. Indianapolis, IN: John Wiley & Sons.

Charette, Robert N. 2005. "Why software fails." *IEEE Spectrum* (September). http://spectrum.ieee.org/computing/software/why-software-fails/.

D'Anjou, J., S. Fairbrother, D. Kehn, J. Kellerman, and P. McCarthy. 2004. *The Java Developer's Guide to Eclipse, Second Edition*. Boston: Addison-Wesley.

DeCarlo, J., et al. 2008. *Strategic Reuse with Asset-Based Development*. IBM Redbook. www.redbooks.ibm.com/abstracts/sg247529.html?Open.

Demir, A. 2004. "Comparison of Model-Driven Architecture and software factories in the context of model-driven development." *IEEE Proceedings of the Fourth Workshop on Model-Based Development of Computer-Based Systems and Third International Workshop on Model-Based Methodologies for Pervasive and Embedded Software*. Washington, DC: IEEE Computer Society, 75–83.

Fowler, M. 1997. *Analysis Patterns: Reusable Object Models*. Reading, MA: Addison-Wesley.

———. 1999. *Refactoring: Improving the Design of Existing Code*. Reading, MA: Addison-Wesley.

———. 2003. *Patterns of Enterprise Application Architecture*. Boston: Addison-Wesley.

————. 2004. *UML Distilled: A Brief Guide to the Standard Object Modeling Language*. Boston: Addison-Wesley.

Gamma, E., R. Helm, R. Johnson, and J. Vlissides. 1995. *Design Patterns: Elements of Reusable Object-Oriented Software*. Reading, MA: Addison-Wesley.

Gonzalez, C., and E. Lane. 2008. "Enabling asset consumability: Is your wardrobe good, bad, or ugly?" *developerWorks* (July). www.ibm.com/developerworks/rational/library/edge/08/jul08/gonzalez_lane/index.html.

Greenfield, J., and K. Short. 2004. *Software Factories: Assembling Applications with Patterns, Models, Frameworks, and Tools*. Indianapolis, IN: John Wiley & Sons.

Hohpe, G., and B. Woolf. 2004. *Enterprise Integration Patterns*. Reading, MA: Addison-Wesley.

Jacobson, I., G. Booch, and J. Rumbaugh. 1999. *The Unified Software Development Process*. Reading, MA: Addison-Wesley.

Jacobson, Ivar, Martin Griss, and Patrik Jonsson. 1997. *Software Reuse: Architecture, Process and Organization for Business Success*. Reading, MA: Addison-Wesley.

Johnston, Simon. 2005. "UML 2.0 Profile for Software Services." *developerWorks* (April 13). www.ibm.com/developerworks/rational/library/05/419_soa/.

Kelly, S., and J. Tolvanen. 2008. *Domain Specific Modeling: Enabling Full Code Generation*. Hoboken, NJ: John Wiley & Sons.

Kerievsky, J. 2004. *Refactoring to Patterns*. Boston: Addison-Wesley.

Koushik, S., G. Vasudeva, G. Galambos, and J. Adams. 2001. *IBM e-Business Patterns: A Strategy for Reuse*. Double Oak, TX: MC Press. Some of the content is also available at www.ibm.com/developerworks/patterns/.

Kovari, P. 2007. "Explore model-driven development (MDD) and related approaches: Applying domain-specific modeling to Model-Driven Architecture." *developerWorks* (September 18). www.ibm.com/developerworks/library/ar-mdd4/index.html.

Kraus, Joe. 2005. "The long tail of software: Millions of markets of dozens." March 9. http://bnoopy.typepad.com/bnoopy/2005/03/the_long_tail_o.html.

Larsen, G. 2003. "Asset based development." http://xml.coverpages.org/Larsen-RAS200311.pdf.

————. 2006. "Model-driven development: Assets and reuse." *IBM Systems Journal* 45, no. 3.

Manolescu, D., W. Kozaczynski, A. Miller, and J. Hogg. 2007. "The growing divide in the patterns world." *IEEE Software* (July/August), 61–67.

Marquardt, K. 2006. "Patterns for plug-ins." In *Pattern Languages of Program Design 5*, edited by D. Manolescu, M. Voelter, and J. Noble. Boston: Addison-Wesley.

Meszaros, G., and J. Doble. 1998. "A pattern language for pattern writing." In *Pattern Languages of Program Design 3*, edited by R. Martin, D. Riehle, and F. Buschmann. Reading, MA: Addison-Wesley.

Miller, Joaquin, and Jishnu Mukerji, eds. 2003. "MDA Guide Version 1.0.1." Object Management Group (June 12). www.omg.org/cgi-bin/doc?omg/03-06-01.

Panda, D., R. Rahman, and D. Lane. 2007. *EJB 3 in Action*. Greenwich, CT: Manning Publications.

Riehle, Dirk. 1997. "Composite design patterns." In *Proceedings of the 1997 Conference on Object-Oriented Programming Systems, Languages, and Applications (OOPSLA '97)*. New York: ACM Press.

Rising, L. 2000. *The Pattern Almanac*. Boston: Addison-Wesley.

Royce, Walker. 2009. "Improving software economics: Top 10 principles of achieving agility at scale." IBM Rational Whitepaper. http://download.boulder.ibm.com/ibmdl/pub/software/rational/web/whitepapers/Royce_SoftwareEconomics_whitepaper3.pdf.

Schneider, S., and R. Lexvold. 2008. "Epiphanies of patterns! A hands-on survey of pattern-related automation technologies." EclipseCon.

Siddle, J. M., and D. Draper. 2008. "How patterns shaped new WS-Notification functionality in IBM WebSphere Application Server 7.0." *developerWorks* (December 23). www.ibm.com/developerworks/architecture/library/ar-wsnpat/index.html.

Smith, J., and D. Stotts. 2003. "Flexible automated design pattern extraction from source code." *Proceedings of the 2003 IEEE International Conference on Automated Software Engineering*, Montreal QC, Canada, October 8–10. Also available at ftp://ftp.cs.unc.edu/pub/publications/techreports/03-016.pdf.

Srinivasan, Harini, James Conallen, and Eoin Lane. 2005. "The requester side caching pattern specification, Part 1: Overview of the requester side caching pattern." *developerWorks* (October 24). www.ibm.com/developerworks/webservices/library/ws-rscp1/index.html.

———. 2006. "Building SOA applications with reusable assets, Part 4: The requester-side caching pattern." *developerWorks* (November 22). www.ibm.com/developerworks/webservices/library/ws-soa-reuse4/.

———. 2008. "The requester side caching pattern specification, Part 2: The requester side caching pattern implementation specification." *developerWorks* (March 13). www.ibm.com/developerworks/webservices/library/ws-rscp2/index.html.

Tiedt, Philipp. 2006. "Building cheat sheets in Eclipse V3.2: Learn about V3.2 enhancements." *developerWorks* (August 8). www.ibm.com/developerworks/opensource/library/os-ecl-cheatsheets/.

Vlissides, J. 1997. "Patterns: The top ten misconceptions." *Object Magazine* (March).

———. 1998. *Pattern Hatching: Design Patterns Applied*. Reading, MA: Addison-Wesley.

Wahler, Michael, Lee Ackerman, and Scott Schneider. 2008a. "Using IBM constraint patterns and consistency analysis: An overview." *developerWorks* (May 20). www.ibm.com/developerworks/rational/library/08/0520_wahler-ackerman-schneider/.

———. 2008b. "Using the IBM constraint patterns and consistency analysis extension: A step by step guide." *developerWorks* (May 27). www.ibm.com/developerworks/edu/dw-r-conpatcon.html.

Yacoub, S., and Ammar, H. 2003. *Pattern-Oriented Analysis and Design: Composing Patterns to Design Software Systems*. Boston: Addison-Wesley.

Additional Resources

Ackerman, L., and C. Gonzalez. 2007. "The value of pattern implementations: Going beyond pattern specifications." *Dr. Dobb's Journal* (May). www.ddj.com/cpp/199204017.

Balduino, R. 2007. "Introduction to OpenUP (Open Unified Process)." www.eclipse.org/epf/general/OpenUP.pdf.

Beck, K. 2000. *Extreme Programming Explained: Embrace Change*. Boston: Addison-Wesley.

Biswas, Rahul, and Ed Ort. 2006. "The Java Persistence API: A simpler programming model for entity persistence." Sun Developer Network (May). http://java.sun.com/developer/technicalArticles/J2EE/jpa/.

Brown, A., S. Iyengar, and S. Johnston. 2006. "A Rational approach to model-driven development." *IBM Systems Journal* 45, no. 3. www.research.ibm.com/journal/sj/453/brown.html.

Brown, W., R. Malveau, H. McCormick III, and T. Mowbray. 1998. *AntiPatterns: Refactoring Software, Architectures, and Projects in Crisis*. Indianapolis, IN: John Wiley & Sons.

Cohen, M. 2002. "An Overview of Scrum." Mountain Goat Software (January 1). www.mountaingoatsoftware.com/presentations/30--an-overview-of-scrum.

Conallen, J., P. Kovari, and L. Ackerman. 2008. "Introduction to DSLs and DSMs, on the Rational Modeling Platform." Rational Software Developers Conference, Orlando, FL, June 1–5.

Cook, S. 2006. "Domain-specific modeling." *Microsoft Architect Journal* (October). http://msdn.microsoft.com/en-us/library/bb245773.aspx.

De Vries, M., and J. Greenfield. 2006. "Measuring success with software factories and Visual Studio Team System." MSDN (November). http://msdn.microsoft.com/en-us/library/aa925157.aspx.

Dmitriev, S. 2004. "Language oriented programming: The next programming paradigm." *onBoard* (November). www.onboard.jetbrains.com/is1/articles/04/10/lop/index.html.

Eadie, S. 2006. "A GSI's perspective of software factories." *Microsoft Architect Journal* (October). http://msdn.microsoft.com/en-us/library/bb245775.aspx.

Eclipse.org. "Introduction to the Eclipse Process Framework." www.eclipse.org/epf/general/An_Introduction_to_EPF.zip.

Fichman, R. 2001. "Incentive compatibility and systematic software reuse." *Journal of Systems and Software* 57, no. 1 (April 27): 45.

Gamma, E., and K. Beck. 2003. *Contributing to Eclipse: Principles, Patterns, and Plug-Ins*. Boston: Addison-Wesley.

Gardner, T., and L. Yusuf. 2006. "Combine patterns and modeling to implement architecture-driven development." *developerWorks* (February 14). www.ibm.com/developerworks/library/ar-mdd2/.

Greenfield, J. 2004a. "The case for software factories." *Microsoft Architect Journal* (July). http://msdn.microsoft.com/en-us/library/aa480032.aspx.

———. 2004b. "Software factories: Assembling applications with patterns, models, frameworks, and tools." MSDN Architecture Center (November). http://msdn .microsoft.com/en-us/library/ms954811.aspx.

———. 2006. "Bare-naked languages or what not to model." *Microsoft Architect Journal* (October). http://msdn.microsoft.com/en-us/library/bb245772.aspx.

Harel, D. 2000. *Computers Ltd.: What They Really Can't Do*. Oxford: Oxford University Press.

Herrington, Jack. 2003. *Code Generation in Action*. Greenwich, CT: Manning Publications.

Highsmith, J. 2002. *Agile Software Development Ecosystems*. Boston: Addison-Wesley.

IBM. 2006. "EMFT JET Developer Guide." http://publib.boulder.ibm.com/ infocenter/rsmhelp/v7r0m0/index.jsp?topic=/com.ibm.rsm.nav.doc/topics/ emftjetdevguide.html.

———. 2007. "Rational Method Composer Plug-ins: RUP for Asset-Based Development V3.0 and Asset-Based Development Governance V1.0." www.ibm.com/ developerworks/rational/downloads/07/rup_abd_gov/.

Jeffries, Ron. "XProgramming.com: An Agile software development resource." www.xprogramming.com.

Koenig, A. 1995. "Patterns and antipatterns." *Journal of Object-Oriented Programming* (March–April).

Kroll, P., and B. MacIsaac. 2006. *Agility and Discipline Made Easy: Practices from OpenUP and RUP*. Boston: Addison-Wesley.

Lane, E. "Pattern (reusable) assets classification." http://eoinlane.blogspot.com/2008/ 03/reusable-software-assets-represent.html.

Larsen, G., and E. Lane. 2006. Building SOA applications with reusable assets, Part 1: Reusable assets, recipes, and patterns. *developerWorks* (March 14). https:// www.ibm.com/developerworks/webservices/library/ws-soa-reuse1/.

Lim, W. 1998. *Managing Software Reuse: A Comprehensive Guide to Strategically Reengineering the Organization for Reusable Components*. Upper Saddle River, NJ: Prentice Hall.

Martin, Robert, D. Riehle, and F. Buschmann, eds. 1998. *Pattern Languages of Program Design 3*. Reading, MA: Addison-Wesley.

Microsoft MSDN. 2005. "Domain-specific languages (DSLs) and software factories." MSDN (November 22). MSDN ARCast, http://msdn.microsoft.com/en-us/library/aa983295.aspx.

Moore, W., et al. 2004. "Eclipse Development using the Graphical Editing Framework and the Eclipse Modeling Framework." IBM Redbook. www.redbooks.ibm.com/abstracts/sg246302.html?Open.

Novotny, O. 2005. "Next generation tools for object-oriented development." *Microsoft Architect Journal* (January). http://msdn.microsoft.com/en-us/library/aa480062.aspx.

Object Management Group. "Model Driven Architecture (MDA) FAQ." www.omg.org/mda/faq_mda.htm.

Portier, B., and L. Ackerman. 2009. "Model driven development misperceptions and challenges." *InfoQ.com* (January 21). www.infoq.com/articles/mdd-misperceptions-challenges.

Poulin, J. S. 1997. *Measuring Software Reuse: Principles, Practices, and Economic Models*. Reading, MA: Addison-Wesley.

Regio, M., and J. Greenfield. 2006. "Designing and implementing a software factory." *Microsoft Architect Journal* (January). http://msdn.microsoft.com/en-us/library/bb245657.aspx.

Object Management Group. "Reusable Asset Specification, version 2.2." www.omg.org/technology/documents/formal/ras.htm.

Royce, Walker. 1998. *Software Project Management: A Unified Approach*. Reading, MA: Addison-Wesley.

Schwaber, K., and M. Beedle. 2002. *Agile Software Development with Scrum*. Upper Saddle River, NJ: Prentice Hall.

Steinberg, D., F. Budinsky, M. Paternostro, and E. Merks. 2009. *EMF: Eclipse Modeling Framework*. Boston: Addison-Wesley.

Swithinbank, P., et al. 2005. *Patterns: Model-Driven Development Using IBM Rational Software Architect*. IBM Redbook. www.redbooks.ibm.com/abstracts/sg247105.html#alsodownloaded.

Voelter, M., B. Kolb, S. Efftinge, and A. Haase. 2006. "From front end to code: MDSD in practice." *Eclipse Corner Article* (June). www.eclipse.org/articles/Article-FromFrontendToCode-MDSDInPractice/article.html.

Wahli, U., et al. 2008. *Building SOA Solutions Using the Rational SDP* (April). IBM Redbook. www.redbooks.ibm.com/abstracts/sg247356.html?Open.

Index

Numbers

80/20 rule, in pattern development, 170

A

ABD (asset-based development)
    identification, production, management, and
        consumption of assets, 5
    key areas of, 137
    overview of, 4, 357
    PBE as specialized form of, 10
    two perspectives on, 5–6
Abstract classes, adding support for, 84–85
Abstract Factory pattern, UML patterns, 24–25
Abstraction
    MDD (model-driven development) and, 214,
        222
    recurring solutions and, 190
Abstraction blinders, pitfalls of Pattern
        Opportunity pattern, 188
Activity diagrams, 138
Actors, LogoAuction application, 49–50
Agile development
    approaches to software development, 3
    OpenUP and, 146
    Oslec Software using, 39
    XP (Extreme Programming) and, 147
Alexander, Christopher, 6, 11–12, 292, 298, 312
Analysis patterns, applying to LogoAuction
        application, 47
AndroMDA, 366
Antipattern pattern
    context, problem, forces, and solution, 184–185
    example and related patterns and guidelines,
        185
    overview of, 157
Architectural design, pattern categories, 353–354
Architectural Discovery feature, RSA (Rational
        Software Architect), 341
Architecture, LogoAuction application
    data architecture, 63–64
    deployment architecture, 59–63
    logical architecture, 56–59
    overview of, 55–56

Artifacts
    code generators producing, 347
    exemplar as key artifact, 242
    relationship to binaries, 259
    significance in exemplar analysis, 204
    storing source and development, 118
    text-based, 226
Asset-based development. *see* ABD (asset-based
        development)
Asset Librarian role, 385–386
Asset repository
    capturing pattern relationships in, 253
    choosing solution for, 259
    deploying patterns to, 410–411
    features to consider, 326–327
    integration of asset repository with
        organizational uses, 249
    overview of, 118
    searching for requirements, 294
    Use an Asset Repository guideline, 299–301
    versioning and, 261
Assets
    identification, production, management, and
        consumption, 5, 137
    integration of asset repository with
        organizational uses, 249
    metadata, 119–120
    reusable, 356
    review process, 120–121
    timing reuse of, 308
    training for managing, 329
Assumptions
    defined, 18–19
    points of variability and, 210
Attributes
    dynamically building for entities, 96
    identifying entity roles for Subsystem Façade
        pattern, 81–82
Auction Management subsystem
    areas of responsibility in LogoAuction
        application, 57–58
    entities and projects, 115
    implementation of, 113
    Start Auction and Close Auction use cases, 124

425

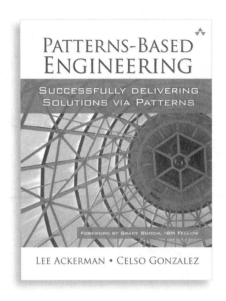